Your Guide to Perpetual Youth

AGE
PROTECTORS

Your Guide to Perpetual Youth

AGE
PROTECTORS

Stop Aging Now

WITH THE LATEST BREAKTHROUGHS THAT

Halt the Life-Robbing Diseases

Erase the Lines of Time

Sharpen Your Mind and Memory

Rekindle Your Youthful Spirit

Edited by Edward Claflin

Rodale Press, Inc.
Emmaus, Pennsylvania

Copyright © 1998 by Rodale Press, Inc.

Illustrations copyright © 1998 by Narda Lebo

The table on page 137 was abridged from *Brain Power* by Vernon Mark, M.D., F.A.C.S., with Jeffrey P. Mark, M.Sc. Copyright © 1989 by Vernon H. Mark and Jeffrey Paul Mark. Reprinted by permission of Houghton Mifflin Company. All rights reserved.

The "Are You Burning Out?" quiz on page 219 was adapted from *Take This Job and Love It*, by Dennis T. Jaffe, Ph.D., and Cynthia D. Scott, M.P.H., Ph.D. Copyright © 1988 by Dennis T. Jaffe, Ph.D., and Cynthia D. Scott, M.P.H., Ph.D. Reprinted by permission.

The "Are You Feeling the Crunch?" quiz on page 231 was adapted from *The Demographics of Time Use*. Reprinted with permission. Copyright © 1991 by American Demographics, Inc., Ithaca, New York.

The four-step guidelines to centering prayer on pages 266 and 267 were adapted from the brochure *The Method of Centering Prayer* by Father Thomas Keating. Copyright © 1995 by Saint Benedict's Monastery. Reprinted by permission of Father Thomas Keating. For more information, contact the Contemplative Outreach, Ltd., 9 William Street, P.O. Box 737, Butler, NJ 07405.

The range-of-motion exercises on pages 284 to 286 were used by permission of the Arthritis Foundation. Copyright © 1997 by the Arthritis Foundation. For more information, please write to the Arthritis Foundation at P.O. Box 7669, Atlanta, GA 30357.

Library of Congress Cataloging-in-Publication Data

Age protectors : your guide to perpetual youth / edited by Edward Claflin.
     p. cm.
    Includes index.
    ISBN 0–87596–454–0 hardcover
    1. Longevity—Popular works.   2. Aging—Prevention—Popular works.
  I. Claflin, Edward.   II. Prevention Health Books.
  RA776.75.A34   1998   97–46595
  612.6'8—DC21

Distributed to the book trade by St. Martin's Press

    4 6 8 10 9 7 5   hardcover

Visit us on the Web at www.preventionbookshelf.com or call us toll-free at (800) 848-4735

Age Protectors Staff

Senior Managing Editor: Edward Claflin
Senior Editor: Matthew Hoffman
Writers: Bridget Doherty, Doug Dollemore, Joely Johnson,
Barbara Loecher, James McCommons, Ellen Michaud,
Kristine M. Napier, Julia VanTine, Selene Yeager
Assistant Research Manager: Jane Unger Hahn
Lead Researchers: Kelly Elizabeth Coffey, Jan Eickmeier
Editorial Researchers: Jennifer A. Barefoot, Elizabeth A. Brown, Lori Davis,
Leah B. Flickinger, Carol J. Gilmore, Jennifer L. Kaas, Nanci Kulig,
Mary S. Mesaros, Deanna Moyer, Staci Ann Sander, Lorna S. Sapp
Senior Copy Editor: Karen Neely
Art Director: Darlene Schneck
Interior Designer: Debra Sfetsios
Cover Designer: Andrew Newman, Darlene Schneck
Layout Designers: Keith Biery, Susan P. Eugster, Pat Mast
Manufacturing Coordinator: Patrick T. Smith
Office Manager: Roberta Mulliner
Office Staff: Julie Kehs, Suzanne Lynch, Bernadette Sauerwine

Rodale Health and Fitness Books

Vice President and Editorial Director: Debora T. Yost
Executive Editor: Neil Wertheimer
Design and Production Director: Michael Ward
Research Manager: Ann Gossy Yermish
Copy Manager: Lisa D. Andruscavage
Production Manager: Robert V. Anderson Jr.
Studio Manager: Leslie M. Keefe
Book Manufacturing Director: Helen Clogston

Thomas Platts-Mills, M.D., Ph.D.

Professor of medicine and head of the division of allergy and immunology at the University of Virginia Medical Center in Charlottesville

David P. Rose, M.D., Ph.D., D.Sc.

Chief of the division of nutrition and endocrinology at Naylor Dana Institute, part of the American Health Foundation, in Valhalla, New York, and an expert on nutrition and cancer for the National Cancer Institute and the American Cancer Society

William B. Ruderman, M.D.

Practicing physician at Gastroenterology Associates of Central Florida in Orlando

Maria A. Fiatarone Singh, M.D.

Assistant professor in the division on aging at Harvard Medical School, associate professor in the School of Nutrition at Tufts University, and chief of the Human Nutrition and Exercise Physiology Laboratory at the Jean Mayer U.S. Department of Agriculture Human Nutrition Research Center on Aging at Tufts University, all in Boston

Yvonne S. Thornton, M.D.

Associate clinical professor of obstetrics and gynecology at Columbia University College of Physicians and Surgeons in New York City and director of the Perinatal Diagnostic Testing Center at Morristown Memorial Hospital in Morristown, New Jersey

Lila Amdurska Wallis, M.D., M.A.C.P.

Clinical professor of medicine at Cornell University Medical College in New York City, past president of the American Medical Women's Association, founding president of the National Council on Women's Health, director of continuing medical education programs for physicians, and master and laureate of the American College of Physicians

Andrew T. Weil, M.D.

Director of the program in integrative medicine of the College of Medicine at the University of Arizona in Tucson

Richard J. Wood, Ph.D.

Associate professor at the School of Nutrition at Tufts University in Medford, Massachusetts, and laboratory chief of the Mineral Bioavailability Laboratory at the Jean Mayer USDA Human Nutrition Research Center on Aging at Tufts University in Boston

Contents

part 2 | Whole-Body Protection

ix

Protecting Your Zestful Youth

If life were a game, most of us would probably admit that we start off playing hard. We go for goals. We strive for achievements. When we get to first base, we turn our eyes toward second. As soon as we steal second, our eyes are on third.

But somewhere along the way, it turns into another kind of game. Not the kind where we're beating the clock or scoring more runs or racing for the finish line. Instead, we start finding that we would like to slow things down a bit. Relish what we have. Pause to smell the flowers. Stop the clock.

If that's the stage you are in, then the tactics in this book are exactly what you need. In Part 1, you'll find 12 Stop-Time Tactics that will help protect your health, your mental alertness, your relationships, even your sense of adventure. In Part 2, you'll find very specific, scientifically proven tactics that can help protect you from a wide variety of physical and emotional problems—ranging from arthritis, cancer, and depression to loneliness, osteoporosis, and vision problems.

You don't need to adopt all these strategies. They are really options rather than requirements. But whether you try many of these practical strategies or only a few, you can be sure that they all contribute to a single purpose—protecting your youth.

To help you make an easy selection of strategies, we have put them under two headings. First are things you can do quickly—often in five minutes or less—and these come under the heading of "Makeover Minutes." Second are the strategies you can use if you have more time and want to go beyond the quick-and-easy approach. These strategies come under the heading of "Long-Term Tactics." Wherever you look, you'll find a wealth of authoritative advice and recommendations that come directly from the experts we inter-

x

viewed and from the latest anti-aging research. Our goal is to give you the tools and toys you need to protect yourself from all the factors in your environment as well as in your mind and body that could be making you feel, act, and look older than you would like to be.

In this book, you'll discover practical ways to trim your waistline, help erase wrinkles, and prevent hair loss. Methods to keep your memory keen and your wits sharp. Skillful, easy ways to attack aches and pains, and after they are gone, prevent them from recurring again. Challenges and adventures that are custommade to help you preserve a youthful outlook. A specific way of praying to feed your spiritual life. Along with each of these is research that shows just how important each factor really is.

And if you need more than general "age protectors," we also provide advice on how to confront age-related health problems. If you have a health condition that runs in your family or one that is steadily sneaking up on you, look in Part 2: "Whole-Body Protection." There, you'll find specific, powerful, disease-fighting strategies recommended by doctors and leading specialists as well as qualified practitioners of alternative medicine. So if you are at risk of arthritis, depression, diabetes, heart disease, or other health problems that are often age-related, you will have ready-at-hand weapons for fighting them.

Best of all, you'll discover that it is unnecessary to follow any rigid step-by-step plan to protect yourself from aging. To protect your youth, experts have discovered, you need to dabble in many things—from morning walks to night classes, from volunteering at city hall to meditating in silence, from preparing a "superfoods" snack to creating a cell-protecting diet, from traveling the continent to gardening in your own backyard.

In fact, this is a book you can turn to anytime for more ideas. And each idea will truly help you preserve your good health and good looks—and protect your zestful youth.

Edward Claflin

Edward Claflin
Senior Managing Editor
Prevention Health Books

part 1

Stop-Time
Tactics

Protect Your Body
with Superfoods

An average of three times a day, every day, you get the opportunity to protect your body from the effects of aging. Over the course of a single year, that's more than 1,000 individual chances to boost your immunity and reverse disease.

What are we talking about here? Simply put, the power of nutrition. The effects that our diets have on our health are no longer disputable. In fact, compelling evidence has been mounting steadily. Studies show the disease-protective effects of wholesome, everyday foods such as fruits and vegetables. Even in this age of convenience when fast foods are being consumed like candy, basic foods are still the best for our health.

That's why Stop-Time Tactic No. 1 is all about your array of food choices. You can protect yourself with food that's no farther away than the nearest supermarket. By homing in on fresh fruits and vegetables, you are likely to live a longer and healthier life. That's the general rule. Specifically, though, you give yourself an injection of youth serum every time you select, prepare, and savor some of the top superfoods. These foods not only nourish you, they also help prevent, postpone, or banish the many kinds of diseases and health problems that can age you faster than you can say, "bacon cheeseburger."

Fortunately, eating right is not just a matter of refusing luscious desserts and turning down deep-fried finger foods. When you go for superfoods, there is much good eating ahead.

3

Peak Nutrition

Every bite of broccoli or apple, every spoonful of whole-grain cereal, every sip of water or skim milk, every taste of tuna fish or tofu is a contributor to your health and a protector of your youth. While we don't often think of food as having magic bullets in the sense that miracle drugs are magic bullets, they really do produce miraculous amounts of prevention, protection, and healing in our bodies.

Some foods protect us by boosting immunity. Others sweep out the digestive tract and keep it in top-notch working order. Still others can help reduce the risk of cancer, protect us from heart attack, maintain brainpower by deterring stroke and memory loss, strengthen our bones, and guard our vision. And, of course, there are some stupendously protective and nutritious foods that are more like golden clouds than magic bullets. Eat them, and you'll do wonderful favors for your overall health. In fact, we'll give you the names of the top 20 protective superfoods—your best insurance against early aging—that can help guard every part of your mind and body throughout your entire life.

The net result of all this good eating? A younger you. That's because food is not just a builder, it is also a protector. And if you eat the superfoods recommended by leading doctors, nutritionists, and dietitians, you are truly using the best tactic there is to protect yourself from aging.

In Part 2 of this book, "Whole-Body Protection," you will find out how to integrate food-smart strategies along with other tactics to protect yourself from specific health conditions. And you will discover even more tips about the superfoods that you find here. But meanwhile, here is what experts have to say about the top foods for overall protection of your youth and health. In the sections that follow, you will find lists of 10 superfoods that will help guard your heart, your gut, your bones, and your brainpower—plus 20 top superfoods to help protect your whole body. These superfoods were selected by Kristine M. Napier, R.D., author of *Eat to Heal: The Phytochemical Diet and Nutrition Plan.*

4

Superfoods to Guard Your Heart

As the most important muscle in your body, your heart can't rest for a minute. Every moment, it is working to squeeze oxygen-rich blood into every body cell, from the top of your head to the end of your toes.

To remain powerful your heart depends on the same oxygen-rich blood supply that it sends out to the rest of your body. When the bloodstream becomes littered with too much fatty debris—as happens when cholesterol levels get out of whack—the heart muscle is first in line to suffer the consequences.

"Eating a heart-friendly diet is one of the most effective ways to prevent artery-clogging heart disease," says cardiac nutritionist Julie Avery, R.D., a registered dietitian in preventive cardiology at the Cleveland Clinic Foundation in Cleveland. "Most important, keep total and saturated fat levels low." (For more tips to help you do that, see Protect Yourself from Heart Disease on page 360.)

Of course, you can drastically lower the animal fat in your diet and increase all the nutrients if you give up eating meat and go on a vegetarian diet. But Avery suggests another strategy. "I encourage everyone to trade some of their meat meals for at least one or two fish meals and one or two vegetarian meals each week," she says.

Including fish is a great heart-protective strategy because fish has much less total fat and saturated fat than most meat. Plus, cold-water fish such as salmon, tuna, and mackerel harbor another heart-disease fighting secret, says Gary J. Nelson, Ph.D., a research chemist at the U.S. Department of Agriculture Western Human Nutrition Research Center in San Francisco. "These fish have fats containing omega-3 fatty acids that help them adapt to the cold water in which they live."

Omega-3s are thought to help the heart in several ways. For one, they might help lower blood pressure. "There's also evidence that omega-3s keep blood from clotting over time," says Avery. That's beneficial because when blood clots overzealously, arteries can become clogged. Other studies have shown that omega-3s buoy up high-density lipoproteins (HDLs), the "good"

know what?

A three-ounce lean, broiled hamburger has 14 grams of fat, 6 of which are saturated. Three ounces of tuna packed in water, about half a can, has less than 1 gram of fat, barely a trace of which is saturated.

5

A Step Beyond Vegetarianism

It's not difficult to see that fruits and vegetables are many of the superfoods that help protect your body from age-related disease and health problems. So you may be asking yourself about the benefits of becoming a vegetarian.

People on the most strict vegetarian diet—called a vegan diet—don't eat any animal products, including meat, fish, eggs, and cheese. Then what *do* they eat?

The key to vegan eating lies in enjoying a variety of foods, says Reed Mangels, R.D., Ph.D., nutrition advisor for the Vegetarian Resource Group in Baltimore. It's very important to choose foods from a range of sources, she says—and that's not only to keep you healthy but also to avoid boredom. Just as no one could live on a regimen of double cheeseburgers, a diet consisting solely of broccoli and brussels sprouts will also be less than optimal.

"You can use the U.S. Department of Agriculture's Food Guide Pyramid as a starting point," says Dr. Mangels. But if you're vegan, you'll be leaving out the meat and dairy products.

"The focus is on the biggest part of the triangle—whole grains and cereals," she says. Grains—from brown rice and oatmeal to whole-wheat bread and pasta—form the foundation of the vegan menu. From there, beans of all kinds, vegetables, and fruits fill out the rest of the menu.

The payoff for following this pared-down diet comes in the form of some impressive health benefits, says Dr. Mangels. Vegans have a low risk for many diseases including diabetes, heart disease, and some forms of cancer. "People theorize lots of reasons why that's so," she says. "Vegans generally get more fiber, more phytochemicals from the vegetables they eat, and fewer pesticides."

cholesterol that helps clear "bad" low-density lipoproteins (LDLs) from the bloodstream.

Fish also serves up good news for people who already have heart disease. If someone has had a heart attack, studies show, eating just two high-omega-3 fish meals each week (7 to 14 ounces total) may reduce the chances of suffering a second, fatal heart attack.

Vegetable protein, especially soy protein, can help keep the pipelines in the heart open, says Mark Messina, Ph.D., a nutritionist, private consultant, and soybean expert in Port

6

Townsend, Washington. Studies suggest that one of the ways it may do this is by helping lower cholesterol levels. Eating tofu, tempeh, and some other meat substitutes is a great way to get more soy protein in your diet.

Soy protein has another great secret: phytoestrogens. "The phytoestrogens seem to help reduce cholesterol levels, especially the more dangerous LDL cholesterol," says Dr. Messina. When heart disease experts at the University of Kentucky in Lexington analyzed the results of 38 studies about the effect of soy protein on cholesterol levels, they found that people who ate an average of 47 grams of soy protein daily had a 13 percent fall in harmful LDL levels and a 9 percent drop in total cholesterol levels.

Minerals such as calcium, potassium, and magnesium are crucial players in the heart-health scenario. In one of its lesser-known roles, calcium is part of a protein that helps regulate blood pressure. Potassium is believed to both prevent and help correct high blood pressure as well as keep your heartbeat steady. And, although there is less than an ounce of it in a 130-pound person, magnesium appears essential to healthy heart function, protecting that vital organ from heart disease as well as helping to control high blood pressure.

There has also been good news about the role played by some ordinary B vitamins in protecting heart health. The stars, some researchers say, are vitamins B_6 and B_{12} and folic acid—and what distinguishes this threesome is the way they make guerrilla attacks on a substance called homocysteine.

Homocysteine is an amino acid that belongs in the bloodstream. But when the levels of homocysteine are too high, it contributes to blocking arteries. Some heart research has shown that if you don't get enough of certain B vitamins—that is, you're not eating enough foods rich in these nutrients—homocysteine levels go up. And there seems to be another reason to get good amounts of these nutrients. "Even if homocysteine levels remain normal, low levels of vitamin B_6 may raise heart disease risk," says Killian Robinson, M.D., a staff cardiologist at the Cleveland Clinic Foundation in Cleveland, who is involved in international research on homocysteine and heart disease.

The food sources of these benign Bs? Well, you can harvest
(continued on page 10)

know what?

Twelve ounces of low-fat tofu has as much protein as a three-ounce hamburger but just 7 grams of fat, only 1 of which is saturated.

7

Top 10 Heart-Protective Superfoods

Many foods offer protection against youth-robbing heart disease, but the best ones are low in total fat, low in saturated fat, and high in omega-3s. And those that are the cream of the heart-protective crop also have B vitamins, vitamin E, and the phytoestrogens like those found in soy (the kind that help keep blood cholesterol levels in check). The high-fliers are also high in the blood-pressure-lowering nutrients calcium, magnesium, and potassium. (See page 34 for more about these minerals.) In the table below, the percentages shown are the percentages of the Daily Value for healthy adults consuming a 2,000-calorie-a-day diet.

The Top 10

1. Spinach, cooked (½ cup)

Vitamin B_6: 11%
Vitamin E: 5%
Folate: 33%
Calcium: 12%
Magnesium: 20%
Potassium: 12%

2. Black-eyed peas, cooked (½ cup)

Vitamin B_6: 3%
Folate: 26%
Calcium: 11%
Magnesium: 11%
Potassium: 10%
Another plus: very low in total and saturated fat

3. Broccoli, boiled (½ cup)

Vitamin B_6: 6%
Vitamin E: 7%
Folate: 10%
Calcium: 4%
Magnesium: 5%
Potassium: 7%

4. Milk, nonfat (1 cup)

Vitamin B_6: 5%
Vitamin B_{12}: 15%
Calcium: 28%
Magnesium: 6.5%
Potassium: 11%

5. Tuna, canned, in water (3 oz.)

Vitamin B_6: 19%
Vitamin B_{12}: 31%
Vitamin E: 7%
Magnesium: 7%
Potassium: 6%
Another plus: an excellent protein source that is very low in total and saturated fat

6. Pink salmon, with bones, canned (3 oz.)

Vitamin B_6: 13%
Vitamin B_{12}: 62%
Vitamin E: 6%
Calcium: 18%
Magnesium: 7%
Potassium: 8%
Another plus: a great protein source that is high in omega-3s

7. Tofu, firm (3 oz.)

Folate: 6%
Calcium: 3%
Magnesium: 6%
Potassium: 5%
Other pluses: a good source of vegetable protein that is very low in total and saturated fat and high in phytoestrogens

8. Wheat germ (2 Tbsp.)

Vitamin B_6: 7%
Vitamin E: 13%
Folate: 12%
Magnesium: 11%
Potassium: 4%

9. Kidney beans, cooked (½ cup)

Vitamin B_6: 6%
Folate: 29%
Calcium: 3%
Magnesium: 10%
Potassium: 10%
Another plus: a good protein source that is very low in total and saturated fat

10. Papaya (1 med.)

Vitamin E: 17%
Folate: 29%
Calcium: 7%
Magnesium: 8%
Potassium: 22%

Runners-Up to the Top 10

1. Swiss chard, boiled (½ cup)

Vitamin B_6: 4%
Vitamin E: 9%
Calcium: 5%
Magnesium: 19%
Potassium: 14%

2. Acorn squash, mashed (½ cup)

Vitamin B_6: 12%
Folate: 6%
Calcium: 6%
Magnesium: 13%
Potassium: 16%

3. Mustard greens, boiled (½ cup)

Vitamin B_6: 4%
Vitamin E: 7%
Folate: 13%
Calcium: 5%
Magnesium: 3%
Potassium: 4%

4. Asparagus, cooked (½ cup)

Vitamin B_6: 33%
Vitamin E: 2%
Folate: 6%
Potassium: 4%

what?

Ever met a
vegetarian?
Some famous
ones include
Carl Lewis,
Mr. Rogers,
Peter Falk,
Steve Martin,
Martina
Navratilova,
and Dennis
Weaver.

plenty of folate (the natural form of the supplement folic acid) from dark green, leafy vegetables and from legumes like peas and beans. For vitamin B_6 specifically, many unprocessed foods such as fish, whole grains, soybean products, fruits, and vegetables are bountiful sources. For vitamin B_{12}, your options are limited because it is found in red meat, and our hearts don't need the artery-clogging saturated fat that's part of that package. But fortunately, the nutrient is in milk, too. And if you drink the nonfat (skim) kind, you will get the benefits of B_{12} without the disadvantages of animal fat.

Vitamin E is another heart-kind vitamin, and it seems to play a couple of roles in heart-disease protection. Because it counters the negative effects of oxygen by-products in the body, vitamin E is often called an antioxidant. It probably acts as a scavenger, gobbling up oxygen-containing substances that make fats turn bad just the way butter can turn bad if it's left out on the counter. In the arteries, vitamin E may prevent the same process in bad cholesterol particles—a process that would make them even more likely to lodge in the heart's arteries. Other research suggests that vitamin E stops excessive blood clotting that can also block arteries.

While some people take supplements to get vitamin E, that might not be the best way. In one of the strongest studies of vitamin E to date, researchers found compelling evidence that the amount reaped from a healthy, low-fat diet is enough to reduce heart disease risk in women. "This is the first study to examine the effect of vitamin E from food instead of from supplements, and the results surprised even us," says chief investigator Lawrence H. Kushi, Sc.D., associate professor of public health, nutrition, and epidemiology at the University of Minnesota in Minneapolis. Postmenopausal women who ate the most vitamin E daily as real food—at least 10 international units (IU)—slashed their risk of heart disease by an astonishing two-thirds when compared to women who ate the least (less than 5 IU daily).

Many vitamin E-rich foods are also high in fat. But if you can choose wisely, you will avoid the fat trap. Some good vitamin E sources that are low in fat are wheat germ, mangoes, asparagus, and whole-grain cereals. The secret is choosing wisely.

10

Tofu Made Easy

A white to off-white, cloudlike cake, tofu hardly resembles the tough, little soybeans that it's made from. Nutritionally, though, tofu contains all of the bean's goodness, and you will quickly discover (if you haven't already) that you can easily prepare delicious dishes containing lots of this health-giving ingredient.

Since it's a rich source of phytoestrogens—and specifically the kind that help protect you from heart disease—you will want to get more in your diet. Yet many people consider it a somewhat exotic (if bland) Asian food.

Fortunately, tofu is no longer the hard-to-find health-food-store specialty that it once was. Now you can pick up a package in the produce section of almost any supermarket. So all you have to do is bring tofu home to dinner. Here are some recommendations from Reed Mangels, R.D., Ph.D., nutrition advisor for the Vegetarian Resource Group in Baltimore.

Keep tofu well-watered. Tofu is very perishable. Refrigerate fresh tofu for up to a week in a closed container of water and change the water every day. If you have kept tofu past its prime, it will smell slightly sour. Discard it.

Marinate away. One of tofu's most characteristic traits is its plainness—that is, fresh tofu doesn't have a very strong flavor of its own. Take advantage of this blandness by marinating tofu in whatever flavor you savor. A soy sauce and ginger marinade is a natural, in keeping with tofu's Eastern origins. But think creatively. An olive oil–fresh basil marinade could be just perfect if you would like to stir those chunks of flavored tofu into spaghetti sauce.

Go eggless. A great way to disguise tofu is to make a mock egg salad. Use cubes of firm tofu instead of hard-boiled eggs. Mix with low-fat mayonnaise and a little mustard or add curry powder for color.

Tempt yourself with tempeh. Tempeh (pronounced *TEM-pay*) is a firm, meatlike patty made from fermented soybeans. In con-

11

trast to tofu's blandness, tempeh has a unique, nutty flavor. You will find the vacuum-packed rectangles in the refrigerator section of health food stores. Be inventive when cooking tempeh—try baking, steaming, or sautéing. And slabs of barbecued tempeh make great veggie sandwiches.

Try a change of texture. Freezing tofu gives it a chewier texture, closer to that of meat. Tightly wrap slices of tofu in plastic and freeze for up to three months. Defrost it at room temperature before you cook it.

Superfoods to Guard Your Gut

Aging means slowing down, and there's nothing that slows you down more than a sluggish intestinal tract. Combating constipation, one of the most annoying problems of aging, isn't just a matter of comfort. It also means sidestepping hemorrhoids and diverticular disease that crop up so frequently with age.

One of the most underutilized secrets to regularity? Dietary fiber. "If fiber were a nutrient, it would be one of the most deficient in American diets," says Cathy Kapica, R.D., Ph.D., assistant professor of nutrition and dietetics at Finch University of Health Sciences/Chicago Medical School. Fiber—often called bulk—is just the indigestible portion of plant foods. Because it is indigestible, it travels through your intestines without being absorbed by your body. This seemingly useless attribute is precisely what makes it such a wonderful disease preventer.

All plant foods generally have two kinds of dietary fiber—soluble and insoluble. But some fruits, grains, and vegetables are better sources of one kind than the other. Soluble fiber, particularly abundant in oats and dried beans, dissolves in the watery contents of the gastrointestinal tract to form a gel. This gel corrals some of the fats, cholesterol, and chemicals in the intestinal tract that would otherwise get absorbed. For example, soluble fiber is great for doing a sweep-up of bile acids, which your body makes from cholesterol and uses to break down fats in your small intestine. Soluble fiber helps carry bile out of the body and can aid in lowering your overall blood cholesterol level.

12

Top 10 Superfoods for Gut Protection

In addition to foods high in fiber, especially insoluble fiber, the best of the intestinal protectors are also high in selenium, which seems to be a help in preventing cancer. Others that are well-liked by your digestive tract are foods rich in vitamins A, C, and E, all important to good immune-system functioning. Makes sense because the immune system has to be strong in your digestive system to stave off cancerous changes. Percentages shown are the percentages of the Daily Value for healthy adults consuming a 2,000-calorie-a-day diet.

The Top 10

1. Bulgur wheat, cooked (½ cup)

Total fiber: 4.1 g.
Insoluble fiber: 3.4 g.
Selenium: 11%

2. Wheat germ (2 Tbsp.)

Total fiber: 2.6 g.
Insoluble fiber: 2.1 g.
Vitamin E: 13%
Selenium: 17%

3. Acorn squash, mashed (½ cup)

Total fiber: 5.4 g.
Insoluble fiber: 4.9 g.
Vitamin A: 6%
Vitamin C: 22%

4. Sunflower seeds, dry roasted (⅓ cup)

Total fiber: 2.7 g.
Insoluble fiber: 1.6 g.
Vitamin E: 107%
Selenium: 48%

5. Whole-wheat bread (1 slice)

Total fiber: 2 g.
Insoluble fiber: 1.5 g.
Selenium: 15%

6. Black-eyed peas, cooked (½ cup)

Total fiber: 4.4 g.
Insoluble fiber: 3.9 g.
Vitamin A: 7%
Selenium: 4%

7. Kidney beans, cooked (½ cup)

Total fiber: 6.6 g.
Insoluble fiber: 3.9 g.

8. Spinach, cooked (½ cup)

Total fiber: 2.2 g.
Insoluble fiber: 1.5 g.
Vitamin A: 74%
Vitamin C: 15%
Vitamin E: 5%
Selenium: 2%

9. Broccoli, boiled (½ cup)

Total fiber: 2.3 g.
Insoluble fiber: 1.1 g.
Vitamin A: 11%
Vitamin C: 97%
Vitamin E: 7%

10. Sweet potato, baked (½ cup)

Total fiber: 3.1 g.
Insoluble fiber: 1.5 g.
Vitamin A: 249%
Vitamin C: 47%

The Super Fluid

In a world of celebrity-sponsored soft drinks, micro-brewed beers, super-hyped sports beverages, and gourmet-flavored coffees, plain water often gets relegated to last choice. And that's too bad, according to Nancy Clark, R.D., director of nutrition services at SportsMedicine Brookline in Brookline, Massachusetts, and author of *Nancy Clark's Sports Nutrition Guidebook, Second Edition*. "Water," she says, "is the ultimate nutrient."

Water is essential to human health. It's possible to survive for weeks without food, but you'll only last a few days without water. Because our bodies are anywhere from 60 to 70 percent water, a shortage can quickly turn into a crisis. Severe dehydration can lead to life-threatening heart disturbances. But even mild dehydration can cause dizziness, fatigue, cramps, and nausea. And for overall digestive health, it's essential as well since you always need the liquid to bulk up soluble and insoluble fiber.

The standard recommendation is at least eight glasses (that's eight ounces, or one cup, each) of water a day for the average adult, says Clark.

Of course, no one's average. Depending on your gender, your weight, your age, your activity level, and the temperature outside, your body's need for fresh water can be even higher.

But don't rely on thirst alone to drive you to drink. "Even if you aren't actually feeling thirsty, you could still need water," Clark says. So strive for that eight-glass minimum—whether you are parched or not.

You can tell how you're doing in the drinking department by monitoring your urine. "Urine should be practically clear," says Clark. "And there should be a good volume of it, too." In other words, if you are not visiting the rest room every two to four hours, you probably need to drink more.

Should you choose bottled water over tap water? Ask your tastebuds, says Clark. "It's important to have good-tasting water around," she says, "because the taste will affect how much you drink." So, if you're reluctant to drink water that comes from the faucet, it is a wise investment to buy bottled or install a filter. Even an inexpensive, low-tech filtering system can make a big difference in water flavor, she says.

But insoluble fiber, particularly abundant in bran cereals, seems the more important fiber when it comes to keeping the colon cancer-free. It works like a sponge, soaking up water in the intestinal tract. Since the spongelike effect makes intestinal

14

wastes much heavier, they move faster through the intestinal tract. "Not only does this keep you more regular, it also may help prevent colon cancer," says Dr. Kapica. Besides ushering out potentially cancer-causing substances, insoluble fiber also cuts down on the number of polyps that form in the gastrointestinal tract. And that's an important service because polyps are small, sometimes precancerous growths that may grow larger if left alone.

As you may have learned when you tried to eat a lot of high-fiber foods, all that fiber—both soluble and insoluble—needs some liquid help for smooth passage. That's why it's also essential to have plenty of water. "Without enough fluid, fiber just can't do its job in the intestinal tract," says Dr. Kapica. For fiber to work well, it needs to soak up fluid to create a bulkier stool. More important, without fluid, too much fiber can cause a blockage.

Makeover Minutes

Get Your Fill of Bountiful Broccoli

When it comes to eating your vegetables, broccoli is one mean green you should indulge in as often as possible. As you may have noticed, it has made the first two top 10 lists—for protecting your heart and helping your digestive system—and it is among the top 20 best foods for overall age protection. (For more information, see "Top 20 Foods for Total Protection" on page 32.) That's because broccoli is a boon to good health in so many ways, says Robert E. C. Wildman, R.D., Ph.D., professor of nutrition and dietetics at the University of Delaware in Newark. "It really might be the ultimate vegetable." This stalky, treelike plant provides vitamins and other potent substances that put it in many of our top 10 lists for its protective power.

Broccoli's deep-green color signals the presence of plenty of beta-carotene. This precursor to vitamin A is known as an antioxidant. In the body, antioxidants put the brakes on molecules called free radicals, tough guys who wander about causing in-

15

Foods to Flee From

Sure, there are a lot of wonderful foods. They will do great things for your overall health and help keep you feeling younger and more energetic. But while you're filling up on these super-foods, it's also important to steer clear of foods that can undermine your good intentions. These are the ones that offer nil in the way of nutrition, while serving up ferocious amounts of fat and cholesterol. If you occasionally indulge in small amounts, these foods won't do much damage. Just be sure they don't make it to your high-rotation list.

Here are some of the worst offenders, say Robert E. C. Wildman, R.D., Ph.D., professor of nutrition and dietetics at the University of Delaware in Newark, and other experts.

Canned meat products. Canned convenience meat made its first ap-pearance on dinner plates during World War II. Innocent-looking enough, the oftentimes pink pork product can contain 24 grams of fat in every little three-ounce serving—nearly the amount found in two ground-beef burgers.

Fettucine Alfredo. Also known as heart attack on a plate, just one serving of this rich, cream-and-cheese-based Italian dish contains 857 calories, 54 grams of fat, and 250 milligrams of cholesterol. And that doesn't include the garlic bread that often goes with it. It's saturated fat all the way—so do your best to keep away.

Pound cake. Ever wonder why it's called pound cake? The name refers to the pound of butter traditionally included in this yellow devil of a dessert. Dense and sweet, this high-calorie choice will fill your arteries

visible damage that eventually leads to aging and increased risk for chronic diseases like cancer.

In addition to its vitamin content, broccoli boasts at least four kinds of phytochemicals, cancer fighters in food that are neither vitamins nor minerals. With names like sulforaphane, phenethyl isothiocyanate, monoterpene, and indole, you might not believe that these are natural ingredients. But in fact, these tongue-twisting, health-enhancing compounds are abundant in nature.

Here are some tips on how you can get more broccoli in your meals every day. These recommendations come from Linda Nebeling, R.D., Ph.D., a nutritionist for the Five a Day for Better Health program at the National Cancer Institute in Bethesda, Maryland.

16

with 44 milligrams of cholesterol per slice. Better bet—forgo the pound cake (and the pounds) and opt for practically fat-free angel food cake.

Spareribs. This all-American meat is too high in fat to justify including in any healthy diet. With nearly 26 grams of fat per three-ounce serving, a double helping of spareribs could easily fill an entire day's fat budget. And with 103 milligrams of cholesterol and high levels of saturated fat, your heart will thank you for sparing the spareribs.

Specialty coffees. Beware of gourmet cappuccinos and mochaccinos made with full-fat milk. According to Ted Lingle, executive director of the Specialty Coffee Association of America, the difference between a 12-ounce whole-milk cappuccino and the nonfat version is as much as five grams of fat. So, if you yearn for latte, be sure to specify the skinny variety. And you won't even notice a difference. Nonfat milk froths up just as nicely as the full-fat stuff, says Lingle.

Premium ice cream. There's nothing like a cool ice cream sundae on a hot summer afternoon. Nothing worse for your waistline is more like it. "The sugar and the fat in ice cream work really well together to make you gain weight," says Diane Grabowski-Nepa, R.D., nutrition educator at the Pritikin Longevity Center in Santa Monica, California. "And it's simply much too easy to overdo it when it comes to portion size." She recommends low-fat or nonfat frozen yogurt as a pretty convincing stand-in when the ice cream urge hits you.

Eat 'em raw. Raw or lightly steamed broccoli has a hearty, satisfying crunch. When dunked into a low-fat dip, this veggie makes a great alternative to chips. So, next time you want to settle down with a bowl of something crispy, go for the green.

Don't forget about soup. Broccoli doesn't have to be relegated to the corner of your dinner plate. Bring it to center stage by letting it star in a pot of soup. Cream of broccoli soup is a whole different way to capitalize on this vegetable. Substitute evaporated skim milk for heavy cream and use a blender to puree cooked broccoli until it's smooth.

Pick some florets. If preparing broccoli seems like a chore, check out the packages of already-trimmed broccoli at your gro-

17

cery store. Florets, the top part of the vegetable with the thick stems already removed, are just right for steaming or sautéing. They may cost a bit more, but you will be more likely to eat them. "Having pre-cut vegetables available is helping a lot of people to eat healthier," says Margaret Barth, R.D., Ph.D., associate professor of nutrition and food science at the University of Kentucky in Lexington. "These products make a big difference to working moms and other busy people."

Superfoods to Boost Immunity

History's most respected five-star general couldn't have planned a more strategic attack. Indeed, your immune system stands ready to fight off potential troublemakers 24 hours each day and from multiple angles. And food is an essential reinforcement on every flank.

"A strong immune system depends on being well-nourished," says Dr. Kapica. As you age, nutritional reinforcements become even more critical because your immune system—like a sentinel starting to snooze—begins to grow weary. Keep it revved up with good nutrition, however, and you may be able to hold off the invaders that take a toll on your youthful energy.

It's easy to understand why the immune system tires and why it demands good nutrition. Multiple immune system representatives—embedded in tissues of the nose, intestinal tract, and lungs—guard every cell and patrol the bloodstream. "Having a properly working immune system is the way to control and stop bacteria and viruses that we're exposed to all the time—before they set up an infection," says Dr. Kapica.

And the immune system keeps continual watch over early cancerous changes in cells. "These tiny changes occur constantly, but the immune system squelches most of them," says Dr. Kapica. All the more reason to keep that system well-supplied.

Feeding the immune system involves a lot more than popping a multivitamin every morning. In fact, your guardian angels are fussy: Overloading your cells with one or another nutrient can actually unbalance the system, and you might get

18

some unpleasant side effects. There are times when taking a lot of one vitamin or mineral can cause more harm than good. But as long as you are getting these nutrients from food rather than from megavitamins, there is little chance that you will upset your immunity with an unbalanced overdose of one particular nutrient.

Good-quality protein is key to good immune system functioning. "Fortunately, Americans generally do eat enough protein," says Dr. Kapica. As we age and the nest empties, however, we are less likely to fix complete meals. "Relying on salads, soups, and toast often means coming up short on protein." Look to fish, lean meat, nonfat milk, and legumes for protein.

The key vitamin players in the immune system are vitamins A, C, and E; biotin; folic acid; and all the B vitamins. You also need certain minerals, including zinc, iron, copper, and selenium (particularly important in cancer-preventive response).

Makeover Minutes

Quick Immunity from the Sea

Seafood is a great low-fat, protein-rich alternative to red meat, says Dr. Wildman. But as we've noted, there are even more benefits to be found in the omega-3-rich "fatty fish" that thrive in the deepest, coldest ocean waters.

For boosting immunity, both tuna fish and pink salmon (with bones) are high on the superfood list because both have plenty of protein, selenium, and the all-important B vitamins in addition to their body-friendly fish oil. Fortunately for those on the go, tuna and salmon are quick and easy to prepare. Here are some suggestions to get more in your diet.

Open a can. Canned tuna and canned salmon are convenient and inexpensive, notes Diane Grabowski-Nepa, R.D., nutrition educator at the Pritikin Longevity Center in Santa Monica, California. To be sure that you're getting the most omega-3 fatty acids possible, choose water-packed seafood, she advises.

(continued on page 22)

19

Top 10 Superfoods for Immunity

The criteria for immunity boosters? All the superfoods on this list are fair to good sources of at least four of the following nutrients: vitamin A, vitamin C, vitamin E, zinc, copper, selenium, B vitamins, and protein. Vitamin E and the minerals get extra points simply because they are abundant in relatively fewer foods. As for the foods with protein, they had to be low in saturated (animal) fat to make this list. Percentages shown are the percentages of the Daily Value for healthy adults consuming a 2,000-calorie-a-day diet.

The Top 10

1. Oysters, steamed (3 oz.)
Vitamin C: 18%
Vitamin E: 8%
Copper: 114%
Selenium: 87%
Zinc: 186%
Protein: 32%
Other pluses: riboflavin, niacin, and vitamin B_{12} (at least 20% of each)

2. Sunflower seeds, dry roasted (⅓ cup)
Vitamin E: 107%
Folate: 25%
Copper: 39%
Selenium: 48%
Zinc: 15%
Protein: 17%
Another plus: niacin (15%)

3. Spinach, cooked (½ cup)
Vitamin A: 74%
Vitamin C: 15%
Vitamin E: 5%
Folate: 33%
Copper: 8%
Zinc: 5%
Another plus: riboflavin (13%)

4. Wheat germ (2 Tbsp.)
Vitamin E: 13%
Folate: 12%
Copper: 5%
Selenium: 17%
Zinc: 16%
Protein: 9%
Other pluses: thiamin (16%) and magnesium (11%)

5. Pink salmon, with bones, canned (3 oz.)
Vitamin E: 6%
Selenium: 40%
Zinc: 5%
Protein: 34%
Other pluses: riboflavin (9%), niacin (28%), vitamin B_6 (13%), and vitamin B_{12} (62%)

6. Kidney beans, cooked (½ cup)
Folate: 29%
Copper: 11%
Zinc: 6%
Protein: 17%
Other pluses: thiamin (9%) and iron (14%)

7. Milk, nonfat (1 cup)

Vitamin A: 14%
Zinc: 6%
Protein: 16%
Other pluses: riboflavin (19%), niacin (10%), and vitamin B$_{12}$ (15%)

8. Tuna, canned, in water (3 oz.)

Vitamin E: 7%
Selenium: 97%
Zinc: 3%
Protein: 50%
Other pluses: niacin (25%), vitamin B$_6$ (19%), and vitamin B$_{12}$ (31%)

9. Papaya (1 med.)

Vitamin A: 9%
Vitamin C: 313%
Vitamin E: 17%
Folate: 29%

10. Swiss chard, boiled (½ cup)

Vitamin A: 28%
Vitamin C: 27%
Vitamin E: 9%
Copper: 7%

Runners-Up to the Top 10

1. Acorn squash, mashed (½ cup)

Vitamin A: 6%
Vitamin C: 22%
Folate: 6%
Copper: 6%
Other pluses: thiamin (14%) and vitamin B$_6$ (12%)

2. Mustard greens, boiled (½ cup)

Vitamin A: 21%
Vitamin C: 30%
Vitamin E: 7%
Folate: 13%

3. Sweet potato, baked (½ cup)

Vitamin A: 249%
Vitamin C: 47%
Copper: 12%

4. Broccoli, boiled (½ cup)

Vitamin A: 11%
Vitamin C: 97%
Vitamin E: 7%
Folate: 10%

5. Black-eyed peas, cooked (½ cup)

Vitamin A: 7%
Folate: 26%
Copper: 6%
Zinc: 6%
Protein: 5%
Another plus: riboflavin (7%)

Magical Accompaniments

Sometimes, the right accompaniment to your main dish can bring along a number of health benefits. None of these accompaniments will ever make it as a main course, but if you use them while you're cooking (in the case of olive oil and garlic) or sip them with your servings (in the case of tea and wine), you will be adding one more dose of health protection to your meal. Here's why.

Olive oil. This is an exception to the rule when it comes to fat. People eating a high-fat diet that gets most of its fat from olive oil have lower blood cholesterol, lower blood pressure, and less incidence of heart disease than if they got fat from other sources. That may be because olive oil is one of the richest food sources of monounsaturated fatty acids, says Robert E. C. Wildman, R.D., Ph.D., professor of nutrition and dietetics at the University of Delaware in Newark. Monounsaturated fat behaves differently in the blood than dangerous saturated fat. The monounsaturated fat tends to lower bad low-density lipoprotein (LDL) cholesterol while maintaining the good high-density lipoprotein (HDL) type. The trick, of course, is to use monounsaturated fats like olive oil in place of saturated fats like butter.

Tea. Research suggests that the cherished teatime of Eastern and European cultures may actually be a very

That's because fatty acids tend to dissolve in vegetable oils. And if the fish is packed in oil, you will lose the fatty acids when you pour out the oil.

Try seafood Italiano. Canned tuna or salmon isn't just for lunch-box sandwiches. This seafood lends itself nicely to many other dishes. Try adding a can of either one to marinara sauce and toss with linguine.

Have some easy sea salad. Mix a can of tuna or salmon with hard-cooked egg whites, boiled small potatoes, and steamed green beans. Drizzle with vinegar and olive oil. In just minutes, you'll have an impromptu niçoise salad.

Superfoods to Save Your Bones

Although your skeleton is a solid structure, the whole framework is alive—and every bone is constantly changing in a process

22

healthy national pastime. Both black and green teas contain flavonoids, compounds that possess protective antioxidant properties. The flavonoids in tea keep dangerous LDL cholesterol in check, reducing the plaque that can clog arteries. And green tea also shows promise as an anticancer weapon. Both green and black teas come from the same plant, but they are processed differently. Animal studies indicate that daily indulgence in green tea could significantly lower rates of lung, stomach, and esophageal cancers.

Garlic. Garlic's heart-smart ability to shrink total cholesterol seems to come from the same place as its heady taste and smell—sulfur compounds such as allicin. Eating just one-half to one clove of garlic per day may lower cholesterol by as much as 9 percent. Adding garlic to your diet regularly may even help ward off a second heart attack, says Dr. Wildman.

Wine. Wine's potential to lower the risk for heart disease has been talked about for some time. Now, research shows that moderate imbibing may also help you keep your wits about you as you age. A French study of 3,675 men and women over age 65 suggests that those who drank three to four glasses of wine per day were only one-fifth as likely to develop dementia or Alzheimer's disease as compared to nondrinkers.

called remodeling. "That means bones need to be fed well every day of your life," says Patty Packard, R.D., a research dietitian at Creighton University and a consultant at the Creighton Osteoporosis Research Center, both in Omaha, Nebraska.

Neglect the feeding of your bones at your own peril: When they finally complain, it may be with a loud crack. That pronounced sign of early aging is the end result of the condition known as osteoporosis, a disease that affects some 10 million Americans, causing 1.5 million fractures yearly. The disease is so common that one in every two women and one in eight men over age 50 will have an osteoporosis-related fracture in their lifetimes.

Though bone building may come naturally when you are at your youngest, you'll probably have to devote more attention to it if you want to keep your youthful bone structure intact. Bones have a propensity to soak up bone-building nutrients

23

Top 10 Superfoods for Bone Protection

For good amounts of calcium, magnesium, phosphorus, and vitamin D, there are probably few foods better than vitamin D-fortified nonfat milk. Nonfat yogurt, while higher in calcium than nonfat milk, is just a runner-up because it doesn't contain the vitamin D supplementation that would help you absorb its calcium. Cheese is almost a worthy top-10 candidate, but doesn't make the list for two reasons:

It not only is lacking in vitamin D but also is fairly high in fat. Tofu, on the other hand, makes this list again for its phytoestrogens, and it is joined by the other great vegetable sources of protein that also have at least two of the essential bone-building nutrients. Percentages shown are the percentages of the Daily Value for healthy adults consuming a 2,000-calorie-a-day diet.

The Top 10

1. Milk, nonfat (1 cup)
Vitamin D: 23%
Calcium: 28%
Magnesium: 7%
Phosphorus: 23%

2. Pink salmon, with bones, canned (3 oz.)
Vitamin D: 117%
Calcium: 18%
Magnesium: 7%
Phosphorus: 28%

3. Spinach, cooked (½ cup)
Calcium: 12%
Magnesium: 20%
Phosphorus: 5%

4. Tofu, firm (3 oz.)
Calcium: 3%
Magnesium: 6%
Phosphorus: 8%
Other pluses: phytoestrogens and vegetable protein

until around age 30. When fed well, they bulk up during this whole time. After age 30, however, the cycle reverses, and bones naturally tend to give up bulk. But you can still give them a helping hand—or rather, many helping glasses and spoonfuls—to help protect your frame from aging. "Whether you are 58 or 88, it's not too late to start building stronger bones," says Packard.

While both men and women suffer bone loss, women have a particular life-cycle challenge that occurs when they reach

24

5. Kidney beans, cooked (½ cup)
Calcium: 3%
Magnesium: 10%
Phosphorus: 13%
Another plus: vegetable protein

6. Yogurt, nonfat, plain (1 cup)
Calcium: 49%
Magnesium: 12%
Phosphorus: 38%

7. Orange juice, calcium-fortified (¾ cup)
Calcium: 23%
Magnesium: 5%

8. Black-eyed peas, cooked (½ cup)
Calcium: 11%
Magnesium: 11%
Phosphorus: 4%
Another plus: vegetable protein

9. Catfish, cooked with dry heat (3 oz.)
Vitamin D: 106%
Magnesium: 6%
Phosphorus: 26%

10. Tuna, canned, in water (3 oz.)
Vitamin D: 34%
Magnesium: 7%
Phosphorus: 23%

Runners-Up to the Top 10

1. Broccoli, boiled (½ cup)
Calcium: 4%
Magnesium: 5%
Phosphorus: 5%

2. Acorn squash, mashed (½ cup)
Calcium: 6%
Magnesium: 13%
Phosphorus: 6%

3. Herring, pickled (2 oz.)
Vitamin D: 97%
Calcium: 5%
Magnesium: 1%
Phosphorus: 5%

menopause, sending the natural hormone estrogen into a nose-dive. In the first five to seven years following menopause, when there is steep estrogen loss, a woman can lose up to 20 percent of her bone mass if she does nothing to prevent it.

Hormone-replacement therapy (HRT), which supplies estrogen as well as other hormones like progesterone, can be a big help in preventing this life-changing bone loss. But whether or not a woman uses HRT, taking calcium remains a key strategy. The National Institutes of Health recommends 1,000 milligrams of calcium a day for postmenopausal women up to age 65 who use HRT. For postmenopausal women who don't use HRT, it is estimated that a calcium intake of 1,500 milligrams a day may limit loss of bone mass.

That mineral is no solo player, however. "As essential as it is, calcium alone can't build strong bones," says Packard. It depends on vitamin D, which helps the body absorb and use calcium optimally. Three other minerals are also needed to lend strength to bones: phosphorus, magnesium, and fluoride. "While bones would at least partially form without enough of these other minerals, they just wouldn't be as strong," she says.

Another food component—the isoflavones found in soy products—may also help out bones, especially in post-menopausal women, says soy researcher John W. Erdman Jr., Ph.D., professor of nutrition at the University of Illinois at Urbana–Champaign.

Dr. Erdman was especially interested in isoflavones because they are in a category of phytoestrogens that seem to mimic the action of estrogen. To study their effectiveness, Dr. Erdman's nutrition research team fed two groups of postmenopausal women a daily dose of soy protein that contained isoflavones. One group received a normal dose of isoflavones and the other group got a richer, elevated level of it. A third group of women received a milk-based protein.

"The results of our initial studies are very exciting," says Dr. Erdman. "In just 24 weeks, bone density in the spine increased 2 percent in the group of women receiving the isoflavone-rich soy protein with the highest amount of isoflavones." That's significant, he points out, because for every 10 percent loss of bone, the risk of spine fracture increases by 50 percent.

Although Dr. Erdman says that we can only theorize why isoflavone-rich soy restores bone mass, he suspects that it's because soy mimics the action of estrogen in bone. It's also possible that soy protein is easier on bones. Soy protein—and all other vegetable sources of protein such as kidney beans and black-eyed peas—have much less of the sulfur-containing amino acids found in meat. In excess, sulfur-containing amino acids tend to pull calcium from bones.

26

Superfoods for Brainpower

Your brain is the center of your universe. It controls every intentional motion you make, every thought you think, every nightmare that wakes you, and every pleasant dream that visits you in sleep. Without a moment's hesitation, it simultaneously and efficiently regulates a host of unconsidered actions like breathing, heartbeat, muscle contraction, and blinking. Whether you are adding a column of numbers or deciding in a split second how to swerve the car to avoid danger, you don't have to give a your brain a second thought: It is always on call for high-speed service.

No wonder, then, that many people worry about brain-related problems like slowed reaction time and memory loss as they get older. And if someone in your family has had a stroke, it's likely that you will begin to worry about that, too.

Keeping your brain in apple-pie working order and protecting it from stroke are high priorities for the young-at-heart and young-in-the-head who want to stay that way. But how can food help you do that?

More than any other organ in the body, the brain depends on a continuous, oxygen-rich blood supply. That explains why a person becomes confused or loses consciousness during oxygen deprivation—and that's exactly what happens when blood flow to the brain is blocked during a stroke. While nourishment alone can't ensure that your brain will get all the oxygen it needs to keep you thinking young, the right foods can certainly help prevent a mind-altering stroke. According to the American Heart Association, atherosclerosis (clogged arteries) and high blood pressure are two of the leading causes of stroke. To discover why, just touch both of the arteries on either side of your Adam's apple—the carotid arteries—and imagine what happens when those pipelines carrying oxygen-rich blood to the brain are blocked. And even if they are only partially blocked by atherosclerosis, your stroke risk rises dramatically. So any foods you eat to help prevent atherosclerosis will also help to protect the awesome computer at the top of those pipelines.

High blood pressure—hypertension—is an even greater risk

Strive for Five

Five a Day for Better Health is the national nutrition program started in 1991 by the National Cancer Institute, located in Bethesda, Maryland, and the Produce for Better Health Foundation, a nonprofit industry partner. Look around, and you will see their slogan appearing everywhere—from colorful logos on plastic produce bags to handouts for public school educational programs. Their hope is to get all Americans to eat at least five servings of fruits and vegetables every day by the year 2000.

The goal is a noble one—no less than the health of the entire nation. The basis of the effort comes from surveys showing that people who get the most vegetables and fruits in their diets have the lowest risk for many illnesses, including cancer and heart disease.

The good news is that most American adults now average about $4\frac{1}{2}$ servings of fresh produce per day— only a half-serving away from the recommended 5. But children are still lagging behind at only about 3 servings daily. "We don't quite understand why children's consumption of fresh vegetables and fruits hasn't increased in the same way as the adults'," says Linda Nebeling, R.D., Ph.D., nutritionist with the Five a Day for Better Health program. "We are putting a lot of focus now on getting kids to eat just as many fruits and vegetables as their parents do."

Here are some expert tips for fitting in five a day.

Get some decent exposure. Just being around fruits and veggies may make you eat more of them, says

factor than atherosclerosis, according to the American Heart Association. And controlling blood pressure is the most important way to lower your risk for stroke, says neurologist James L. Napier Jr., M.D., associate clinical professor of medicine at Case Western Reserve University School of Medicine in Cleveland.

Fortunately, blood pressure can often be controlled by eating healthier, the American Heart Association reports, and you don't need to eat boring, tasteless, unsalted food either. But you do need to favor an ideal combination of food.

In a ground-breaking, nationwide diet and hypertension study called the Dietary Approaches to Stop Hypertension (DASH) study, researchers divided nearly 500 adults with and without high blood pressure into three groups and fed each

28

Dr. Nebeling. "Put them at eye level in the fridge so that it's the first thing you see when you look in there," she says. And that way your kids will be more likely to crunch a carrot rather than a Clark bar.

Try dried. Dry fruit is an option that many people overlook. Just a quarter-cup raisins or a quarter-cup dried apricots counts as a whole serving of fruit. Keep dried fruit in your desk or send it to lunch in your child's backpack. "It won't go bad on you, and it's a much better choice than those sugary fruit leathers," says Dr. Nebeling.

Make a presentation of it. Stark string beans staring from your plate aren't very exciting. But a cozy bowl of homemade vegetable soup, some steamed broccoli draped with melted low-fat Cheddar, or a cool blueberry smoothie for breakfast are anything but boring. The challenge is to add fruits and vegetables to your diet in ways that make you want to eat more of them. "We're not just talking about salad here," says Dr. Nebeling.

Do a serving size-up. One serving of vegetables or fruit is a lot smaller than most people think, says Dr. Nebeling. A medium-size banana or apple, a half-cup cut-up fruit, or just a quarter-cup dried fruit all count as a full fruit serving. And a half-cup cooked beans or vegetables, or one cup raw salad greens make the grade as a complete vegetable serving. So, don't think you have to eat truckloads to hit that five-a-day mark, says Dr. Nebeling. And remember, five is a minimum—more servings are even better.

group a different diet. One group ate a typical American diet that was low in fruits and vegetables but accompanied by high-fat dairy products, so the total diet was high in fat content. The second group ate a diet high in fruits and vegetables but skipped the dairy foods. The third group was given a combination diet that was high in fruits, vegetables, and low-fat dairy foods—overall, a low-fat diet with ample dairy in it. Sodium intake averaged about three grams daily in all groups, and all participants maintained their usual weight during the study.

"The combination diet produced striking reductions in blood pressure," says researcher Lawrence J. Appel, M.D., associate professor of medicine, epidemiology, and international health at Johns Hopkins University in Baltimore. All types of

(continued on page 32)

Protect Your Body with Superfoods

Top 10 Superfoods to Protect Your Brainpower

To help lower your blood pressure—that all-important factor in warding off stroke—you will want to favor the fruits, vegetables, and low-fat dairy foods that make up an ideal combination diet. Many of these are high in the calcium, magnesium, and potassium that you need for blood pressure control—mixed, of course, with the other food ingredients that also help out. For memory-boosting and brainpower nutrients, you can add superfoods that are high in vitamins B_6, B_{12}, C, and E—as well as folate and beta-carotene. An extra advantage to this list is that all of these foods are naturally low in sodium and fat, two important factors to consider in keeping blood pressure low. Percentages shown are the percentages of the Daily Value for healthy adults consuming a 2,000-calorie-a-day diet.

Top 10 Foods

1. Milk, nonfat (1 cup)
Vitamin B_6: 5%
Vitamin B_{12}: 15%
Vitamin C: 4%
Folate: 3%
Calcium: 28%
Magnesium: 7%
Potassium: 11%

2. Spinach, cooked (½ cup)
Vitamin B_6: 11%
Vitamin C: 15%
Vitamin E: 5%
Folate: 33%
Calcium: 12%
Magnesium: 20%
Potassium: 12%
Another plus: high in beta-carotene

3. Black-eyed peas, cooked (½ cup)
Vitamin B_6: 3%
Vitamin C: 3%
Vitamin E: 1%
Folate: 26%
Calcium: 11%
Magnesium: 11%
Potassium: 10%

4. Acorn squash, mashed (½ cup)
Vitamin B_6: 12%
Folate: 6%
Calcium: 6%
Magnesium: 13%
Potassium: 16%
Another plus: high in beta-carotene

5. Pink salmon, with bones, canned (3 oz.)
Vitamin B_6: 13%
Vitamin B_{12}: 62%
Folate: 3%
Calcium: 18%
Magnesium: 7%
Potassium: 8%

6. Kidney beans, cooked (½ cup)
Vitamin B_6: 6%
Folate: 29%
Calcium: 3%
Magnesium: 10%
Potassium: 10%

7. Orange juice, calcium-fortified (¾ cup)

Vitamin B$_6$: 5%
Vitamin C: 103%
Folate: 8%
Calcium: 23%
Magnesium: 5%
Potassium: 11%

8. Papaya (1 med.)

Vitamin C: 313%
Vitamin E: 17%
Folate: 29%
Calcium: 7%
Magnesium: 8%
Potassium: 22%
Another plus: high in beta-carotene

9. Bok choy (Chinese cabbage), cooked (½ cup)

Vitamin B$_6$: 7%
Vitamin C: 37%
Folate: 9%
Calcium: 8%
Magnesium: 3%
Potassium: 9%
Another plus: high in beta-carotene

10. Potato, baked (½ cup)

Vitamin B$_6$: 9%
Vitamin C: 13%
Folate: 1%
Magnesium: 4%
Potassium: 7%

Runners-Up to the Top 10

1. Broccoli, boiled (½ cup)

Vitamin B$_6$: 6%
Vitamin C: 97%
Vitamin E: 7%
Folate: 10%
Calcium: 4%
Magnesium: 5%
Potassium: 7%

2. Wheat germ (2 Tbsp.)

Vitamin B$_6$: 7%
Vitamin E: 13%
Folate: 12%
Magnesium: 11%
Potassium: 4%

3. Banana (1 med.)

Vitamin B$_6$: 34%
Vitamin C: 18%
Magnesium: 9%
Potassium: 13%

4. Vegetable juice, low-sodium (6 oz.)

Vitamin B$_6$: 9%
Vitamin C: 56%
Vitamin E: 2%
Folate: 7%
Magnesium: 4%
Potassium: 7%
Another plus: high in beta-carotene

5. Tofu, firm (3 oz.)

Magnesium: 6%
Potassium: 5%

Top 20 Foods for Total Protection

One thing's for sure: If you tried to eat all the foods on the top 10 lists, you would be in for a healthy feast of gargantuan proportions that could help fend off age-related diseases. But many of those foods may be dark leafy greens; high-fiber, high-nutrient fruits and vegetables; and some whole-grain foods that you rarely shop for. So maybe you'd like a head start on your next shopping list.

That's exactly what you'll find here. This top 20 list is literally the best of the best—the 20 foods that have unquestionable star-quality when it comes to body and mind protection. But, of course, these remarkable 20 won't serve you unless you serve *them*—not necessarily at every meal but certainly as often as possible. So, along with this highly recommended list, we have also included some suggestions for preparing and serving provided by Kristine Napier, R.D., author of *Eat to Heal: The Phytochemical Diet and Nutrition Plan*.

The Top 20

1. **Spinach.** If it's fresh, wash it thoroughly and steam it gently. Or just open a box of frozen spinach and microwave or steam. For extra zest, give each serving a squeeze of fresh lemon. Go for a cup at a time.

2. **Nonfat (skim) milk.** Get at least two cups daily. If you are used to whole milk or low-fat (1% or 2%) milk, be patient. It might take a while to get used to the taste of skim, but for all the fat calories you save by drinking the nonfat variety, it's worth getting used to.

3. **Wheat germ.** Sprinkle it on cereal, mix it into quick breads, stir it into calcium-fortified orange juice.

4. **Canned pink salmon with bones.** Eat it from the can, add it to salad, or warm it up as salmon loaf.

5. **Kidney beans.** Open a can, rinse, drain well, and throw those red gems on top of your salad or into chili. If you have the time, cook the beans from scratch.

6. **Papaya.** Wash, slice, and enjoy.

7. **Black-eyed peas.** Open a can, rinse, and drain well. Add the peas to soups and stews. Don't hesitate to cook from scratch if you have the inclination.

8. **Canned tuna.** Always buy the water-packed variety. After you have

people benefited—not just men or women or people of only one race—and within just two weeks of starting the diet. "If all Americans ate this way, the returns could be huge," he concludes.

32

drained the tuna, add to a salad, or stir into a casserole. If you're making a tuna sandwich, substitute low-fat for high-fat mayonnaise, be sure to use whole-wheat bread, and add a thick slice of tomato.

9. **Broccoli.** Open a bag of frozen broccoli and microwave it a very short time. Or buy it fresh and steam it. Enjoy as is, or puree into soup with nonfat milk.

10. **Acorn squash.** Bake, peel, and mash with nonfat milk and nonfat cream cheese.

11. **Tofu.** Buy the extra-firm, light variety for stir-fries, and then experiment. Tofu picks up the flavor of whatever you put it with. Garlic, ginger, and tamari are all great complements. Stuff the firm, light variety into lasagna after mixing it with some reduced-fat mozzarella and lots of oregano, basil, and garlic.

12. **Bulgur wheat.** Don't avoid this incredibly easy-to-prepare food. Just add boiling water, black pepper, and lemon juice. Then cover and let it steam to its golden tenderness in just 30 minutes. Add lots of chopped tomatoes, chopped onions, and just a touch of extra-virgin olive oil for a filling lunch.

13. **Whole-wheat bread.** Make this the bread staple in your home and use it exclusively. Find a great bread bakery that uses excellent whole-wheat products.

14. **Sweet potato.** Bake in the skin, peel, and sprinkle with brown sugar. Or bake and refrigerate it. Cut off a thick, cold slice when you are looking for something sweet.

15. **Swiss chard.** Steam and enjoy with lemon juice. Or chop finely and use it in soups with kidney beans, black-eyed peas, lentils, and tomato sauce.

16. **Nonfat yogurt, plain.** Have several cartons on hand for a quick snack.

17. **Bok choy.** Stir-fry with tofu and your favorite herbs and spices.

18. **Tomato.** Cut, chop, or eat whole, however you like.

19. **Cantaloupe.** Wash, peel and enjoy the sweetness.

20. **Sunflower seeds.** Buy them dry-roasted. Enjoy them for a snack or toss on any salad.

So what was it about the DASH way of eating that pushed down the mercury on the blood pressure dial? "We can't be sure, but what we can say is that the diet is very healthy and should be helpful in preventing other medical problems, such as cancer and osteoporosis as well as high blood pressure," says Dr. Appel.

Other research has shown that potassium, magnesium, and calcium could also play roles in keeping blood pressure down. Potassium may help the body get rid of excess sodium, which can raise blood pressure in salt-sensitive individuals. It may also reduce the urinary loss of calcium and magnesium, both of which may also have protective effects on the body. Magnesium may help relax blood vessel walls, which decreases pressure when the heart beats. Calcium contributes to maintaining normal blood pressure by helping to transmit messages from the outside to the inside of cells.

The only catch is actually a bonus: You have to eat real food to get these benefits. "Supplements just don't seem to have the same effect on blood pressure," says Dr. Appel. He believes the difference is explained by the way the minerals and many other health-promoting substances in food work together. It may not be just the minerals; it's possible other substances in food, such as fiber, folate, and phytochemicals, may be working together to drive down blood pressure, according to Dr. Appel. To help avoid stroke, he urges people to eat four to five servings of vegetables, four to five servings of fruits, and three servings of nonfat dairy every day. ("And if you are on medication for blood pressure, be sure to take it," Dr. Appel adds. "While diet can control many people's blood pressure, millions of Americans still need to be on drug therapy.")

But of course it's not just stroke that can interfere with clear thinking. As we age, the ability to remember often seems to dwindle. When we're not only losing our keys but also forgetting when we last saw them, we may start to wonder what's up—and how to stop it. And we know intuitively that elderly people who seem youngest in years seem to maintain their memories and brainpower.

Is there any way that the right, nutritious foods can help you keep this fabulous gift of quick, clear thinking as you age? Maybe there is, say researchers at the Jean Mayer U.S. Department of Agriculture Human Nutrition Research Center on Aging at Tufts University in Boston.

Led by former Tufts psychologist Karen M. Riggs, Ph.D., Tufts researchers studied how 70 healthy men age 54 and older performed on tests of mental functioning. Dr. Riggs's team also measured the amount of certain B vitamins that the men had in their bloodstreams and correlated the two bits of information, turning up interesting results. Those men with the lowest levels of vitamin B_{12}, folic acid, and vitamin B_6 did not perform as well on certain mental acuity tests. "While more research is warranted, there is no doubt that everyone should get the current recommended dietary allowance for these three B vitamins," says Dr. Riggs.

Even more findings implicate food in mind maintenance. Swiss researchers have turned up evidence that people with the highest blood levels of vitamin C and beta-carotene may also protect their mental functioning and memory. They found that healthy 60-year-olds with the highest blood levels of these important antioxidant nutrients score higher on memory tests. Most of the study participants with the highest blood levels got them from eating real food, not from supplements.

Elsewhere in the world, Dutch researchers uncovered similar findings about beta-carotene and how it protects mental processes involving memory, judgment, perception, and reasoning. Yet another study—this time of Japanese-American men living in Hawaii—points to a role for the antioxidant nutrients vitamin E and vitamin C in forestalling losses in mental function.

While research teams are still thinking through why antioxidant foods keep them thinking clearly, they hypothesize that antioxidant nutrients or something else in antioxidant-containing foods may protect fragile brain cells from oxidative damage. This type of damage can break down neurons, which can keep them from properly transferring signals that translate into thinking. Of course, antioxidant nutrients might also keep blood vessels clear so that oxygen-rich blood can flow at full force to the brain cells—also necessary to keep them working their best.

know what?

Researchers say there would be 27 percent fewer strokes in the United States if people ate the combination diet of fruits, vegetables, and low-fat dairy products.

35

Never, Ever Get a Potbelly

We all know people who look and act young, seem to snack whenever they want, and never have big ups and downs in their weight.

Envy them?

If you're not a member of their semi-exclusive club, there's a good chance you keep wondering, "How come *they* can do it when I can't?"

Well, good genes are part of the answer, but it's also likely that these energetic friends of yours eat the right foods—lots of fruits and veggies and little fat—and exercise at home and on the job. They use stairs rather than wait for elevators, they take walks at lunch, and they pedal a bike or swing a tennis racket on the weekends. In short, they are physically active.

However they do it, these folks maintain a balance between the calories they take in and the calories that go out. And that's a balancing act of major proportions—since the average person eats about 2,000 pounds, or a pickup-truck-load, of food each year.

That truckful of potatoes, pasta, chips and salsa, bread, brownies, and everything else contains some 800,000 calories of energy. Surprisingly, it doesn't take many calories to tip the scale in the wrong direction. If you take in just 100 extra calories a day—the amount in a single tablespoon of mayonnaise—you could gain 11 pounds in one year. On the other hand, if you went out for a brisk 30- to 40-minute walk each day, you would burn about 100 calories and lose that 11 pounds in one year.

36

Although this formula is a bit simplistic (not everyone acquires or expends pounds at that rate), it shows how small changes in calories over time can make a big difference in your weight. Even if that spare tire seems to be written into your destiny (everyone in your family has one), your belly won't inflate overnight. It's a gradual process.

Perhaps you're past your twenties or thirties and wondering why the pounds don't come off so easily. There are good reasons: You probably aren't as active as you once were, and you don't burn calories as efficiently as you once did either. That's because the less active you are, the less muscle or lean body mass you have, which is your calorie-burning machinery.

Be Slimmer, Stay Younger

There's more than waning youth associated with a swelling midsection. A potbelly—or what doctors call upper-body obesity—is associated with several age-related afflictions: Type II diabetes, high cholesterol, high blood pressure, gallbladder disease, heart disease, some forms of cancer, stress to weight-bearing joints, and ultimately, a decreased life span.

Although a slimmer waist doesn't guarantee perfect health, your risk of having these problems will certainly be lower if you maintain a healthy body weight, says William Hardy, M.D., medical director of the weight-management program at Crittenton Hospital in Rochester, Michigan. "In general, overweight people don't live as long. Most of the old-timers you see walking around are pretty slim," he says. "When you decrease the risk associated with being overweight, chances are that you will live longer."

A number of important studies support Dr. Hardy. In an American Cancer Society 12-year cancer-prevention study of 262,000 women and 62,000 men, researchers concluded that adults between ages 30 and 74 have a higher risk of premature death if they are overweight. And those who are most in jeopardy are already carrying extra weight in their thirties and forties. The risk of dying from cardiovascular disease was particularly high among those who were overweight in this age range—nearly 10 percent greater than for people in the healthy weight ranges.

know
what?
Between her midtwenties and mid-forties, an average-height American woman gains eight pounds. The average-height American man gains six pounds in the same span of years.

37

Getting Back to a Younger Weight

Diana Bolkas considered herself a chubby 14-year-old. But that was when she weighed only 140 pounds.

Eleven years later, the five-foot four-inch Bolkas tipped the scales at 175 pounds. Not comfortable pounds either. She not only felt sluggish and depressed with her weight gain but also was fearful for the future. Members of her immediate family were overweight and some suffered from Type II, or non-insulin-dependent, diabetes, an illness that is often associated with obesity. If she couldn't turn the tide of weight gain, Bolkas knew, she was soon going to have the same health problems as her much-older relatives.

"I felt I was losing control over my body, and I couldn't accept the idea that I was meant to be heavy all my life," says Bolkas, a media manager for an advertising firm in New York City. By the age of 25, she had tried a number of diets. "I was really scared because nothing had worked so far," she recalls.

Bolkas eventually went to a registered dietitian who told her to forget dieting. Instead, the dietitian showed her how to cut the fat in her meals by making substitutions, eating smaller portions,

Not only are you likely to live longer if you maintain a healthy weight, you are also likely to ward off the bevy of diseases that can steal your youthful energy as slyly as a pickpocket. The higher the weight and the earlier you gain it, the more you are at risk of getting hit with a number of diseases that often signal the onset of older age, according to a scientific review conducted by a New York City doctor and obesity researcher. Among the grim visitors to come knocking early on the doors of the overweight are coronary heart disease, gallbladder disease, respiratory disease, some types of cancer, gout, and arthritis.

In fact, excess weight can be blamed for as many as 300,000 premature deaths annually, according to a survey of 30,000

and changing the way that she prepared and thought about food.

"Mine was a typical American diet. Lots of desserts and sweets," Bolkas explains. "When I would go to the store, I'd buy everything low-fat and think it was okay to eat all I wanted."

What Bolkas learned was a lifelong strategy for eating better and a gradual method of losing weight. It took her 18 months to drop 35 pounds. As her weight gradually decreased, she began to feel as if she had recovered the vigor and energy of a younger person. Getting off the commuter train at Penn Station, she dashed up the stairs instead of riding the escalator. At the gym, exercise became more of a joy than a burden.

Bolkas says she still eats sweets occasionally, but her new habit is to order or prepare foods that are lower in fat instead of the high-fat foods she used to consume. "I no longer eat so much that I feel I have no energy or stamina," she adds.

Feeling content with her new 140-pound body, Bolkas happily accepts the fact that she's never going to be a petite size 4 with a 20-inch waist. Nature just gave her a large frame, but she feels a lot different about that frame than when she had an extra 35 to 40 pounds on it.

adults by the National Center for Health Statistics. During the survey, which was conducted between 1991 and 1994, doctors were alarmed to discover that 49 percent of American women and 59 percent of American men were overweight.

Get rid of that extra weight, and you'll not only live longer but live better, adds Dr. Hardy. People who maintain healthy body weights tend to be more active, eat the right foods, feel younger, and maintain the winning edge when they do get an illness.

Take joint pain, for instance. "Let's say you have arthritis of the weight-bearing joints and you're 30 pounds overweight. That's like carrying around two bowling balls with every step. Imagine the pressure on your joints," says Dr. Hardy. "If you lose those 'bowling balls,' you're obviously going to feel much better."

As you age, then, excess weight becomes more of a health concern. Unfortunately, at the same time the pounds are easier to put on, they are also harder to take off. The much-heralded weight-loss solution—switching to a low-fat diet—can certainly help you win the game. But low-fat is just part of the bigger stop-time tactic. Whatever else you do, you also have to pay attention to the total calories.

Where Calories Get Too Comfortable

The tendency to widen out as you age is primarily due to changes in your resting metabolism and your physical (or calorie-burning) activity. Resting metabolism is the amount of energy you use to power a whole range of vital body functions. Blood pulses through your system. Eyes blink. Lungs expand and contract. Your heart beats calmly. And your body temperature rides along at a thermostatic setting just under 100 degrees.

All these mechanical and thermometric functions require a base level of energy. You need a lot of calories to keep the heat at that level—and most adults burn 60 percent of all calories just for basal metabolism.

You use another 10 percent of calories to digest and metabolize food. One to three hours after a meal, the nutrients in your bloodstream and the food in your stomach and intestines produce heat in a process called the thermic effect of food. The amount of burn varies with the type of food. Your body needs more calories to breakdown a steak than a banana and very few calories are expended in breaking down fat or simple sugars.

With the remaining calories, you fuel physical activity, everything from line dancing to playing the piano to shoveling snow. Every activity has a calorie cost, but as you might guess, not all activities are equal. If you arc a would-be Pavarotti or Beverly Sills, breaking into operatic song during your morning showers, you use twice as many calories per hour as you would sitting and staring at Willard Scott's pate on the *Today* show.

If you're moving your whole body in an activity like walking, bowling, dancing, or playing golf, the energy you expend is greater if you have more weight to move around. A 143-pound man who walks three miles in an hour burns 222 calories. A lighter person, a 110-pound woman, burns only 180 calories going the same pace.

Once the daily business of breathing, eating, singing in the shower, and moving about are met, any unused or surplus calories get stored away, mostly in the form of fat. The law is written in the book of inevitability: Take in more calories than you use, and you will gain weight.

Burn Before You Bulge

Resting metabolism differs among people because of age, physical condition, the amount of muscle and fat in the body, and gender. At birth, you had a very high metabolism that made you cry out for food every few hours. Two years later, you were a mini-tornado of energy, but internally your metabolism was already beginning to slow down. With the exception of a brief period during puberty when your metabolism rises, the slowdown continues for the rest of your life.

That decline is slight until you reach your thirties, when metabolism slows by 2 to 5 percent per decade. By age 55, you require 145 fewer calories per day than you did in your midthirties. For that reason alone, if you haven't cut back on calories or increased your activity level to burn more calories, you're going to find yourself walking around with a couple of bowling balls' worth of fat.

With this new dimension added to your girth, you're likely to look older and feel more burdened. Worst of all, the just-for-kicks physical activities that you used to enjoy are likely to become more of a chore—whether you are wading into a rushing stream to cast a fly, playing tennis in a foursome, or trekking the outlet malls in search of great bargains.

The fact that your metabolism slows down as you age is closely related to the loss of muscle. If you are fit and active, you probably have a relatively higher resting metabolism than your overweight, out-of-shape neighbor asleep in his hammock. As you age, you lose the toned-up, hard muscles of youth and instead build up stores of fat on your thighs, belly, and buttocks.

know
what?

There's cause for concern if your waist circumference is greater than 40 inches, doctors say. Fat stored around the abdomen has been linked to cardiovascular disease and is more risky than fat stored around the hips and thighs.

41

If you are a man, you are more likely to get a potbelly. If you are a woman, the weight usually accumulates down lower—on the hips and buttocks.

That flab, unfortunately, is not as metabolically active as muscle. While muscles contract, stretch, generate heat, demand blood, and burn calories, your fat just sort of sits there in storage.

Because most men are more muscular than most women, males generally have a higher metabolism. Women, because of their naturally higher percentage of body fat, tend to have a 10 to 12 percent lower resting metabolic rate than men.

Where Your Body Balances Out

Your genes as well as your gender has an influence on the way you pack extra pounds. There is some scientific evidence that all people—thin or fat—have setpoints for their weight. In other words, you weigh what your body "thinks" you should weigh. If you overeat, your body may tell you to cut back. If you take in too many calories, metabolism naturally revs up to burn away the excess. And if you try to cut back during dieting, your body slows its metabolism as a way to defend its weight.

If you are obese or underweight, your problem may lie with a biological setpoint that is fixed too high or too low. Even though your weight may be judged "unhealthy" by doctors—because heavier people statistically have more health problems— your body believes it is storing up reserves at the proper level.

Of course, there is often an obvious genetic connection. If your mom or dad was always fighting the fat war, you probably will, too. But even though metabolism is somewhat in the genes, that doesn't mean that you can't do anything about it, says Arthur Frank, M.D., director of the obesity-management program at George Washington University in Washington, D.C. "You can learn to manage your metabolism," he says. "In other words, you have to deal with it."

One way is to exercise. When you're active, you temporarily rev up your metabolism and burn additional calories. If you exercise briskly, the burn may last for several hours af-

42

terward. This results from your muscles using more calories to recover and repair themselves.

Rev It Up

If you work out at least three times per week, you'll likely increase lean body mass (a fancy name for muscle), which burns more calories than fat. Strength training—such as light weight lifting—can be an important part of your stay-young, stay-fit, weight-loss program.

And if you work out while you're reducing your intake of calories, you'll maintain or increase the muscle you already have. In other words, you really need some convenient form of regular exercise if you're eating less. Because if you don't keep up the calorie burn, you'll lose muscle as you shed pounds,

How to Ballpark Your Calorie Counting

Some calorie counting can be done using the ballpark method—just looking at food labels and making some rough estimates. Start scanning labels, and you can quickly familiarize yourself with what's high and what's low.

As for the unlabeled fresh foods in the produce department, you can be sure that most legumes, fruits, and vegetables are lower in calories than most packaged and prepared foods. Fast food, at the other extreme, is likely to be off the charts when it comes to calories. So take that into consideration when you do your ballpark calculations. And figure that any gooey, oily, dense, or sweet packaged foods are much more likely to be high in calories than raw foods.

For a more exact tally, you can get calorie counts by reading nutrition labels on bottles or packages. Or you can use a calorie guide, such as *Bowes and Church's Food Values of Portions Commonly Used*, that includes brand-name foods, fast foods, and common restaurant meals, says Gail C. Frank, R.D., Dr.P.H., professor of nutrition at California State University, Long Beach, and co-principal investigator of the Women's Health Initiative at the University of California, Irvine, Medical Center in Orange, California.

which means that you'll lose some of your body's natural ability to burn calories even as you're losing weight.

So if you aren't in the mood to carefully count calories, be sure to keep exercising in ways that keep your muscles in shape. As long as you do that, you will keep on burning calories even when you are eating less.

Inching toward a Banished Belly

Dieting also changes metabolism, but not in a helpful way. When you cut calories, your body responds by lowering metabolism. In fact, your resting metabolism can plummet as much as 45 percent when you diet.

When you stop exercising and stop watching calories, your resting metabolism usually returns to normal, says Dr. Frank. When that happens, most people gain back their weight—and sometimes very quickly. The setpoint nudges your weight back up to its old level.

"You can get some control over a weight system that is set wrong, but you have to keep after it," says Dr. Frank. "The problem doesn't go away after you've lost the weight."

At the beginning of any weight-loss program, you will need an idea of how many calories you should be taking in each day. Remember that these numbers are just averages, but they will help you understand how one more dab of peanut butter on your toast or one less flight of stairs at the mall may be contributing to the midsection expansion. Perhaps you need to push away dessert or stop heaping sour cream on your potatoes. Or, maybe you just need to turn your evening stroll into a two-mile, faster-paced power walk. More than likely, you need to do some of both.

Which is really no chore. As soon as you start to reap the benefits of this age-protector tactic, you'll realize that being a lighter weight also helps you feel like a more youthful you.

Some Shape-Up Math

There's a quick way to calculate your daily calorie need based on your activity level, but first you'll have to judge how ac-

know what?

A fresh salad with two tablespoons fat-free vinaigrette dressing has 48 calories. Use two tablespoons ranch dressing instead of the vinaigrette, and the same salad weighs in with 183 calories.

44

tive you are. Researchers use the categories "sedentary," "moderately active," and "active." To figure out which category best describes you, think about your level of physical activity in the past six months to a year.

A sedentary person is someone whose job is not physically demanding, who rides rather than walks, watches a lot of television, doesn't like being involved in physical activities like walking or hiking, and may find physical exercise uncomfortable. The moderately active individual walks occasionally, works around the yard and house, and may play softball, ride a bike, or participate in some other recreational physical activity more than once a week. An active person exercises vigorously at least three times a week for 20 to 30 minutes and looks for ways to burn more calories during the day by walking briskly and climbing stairs rather than whiling away flights of potential exercise on escalators and elevators.

To guesstimate your daily calorie requirements, you need to begin with a reasonable target weight range. An easy guideline is to allow 100 pounds for the first five feet of your height, then add 5 pounds for every inch over five feet, says Doris Derelian, R.D., Ph.D., former president of the American Dietetic Association. Once you have this figure, add 10 percent to find your upper range and subtract 10 percent to find your lower range. For example, a woman who is five feet four inches tall should weigh approximately 120 pounds, plus or minus 12 pounds. That makes her healthy weight range 108 to 132.

With your target weight in mind, think, too, about the activity level you're at right now—using the criteria for sedentary, moderately active, or active. With this information in mind, you can judge your daily calorie requirements. Multiply your target body weight (in pounds) by the number below associated with your activity level to figure out your daily caloric requirements.

Sedentary woman: 12
Sedentary man: 14
Moderately active woman: 15
Moderately active man: 17
Active woman: 18
Active man: 20

But even if you don't take time to do this math, there's an instinctive way to know whether you're getting too many calories every day. The fact is, most folks have a pretty good idea if they are overweight, says Tina Ruggiero, R.D., health and nutrition editor of the *Richard Simmons and Friends* newsletter. The trick, however, is to come up with some reasonable weight-loss expectations without trying to be something you are not.

"Throw out the image of the ideal woman that you see in magazines and ask yourself, 'What was my weight when I felt most comfortable? When did my clothes fit best?'" advises Ruggiero. "That may be your ideal weight, and it may be 10 pounds above what some chart says you should weigh. A healthy weight is one that you can maintain by eating right and being active."

Target the Fat

Whether or not you start counting every last calorie, there's an easy way to make a big dent in calorie consumption. Just take aim at the fat in your diet.

Fat contains 9 calories per gram, twice as many calories as you get from the same amount of protein or carbohydrate. Picture a cup of flour (mostly carbohydrate) and cup of cooking oil (all fat). The cup of oil contains about 2,000 calories while the flour has just 455 calories.

"Fat packs a big punch when it comes to calories. That's why it really is important to watch what kind of food you're eating," says Gail C. Frank, R.D., Dr.P.H., professor of nutrition at California State University, Long Beach, and co-principal investigator of the Women's Health Initiative at the University of California, Irvine, Medical Center in Orange, California. "Cut the fat, and you'll cut calories."

But dietary fat isn't just a culprit because it is high in calories. Fat in food is more easily turned into body fat. Your body has to burn (or metabolize) 25 percent of the calories contained in carbohydrates and protein in order to turn them into body fat. Not so with the calories that come from fat. Fully 97 percent of calories from fat in the diet is available for immediate storage.

46

In other words, your body is very efficient at storing fat. That butter on your toast is like a sports car zooming down the expressway with nary a cop in sight. It's going to get to your belly or backside fast—and with no detours.

Most Americans get 37 percent of their daily calories from fat. That's average, so if you eat pretty much what your neighbors eat, you're probably somewhere in that range. And that's a long way from ideal. The American Heart Association says that fat should be no more than 30 percent of daily intake. And other experts say that you should get fewer than 25 percent of your calories from fat.

Most people recognize that the percentage of fat is very high in foods like whole milk, cheese, and marbled steaks. And you're probably aware that peanuts, salad dressings, mayonnaise, cream sauces, gravies, cookies, and many baked goods like croissants and doughnuts are classic fat traps. Many foods that are high in sugar are also high in fat. And baked goods are likely to be made with eggs, butter, and oils—the high-fat troika that can ride roughshod over your best fat-cutting intentions.

Makeover Minutes

Cutting Fat and Calories

Since most of us get our daily food supply from the supermarket, we have to face a staggering array of tempting choices that line the shelves of those gleaming aisles. So rule number one is: Don't go to the store hungry.

"The supermarket is the first place to start to cut fat and calories from your diet, but you won't do a good job of it unless you have a plan," says Debbie Stafford, R.D., a research dietitian in the Lipid Research Clinic at the Baylor College of Medicine in Houston.

Here are some small changes in shopping habits suggested by Stafford that can make a big difference in calorie consumption.

Make a list. Sit down with a cookbook and put together a

47

low-fat meal plan for the week. Make a list of all the ingredients you need and be sure to take it with you to the store. "When you have a list, you're more likely to stick to it and not get caught up in buying things on a whim," Stafford says.

Shun the promo and read the label. When you're selecting packaged food, ignore the promotional labeling on the front that may proclaim "No Fat" or "Low-Fat." Even if the food is low in fat, says Stafford, that doesn't mean it's low in calories. Turn to the nutrition label on the back to find out what's really up.

Be serving-conscious. The nutrition label will also tell you the serving size—and that's an important factor when you are watching your intake. For quick estimates, remember that one ounce of cheese is about the size of your thumb, says Dr. Gail Frank. And one serving of fish, beef, or poultry is just three ounces—about the size of a deck of cards.

Be a bottom-feeder. Load your cart with items from the bottom of the food pyramid. They are whole grains, vegetables, fiber, and fruits—foods that contain little fat and lots of carbohydrates, notes Stafford. Plus you get an extra benefit. These foods are cheaper than most meat, dairy, and packaged products, so you'll be cutting your grocery bills while reducing your waistline.

Avoid temptation. Stay away from the aisles where you may lose your resolve, advises Stafford. Chips, soft drinks, and baked goods are the badlands of supermarket territory. Leave them to other hunter-gatherers and spend more time in the fresh fruits and produce section.

Change gradually. As you ease into new frontiers of dietary change, focus on the foods you eat most frequently, especially the ones that are naturally high in fat, such as cheese, milk, margarine, or favorite frozen meals. If you're a cheese-lover, for instance, start choosing cheeses made from skim rather than whole milk. One slice of whole-milk American cheese contains 4.5 grams of fat and 60 calories, while skim American gives you 0 grams of fat and 30 calories.

"Then, on the next shopping trip, you concentrate on changing something else," suggests Stafford. "Some people are more successful by combining little assignments."

48

Brand your favorites. Shopping for low-calorie foods becomes a lot swifter when you screen the brands and make a mental list of the ones you want. At first, for instance, you may spend 15 minutes reading the nutrition labels, says Stafford. Once you have found the lower-calorie product, make it your brand.

Think lean. You don't have to become a vegetarian to cut fat. "When I tell people that it's okay to eat beef, they find it very comforting," says Stafford. "People should continue to eat the food and meals that they like but substitute with lower-fat items."

If you like meat, simply choose leaner cuts, trim off visible fat before cooking, and don't eat portions larger than three ounces at one sitting, she says. Remember, lean beef has little marbled fat. Because ground meat is processed, it can be higher in fat than other cuts of meat. Most poultry is lower in fat than red meat. Good choices in beef are top round, shank cross cuts, and sirloin; in lamb, shank, foreshank, and leg; in pork, tenderloin and cured ham; and in poultry, chicken breast and turkey white meat.

Makeover Minutes

Keys to Healthy Cooking

At home in your kitchen, with your cookbook open to your favorite recipe, there's something else you can do to lower the fat and calories in your diet. Many traditional recipes call for more sugar, eggs, oil, and high-fat ingredients than are necessary. "Often you can cut back, eliminate, or make substitutions for these ingredients and still not sacrifice taste or consistency," says Ruggiero.

Fortunately, good substitutes don't change the taste of food very much. And it's easy to get used to bringing them into your cooking. Here's what experts in fat- and calorie-cutting cuisine recommend.

49

Put the Skids on Grease

All cooking oil is fat and is loaded with calories—about 120 calories per tablespoon. It is one of the biggest sources of hidden fat in the American diet.

Because oil is a necessary cooking ingredient in many prepared foods, it's hard to eliminate from your diet completely. You can easily use healthier oils—and cut back on all oils—when preparing food in your own kitchen, says Mary Kay Mitchell, R.D., Ph.D., professor of human nutrition at Ohio State University in Columbus.

Choose cooking oils low in saturated fats and high in monounsaturated and polyunsaturated fats, she advises. Monounsaturated fats help lower total cholesterol while saturated fats raise cholesterol, contributing to clogged arteries and setting the stage for heart disease, says Dr. Mitchell.

Your healthiest choices, according to Dr. Mitchell, are olive, canola, safflower, rice bran, corn, and peanut oils. Avoid coconut oil, palm oil, cottonseed oil, lard, and vegetable shortening due to their high amounts of saturated fat.

Dr. Mitchell advises against using butter or margarine to add flavor. "Regular margarine is high in fat, and diet margarine has a lot of water content, so it really doesn't work well as a replacement," she explains. "If you're looking for flavor, use oils with strong natural flavors like olive oil or ones that have been seasoned with herbs."

Yank the yolks. Whole eggs are loaded with cholesterol. Discard the yolks and use only the egg whites, which are low-calorie, high-quality protein. If you still want yolks, try using one instead of two when you are making an omelet. In scrambled eggs, you can even use one yolk with three or four egg whites.

Get less nutty. If a bread or roll recipe calls for a cup of nuts, try using just a third or half a cup. You probably won't miss the extra nuts, and you'll cut down on fat significantly. Nuts are very high in fat. Just one ounce of most types exceed 160 calories. The lone exception is chestnuts, which have just 70 calories per ounce.

Wean yourself from "whole-someness." Skim or nonfat milk has all the calcium and nutrients you need, but weaning your-

Your other choice is to simply cut back. Here are some ways to get the grease out.

Wipe it thin. Rather than pouring oil into a pan, apply it lightly with a brush or a paper towel. You need just a thin coating to keep food from sticking. "Food doesn't have to float for oil to do its work," says Dr. Mitchell.

Get misty. Firing a short burst of nonstick spray oil (like Pam) into your pan adds almost no fat or calories because you apply so little. If you don't like an aerosol spray, make your own mist by dispensing oils from a reusable spray bottle.

Go nonstick. Instead of using a cast-iron or stainless steel skillet, use a skillet with a nonstick coating. With this type of surface, you will need only a smidgen of oil to keep food from sticking to the pan, Dr. Mitchell points out.

Stir in a surrogate. In many recipes, you can use half the amount of oil called for or substitute an equal portion of nonfat sour cream or nonfat yogurt without substantially changing the flavor and texture of the food. "Make sure you use plain yogurt without flavoring," advises Dr. Mitchell.

Measure better. If you must use oil to make a recipe work, be sure to dole it out with a measuring spoon rather than just pouring in a "splash of oil." A precise tablespoon is usually less than you use when you just add that splash, says Dr. Mitchell.

self from the taste of whole milk may take time. If you like whole milk on your cereal, for instance, try mixing it with skim before you pour it on. Gradually add more skim each day, until you eliminate whole milk altogether. You'll save 71 calories for every eight-ounce glass you drink or pour on your cereal.

Use your yogurt. If a recipe calls for sour cream, buy a nonfat variety or try using low-fat or nonfat plain yogurt instead. In most recipes, you can't tell the difference, says Ruggiero.

"I make a nonfat yogurt cheese by putting nonfat yogurt into a strainer over a bowl in the refrigerator," she explains. "The liquid drains into the bowl, and I'm left with a hearty cheeselike spread for regular and sweet potatoes. And it has the added bonus of being high in calcium."

51

Try jelly. Butter is all fat. Use it sparingly or not at all. Jelly, marmalade, or cinnamon on your toast or English muffins is a better choice.

Marginalize the margarine. Margarine isn't really a better choice than butter because its calories come from fat, too. If you must use margarine, pick a light or diet variety to cut down on the number of calories per serving.

Makeover Minutes

Low-Fat Cooking

Often it isn't the food you eat but how you prepare that food that makes it high-calorie. Fresh fish can be a good low-calorie meal, but if you dip the fillet in beer batter, bread it, and drop it into a pan of oil, you're loading it with fat. There are many ways to cook fish—and other food—that will make sure you don't add calories in the process.

To go the low-fat cooking route, you need the right utensils, along with some alternative cooking methods that dodge pitfalls such as high-fat frying. Here are some of the ways and means that expert cooks recommend.

Broil without oil. Instead of breading and deep-frying that fish fillet, turn to the grill-pan in your oven or fire up your backyard barbecue. Grilling is even better for meat since it allows the fat to drip down rather than being soaked up by the meat. Another bonus is the rich, smoky flavor the grill will impart to your usual meal.

If you're grilling in your kitchen, use a slotted broiler in your oven or a ribbed, cast-iron frying pan on the stove top. Broiling a 3½-ounce top sirloin instead of frying it in a pan eliminates close to 60 calories.

Steam your veggies. Steam-cooked vegetables come out crunchy—not limp—with all the nutrients locked in. And if they have more flavor, you won't even want to add butter or margarine. You can steam your veggies in a microwave steamer or

52

Getting a Boost from Medical Nutrition Therapy

Although it's not always necessary, there are good reasons to seek out professional help when it comes to weight loss. If all your weight-shedding attempts have resulted in adding pounds rather than subtracting them, the support of a doctor or a registered dietitian may be just what you need to slam the brakes on weight gain.

Many doctors and registered dietitians today offer nutrition or weight-management counseling called medical nutrition therapy (MNT).

During MNT, the health professional will take some basic body measurements—body mass index, waist-to-hip circumference, and skin-fold measures—to determine the amount and distribution of fat on your body. You'll also have your blood pressure, cholesterol levels, and blood sugar checked, and you'll be asked about your relatives to find out whether obesity, diabetes, and heart disease tend to run in your family.

"A health assessment like this begins to tell me if someone is at nu-tritional risk. For example, if you have a family risk of diabetes, then weight can be a real concern," says Gail C. Frank, R.D., Dr.P.H., professor of nutrition at California State University, Long Beach, and co-principal investigator of the Women's Health Initiative at the University of California, Irvine, Medical Center in Orange, California.

MNT also puts your eating behaviors under scrutiny. You'll be asked questions like: Do you skip breakfast? Graze throughout the day? Snack in the evening? Eat sweets and desserts? Drink alcohol daily?

"I've counseled some people who drink 10 cans of soft drinks a day. That tells me a lot," says Dr. Frank. "When I know where their calories are coming from, especially those excess calories, I can make recommendations. Then we'll see what foods they are willing to give up or replace with better, healthier choices. Monitoring their body weight and blood cholesterol and glucose levels will tell if we are successful in lowering their risk for chronic disease—heart disease, hypertension, and diabetes, to name a few."

use a stove-top stainless steel steamer. Both hold vegetables just above boiling water.

Sizzle in water. If you don't steam your veggies, sizzle them in their own juices rather than in fat-laden oil. Vegetables con-

53

tain lots of water. Put them in a nonstick pan, cover, and cook on very low heat. When done, they should be tender but not droopy.

Pour off the grease. Because fat is lighter than water, it rises and accumulates at the top of soups and stews. Use a ladle to skim it off. If you store your homemade stew in the fridge, check the surface after it has been chilled. If some fat has hardened on the top, you can easily lift off that fatty layer before you reheat for serving. You can also use this technique to reduce fat in gravies and sauces.

Makeover Minutes

Filling Up, Not Out

Frequently, we either view food as an enemy—or just something to eat because it's there, says Mary Kay Mitchell, R.D., Ph.D., professor of human nutrition at Ohio State University in Columbus. "A lot of us eat anytime, and we eat all day—no matter whether we are hungry or not. We don't follow our body's own cues."

Getting control over our eating means changing attitudes about the ways we consume food and think about food, says Dr. Mitchell. Here is what she recommends if you want to avoid the pitfalls of overeating.

Relish the occasion. All-you-can-eat buffets and triple-cheeseburgers are signs of the times, but that doesn't mean you have to join in the high-fat, high-calorie food fest. Treat a meal like an event. Slow down and enjoy the tastes and smells of the food, recommends Dr. Mitchell.

Put less on the plate. When you sit down to a home-cooked meal, put a reasonable amount on the plate, she says. If you're still hungry, you can always go back for more. But if you load up your plate at the very start, you're likely to feel as though you have to finish it all.

Push the plate away. You may have been taught that it was

54

bad manners not to leave an empty plate, but it may be bad for your health. Restaurants pile on huge portions that encourage overeating. Practice moderation.

Slow down. If you eat fast, you're more likely to overeat because your body doesn't have enough time to send you signals that you are full—signs that nutritionists call signals of satiety.

"Slow eating encourages moderation. It gives your mind time to catch up with the body," Dr. Mitchell explains. "When you eat fast or all the time, you change your satiety mechanisms. They just don't work to tell you to stop."

Look Younger,
Feel Younger

Aging sure ain't what it used to be.

Thank God.

It wasn't so long ago that men and women started to put on weight, wrinkle up, and hunch over by their midthirties. When they got to 40, that was really middle age. And after that? Dust off Grandma's rocking chair; it's over-the-hill time.

Well, no more. All you need do is to take one look around at all the baby boomers hiking and biking into their fifties and sixties, and you can see the sea of change in attitudes about age and aging.

Whether we're in the boomer group or just a tad older, we all share an increased desire to look as young as we feel. It's no secret that most of us would like to escape the telltale traces of time taking its toll. And many anti-aging experts—from personal trainers to cosmetologists and dermatologists—are eager to help us look younger. Although the fountain of youth is still a long way off and a little wear and tear will always be a sign of an actively lived life, scientists are constantly discovering more and better ways to keep Father Time from leaving his mark.

We understand better than ever what causes appearance to change. Why our pearly whites lose their luster, our lustrous locks turn to shades of gray, and our tall, straight spines begin to bend with the years. We also know how to prolong, prevent, and sometimes reverse these changes. So here are some up-to-date tips from experts on what you can do now for your skin, hair, teeth, and posture—as well as long-term strategies to keep you looking younger than the passing birthdays say you are.

56

Appearance Is Skin Deep

It is one of the most remarkable organs ever created. Taut enough to use as a drum. Supple enough to yield to a loved one's touch. An all-encompassing covering that protects you and keeps you warm. For better or worse, though, your skin is also the first thing you see when you look in the mirror—which makes you acutely conscious of how you're appearance is faring.

Unfortunately, your skin takes the brunt of abuse from the elements. Like a pair of your most beloved blue jeans, countless hours of stretching, rubbing, bending, washing, and running around in the wind and sun take their toll. And like your best denims as well, skin wrinkles, sags, thins, and fades over time. As more of our population enters the time of life when these signs begin to show, the demand for solutions increases. Procedures that make people look younger—like Retin-A treatments and chemical peels—have been on the rise since the early 1990s. And by about the middle of the decade, the demand for face-lifts surged ahead by 178 percent in just five years.

But if you understand what happens to transform your skin from baby-bottom smooth to a little rough around the edges, you can put the brakes on many of these ravages of time and keep your skin looking younger at any age.

The skin is made up of two distinct layers: the dermis and the epidermis. The deeper layer is the dermis. Rich with blood vessels, the dermis acts like a liaison between your skin and all the stuff below the surface, such as your muscles and fat.

Your dermis also contains a support network made up of collagen and elastin. Its collagen acts like a protein scaffolding. The fibers known as elastin, as their name implies, give your skin its elasticity and resilience. Directly on top of the dermis is the outer layer, the epidermis. This is the visible skin, and the first to show signs of wear and tear. The epidermis is about as thin as a page of this book—and it's made up of both dead and living cells. The cells that make up the epidermis are called basal cells. These cells evolve into keratinocytes, which are like the salmon of your skin because they "swim" their way up to the surface of the epidermis, where they die and form a

Amazing Face

In a business where the average model is washed up at age 30, Gabrielle von Canal is a rarity. Blonde-haired and blue-eyed, Gabrielle—now in her fifties—has been on the covers of *Harper's Bazaar*, *Town and Country*, *Woman's Day*, and *Prevention* magazines. She is every bit as busy now as she was in her wrinkle-free twenties.

A model since 1963, Gabrielle is a firm believer in the cardinal rules of skin care. After gently cleansing and moisturizing, she applies a sunscreen with a sun protection factor (SPF) of 15 every day, regardless of the weather or the season.

Doing print ads for Oil of Olay, Revlon, Max Factor, and Lancôme, among others, Gabrielle is living proof that true beauty has no age. "A woman becomes her most beautiful at 30. Something inside and out comes together at that age. If you have good genes and lead a healthy life, there's no reason you can't look terrific at 40 and 50."

Her career did hit one lull when she was in her thirties, Gabrielle admits. "That's when you're considered too old to be young, yet too young to be older," she says. But in her forties, she got work again—in part because many older models had left the profession for marriage and kids.

And Gabrielle has found her niche as a model whose good looks appeal to older women seeking youth-enhancing moisturizers and skin creams. But that doesn't mean the New York City resident has flawless skin. "I've never had plastic surgery," she says. "I have wrinkles, but wrinkles are not what makes you old. People overlook them."

protective coat of dead cells, known as the keratinized layer. As this layer is shed, you continually replenish it with more skin.

For the first 30 years of life, this skin cycle works just fine, and your skin is able to fend off the elements, while constantly regenerating itself. But a legion of forces, including the environment and age, interfere with this process, says Howard Luber, M.D., of Southwest Skin Specialists in Scottsdale, Arizona. "Sun

58

exposure, the pull of gravity, constant facial expressions, reduced collagen production, the loss of skin elasticity, and muscle weakening cumulatively contribute to what's known as the photo-aging process."

You also lose some of the fat padding on your face, which not only contributes to wrinkling but also causes you to lose a bit of the coloring you had when you were younger. Plus, you'll notice other small changes in your skin coloring from years spent in the sunshine. On the backs of your hands, for instance, you might notice small, round spots—yellow, black, or brown in color—commonly known as liver spots or age spots. They're the result of a buildup of melanin or pigment from sun exposure. Similarly, you may notice some blotchiness on your face where built-up pigment has become unevenly distributed, says Seth L. Matarasso, M.D., associate clinical professor of dermatology at the University of California, San Francisco, School of Medicine.

Makeover Minutes

Stop the Damage

The key to battling time as it scuffles with your skin is to arm yourself with the all the right weapons. Even if you have a trusted collection of makeup, you may need to consider some changes in brand, style, or routine to keep your skin looking young. In fact, skin-care experts and cosmetologists say that the same makeup you have been using for years may actually make your skin look older instead of younger.

You'll be amazed at how taking just a few minutes a day to pay attention to your skin and your appearance can make a radical change for the better. Try the following, and you'll see the difference in almost no time at all.

Say cheese. Before you try cosmetics and creams to keep your young appearance, try a positive attitude and a smile, says Gabrielle von Canal. She should know. A Ford model, who defies the odds by making her living as a model while in her fifties,

59

Gabrielle emphasizes attitude over everything for improving your appearance. "Check yourself out for what you like," she advises. "Maybe you have good hair or a young-looking body. Whatever it is, if you feel good about just one thing, it can make you look young. It's an energy, an attitude, that you have inside. If you feel like you're old and over-the-hill at 40, then you will be, regardless of makeup or face creams. If you don't care about age, then it won't matter. It's as simple as that."

Shun the sun. Starting this minute, if you decide that you'll always have protection against the sun, you can prevent scores of wrinkles and skin blotches that would otherwise crop up on your complexion 10 years from now, says Grant Anhalt, M.D., professor of dermatology at Johns Hopkins University in Baltimore. Most of the signs of aging that you see on your skin today are from hours spent basking unprotected beneath the cruel sun during your youth. Ultraviolet (UV) radiation from the sun's rays penetrates the nucleus of each cell, causing damage that makes it harder for the cell to produce collagen and elastin. After a while, your skin can't regenerate itself as it should, says Dr. Anhalt. Without new skin to replace the old, your face can begin to look weathered and lined.

Because the skin damage caused by sunning is slow and cumulative, you don't see the bad side effects until 5, 10, even 30 years down the road, says Dr. Anhalt. That's why it's important to start smart sun habits today.

Aim high. "When it comes to sun protection factor (SPF), you should wear the highest SPF you can find," says Joseph C. Kvedar, M.D., assistant professor of dermatology at Harvard Medical School. He tells people to use at least SPF 30 and to apply it at least 20 minutes before initial sun exposure.

Guard against both ultraviolet rays. Though most people think they're safe if they just protect against UVB rays—the ones known to cause the most burning and damage—you need to buy a sunscreen that protects against the shorter, nonburning UVA rays as well, says Dr. Kvedar. Check the labels and opt for a full-protection sunscreen with an SPF of at least 30. Studies show that UVA rays can cause considerable damage to the elastic content of the skin, even if they don't cause a burn.

60

Stay out of the salons. Tanning salons rely on the UVA rays, explains Dr. Anhalt, which penetrate more deeply into the skin than UVB rays. "If you undergo longer exposure to a more penetrating ultraviolet ray, does it do any less damage? Common sense says probably not."

Make skin guarding a daily habit. "You should apply sunscreen to your face, neck, and hands first thing in the morning, before you apply your makeup, any time you plan on being outdoors—not just for long-term sun exposure," says Dr. Kvedar.

And don't forget to protect your lips and around your eyes since they are particularly sensitive to the damaging effects of the sun, adds Dr. Anhalt.

Go undercover. For added protection around your eyes, try a fashionable pair of wraparound sunglasses, says Dr. Anhalt. "They'll also help prevent wrinkles by keeping you from constantly squinting into the sun." For even better results, wear a hat, too.

Hit the bottle. If you must look like George Hamilton after a stint in the tropics, then try a bottled tan, suggests Dr. Matarasso. "Liquid tanners are getting much better, and their colors look more realistic. But don't think the tanner protects you from the sun. You will still have to wear sunscreen."

Try some vitamin C and see. Another reason that scientists believe that the sun damages our skin is that sunlight generates so many free radicals. Free radicals are oxygen molecules that have been stripped of an electron, which throws them off balance. To stabilize themselves, these injured molecules steal electrons from your body's healthy molecules, making themselves better but leaving more free radicals in their wake. Unstopped, this free radical free-for-all eventually causes cell and tissue damage, and along come wrinkles.

To keep these molecular pirates from doing their dirty deeds, antioxidants, like vitamins C and E and beta-carotene, help counteract their effects, says Dr. Luber. That's why investigators developed a vitamin C cream called Cellex-C. Available in cream, gel, or serum, Cellex-C contains a 10 percent solution of a form of vitamin C known as L-ascorbic acid, which some scientists believe you can slather on your face daily to mop up

know what?

Your skin is only $^{15}/_{1000}$ to $^{21}/_{1000}$ of an inch thick, but you have an awesome amount of it—about 20 square feet weighing nearly 10 pounds. In a lifetime, you shed about 40 pounds of skin.

61

those cell-pillaging free radicals before they can harm your skin. You won't find Cellex-C at a drugstore. For a supplier near you or to place an order, you can write to Caleel-Hayden, L.L.C., at 518 17th Street, Suite 1700, Denver, CO 80202. (Be sure to include your ZIP code in the letter.)

Though it's too early to know how effective Cellex-C really is, one very small study found that five people who used the cream on half of their faces every day for up to eight months reported less wrinkling on the treated half than on the untreated half. "Cellex-C is an exciting story in skin care," says Dr. Luber. "It will be interesting to see if long-term use of topical vitamin C reduces the incidence of skin cancer and its precursors."

Scientists believe that this cream not only may protect against free radicals but also may trigger cells to make more collagen, which would help keep the skin smooth and firm from the inside out. Though L-ascorbic acid is the same active substance that is found in citrus fruits, rubbing orange juice on your face won't do the trick. Neither will taking vitamin C supplements. You can't even get close to the concentrations you need by either method. You need the direct vitamin C solution, says Dr. Luber.

Make it moist. Though a moisturizer will not erase your wrinkles, it will lessen their appearance and protect your skin. Moisturizer for the face is like clothing on the body, says Annette Law, an aesthetician at Annette Law Aesthetics at the Four Seasons Hotel in Philadelphia. "Apply several thin layers throughout the course of the day. It protects your skin against heat, wind, cold, and the elements in relation to your personal activities and environment." Moisturizer is especially important as we age because our skin has less flexibility to expand and contract with weather changes, says Law.

Law suggests moisturizing several times a day. Buy a little spray bottle to keep with you, then spray your face with water during the day and apply moisturizer to your damp skin to lock in the water. Also, don't use soap to wash your skin. It's too harsh and drying. Instead, use a cream makeup remover or a gentle liquid cleanser made especially for the face.

Check the acids. Studies show that in the right concentra-

62

tion, the mild acids found in fruits, sugarcane, and milk can actually reverse some of the earliest signs of aging. These acids, known as alpha hydroxy acids, include glycolic acid and lactic acid. They work by peeling off the very top layer of skin, leaving the fresher, less-wrinkled layer for all the world to see.

Alpha hydroxy acids are available over the counter in creams, lotions, and gels of varying concentrations. The higher concentrations (around 20 percent) are more likely to cause irritation in people, particularly those with sensitive skin, says Dr. Luber. In one small study, researchers had 10 women apply a 5 percent lactic acid cream and 14 women apply a 12 percent lactic acid treatment twice a day for three months. Though both groups noticed appreciable changes on the skin's surface, only those applying the stronger solution saw their dermis—the supporting layer—actually become thicker. Still, for those who can't take the higher acid ranges, 5 to 8 percent glycolic or lactic acid creams can effectively reduce some of the signs of sun damage like blotchy complexion and rough skin, according to studies. And even if your skin isn't sensitive, it's a good idea to use a 5 percent cream for the areas around your eyes. Don't apply the cream directly to your eyelids, however.

Make way for Retin-A. First used as an acne medication, Retin-A has proved to be what countless people were looking for to help skin problems associated with aging, like wrinkles and blotchiness. Retin-A is a vitamin A derivative that has been approved for long-term correction of fine lines, says Dr. Matarasso.

This prescription cream works by attracting collagen-making cells closer to the surface of the skin. "It produces a thicker and healthier epidermis," says Dr. Luber. "And if you continue to use it, you can help preserve the skin and slow down the normal aging process."

Retin-A also actually seems to reverse signs of sun damage, according to research. In one study conducted at Royal North Shore Hospital in St. Leonards, Australia (the Land Down Under, where the sun can be scorching), scientists asked 62 people with sun-damaged skin to use a 0.05 percent Retin-A cream. In the trial group, people applied the cream to their faces, necks, left forearms, and hands for 24 weeks. In another

63

**know
what?**

In ancient
Rome, where
a very pale
complexion
was consid-
ered ideal,
women used
white lead
and chalk to
whiten their
skin.

group, people applied a dummy cream to the same areas for
the same length of time. When the researchers and the study
volunteers examined their complexions at the end of the study,
skin wrinkles, blotchiness, age spots, and roughness improved
markedly among the Retin-A folks but not among those using
the fake cream.

When it first became available, Retin-A was too strong for a
lot of people's skin and caused irritation. Now it's available in a
gentler prescription cream called Renova. But some people are
still sensitive to Renova at first, so you should use it every other
night, instead of daily, until you have adjusted to it. Apply just a
pearl-size amount to a completely dry face—being especially
sparing on the sensitive areas around the eyes and mouth.

Change your spots. Bleaching creams range in strength from
the mild Porcelana, which is a 2 percent cream, to a much
stronger 20 percent, prescription-only solution, says Dr.
Matarasso. All contain the active ingredient hydroquinone,
which interferes with the enzyme your skin needs to produce
melanin, or your skin's pigment. Applying bleaching cream every
day to your age spots in conjunction with a good sunscreen can
help make the spots fade over several weeks. For particularly
dark or stubborn spots, you may want to ask a doctor about combining Retin-A with a hydroquinone cream to speed the fading
along, says Dr. Matarasso. And remember, without using sunscreen, you'll never get that spot out. In fact, it'll darken.

Doll up by daylight. No matter how much you dodge the sun,
you may still want some cosmetics to help your lips, eyes, and
cheeks look younger. To make that makeup as natural as possible, you need natural light, says Gabrielle.

Position a mirror near a window and apply cosmetics with
the benefit of natural daylight, she suggests. If you put on
makeup trusting the reflection you see in a lightbulb-lit bathroom mirror, you might end up looking like a circus clown when
you step out into natural light.

Prime your lips. Older lips tend to stay creased even when
you're not puckering them, says Stefanie Grizzelle, a makeup
artist with the Vidal Sassoon Salon in Beverly Hills, California.
To keep your lipstick from bleeding into the fine, feathery lines

64

around your lips, first apply a foundation-like primer on both lips. (A concealer—the same as an under-the-eye concealer—works best, according to Grizzelle.) After you have applied the primer, pat both lips with translucent powder, and then apply your lipstick.

Go soft on the eyes. Dark-colored eye makeup draws attention to wrinkles, says Grizzelle. Also, avoid frosty or metallic eye shadows, which highlight the crepelike quality of the eyelid skin. Stick to soft brown in eyeliners and tan and peach eye makeup, she suggests. These natural earth tones are the best way to go.

Weaken your foundation. Piling on foundation is like pointing a neon sign at your wrinkles, says Gabrielle. Instead, dip a fine brush in yellowish foundation and dab it on skin blotches and brown spots to even them out, she says. Then take a damp sponge and apply foundation to the entire face, making sure to match the color of your neck so there's no obvious line along your jaw. Blending thoroughly is the most important step. Finish it off by applying a translucent powder.

Brush up on blush. With a couple sweeps of a blush brush you can restore some of the color that may have faded from your cheeks, says Gabrielle. Smile, then apply blush to the highest plane of your cheekbones, moving the brush upward. Women in their twenties sometimes put blush under their cheeks, but that is not advisable in later years, she says. That makes your cheeks look too hollow.

Long-Term Tactics

For Youthful Skin

While the suggestions below aren't as quick and simple as rubbing a cream or lotion on your skin, over time they can be even more effective. Here are some options that may require more patience, but they'll help you get great-looking skin if you stick with the program.

65

Skip the smokes. Heavy smokers often end up with a distinctively haggard look called smoker's face, observes Jeffrey Smith, M.D., assistant clinical professor of dermatology at Loma Linda University in California. Smokers' wrinkles are deeper than nonsmokers', their faces look more gaunt, and the color of the complexion is gray or slightly yellow, he says.

Nicotine from the cigarette causes blood vessels to constrict, and those constricted vessels block some oxygen from reaching the skin. "When you smoke a single cigarette, the constriction lasts for hours after you have stopped," Dr. Smith says.

Doctors also say that smoking fragments elastin, which are the long smooth fibers of protein that give skin its resilience. Adding injury to insult, smoking also impairs your body's wound-healing ability and increases your chances of developing some types of skin cancer. Although Dr. Smith urges people to give up cigarettes entirely, he says that even cutting back seems to improve the quality of complexion and the skin's ability to heal.

Ask your M.D. about HRT. Hormone-replacement therapy (HRT) has received many accolades from the medical community for protecting postmenopausal women from heart disease as well as other age-related complications, such as osteoporosis. Now scientists are finding that it can help your skin stay younger as well. They have discovered that the estrogen used in HRT can affect wrinkles and dry skin.

In one study of 3,875 postmenopausal women, epidemiological researchers from the University of California, San Francisco, School of Medicine; the University of California, Los Angeles (UCLA), School of Public Health; and the division of geriatrics at the UCLA School of Medicine studied the results of the First National Health and Nutrition Examination Survey and found that women who used estrogen prior to the study were 25 percent less likely to have dry skin and 30 percent less likely to have wrinkles as were women who had not used estrogen. "There's no magic to it," says Dr. Luber. "Estrogen simply retards the normal aging process in women, from their oil-producing, sebaceous glands to their blood vessels. If you allow them to continue taking estrogen after their bodies stop producing it, you

66

can continue protecting them from that degeneration. And that means healthier, better-nourished skin."

Despite this benefit, hormone-replacement therapy is not something you would do just for cosmetic reasons. The treatments affect a woman's entire hormone system, and some women dislike the side effects of the treatment—and worry about the elevated risks of uterine and breast cancers. Most doctors agree that whether or not a woman needs hormone therapy is a decision that should be made carefully by a woman and her doctor, depending on her medical history, not for skin care alone.

See a professional. If you're serious about eliminating facial flaws for good (or at least for a long time), you might want to investigate the options a plastic surgeon can offer. Plastic surgery doesn't necessarily mean a face-lift. In fact, quick and painless laser treatments can wipe out surface wrinkles and can also give a more uniform color to the skin, minimizing brown and red spots and other imperfections. People with very dark skin and Asians, however, do not do well with laser surgery because their skin becomes blotchy.

"The laser is the most dynamic and dramatic method of eliminating the smaller imperfections of the skin," says Michael

The Eyes Have It

If you have ever wondered where age betrays itself, just ask the guesser. A featured performer at some carnivals and sideshows, the guesser is someone who literally reads your age.

The secret?

"It's all in the eyes," says Greg Scheid, operations manager at Cedar Point, an amusement park in Sandusky, Ohio. Scheid, who has trained about 100 guessers in his time, says that the lines around the eyes speak volumes about age.

"Look at the road maps around the eyes, and you'll see the number of lines there," says Scheid. "With experience, a guesser can accurately guess the age 70 to 80 percent of the time."

So grab your sunscreen and put on your shades next time you're heading for the great outdoors. By protecting that tell-all skin around your eyes, you'll make it harder for any guesser to guess your age.

Sachs, M.D., a plastic surgeon and director of research at New York Medical College in New York City. "It's amazing. When you put the laser on the face, the skin tightens before your very eyes."

During laser treatments, the doctor removes the top layer of the skin with a computer-controlled pulse of "hot" light that cools off so quickly that it never burns the skin, says Dr. Sachs. But the heat it produces is enough to shrink the collagen fibers that give skin its bounce. That quick burst pulls sagging skin taut again. The treatments can help ease the vertical lines running from the nose down to the mouth, zap the crow's-feet around the eyes, and obliterate forehead lines. Lasers can't be used on the extremely delicate skin of the neck, however.

The procedure can cost between $3,000 and $6,000 if you have your whole face done. After treatments, the doctor may apply a layer of antibiotic-filled Vaseline, according to Dr. Sachs. Healing takes 7 to 10 days, but the face can stay pink for up to three months. After laser treatments, you don't have to avoid the sun if you want to keep your younger-looking skin wrinkle-free, but make sure you slather on a sunscreen of SPF 30 or higher at least 20 minutes before you head outdoors.

Hair Today, Salon Tomorrow

Like a nation of modern-day Samsons, men and women invest a great deal to protect their crowning manes—especially when those full locks begin to thin, turn gray, or fall out. Just click the tube to any late-night infomercial, and you'll see there is little we won't do to have more or better hair. We'll spray it on, paint it on, glue it on, weave it on, sew it on, dye it, bleach it, and highlight to the point that it's a miracle that any of us have any hair left. And while we're doing all that, the pharmaceutical companies are frantically trying to find a "cure" for baldness—investing $200 million to $300 million each year in a race to guarantee fulsome hair for all.

Though hair is technically "dead," it is also quite alive. An extension of your epidermis or outer layer of skin, hair "grows" as the hair follicle cells absorb nutrients and amino acids. After these cells push upward, they slowly die, forming a hard protein known as keratin. The keratinized cells, in time, continue to push upward, creating three layers known as the medulla (the core), the cortex (the middle layer), and the cuticle (the outer layer). The average human head contains 80,000 to 120,000 strands. Apart from their distinctive colors—defining whether you're to be a blonde, brunette, or redhead—these ample locks serve to keep your head warm, so you're better able to regulate your body temperature.

Like leaves on a tree, your hair goes through stages. It grows, it rests, then it sheds. About 10 percent of all your hair follicles are resting or shedding at any given time, so even younger folks lose 50 to 100 hairs a day.

As we get older, the cycle between growing and shedding shortens, so hair stays in the resting and shedding stages longer, explains Dominic A. Brandy, M.D., clinical instructor of dermatology at the University of Pittsburgh School of Medicine, director and founder of American Medical Hair Restoration Associates, and author of *A New Headstart!* After about the first 30 years of life, hair strands also become thinner and start to lose their color, he says. With age, the cells in the follicles start to shrink, and they stop producing melanin—the pigment that gives your hair its characteristic color. Balding occurs when the hair follicles degenerate to the point where they cease to produce hair.

Though we can all expect some hair loss, graying, and thinning as we age, many people make a beeline to baldness. No one knows why some people bald quickly while others don't. But some of the culprits are known. Whether you're male or female, you're more likely to bald if you have an abundance of male hormones, particularly a derivative of testosterone known as dihydrotestosterone (DHT), says Dr. Brandy.

"Dihydrotestosterone is formed in the hairs' oil glands," explains Dr. Brandy. "It forces the hair shaft to grow shorter and finer until eventually there's nothing left." Researchers aren't sure why testosterone changes into dihydrotestosterone. These chemical changes happen in everyone, including women, but people who are most sensitive to the substance experience the most hair loss as a result, according to Dr. Brandy.

69

"Women are protected until they reach menopause because estrogen counteracts the effects of dihydrotestosterone," says Dr. Brandy. "After they stop producing estrogen, if they've inherited a sensitivity to dihydrotestosterone, they're just as susceptible to thinning hair as men are."

So you can expect to lose some hair as you age, and there's likely to be some graying and thinning. But that doesn't mean you just have to sit back and watch it happen. Science and technology have come a long way. Here are some strategies for keeping your topknot in top-notch shape as the birthdays roll by.

Makeover Minutes

For Your Mane

By giving your tresses just a few minutes' attention, you can greatly improve the appearance of your pate, say hair and style experts. Try one of these approaches and see.

Shampoo, rinse, and repeat. Despite what your grandmother might have told you, your hair will not fall out if you shampoo too much. Dr. Brandy recommends that you shampoo your hair daily, especially if you have a tendency for male or female pattern baldness. Some researchers speculate that the baldness-inducing dihydrotestosterone can build up in the scalp if you don't shampoo every day. "I don't know how valid a theory it is," says Dr. Brandy—but in any case, he thinks daily washing is a good idea.

Make your gray glow. Many men and women would love to proudly display their gray but find that it never looks as vibrant as their darker hair did. "That's because gray hair gets dull and dirty before other shades do," says Philip Kingsley, trichological consultant to celebrities, such as Mick Jagger and Ivana Trump, and author of *Hair: An Owner's Handbook*. "So, it's especially important for people with gray hair to shampoo every day. Even better, you should also condition every time you shampoo because gray hair tends to be drier," he says.

70

Add a dab. Older, finer hair is harder to make appear full, says Kingsley. To give you a fuller, healthier look, add some blow-dry gel or mousse to help protect your hair while you blow-dry it, says Kingsley.

Coat your locks. If your hair is starting to thin, reach for an over-the-counter hair thickener, says Kingsley. "These products work by coating the hair shaft. Though they certainly don't grow hair, they can make an appreciable difference in the appearance of its thickness."

"One shampoo that people in my practice frequently praise for coating the hair and adding thickness is Mane and Tail Shampoo, adds Dr. Brandy. Originally designed for horses, this shampoo became popular enough among their two-legged riders that it's now available in drugstores.

Pump up the volume. To add volume to your thinning locks, blow-dry your hair while it's parted in its usual place. Then once it's dry, part it in a different place and see how much lift it gives your hair, says Alex Ioannou, co-owner of Trio Salon in Chicago. "Anytime you can distort your roots, you get more volume. Just be sure to keep your blow-dryer and brush moving constantly to avoid overdrying your hair since older hair is already dry."

Lighten up. Along with your hair becoming thinner as you age, your complexion loses some of its color. To reduce the contrast, go a shade or two lighter than your natural hair color, especially if you have naturally very dark hair. That's because dark colors call attention to gray or thinning hair. And it also heightens the contrast with a pale scalp and complexion, notes Dr. Brandy.

If you're only partially gray, you might not require constant, overall coloring. Instead, try highlighting, lowlighting, or both, suggests Judith Ann Graham, a member of the Association of Image Consultants International and an image consultant in private practice in New York City. Highlighting bleaches the gray and adds new color to it. Lowlighting means that you apply color to the gray to give your hair a more uniform look—and then you don't need to maintain highlights. That way you can camouflage most of your gray hairs without having to worry about constant touch-ups.

know what?

Dying to try a new dye? Ancient Assyrians colored their hair with gold dust, gold thread, and scented yellow starch. Romans dyed their hair black with St.-John's-wort, myrtle, and walnut husks.

71

Stay colorful. The one thing you don't want to do, however, is go blonde just because you're getting older, says Damien Miano, co-owner of Miano-Viel Salon and Spa in New York City. "While it makes sense for someone with thinning hair to decrease the contrast between their scalp and hair by going a little lighter, it does not make sense for everybody. You want to maintain some contrast between your skin and hair to bring out your features and have a younger, not a washed-out, appearance," he says.

Be a trend-softener. You can have the newest, latest look without any appearance of fabricated youth if you adapt the latest trends in hairstyles and soften them for yourself, says Miano. "A good stylist can do this for you. It creates an attractive, current look without the harsh effects that trendy styles often have on older women."

Do the blue. Another minor pitfall with going gray is that gray hair can take on a yellow tint, especially if you perm it or if you are around someone who smokes. To wash that yellow right out of your hair, Kingsley recommends using a blue-colored shampoo because the blue dye will create an optical illusion that hides the yellow tinge. Naturally, this will take some fine-tuning so that your hair doesn't seem to take on a bluish cast. If you're trying this out, have a trusted friend or hairdresser give you an honest appraisal and adjust the blue factor accordingly.

Derail that ponytail. A popular trend for balding men is to grow their hair long in the back to compensate for a thinning top, says Lisa Cunningham, an image consultant in private practice and a continuing education instructor at the Fashion Institute of Technology in New York City. "As if growing it long and putting it in a ponytail will look like they have more hair. It just looks like your hair is sliding down the back of your head," she says. "Keep it short overall."

Become balder. For men, the solution to pattern baldness may be as simple as a morning shave. "If you have a nicely shaped head and features, the answer might be to pull a Michael Jordan or Yul Brenner and shave your head," says Cunningham. "That looks very sexy and is really easy to keep up."

72

Long-Term Tactics
To Stop the Loss

When you're into keeping your hair for the long haul, sometimes long-term measures are in order. Here are some tips to make the most of your hair through the years.

Gain some Rogaine. As soon as you become concerned about male or female pattern hair loss, reach for some minoxidil (Rogaine), says Dr. Brandy. This over-the-counter product "does seem to help slow the hair shedding process for almost all people," he says. "I use it myself."

Unfortunately, if your problem is a receding hairline, minoxidil probably won't do you much good. It's most effective for people who develop a bald patch on top of the head.

Rogaine works with women, too. In a dermatology study at the University of Texas in San Antonio, researchers found that of 256 women with pattern baldness, those who applied a 2 percent topical minoxidil solution for 32 weeks were likely to get good results. Thirteen percent of those women got moderate hair growth, and another 50 percent saw some improvement, though minimal.

Eat for the hair of it. Like everything from your heart to your skin, your hair will be at its healthiest when you are following a healthful diet, says Kingsley. "That means no extreme dieting and no overloading on junk food. You should also be sure to eat protein with every meal because hair is made of almost 100 percent protein," he says.

While you're busy adding protein to your diet, you might also want to cut some of the fat, suggests Dr. Brandy. "Studies in Japan have shown that as Japanese men eat fewer low-fat foods like rice, fish, and vegetables and eat more high-fat foods like red meat and dairy products, they are seeing a dramatic increase in male pattern baldness."

Some scientists suggest that dihydrotestosterone is formed in the oil gland and follicle of the hair. They say that the more fat you eat, the more active those oil glands become. Logically, more oil, thus more dihydrotestosterone, could mean more hair

73

You Wear It Well

You can have skin as fresh as morning dew and hair as black and shiny as coal, but if you're sporting a jacket you bought while Roosevelt was still in office or a dress that was fashioned after Jackie O., you won't be conveying a youthful appearance, no matter how good the rest of you looks.

Figuring out the subtleties of dressing is tricky, concedes Judith Ann Graham, a member of the Association of Image Consultants International and an image consultant in private practice in New York City. And the challenges get even trickier when you're over 50, she notes. One problem is that manufacturers are youth-obsessed, she says. "People who are 50 and over want good, comfortable clothing that fits well, but there's just very little of it out there."

As you get older, your body changes—and that's more than a subtle change in size, notes Graham. Count on a thicker waistline and a flatter rear end—and your height will probably decrease a bit. So it's unlikely that you'll be able to wear the kinds of clothes you have always worn. Image consultants advise both men and women to change their clothing style as they age to keep looking their best. Here are some strategies that wear well with age.

For women

Be bold. Too many people buy into the belief that you have to wear soft pastels as you get older. "But you've earned the right to wear bold colors," says Graham. "It has a look-at-me, youthful effect."

Pad your shoulders. When your shoulders are broader, the rest of you can't help seeming smaller, says Graham. To help create a contrast to make your hips seem smaller, add shoulder pads to blazers and even blouses. Your goal is to balance out the shoulder and hip lines so that you don't look like a linebacker for the Eagles.

Don't let yourself down. Your breasts naturally hang lower as you age, which can give you a less-than-flattering appearance, says Lisa Cunningham, an image consultant in private practice and a continuing education instructor at the Fashion Institute of Technology

loss, says Dr. Brandy, though he adds that more research is needed to prove that connection.

Try transplant. The most popular long-term solution to permanent hair loss is hair grafting, says Dr. Brandy. "Grafting is the

in New York City. "One of the best things an older woman can do is buy the best underwire bra that she can get her hands on. A youthful bust point is about 2½ inches from under your arms."

Put your arms up. The higher the armholes of your garment, the taller and slimmer you'll look, says Cunningham. Avoid any dress that's cut so the body of the dress and the sleeve are all one piece, forming a bat wing or web. That puts a lot of fabric in your midsection and makes you look thicker.

Skirt the issue. You should be able to find a happy medium when it comes to skirt length, says Graham. A skirt that's too short sends a message that you don't want to be taken seriously, but if the skirt goes to your knees, it will make your legs look short and dumpy. The best rule of thumb: no more than two inches above the knee. If you are a tall woman, take advantage of the long, sweeping skirts popular nowadays.

For men

Sideline that suit. Men hang on to their suits far too long, says Cunningham. "Menswear doesn't change a lot, but lapels go in and out. I'd say get a suit every three to five years, and don't wear one that's over 15 years old unless it's a real classic."

Have a fit. As a man's midsection starts expanding, he goes up in waist size, but the majority of men today would prefer pushing their waistbands below their natural waistlines instead of purchasing larger trousers. As a result, the pants hang low in the front, giving an aging, sagging-crotch appearance, and too high in the back, says Cunningham. To avoid the droop, have the pants tailored to fit your dimensions.

Don't go for a ride. As your shoulders start sloping, you'll find that your jacket rides up in back, says Cunningham. When you have your jackets fitted, don't suddenly develop perfect posture. Just stand the way you normally do.

Nix the mix-and-match. Men make the mistake of wearing a modern suit with an old tie or vice versa, says Cunningham. The widest part of the tie should be the same width as the lapel of the jacket.

cornerstone of hair transplantation. It is simply taking hair from areas of the scalp that aren't sensitive to the effects of dihydrotestosterone and transplanting them onto the balding areas. The effects can last a lifetime."

75

Early hair transplants sometimes produced a "baby doll" look, with hair plugs containing 10 to 20 hairs implanted into the scalp. But today the grafts are smaller—1 to 8 hairs—and the implants are much closer together. The result is a much more natural look, says Dr. Brandy. The main drawback is the price. A typical hair restoration involves transferring about 6,000 hairs or 1,500 to 1,700 grafts, says Dr. Brandy. At the usual price of about $10 per graft, the total cost to put your hair back in its rightful place is a hair-raising $15,000 or more.

Grin and Bare Them

In days past, long before tooth-hardening fluoride made our everyday drinking water a cavity-fighting cocktail and people kept dental floss in their medicine cabinets, many more people needed glasses—for their false teeth.

Permanent tooth loss and dentures, while not things of the past, have become much less common, primarily because dental care has become so much more effective. "Dentistry has been trying really hard to eliminate itself," says Clifford L. Thomas, D.D.S., assistant clinical professor of periodontics at the University of Michigan in Ann Arbor. "Fluoride and advances in preventive dentistry have been really important," he notes. "More people are keeping their teeth for life."

But lifelong chompers need maintenance. Most major highways wouldn't hold up under the kind of daily grind we put our teeth through. There's the pressure from chewing. The acid baths we give them with carbonated sodas and acidic foods. And your hardworking teeth need to endure constant changes in temperature as you munch piping hot food and gulp down icy cold beverages.

All those years of chomping take their toll. You'll develop hairline cracks or grooves, called microcracks. Though generally harmless, these microcracks become more noticeable as you age. Teeth also change color as we get older. Over time, the nerves that nourish our teeth shrink, and the shortage of nourishment causes teeth to darken. Compounding matters,

76

the white part of our teeth—the enamel—gets worn aw
leaving the yellow-tinged underlayer showing through. As tl
underlayer, which is called dentin, becomes more visible, tee
get a yellowish cast.

That's a whole lot of dental assault to overcome. But with a
little effort, you can put some of the white back into your
pearlies. Here are some suggestions.

Makeover Minutes

Whitening Up

Though most strategies for improving the appearance
of your teeth take a bit of time and cost, here are a couple of
quick tricks to making your choppers look their best in a flash.

Try a lipstick trick. Choose a lipstick tint that will make your
teeth look whiter by contrast, advises Linda Stasi, co-author of
Boomer Babes and former beauty and health editor of *Elle, Cos-
mopolitan,* and *New Woman.* "Light lipsticks bring out the yellow
cast of teeth," she notes. Better choices are medium shades like
corals or light reds.

Figure in skin, too. In choosing lipstick color, you also need
to pay attention to the color of your skin, says Graham. If you
have warm-toned peach skin, go with a burnt salmon or a cinnamon lipstick to make your teeth positively dazzling. But if you
have pink-toned skin, those same shades can bring out the yellow in your teeth, so Graham recommends that you find lipstick
with a pink cast to it.

Use a gentle touch. Since yellowing teeth are caused, in part,
by the wearing away of enamel, don't scrub your teeth as if you
were scouring a pan, cautions Dr. Thomas. "Be very gentle with
your toothbrush. If you can't get the stuff off with a gentle massaging motion, it's not coming off. You don't want to wear away
your enamel during toothbrushing."

Abstain from stuff that stains. Avoid staining substances like
coffee, tea, and tobacco, which can find their way into the mi-

77

crocracks of your enamel and make your teeth lose their luster, says Stephen Fassman, D.D.S., general dentist and attending professor in the department of surgery at New York University Medical Center in New York City. And if you don't brush and floss, you're just asking for more staining since plaque and tartar also collect the telltale tints of tobacco, coffee, and tea. Brush and floss your teeth in the morning, at night, and after every meal, he advises.

Long-Term Tactics
For Healthier Teeth

Since healthy, good-looking teeth are a lifetime investment, it pays to develop tooth-sustaining tactics. Here are some strategies for making your smile look its best, no matter what your age.

Bleach your bite. For a whiter bite? You can bleach your teeth. But don't be fooled by those so-called bleaching toothpastes, warns Dr. Thomas. "They have very minimal, if any, effectiveness. In short, they're a colossal waste of cash."

A better choice is a 15 to 22 percent carbamide peroxide solution that you can get from your dentist, says Dr. Fassman. This prescription-only bleach whites out superficial stains on the enamel and also can penetrate to dissolve stains deeper within the tooth. Results can last a few years.

Your dentist can do the bleaching in his office—or you can take it home and do it yourself following your dentist's guidance. Either way, your teeth can end up looking up to three shades whiter than they did before.

With the do-it-at-home bleaching procedure, you apply the bleaching solution and then protect it by wearing a specially fitted mouthguard. For about two weeks, you'll be wearing the mouthguard for a couple of hours every night while the solution goes to work. The cost is between $350 and $500 to bleach all your teeth, depending on whether an office visit is included.

78

While it's more expensive to have your dentist do it, the procedure takes less time; often, it can be done in one visit. And the in-office procedure is less irritating to the gums. The dentist paints the bleaching solution onto your teeth and applies a protective chemical to your gums to avoid any irritation. The bleach remains on the teeth for about a half-hour. (Apart from the additional time required for the home procedure, there's likely to be some gum irritation from the whitening solution.)

Not everyone is a candidate for bleaching, however. If your teeth have always had a yellow or gray cast, bleaching won't work a transformation. And tooth bleaching isn't very effective if you have deep brown, orange, or gray stains. These dark stains sometimes become permanent when someone has received certain types of antibiotics, like tetracyclines, as a child.

Come clean of nicotine. "Smoking is the single worst thing you can do for the health and appearance of your teeth and gums," says Dr. Thomas. "It not only stains your teeth—the nicotine also suppresses the immune system. The nicotine concentrates in the fluids around the teeth, which hinders proper healing. Smoking also masks disease. Your gums look very pink and healthy despite any periodontal disease you may have in the works."

Buy a bond. A permanent solution for discoloration is to have a dentist put porcelain laminates on your teeth, says Dr. Fassman. The dentist removes a small portion of enamel from the front and biting edge of the tooth to make room for the laminates, which are bonded to the teeth. One drawback is that they are somewhat fragile and may chip. In addition, getting laminates means a lifetime commitment to laminates, with the cost of bonding averaging about $750 per tooth.

Getting a Leg Up on Varicose Veins

Maybe you have had great legs your whole life. Or maybe you haven't. Either way, the last thing you want is a bunch of big, blue veins popping up and making your legs look like a road map from your toes to your tokess.

The spindly eyesores commonly known as varicose and spi-

79

der veins are a fact of life for most women over the age of 40, and many over-40 men get them as well. In fact, by age 40, 54 percent of women and 23 percent of men develop these blue-blooded veins on their legs. And by age 50, 64 percent of women and 42 percent of men will have varicosity. And the annoyance factor is more than what meets the eye. Not only are varicose veins unsightly, they can also throb and hurt and are often accompanied by swelling of the lower legs.

Varicose veins generally protrude from the skin of the lower legs below the knee, though they can occur anywhere on the leg. As you age, some of the valves in the main veins that carry blood from the legs back to the heart begin to malfunction. Trapped blood begins to pool in one spot rather than flowing smoothly uphill. Where the vein pops out, you'll see a varicose vein. Many factors can weaken the valves—including excess blood flow caused by pregnancy or the extra strain on blood vessels if you're overweight. Heredity is also a factor.

Some people are prone to smaller, less painful spider veins. These are dilated capillaries that look like red, blue, or purplish threads just below the surface of the skin. They usually form tiny spiderweb-like networks on the thighs, behind the knees, or inside the ankles. No one really knows why spider veins happen. About 80 percent of the time, people who have varicose veins also have spider veins.

Makeover Minutes

Easing the Leg Pressure

Because of the heredity factor, you are much more likely to have veiny protuberances if your mother or father did. But even so, you don't have to sit idly by as they map their way across your legs.

By setting aside just a few minutes a day to try these simple do-it-yourself remedies, you can soothe and relieve achy, bulging varicose veins.

Put your tootsies up. Varicose veins tend to bulge because of stagnant, trapped blood, notes Ben H. Douglas, Ph.D., assistant vice-chancellor of graduate studies and professor of anatomy at the University of Mississippi Medical Center in Jackson and author of *Ageless: Living Younger Longer.* To help empty the blood that is pooling in your lower legs and to reduce swelling and pain, it helps to raise your legs. "Just raise them over the level of your heart." You can be on a couch with your feet raised on a couple of pillows. Or lift your legs up on the back of the couch for a few minutes a day, suggests Dr. Douglas.

Hose them down. Support hose may not have a glamorous image, but they're one of the best forms of temporary relief for varicose veins, says Dr. Matarasso. These heavy nylon hose squeeze the leg and put pressure on the veins, which prevents their distending. Because support hose are thick, women don't have to worry about veins showing. The best support hose are available through prescription, says Dr. Matarasso. So ask your doctor about them.

Horse around. The natural substance escin, extracted from horse chestnut, can help to soothe distended and achy veins, says Earl Mindell, Ph.D., author of *What You Should Know about Natural Health for Women.* You can buy it in a powder form at health food stores. Dilute a half-teaspoon in 16 ounces of warm water and gently rub the mixture on your sore veins, he advises.

Long-Term Tactics
Caring for Your Calves

While there are many ways to camouflage the appearance and ease discomfort of varicose veins, making them go away for good is not so easy. But still, there are steps that you can take. Here's what the experts recommend.

Drop the weight. Yes, we know that's easier said than done, but relief from painful, bulging veins is yet another benefit of shedding excess pounds. Being overweight puts additional pres-

81

sure on the valves of your legs, says Dr. Mindell. "Imagine carrying around a couple of bowling balls. Wouldn't that increase the pressure on your body? Extra weight makes it that much harder for the blood to make its way out of the lower legs."

Beef up your calves. Because varicose veins cause blood to pool in your lower legs, you need to find a way to move the blood back up to the heart, says Dr. Douglas. That means building up your calves, which act as the pumps that propel blood upward when the muscle is contracted. As little as 20 minutes of walking four times a week can help keep your calves primed, says Dr. Mindell.

Inject them. If all else fails, see your doctor whenever varicose veins are making you blue. Varicose and spider veins are easily treated with a procedure known as sclerotherapy, says Dr. Douglas. "A doctor injects a solution that irritates the lining so that the vein (or capillary, in the case of spider veins) fuses and is no longer visible." When this is done to varicose veins, other veins in the leg take over the work of the fused vein, he explains. Depending upon the size of the vein, it may take about three months to erase the blue bulge of the once-working vein.

Straighten Up and Shed Years

"Nothing—not gray hair, not lines on your face—adds years to your appearance the way poor posture does," says Lucien Martin, D.C., a chiropractor in private practice and a specialist in biomechanics in Santa Monica, California. Getting your posture lined up gives you other health benefits as well. "Bad posture seriously affects your physical stamina by stunting your lung capacity. You can increase your lung capacity by up to 30 percent just by correcting your posture," he says.

Sometimes we aren't even aware of poor posture—and the difference it makes in appearances—until we see blinding evidence. "I was at a networking event talking to two other people when someone snapped my picture and sent it to me," says fifty-something New York City resident, Margo Krasne, director of the "Speak Up!" program and author of *Say It with Confidence*. "The other woman in the picture looked wonderful, and I, who thought I had been standing like an elegant model,

82

The Alexander Technique: Learning to Be No Slouch

It's no secret what bad posture looks like. Picture a comma—with the top of the comma formed by head and neck, and the abdomen protruding down below. But according to some schools of thought, simply by fixing your posture, you can end many hard-to-solve medical problems, like chronic back, shoulder, and neck pain.

One way to straighten up for better health is with an educational approach called the Alexander Technique. Developed at the turn of the century by Tasmanian actor F. M. Alexander as a way of strengthening his voice for working on the stage, the Alexander Technique emphasizes the relationship between your head and neck, says Galen Cranz, Ph.D., a teacher of the Alexander Technique and professor of architecture at the University of California, Berkeley.

"In biweekly sessions with a certified Alexander Technique teacher, you focus on relaxing your neck so that your head goes forward and up while your back lengthens and widens," she notes. Your teacher watches how you move—often resting his hand on the back of your neck to remind you to keep that area free.

By learning better head/neck coordination, you reduce pressure on your back, neck, and shoulders. Relief comes when your head is no longer locked, says Dr. Cranz. Also, breathing improves because the chest isn't collapsed and the diaphragm (the sheet of muscle between your abdomen and chest) expands better. Dr. Cranz says it usually takes about 25 sessions to ingrain the technique so that it becomes second nature. Prices average between $35 to $50 for a private session, she adds.

looked pregnant. From that moment on, I began to correct my posture."

Krasne discovered what a difference it makes: People often think she's younger than her years, she says. And in her professional role, she teaches others how they can lose years (as well as gain confidence) just by the way they carry themselves.

Everyone can reap the benefits of standing up straight, says Dr. Douglas. "You'll see a 70-year-old who has a brisk pace and stands upright who looks younger than a 50-year-old who slouches," he says. "Bad posture makes you round your shoulders and stick out your abdomen. It can also decrease the volume of your chest cavity and give you the I'm-getting-old look."

To Better Your Posture

We all have perfect posture until the age of two, when we start modeling our movements and mannerisms on Mom and Dad, say experts. But even if you have been slouching so long that it's a deeply ingrained habit, you can take conscious steps to straighten up. In fact, one of the hardest things about improving your posture is remembering to try. The following are some key ways to keep from being a slouch.

Check yourself out. To remind yourself about good posture, check your reflection in store windows as you walk down the street, suggests Krasne. Also, tell some of your more vigilant friends to keep an eye on you and provide gentle reminders when your start to droop.

Go with the flow. Posture is a fluid movement, not a locked static position, says Krasne. "Think of it as an upward stretching of the spine and not just a standing position. Forget the military pose with your chest and chin sticking out. Just make sure that you don't let yourself sink into your stomach."

To learn how to feel that stretching in your spine, Krasne suggests this exercise: Walk forward. As you step, stretch the top of your head toward the ceiling, keeping your chin and head level. Think of your head as moving toward the ceiling, your shoulders moving to the outside walls, and your legs stretching to the floor. Then concentrate on feeling that same stretching as you walk and move normally.

Prop yourself up. When you sit at a table, you tend to collapse your shoulders, which forces you to sink into yourself, says Krasne. "I put my arms on the edge of the table or on the arms of the chair and stretch my spine," she says. "Sitting straight up takes energy, so use whatever props you need."

Seat yourself. Most people let their pelvis roll too far backward when they're sitting—in part because their feet don't comfortably reach the floor, says Galen Cranz, Ph.D., a teacher of the Alexander Technique and professor of architecture at the University of California, Berkeley, and author of *The Chair: Re-*

84

thinking Culture, Body, and Design. "Most traditional flat chair seats are too high," she notes. To correct for the height, move the bones of the buttocks out near the edge of the seat. That way, says Dr. Cranz, your knees are lower than your hip sockets, which helps your pelvis and spine balance properly and allows your feet to be flat on the floor.

Long-Term Tactics
For Upright Living

If you want to walk tall into your golden years, you'll want to get some daily practice. Here are some exercises that will improve your posture over time. "The hitch is that you must work posture exercise into your schedule every day, like you do brushing your teeth, or else it won't do much good," observes Dr. Martin.

Power up. Exercise boosts the vital leg, back, and stomach muscles that help support good posture, says Dr. Douglas. "People who exercise tend to stand straight because it makes breathing easier for them," he says. Dr. Douglas recommends increasing your breathing capacity and overall stamina by walking for at least a half-hour four times a week.

Dr. Douglas also recommends that you do daily abdominal crunches to strengthen your back, as shown on page 117. Start off by doing as many crunches as are comfortable, even if that's just three, he says. Then increase the number—say, to five crunches the next week—and work your way up until you can do about 30 every day.

Hang around. Gravity is your foe. It tries to pull your head and spine forward and down. But you can fight gravity by marshaling its force to your advantage. "You can counteract these effects with one simple piece of equipment—a stretching bar," says Dr. Martin.

A good stretching bar is the kind of chin-up bar that you can buy in a fitness store. Mount the bar in any doorway at a height

85

such that your feet rest comfortably on the floor while you're holding on to the bar. Any time you can take a break, hang from the bar by your hands, Dr. Martin suggests. Keep your feet flat on the floor and bend your knees to let your upper body stretch straight down. When you're doing it right, you should feel the weight of your buttocks stretching your spine, he says. It only takes a few days of this before you'll begin to notice the elongation of the spine, Dr. Martin says.

Build your bellows. When you lift the chest with a breath, you move the vertebrae of the upper back, says Dr. Martin. "There's a lot of talk about breathing with your belly like they do in yoga. But to help your posture, you should also be sure to breathe so that you expand your upper chest," he says. This kind of breathing is especially important for people who spend most of their time with their upper vertebrae slumped over a desk, he says. "You need to lift those vertebrae on a regular basis."

Stop-Time Tactics

Stop Aches
and Stay Limber

What if a man—say an old man with a flowing white beard, a robe, and a lined, wise-looking face—said to you, "I know how to have more energy, beat depression, boost your immune system, suffer fewer aches and pains, have better sex, lower your blood pressure, and prevent osteoporosis, arthritis, Type II diabetes, heart disease, and some forms of cancer. With this knowledge, you will feel younger and live longer."

You might jump up, seize this wise person by the collar and bark, "What? How? Quick, point me to this fountain of youth. I must know. Please!"

The sage whispers, "Exercise, exercise, exercise."

"What?" you cry. "I thought you were talking about a new drug, a nutritional, herbal supplement, a nonfat candy bar, a diet based on peanut butter and light beer. You mean you want me to do something? Aaughh..."

In disgust, you let the old man go, sink back into your chair, channel-surf to *Oprah*, and mutter something about a false alarm.

The sage shuffles back to his mountaintop but calls out for a final time, "Get off the couch and live."

Savoring Sage Advice

The sage knows—as sages do—what he is talking about. After many years and hundreds of scientific studies, the evidence is clear and irrefutable: Exercise and activity are the best preventive medicine for both mind and body. Live an active life, and you'll live longer and live better, says Russell R. Pate, Ph.D.,

87

The Sizzle of "Sexercise"

Jog for sex.

No, it's not a slogan for a kinky new fund-raiser or any reference to walking the streets, but a darn good reason for you or that disinterested partner of yours to start exercising. Why? Because people who are physically active also tend to get more...well...sexually active. One form of exercise apparently leads to the other.

Exercise has long been known to boost energy and suspected to enhance libido, but a study done with nonexercising, middle-age men at the University of California, San Diego, finally found that putting the low-key putterers on a program of moderate to intense aerobic exercise—biking and jogging, for instance—improved their frequency of sex, performance, and number of orgasms.

Aerobic exercise apparently boosted the men's levels of testosterone—the hormone that's notoriously related to men's sex drive. In addition, exercise enhanced blood flow throughout the body, which enabled the men to have more long-lasting erections, says David Case, Ph.D., research specialist in the department of psychology at the University of California, San Diego.

"We haven't studied the hormone effect in women, but it may be similar," says Dr. Case. "And like a man, a woman who exercises may be reducing her level of stress. Feeling more relaxed, she may be more likely to be interested in having sex."

Both genders probably get other benefits from sex-boosting aerobic exercise, he theorizes. The men in the San Diego study may have been feeling better about themselves and their bodies, says Dr. Case. If you're exercising, you're probably losing some of your waistline, toning up muscle, and looking more attractive to the opposite sex, or your svelte figure may make you more confident and more frisky.

"It's probably a combination—everything from social interaction to physical and psychological changes within the individual," says Dr. Case. "What we do know is that exercise is good for your sex life."

Make that moderate exercise, however, says Dr. Case. A lot more exercise *doesn't* mean a lot more sex, he notes. Highly conditioned athletes can actually lose interest in and have less sex. "Maybe they're just too exhausted," he comments.

professor and chairman of the department of exercise science at the University of South Carolina in Columbia.

Aging and many of the diseases and conditions associated with growing older can be offset, delayed, and even prevented

88

through physical activity. You really can be younger than your years, maintains Dr. Pate.

"Your body has evolved to be active, and when you aren't, it doesn't do well. In fact, it is surprising just how badly we do when we're not active," says Dr. Pate. "You can get old well before your time."

The ultimate consequence of being active is that you'll probably live longer than your neighbor. When it comes to longevity, physical activity is powerful medicine—so powerful that even people who smoke and have done so for years are less likely to die of a heart attack if they stay active, according to a Swedish study. The researchers monitored 642 men over a 25-year period and found that smokers who engaged in vigorous leisure activity were 40 percent less likely to die of heart disease than smokers who did not exercise vigorously. (That's not to say that it's okay to smoke if you exercise, but the study shows the protective effect of exercise.)

Exercise can even help combat some types of cancers. A long-running study of nearly 18,000 male alumni of Harvard University found that men who were more physically active had less risk of getting colon cancer. And researchers in Norway found that among women—especially young women before menopause—physical activity at work and during their leisure hours was associated with a reduced chance of getting breast cancer.

The Wonders for Women

In fact, if you're a woman, exercise may be extra-important to you. Women tend to have more problems than men with some chronic conditions like obesity, heart disease, osteoarthritis, osteoporosis, autoimmune diseases, and depression, says Doralie Denenberg Segal, a physiologist at the National Institutes of Health in Bethesda, Maryland.

"A lot of these problems begin after menopause. So if you haven't been exercising, then you really need to get off your duff when you hit middle age," says Segal. "As women get older, they are much more compromised by these diseases than men."

Osteoporosis is a disease that hits women three times as frequently as men. One of the dreaded signs of aging in women

know what?

Between ages 18 and 29, women are less likely than men to exercise regularly. Between ages 45 and 64, more women than men exercise more than five times per week.

89

Feeling Fine at 50

Approaching 50, gaining weight, working a job no more physically demanding than sliding around a computer mouse, and having a major health scare finally convinced Marc Linn to "get off my duff" and start exercising regularly.

"I looked in the mirror and saw someone who was getting old—and looking old—before his time," recalled Linn, a computer consultant from San Diego. "I was really slipping, and I realized that I'm subject to the same rules as anyone else."

Like 54 percent of all Americans, Linn exercised occasionally, but not frequently enough to do much for his health or weight.

Over the years, Linn had belonged to a health club, learned to row, taken a Jazzercise class, and even done some bike riding for a time. But as the years passed, the frequency and range of his activities began to dwindle. He eventually lapsed into a state of inactivity—although, he admits, he always had this nagging feeling that he should be doing a lot more.

"You'd have to be living on another planet not to know that you need to exercise," he says. "Yet, there was an emotional, rebellious part of me that said, 'If you're telling me I have to, then I'm not going to.' Besides, it just wasn't high on my list of things to do. I felt I didn't have the time."

His flagging interest in exercise was accompanied by less job activity, too. During his twenties and thirties, Linn had led a very active life working at outside sales, often six days a week, and he was always on the go. But at 40, he became a "freelance computer guy," and as he spent more

is that rounded upper back known as dowager's hump. This signature of advanced osteoporosis results from bone loss that actually begins in women around age 35. Eventually, the reduced bone mass becomes less dense and progressively more prone to fractures. Premenopausal women lose an average of 0.25 percent to 1 percent of the bone mass per year. Bone loss can reach 2 to 3 percent or more for up to seven years after menopause. But if you're a physically active woman, that rate can be reduced.

90

time in front of the video screen, he started to gain weight. He put on 50 pounds, and his total weight, 200 pounds, just didn't match his five-foot five-inch frame.

Then Linn had some blood work done. The doctor found a problem with his prostate. Though the problem turned out to be an infection, rather than cancer, Linn had some deep, life-altering thoughts.

"I felt the jig was up," he recalls. "And I made a vow that if this thing turned out all right, I would get my butt moving. I was 50 and fat; I really wanted to be 50 and fit."

The most fitness fun he had had was Jazzercise, so he bought a portable stereo, a lot of "baby boomer–type" music, and an electronic heart monitor. Accompanied by the steady beat of familiar music, he started taking walks in a nearby park.

Typically, Linn warmed up with some slow music, did some martial arts moves to get loose, then tuned in to heavy-beat music for a hard, intensive walk lasting from 30 to 45 minutes.

"The music has been the real key for me. I need something to keep me moving. I get bored easily," comments Linn.

At home, he does some aerobic dancing, mixed with some light weights; performs chin-ups; and does some abdominal crunches.

Within six months of starting his program, Linn dropped 20 pounds, toned his muscles, and noticed that he felt much younger and more energetic.

"I've found that you can't do anything about your age, but you don't have to stop having fun or doing things because you're 50. Exercise has taught me that."

"The good news is that you can help prevent osteoporosis by engaging regularly in weight-bearing activity and resistance training," says Segal.

"For starters, find some activity that you really enjoy. Tie on a pair of sneakers and regularly hit the bricks for an evening walk or enroll in a folk dance class or join a contra-dance group or an aerobics class," suggests Segal. "If you make a physically active lifestyle part of your daily routine, you may be climbing

91

mountains at an age when your friends are comparison-shopping for rocking chairs."

Simply put, exercise is the equivalent of a miracle drug, good for just about everything and everybody, says George McGlynn, Ed.D., chairman of the department of sports and exercise science at the University of San Francisco.

"Everyone can benefit from exercise. Just because your parents and grandparents lived long lives doesn't mean that you can just sit around and expect to live a long life, too," comments Dr. McGlynn. "Even if you have good genes, you can screw up everything by eating a bad diet, smoking, drinking, and not exercising. Do all of those things, and you may encounter unwanted health problems."

Dodging Whole Decades

Human beings really have two ages: the chronological, candles-on-the-cake age, which reminds us how long we have been padding around the planet, and a physiological age, which is a more accurate measure of fitness. That physiological age is also a good indicator of whether you are likely to be around to blow out the candles, with gusto, on your 100th birthday.

Of course, some effects of physiological age need to be accepted with good grace. Your muscles and tendons probably don't stretch like they once did when you were making moves during the days of hopscotch, jump rope, and one-on-one pickup games on the playground after school. Maybe you can't run as fast or as far because your heart and lungs just don't have the capacity they once did.

If you're over 40, don't be surprised if a day of weeding the garden brings aches and pains to muscles that you forgot you had. In medical terms, you lack flexibility, aerobic fitness, and muscle strength—the three physical categories where exercise can do a world of good, says Dr. Pate.

When it comes to aging, it's difficult to know what is natural and what results from sitting around. A lot of supposedly age-related changes in the body—like the loss of muscle strength, stiff tendons and joints, lack of zip, and a less-efficient heart—are

92

more a matter of *deconditioning,* which is the term doctors use for being out of shape.

According to the National Institutes of Health Consensus Statement on Physical Activity and Cardiovascular Health, one in four adults (more women than men) are sedentary. Another one-third of adults don't exercise often enough to derive health benefits. Even though you may hear more about physical fitness, the statistics show that fewer of us than ever are exercising, says Greg Heath, D.Sc., a physiologist and nutritionist who is acting chief of the cardiovascular health branch in the division of adult and community health at the Centers for Disease Control and Prevention in Atlanta.

In the last few decades, Americans have created a leisure-oriented environment where we have numerous highways and malls, and suburbs accessible only by cars. We blow our leaves out of the yard rather than wield a rake. Office work is easier, too. Why walk down the hall with a memo when you can e-mail a message to your colleague?

"Nobody has to get off their fannies anymore, and that's the result of a philosophy that says, 'what's good is easy, and what's easy is better,'" says Dr. Heath. "First, we eliminated vigorous exercise, now we are eliminating moderate activity as well. There really is cultural conditioning going on here. As we get older, we think we have to take it easy and give up the physically active things we used to do."

So maybe you have let your bike rust in the garage. Perhaps you walk by the playground instead of joining in a pickup game of basketball, or you recently decided that the lawn was just too much to take care of, so you hired the kid down the street. Besides, many of us just feel like we're too busy, and on top of all the other things we have to do, we don't have the time or the inclination to exercise.

Helping You Live It Up

There's another reason to stay limber and active that has as much to do with a youthful state of mind as a youthful condition of body. Have you ever looked out the window on a cold, wet

93

The Energy Measure

Whenever he's doing physical exams, Karl Hempel always asks his patients, "How's your energy level?"

"The answer to that question tells me a lot about their general health and fitness," says Dr. Hempel, an M.D. who has a family practice in Tallahassee, Florida. "If your energy level is okay, then most other things are, too."

The energy question is important, too, because feeling pooped out, achy, and tired are probably the most common complaints that general practitioners hear from patients each day, says Donald R. Frey, M.D., chairman of the department of family practice at Creighton University in Omaha, Nebraska.

This weariness can result from stress, thyroid problems, or even clinical depression, but the most common cause is simply lack of conditioning and fitness, says Dr. Frey.

For folks who are deconditioned—a polite medical term for being as soft as the Pillsbury Doughboy—the physical demands of your daily routine can seem overwhelming. Warning signs include your feeling whipped from dressing the kids, making dinner, commuting, climbing stairs, sitting at work, or, in many cases, just lying around the house, says Dr. Hempel.

"I have people tell me, 'I'm tired all the time, and when I come home from work, I have to take an hour-long nap before I can do anything,'" relates Dr. Hempel. They are feeling old well before their time. "When I hear these kinds of complaints from young or middle-age adults, an alarm bell goes off. These are folks who probably need to get more exercise."

Once he makes sure that serious medical conditions such as diabetes, depression, thyroid problems, or anemia are diagnosed and treated, Dr. Hempel prescribes moderate exercise as a remedy.

"I normally recommend that they start walking, but it doesn't really matter what exercise they do as long as they do something and do it consistently," says Dr. Hempel.

At first, many of his patients are skeptical. Will they really gain more energy by expending more energy? But many give it a try because the doctor ordered it. After a few weeks, if they have faithfully followed the exercise prescription, they are convinced.

"They feel better, they have more energy, and they are doing more," says Dr. Hempel. "Some of them come in here all fired up, wanting me to recheck their cholesterol levels."

morning, watched a jogger running through mud puddles, and wondered, "Why run in this weather?"

Well, that jogger probably knows that going for an early run gives her a psychological lift that will be with her the rest of the day. She may approach her job, housework, or child-care duties with less anxiety, more confidence, and in a generally better mood.

"Just how exercise improves your mood and psychological health isn't clear. We don't know the actual mechanisms," says Jack Rejeski, Ph.D., professor of health and exercise science at Wake Forest University in Winston-Salem, North Carolina. "But people do feel mentally better when they exercise. They are more energized and content, and if they have anxiety, anger, or stress, the exercise often brings them some release, some feeling of peacefulness."

The psychological benefits of physical activity may come from changes within the brain's own chemistry—from the increased production of serotonin and other neurotransmitters that improve communication between brain cells, says Dr. Rejeski. Many of the drugs routinely given to depressed people attempt to boost levels of neurotransmitters, he observes.

"Exercise seems to create similar chemical changes in the brain," says Dr. Rejeski. "But just like the drug therapies, it takes some time for that to happen. So you have to get into a program of exercise and stick with it."

Some studies have shown that moderately depressed people improve their mental outlook when they participate in walking, jogging, and weight-lifting programs. If you're on medication, that doesn't mean you should toss it out and go jogging, but you may want to consider exercise as another therapy for feeling blue, says Dr. Rejeski.

Long-term changes in brain chemistry take time, but you can feel more revived and charged up from just a single dose of exercise. And you don't have to run 10 miles or unload a ton of bricks to get this psychological high. It comes with very moderate levels of activity, says Dr. Rejeski.

"You need to put some demands on your body, but you need not strain or work out to the point of fatigue," he explains. "Taking a brisk walk for 30 minutes or so is usually enough."

know what?

Emma Gatewood hiked the entire Appalachian Trail, from Maine to Georgia, at age 67. She enjoyed it so much that she had hiked it twice more by the time she was in her midseventies.

95

Of course, if you keep up these single doses of exercise, you're going to get into better shape, maybe lose some weight, and find yourself doing things that you may have thought you were too old or too weak to undertake. Many people get a psychological boost from exercise because being in better shape gives them more control over their environment—in this case, their bodies, notes Dr. Rejeski.

"Imagine if you had had a heart attack, you might feel pretty vulnerable, anxious, and scared for a time. But if you started an exercise program, you'd probably get more confident and feel more in control," he explains. "That's going to give you a whole new mental outlook."

Never Mind Gym Class

To you, formal exercise may be drudgery, sweating bodies, weight machines shaped like predatory bone-mashers, and preening figures leaping rhythmically in front of mirrors. And maybe your eyes glaze over when you hear terms like *maximal heart rates, frequency,* and *intensity loads.*

When the simple act of exercise gets that complicated, it's just easier to avoid.

"I think we have been too hung up on how many minutes you have to work out, how many days per week, what your heart rate ought to be," says Dr. Pate. "You need to take a broader view of what exercise is. It's simply physical activity."

According to the latest exercise recommendations from the U.S. surgeon general, you'll get significant health benefits with moderate amounts of physical activity on most days (not necessarily every day). How long you exercise depends on how vigorous the activity is. The more vigorous, the less time it takes the get the required amount of exercise. You could wash windows for 45 minutes, take a brisk 30-minute walk, swim laps for 20 minutes, or shovel snow for 15 minutes. It all counts, and you don't have to get your exercise all in one session. Ten minutes here, 10 minutes there add up.

"The important thing isn't exactly what you do, but that you

96

do it regularly," says Dr. Pate. "The accumulation of activity over weeks and years is what really counts."

Whether you decide to play more and work harder or to undertake a structured exercise program, your goal, says Dr. Pate, should be to improve those three areas of physical fitness that we mentioned before—flexibility, aerobic conditioning, and muscle strength.

Good Going

Sometimes, you can cover all the bases with just one exercise. Walking, for instance, is an excellent exercise for your heart, builds up muscles in your lower legs, and loosens up tight back muscles. Done at a brisk pace, walking can strengthen your heart and lungs, says Dr. McGlynn.

If you want more strength in your arms or chest to improve your golf swing—or you want the kind of flexibility that lets you return a swift tennis serve without injury—you'll need to get more specific with your workouts and more dedicated to a schedule, according to Dr. McGlynn. Perhaps you'll start a weight program three times a week and take a yoga class to limber up those aging tendons. And if you have a history of heart disease in your family, you will need extra action to maintain normal blood pressure, cut stress, and control your weight enough to give you the protection that you are looking for.

"It really depends on what your goals are and how fit you want to be," says Dr. McGlynn. "You should do activities that are fun and give you an overall workout. It's good to try a lot of different things."

So whether you want to chop your own wood for next winter's cold nights, strap on a pair of in-line skates and join the youngsters down on the boardwalk, or just have enough energy so that you're not falling asleep during babysitting duty while reading *Goodnight Moon*, you probably need to bend, lift, and move a little more than you have in the past. One caution, however: If you haven't been exercising much, and you're about to start a more energetic daily routine, it's advisable to get a checkup with your doctor before you begin.

97

Start the Action

"For a lot of us who lead really busy lives, the best way is to set aside some time and go out for a jog, swim laps, or lift some weights," says T. Jeff Chandler, Ed.D., of the Lexington Clinic Sports Medicine Center in Lexington, Kentucky. "But you have to make it part of your routine—and whatever you do, it has to be enjoyable." Here are a few suggestions for getting started on an exercise program.

Individualize your exercise. The best exercise is one that you will do for the rest of your life. If jogging looks painful to you, it probably will be. If you have never skied, you probably don't want a cross-country ski machine. And if you feel strange in a health club, don't join one, advises Robert Abelson, Ph.D., a certified health and fitness instructor who teaches adult exercise and weight loss at the University of California, Los Angeles, Extension Center and at adult classes in Torrance, California.

What are your choices? Well, maybe you can go for a swim, a walk, or a hike. Ride a bike on the boardwalk. Dance in your basement to your old 1960s albums. Just experiment and find something that you like to do, advises Dr. Abelson.

Turn off that infomercial. Don't invest a lot of money in exercise equipment or a health club membership as a way to get motivated. "I always tell people to start with an activity that is simple and inexpensive," says Dr. Abelson. "Before joining a health club, look into classes and memberships at the YMCA, local parks and recreation departments, and walking clubs."

Later, as you get more knowledgeable about exercise, you can think about making more investments in equipment, Dr. Abelson advises. Look in the classifieds. You'll find dozens of exercise machines—probably unused.

Start the habit. You ought to walk before you run, says Karl Hempel, M.D., a family practitioner in Tallahassee, Florida. Walking is probably the easiest, most sensible pursuit for anyone starting an exercise program.

98

"I tell my patients who are out of shape to start by walking for just five minutes a day. Go down the block and back and see how you feel," says Dr. Hempel. "When you feel able, gradually build up the distance and pick up the pace."

Dream of Jeannie. If walking seems boring, make your own movie, says Howard J. Rankin, Ph.D., a clinical psychologist and director of the Carolina Wellness Retreat, a private clinic located in Hilton Head, South Carolina, where people come to learn about exercise and motivation. He tells his clients to practice daydreaming 10 minutes a day. While you're walking, build your vacation house, remember an event from childhood, or fantasize about your fondest love. "You daydream better when you move," he says.

Clamp on headphones. If you would rather listen than daydream, you can check out the ball game, listen to a taped book (most public libraries have tapes on loan), or kick on some good walking jams. It's not advisable to wear headphones when you are trekking near heavy traffic, but indoors or on a walking path, an "earphonic symphony" can set some rhythm and tune to your pleasant pace.

"Whether you are daydreaming or listening to music, exercise can be a little departure from the everyday stuff," Dr. Rankin says. "View it as a reward to yourself."

Becoming a Flexible Flyer

Once you have started to get more exercise in your life, you'll automatically become more flexible, says Bryant Stamford, Ph.D., director of the Health Promotion and Wellness Center at the University of Louisville in Kentucky. Just getting more active by taking a walk in the morning, going out dancing once in a while, and reaching up for those cans of peas—even if it hurts—can help you loosen up.

"Flexibility is one more of those areas where you can get back much of what you lost through inactivity," says Dr. Chandler. But, he adds, if you're really looking to concentrate on particular areas and trouble spots—the lower back, neck, and thighs—you should opt for some sort of stretching program.

know what?

A skeletal muscle like your biceps can shrink by one-third or expand by one-third. A smooth muscle—like your intestinal muscles—can double in size or shrink by half.

99

How often do you need to do a stretching routine? While needs differ for each person, Dr. Chandler says that a routine of 15 to 30 minutes done two or three days a week is probably sufficient for you to see real improvement. Eventually, you'll be able to pick up dirty laundry without feeling tightness or discomfort in the lower back muscles—and you'll have the flexibility to avoid muscle pulls and aches that might come after a weekend of downhill skiing.

If this sounds too much like exercise to you, think of it as a relaxation routine, suggests Dr. Chandler. Stretching is like a good massage, a way to relieve the accumulated stresses and tension of work, freeway driving, and family demands that tighten up muscles.

If you're the weekend-warrior type who tries to build a patio on Saturday or a 40-year-old tennis player who competes with the twenty-somethings, you need to limber up before going into battle. The risk of tearing muscles and tendons that once responded like putty is pretty high no matter how active you have been, says Dr. Stamford. Aging athletes need to pay more attention to their flexibility.

"If you're going to keep playing sports, you have to pay some dues to earn the right to do that safely," says Dr. Stamford. "You should be doing a bona fide stretching program."

Your Next Flex

Even if you don't swing a tennis racket or climb rocks on vacation, you may still want to go beyond normal flexibility and get back to the flex of a rubber band. To get that loose again, you have to perform your stretches with real concentration and vigor, says Dr. Stamford. Here are a few of his tips for the athletically inclined.

Warm up first. Most folks think that stretching is the warmup, but you're more likely to injure yourself if you stretch when your muscles and tendons are cold, says Dr. Stamford. Picture a rubber band in the refrigerator or warmed up in the palm of your hand—which do you think will be more pliable?

Walk briskly for a few minutes or even jog lightly to warm up the tissues, and then go into your stretching routine. You'll get more stretch, says Dr. Stamford. Follow the warmup with some light stretching—and then, after you exercise, stretch again, more aggressively.

Go slow. Stretching should be a fluid, gentle motion where you get into a stretch and hold the position once you feel some tension. The tension should be a bit uncomfortable, but not painful, says Dr. Stamford. As you are stretching, you might be tempted to put a little bounce into the motion. Dr. Stamford cautions against it. If you bounce or jerk, you might tear a muscle, he says.

Hold that stretch. When you get into a stretch position, hold it for at least 30 seconds—and try to work up to two minutes. You should feel some tightness, but not pain. After 15 seconds or so, the muscles and tissues will probably give a little more. Most folks hold a stretch for only a few seconds, but if that's your style, make sure that you hold the stretch longer. A few seconds' stretch doesn't really extend the muscle enough, says Dr. Stamford. While you are stretching, breathe as naturally as you can, he says.

"Think of your muscle as a piece of clay. What you're doing is molding the muscle into a shape, and you need more than a few seconds to do that. You have to tax it and make it want to change," he says.

Do an eight-part routine. A good stretching routine—like the following one—works all the major muscle groups of the body from the Achilles tendon at the back of your calf to the trapezius muscle at the lower neck. Doing a full-body routine gets you loose and limber all over, and that's important because you use lots of muscle groups in most activities, says Dr. Chandler. If you're lifting a child, for example, you're using not just your biceps but also your lower back, legs, and even neck muscles.

When doing the routine, try to hold each stretch for at least 30 seconds, if possible, and make sure to work both sides of the body. All these stretches are worth doing anytime, even for a few minutes when you don't have time for a full workout, says Dr. Chandler.

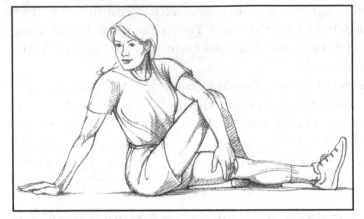

1. Outer Thigh and Torso Stretch

▲ Sit on the floor with your legs extended in front of you. Lift
your right leg and cross it over your left, bending your right
knee so that you can place your right foot on the outside of
your left leg as shown. Lean back on your right arm and turn
your upper body 90 degrees to the right. Use your left elbow
to press the outside of your right knee. Hold, then switch positions to stretch the other leg and side.

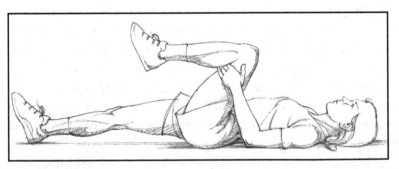

2. Buttocks Stretch

▲ Lie on your back with both legs flat on the floor. Grasp the back of
one thigh and lift and bend the knee toward your chest until you feel
the muscles in your buttocks and lower back tighten. Hold, then
switch positions and repeat with the other leg.

102

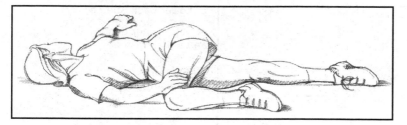

3. Lying Side Stretch

▲ Lie flat on your back. Bend your left leg across your body to your right side as shown. With your right hand, hold your left knee down and roll your head and shoulders back to the left. Hold, and then switch positions to stretch the other side.

4. Calf Stretch

▶ Stand a few feet from a wall with your feet shoulder-width apart. Rest your hands against the wall. Place your right foot forward, and then bend your right leg while extending your left leg behind you. Keeping your back straight and both heels flat to the floor, push your hips toward the wall. You should feel the stretch in the lower part of your extended leg. Hold, and then switch positions to stretch the other leg.

Stop Aches and Stay Limber

5. Lower Back Stretch

◀ Get on your hands and knees with your hands directly under your shoulders.

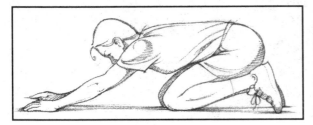

◀ Keeping your hands in place, sit back on your heels. You will feel the stretch along your back. Your arms will be outstretched in front of you.

6. Hamstring Stretch

▶ Sit on the edge of a bed or bench with your right leg extended in front of you and your left foot on the floor. Slide your right hand down your right leg toward your toes, reaching as far as is comfortable. Hold, and then switch positions to stretch the other leg.

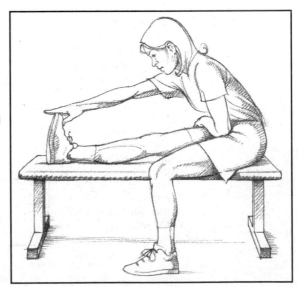

104

7. Arm/Shoulder Stretch

▶ Stand in a doorway, grasping the left and right sides of the door frame at about shoulder height. Lean forward while keeping your chest up and chin in. Gradually straighten your arms as you lean farther into the stretch.

8. Overhead Shoulder Stretch

◀ Stand with your feet shoulder-width apart. Raise your right arm overhead and bend it at the elbow so that your right hand rests behind your shoulder blades. Put your left hand on your right elbow and push down gently so that your right hand slides farther down your back. Hold, and then switch positions to work the other arm.

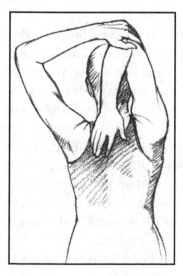

105

Stretching Opportunities

No matter if you choose to work a more formalized routine or just wing it, here's some general advice on stretching from exercise physiologists.

Work your way up. For most people, the important areas to stretch are the lower back, hips, and legs—basically everything from the waist down, says Dr. Chandler.

"These areas most affect your long-term function. The lower body is what gets you from one place to another. Stretching the shoulders is fine, too, but most of us aren't going to go out and pitch a ball game," says Dr. Chandler.

Try sitcom stretching. There is no better place to stretch than in front of the TV. You can easily go through a routine while watching your favorite half-hour show.

"This way you don't have to make time for stretching. You do it while you're doing something else that is enjoyable," says Dr. Chandler.

Expect a little tightness. When you go into a stretch position, you ought to feel some discomfort, but not pain. If it really hurts, back off a bit or try another stretch position that works the same muscles, says Dr. Chandler.

"Ease into it, so you don't get really sore," he says. "After a couple of months, when you have gained more range of motion, you shouldn't have much discomfort."

Customize your stretches. We all stretch unconsciously, all the time, because we can feel tightness in our bodies. Think about your tight areas and how they limit your activities. Do you have difficulty bending over? Can't sit on the floor cross-legged with the grandkids? These are the areas where you especially need more flexibility, says Dr. Stamford.

"Take each joint in a commonsense way. Ask yourself, 'How does the joint operate and what does it allow me to do?' and then do it," says Dr. Stamford. "I once had an 87-year-old man tell me that a few times a day, he lies down on the floor and then gets up. He thought that used most of his muscles and helped him stay flexible. For him it was a perfect exercise."

Reach for the stars. Think about everyday activities that require flexibility, and then mimic the motions. Pretend you are reaching up to grab something off a high shelf or bending to pick up a basket of laundry, suggests Dr. Stamford.

Finding Your Pace

Now that you're loose as a goose, maybe you feel ready to go out and jog a mile.

Think again. If you haven't exercised for 20 years, the last thing that you want to do is try to jog. If the paramedics aren't picking you up, you may have to wait for a good Samaritan like Dr. McGlynn to come along.

Dr. McGlynn was in a park in San Francisco when he saw a fifty-something runner jogging down the path.

"He was wearing a sweatsuit, had weights in each hand, and his face was bright red. He looked terrible," recalls Dr. McGlynn. "I said, 'What are you doing?' The jogger said, 'I'm trying to lose weight.'"

Dr. McGlynn suggested to the jogger that he put down the weights, get rid of the sweats, and first see a doctor for a physical exam. Like many people, the man's conception of exercise was that he had to run himself into the ground to do any good. "It's a strange way to think about exercise, and it's not at all true," he adds. "Just doing a moderate amount of exercise three to five days a week, instead of none at all, can do you a lot of good."

Exercise should be fun, not torture, and physical activity can be a natural part of your day, says Dr. Rankin. "A lot of folks think it's a lot of huffing and puffing—that you have to go work out. It's all that high-performance stuff they see on TV, abs of steel, buns of whatever. It all looks so daunting."

If you are not currently exercising, think first about just increasing your daily activity levels and meeting the minimum standards set down by the U.S. surgeon general—ranging from 15 minutes of vigorous activity to 60 minutes of slow activity daily. Remember that you can get your recommended amount of physical activity by accumulating it in short bursts that are several minutes long, says Dr. Rankin.

107

Chores with a Payoff

If you want some quick and comfortable exercise, here are suggestions from Dr. Rankin.

Go retro. Labor-saving devices for the yard and home can border on the ridiculous. Do you really need a rototiller to dig a small garden? Pick up a spade, advises Dr. Rankin. Retire the whirling weed whacker in favor of a pair of hand clippers. Your neighbors will be grateful if you use a rake and broom instead of a motor-driven leaf blower—and your body will benefit, too.

"I know it goes against the grain of making everything easier," says Dr. Rankin. "When I bought a push mower, all my neighbors thought I was nuts. But it cuts the grass very well, and I get a nice workout every time I mow."

Clean the house. You say that you don't have time to clean the house because you have to go to the gym. Skip the aerobic class, put on some rock 'n' roll, and get the benefit of flexing with cleaning.

Housework is great exercise—especially when you do it fast and hard, says Dr. Rankin. You get the best aerobic workout when the activity lasts for several minutes. So rather than vacuum one room in turn and then stopping, save up the rooms and do the whole house at once, he suggests.

Stroll with the phone. No one's tied to the gossip bench anymore—not if you have a portable phone. Get out of that chair, stroll around the room, climb the stairs, or walk around the outside of the house while you chat, says Dr. Rankin. "If you spend hours on the phone each day, just think how much exercise you can get."

Upping the Ante with Workouts

Putting some effort back into your life will give your lungs a workout, build a stronger heart, and improve your circulation. But to get a good cardiovascular or aerobic workout, you may have to tax yourself a bit more, even break a sweat, says Donald

108

R. Frey, M.D., chairman of the department of family practice at Creighton University in Omaha, Nebraska.

Aerobic exercise requires that you elevate your heartbeat beyond its resting rate. You can easily do that by walking briskly, in-line skating, riding a bike, dancing, going for a swim, or doing other moderate-to-heavy exercise like chopping wood. You get the most aerobic benefit by raising your heart rate to 50 to 75 percent of your maximum heart rate. Maximum heart rate changes with age. For example, the max rate for a 60-year-old person is about 165 beats, so if you are around that age, the target zone for aerobic benefit is between 80 and 120 beats per minute. And remember, you should try to exercise at least three times per week for 20 to 40 minutes.

If you want to make sure that your heart rate is up, you could take your pulse while you exercise, but it's probably not necessary to be so precise, says Dr. Frey.

"Just keep a couple of rules in mind. You should be working hard enough to break a sweat, but not so hard that you can't carry on a conversation with an exercise partner," he says. "In other words, you might be a bit breathless but still able to talk."

If your heart feels as though it's going to jump out of your chest, then slow down, says Dr. Frey. You're probably overdoing it.

Testing the Ticker

The biggest way to avoid that pounding-in-the-chest feeling is to never do anything that taxes your heart muscle. A lot of us follow that strategy, so we don't realize how out-of-shape our lungs and heart are until we try to climb the stadium stairs at a football game or tromp through the woods on the first day of spring. It's when we are huffin' and puffin' like the Big Bad Wolf that we learn our ticker isn't up to the task.

"Weakness with the cardiovascular system is much more apparent when you are stressing the heart with activity than when you are simply resting," says John R. Stratton, M.D., professor of cardiology at the University of Washington in Seattle. "When you're sitting around, you probably don't notice any problems."

Set the Tone Early

Activity stimulates your metabolism, enhances circulation, and pumps up the blood flow to all areas of the body. That's why exercising first thing in the morning often sets the tone for the rest of the day, says Donald R. Frey, M.D., chairman of the department of family practice at Creighton University in Omaha, Nebraska.

When your muscles are warmed up, stretched out, and limber, you're able to do more and shake off that creaky, feeling-my-age stiffness.

"A lot of folks say it takes a while for them to get going in the morning. But if you try exercising first thing—like going out for an early-morning walk—you'll get revved up more quickly," says Dr. Frey.

Not only will you jump-start the body, you'll pump up your brain as well. Exercise apparently causes the brain to release substances that improve communication between brain cells and give you a sense of well-being.

"Your brain literally works better," says Dr. Frey.

You do need to make some allowances, notes Dr. Stratton, because your heart changes with age. When you're older, it doesn't contract as well, its beat has slowed, your arteries are a little stiffer, and you get less blood output with each beat. These same age-related changes can also occur when you don't exercise, however. The American Heart Association says that physical inactivity is a major risk factor—along with smoking and a high-fat diet—for developing coronary artery disease.

The good news is that it's never too late to start moving and get the benefits of cardiovascular conditioning, says Dr. Stratton. "People who have been really sedentary for a long time probably have the most to gain."

Dr. Stratton and his colleagues at the Seattle Veterans Administration Medical Center studied 13 men between the ages of 60 and 82 years and 11 men who were 24 to 32 years old. Both groups were free of heart disease. The men walked, jogged, or biked for 45 minutes, four to five times a week for six months.

Although there were still differences in the hearts of the two groups (the young folks clearly had stronger and better hearts),

110

the older men made significant gains in the efficiency and strength of their hearts. In other words, their hearts responded to exercise just like a younger person's.

Long-Term Tactics

For a Limber Lifestyle

The best way for you to ensure that you're getting adequate conditioning is to set aside a time to exercise three to four days a week, says Dr. Abelson.

"The goal in my class is to just get you moving and keep you moving for at least 20 minutes so that your heart and lungs are working harder," says Dr. Abelson. "It doesn't matter how you do that. You could be biking or line dancing or whatever. Just do what you like to do."

Here are a few activities that Dr. Abelson usually suggests to his students.

Go for a walk. Walking is probably the best, easiest, simplest, and least expensive way to get a cardiovascular workout. If you can walk, you can exercise. To get the most aerobic benefit—that is, get oxygen really flowing through your bloodstream—you need to walk at a brisk pace (about three miles per hour) for 20 to 30 minutes, at least three times per week, says Dr. Abelson.

Dance for your heart's content. You can dance your way to health. Whether it is tap, folk, ballroom, ballet, square, line dance, or just getting down and boogying, dance is good for you. All the basic advice of aerobic conditioning applies here. The more vigorous and sustained the dance, the better, says Dr. Abelson. In other words, the dance floor sweep of the waltz has more aerobic benefit that the stand-in-one-place, grab-your-posterior Macarena.

Take to the water. Aquacise is basically calisthenics and aerobics done in water that's at least waist-deep. The buoyancy of the water relieves a lot of stress on joints and gives some resistance to the movement. Ever try to run across the pool?

111

"If you have joint or ankle problems or are really over-weight, it's a great, safe way to get started exercising," says Dr. Abelson.

Muscling Up

Once you are out of the pool or back from your walk, you may want to finish your workout by grabbing a dumbbell and doing a few curls and presses. Weight or resistance training is not restricted to those sweating guys hanging out in the weight room or those chiseled, Apollo-like hunks on the front of *Men's Health* magazine.

Young women who never made it through week 4 of aerobic dance class are now hoisting a few weights to stave off the effects of osteoporosis. And some nursing-home patients have been able to toss aside the walkers and get out of their wheelchairs after a few weeks of strength training.

"Strength training has really been an area where women and older people shied away, but no longer. Research has shown that resistance training can do a lot to keep us young and strong," says LaDora Thompson, Ph.D., a physical therapist in the department of physical medicine and rehabilitation at the University of Minnesota Medical School, Minneapolis.

Anyone can get stronger. Even people who are 90 years old or have been couch potatoes for decades can build up their muscles and see dramatic results, says Dr. Thompson.

"There doesn't seem to be an age limit on getting stronger. You may not be able to get as strong as you once were, but if you want to still be golfing and walking the course at age 80, there's no reason that you can't stay strong enough to do it," says Dr. Thompson.

And all of us can use some strengthening because we have natural deterioration of muscle and bone as we age. Beginning in your midforties, unless checked by exercise, your muscles will begin to shrink at the rate of 1.5 percent per year. In a 20-year period, you can lose 30 percent of your muscle mass, and what normally tends to replace that lost muscle is fat.

Unfortunately, you get weaker as you get fatter. And that's

112

true even if you look lean and can still fit into your wedding dress or your old army uniform. "Looks can be deceiving. If you have lived an inactive life, you'll be carrying more fat than muscle. Part of that is natural aging, but mostly it's a matter of not being active," says Dr. Thompson.

And after you turn 70, you can lose an additional 30 percent of your muscle strength in just a decade, which makes it more likely that you will be unable to live on your own.

"There's a lot of benefit to keeping your strength up and maintaining your muscle mass," says Roger Fielding, Ph.D., assistant professor of health science at Sargent College of Health and Rehabilitation Sciences at Boston University. "I think it's important for people to realize that strength training is something that you should make part of your life. You want to maintain muscle for as long as you can."

Meeting Resistance

If you're a woman, you may have even more to gain than a man from resistance training (which means working with any kind of weights in your workouts) since women naturally have less muscle and more fat than their male counterparts. Resistance training also keeps bone dense and strong, says Dr. Fielding, so it's a good weapon against osteoporosis.

"When you lift weights or do a lot of walking, the resistance or load you put on your bones forces them to adapt and increase their mineral content," Dr. Fielding explains. "If you exercise when you're young, you can build up your bone density before menopause. By exercising when you are older, you can slow down the rate of loss due to aging."

In a study at Tufts University in Boston, researchers put 20 postmenopausal women (ages 50 to 70) through two 45-minute weight-training sessions per week for one year. Bone density in the spine and the thigh of the weight lifters increased by about 1 percent, while a control group of sedentary women who did not exercise lost an average of 2.1 percent of their bone density at those two sites during the same period. The exercisers improved their muscle strength up to 77 percent.

113

Stay Strong, Stay Active

With strong bones and muscles, your legs won't ache and complain on Sunday morning after a night of cutting the rug at the spring dance. You'll be able to walk those four blocks to church and later spend the afternoon chasing your kids or grandkids around the zoo.

"The leg muscles are probably more important to keep strong than anything else," says Dr. Thompson. "They are what get you from place to place, and that's why walking is a great exercise. We find that people get weaker in their lower extremities as they age, but that's probably because you're just not moving around like you did when you were younger."

Makeover Minutes

For Firming and Flexing

To get the resistance training you need, you don't need to head for the gym and lift weights with the hotshots. Here are ways to get resistance training without weights and machines.

Carry your own books. If a routine of calisthenics sounds tedious, just make weight training a natural part of your day, suggests Dr. Stamford. Take a cardboard box, put in a few books, and put it on your nightstand next to your bed. When you wake up, carry the box to the kitchen. Later on, move it to the front hall or the living room—or carry it upstairs or downstairs.

"Each time you see the box, just pick it up and move it. By the end of the day, you'll have gotten your strength training," says Dr. Stamford. "And as you get stronger, just add more or heavier books."

Make a medicine ball. Buy a soft plastic or rubber playground ball, six to eight inches in diameter, at the bargain store. Remove the plastic plug, let it deflate, then partially fill the ball with water, and replace the plug. Now you have an easy-to-hold, three- to six-pound weight.

You can toss it from hand to hand, press it over your head, curl it like dumbbell, throw it to a partner, or hold it against your chest and squat to a sitting position, says Dr. Chandler.

114

"Just use exercises that feel good to you," suggests Dr. Chandler. "I like to lie on my back and do pullovers, chest presses, and triceps extensions."

Give me five, soldier. Even if you have never been in the military, you probably think of pushups, jumping jacks, and calisthenics when you hear the words *basic training*. Soldiers build muscles and endurance with little more than their body weight. With different routines of calisthenics, you work a full range of muscles: squats for the legs and hips, stomach crunches for the lower back, and pushups for the arms and chest. Here's how to do five of them.

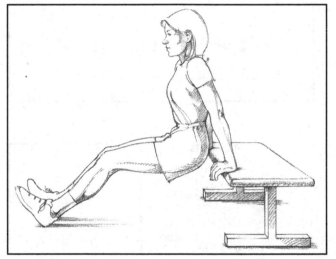

1. Chair Dips

◀ With your arms extended behind you, place your hands on the edge of a bench or a sturdy chair. Your arms should be straight, while your legs are out in front of your body and slightly bent.

▶ Slowly lower your torso by bending your arms at the elbows. Then to return to your starting position, raising your body by straightening your arms. Repeat 2 to 15 times.

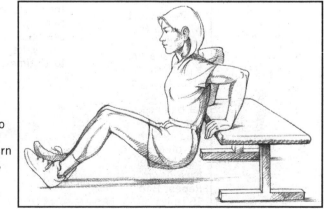

2. Bent-Knee Pushups

◄ Lie facedown on the floor with legs and feet together, knees bent, and feet off the ground. Place your hands flat on the floor, fingers pointing forward, parallel to your shoulders, with your elbows bent slightly away from your body. Keeping your knees bent, slowly push up until your arms straighten.

▶ Lower slowly until your chest is close to the floor. Push yourself back up again. Repeat 2 to 15 times. (If these are too difficult, try inclined pushups. Stand several feet from a wall, arms straight and palms against the wall at shoulder level, heels slightly raised. Bend your arms at the elbows and bring your forehead to the wall, keeping your back straight.)

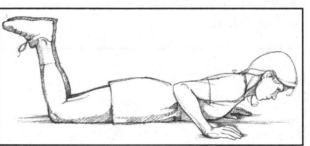

3. Heel Raises

◄ Stand erect with your feet shoulder-width apart on a platform or step. Using a chair or wall for balance, rise on your toes as high as you can. Slowly lower back down. Repeat 2 to 15 times.

4. Squats

▶ Stand with your feet shoulder-width apart. Place your hands on your hips, keep your back straight, and lower yourself to the squat position. Raise yourself back up slowly. Repeat 2 to 15 times.

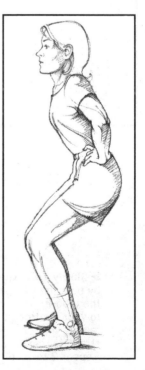

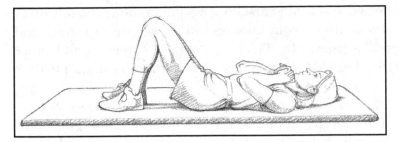

5. Abdominal Crunches

▲ Lie on the floor with your knees bent and your feet planted on the floor. Clasp both hands and rest them under your chin.

▲ Lift your shoulders three to four inches off the floor by contracting your stomach muscles. Keep your neck straight and the small of your back flat on the floor. Repeat 2 to 15 times.

Weight Up!

To build upper-body strength, you will want to lift weight that stresses the muscles. But before you start weight training, be sure to check with your doctor.

The standard recipe for weight training says that you should work out with weights that are 80 percent of the maximum weight you can lift one time. With these, do three sets—8 to 10 repetitions per set. In other words, if you can bench press 100 pounds one time, then you should be able to lift 80 pounds 8 to 10 times. The last couple of lifts should be difficult, but over a few weeks doing these sets, it will get easier, says Dr. Fielding. You will need to determine how much to lift for each weight-lifting exercise that you do, he says.

117

"When you find yourself being able to do three sets of 24 to 30 repetitions, your muscles will have gotten stronger and bigger," suggests Dr. Fielding. "Now it's time to add more weight." Increase the weight so that it is again difficult to do 8 to 10 repetitions.

When you begin working with weights, you'll want advice from a certified physical trainer at the local health club or gym. Once you have the basics, though, you can get your own weights and do these workouts at home. Lift what feels comfortable but challenging, too, recommends Dr. Fielding.

Here are three exercises that will get you started.

1. Upright Rows (with weights)

◀ Stand with feet shoulder-width apart. Grasp a dumbbell in each hand. Hold the dumbbells in front of your thighs with your palms facing your body.

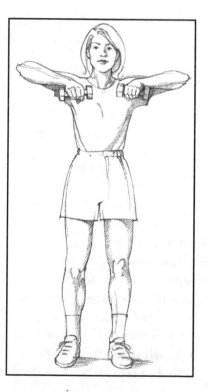

▶ Pull the dumbbells up, bringing your elbows out to the sides until they are even with your ears. Pause, slowly lower the weights to the starting position, and repeat.

118

2. Biceps Curls (with weights)

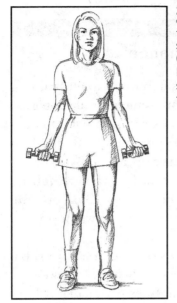

◀ Stand with your feet shoulder-width apart. Grasp a dumbbell in each hand and hold them at your sides with your palms facing forward.

▶ Raise the weights until you're holding them at shoulder height. Lower them slowly, then repeat.

3. Military Presses (with weights)

▼ Sit in a chair with a back support. Start with a dumbbell in each hand. Bending your arms at the elbows, raise the dumbbells to shoulder height, palms facing forward.

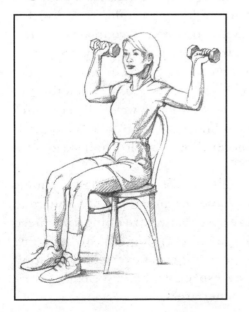

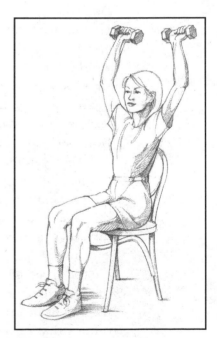

▲ Raise the weights over your head by straightening your arms until they are fully extended. Lower slowly and repeat.

For Muscular Maintenance

Whenever you use weights, it's important to make lifting as effective and safe as possible. Here are some overall strategies.

Puff a little. When you are actually exerting yourself to lift a weight, don't clamp down and hold your breath. By holding your breath, you might cause unusual rises and falls in blood pressure that can be dangerous, particularly if you are getting up in years, advises Dr. Fielding. "You want to relax, breathe through the exercise, blowing out air or exhaling when you are making an exertion," he says.

Choose what you move. Free weights or machines? It probably doesn't make any difference for general health. Free weights may require a little more balancing and finesse to manage them well, whereas machines can be a lot easier to use and safer, says Dr. Fielding.

Get your technique down. When you're first trying a new exercise, for the first one or two sessions, start with just enough weight so that you can do 20 repetitions with relative ease, says Dr. Fielding. Concentrate on using only the muscles that the exercisc is designed for. If you are doing a two-hand curl with a barbell, for instance, you want to use only your arms to lift. Don't jerk the weight or use your back muscles to lift it.

When you put all the strain on your back, you aren't getting the benefit of the exercise, says Dr. Thompson. "It's the full range of motion that counts, not how much weight you can lift," she says. "The movement should work the muscle through its full range, and your movements should be slow and steady, not jerky or abrupt."

Look good all over. The ability to lift well and build stamina requires that you use lots of different muscles. When you go to the gym or health club, make sure that you're doing a balanced routine that works all the large muscle groups in the body, says Dr. Fielding. Be sure to do arm and chest exercises and don't neglect the rest of your body, especially the lower extremities, while you're building those other areas.

120

Getting Started and Sticking with It

Exercise, the miracle drug of age protection, requires one additional ingredient to really make it work. The ingredient is "stick-to-it-ive-ness."

"You have to make activity a real part of your lifestyle. It has to be important to you; otherwise, you won't make it a habit," says Dr. Rankin.

Here are some suggestions for getting the hang of the exercise habit.

Think bleak. If you truly want to get motivated and stay motivated, keep those bad feelings that you have about being a couch potato uppermost in your mind, advises Dr. Rankin. Negative motivation works if you let it. If you can't fit into your swimsuit anymore, remind yourself of that. If your cholesterol level has soared over 200, keep in mind that this is literally a lifesaving activity.

"Most us don't like to think about uncomfortable, bad things, so we just let it fade away," says Dr. Rankin. "You have to keep confronting yourself with it."

Has it been a while since you could fit into some favorite clothes? If you have a party dress that doesn't fit anymore, try hanging it on your bedroom door where you see it every day, suggests Dr. Rankin. Put pictures on the wall of a time when you looked especially dumpy. Tape your 200-plus cholesterol count to the bathroom mirror.

Talk to yourself. Ask yourself why you want to exercise. Is it to look younger? Feel more energetic? Meet good-looking people at the gym? In addition to the negative, you also want reminders of the positive consequences, says Dr. Rankin.

A father might say, "Unless I get in shape, I won't be able to take my son on that pack trip to Wyoming next year." A single woman might remind herself, "If I work out at the gym, maybe I'll meet a man who hoists weights instead of beer mugs."

"'There are lots of reasons to exercise, but what are yours? You have to know why you want to do it," says Dr. Rankin.

Rhyme to run. You can keep these motivations in mind by putting them into catchy, funny phrases like "Arteries go splat

121

when you fill them with fat" or "An exercise session fights depression."

Make those rhymes personal, Dr. Rankin suggests. If you want to get in shape because you want to go backpacking in the mountains, try something like "To reach the top, I have to hop," or "If I don't reach the peak, I'll be a geek."

These mnemonic devices might sound corny, but they work by keeping motivation strong when the temptation is to blow off an exercise session, says Dr. Rankin.

And just so you don't forget to say these rhymes to yourself each day, Dr. Rankin suggests that you link them to everyday sounds. "That way, every time you hear the sound of a phone ringing, a car starting, or water running, one of these phrases runs through your mind," he says.

Track your efforts. People new to exercise often expect instant results, but the reality is that it takes months before stronger muscles, smaller bellies, and greater endurance reveal themselves, says Dr. Heath.

"However, if you keep records of your exercise efforts—distance walked, weight lifted and number of repetitions, minutes of activity—you'll have more immediate and objective ways to prove to yourself that you are getting stronger and healthier," says Dr. Heath.

Don't knock yourself out. Getting into the habit doesn't happen overnight, and that's why so many people trying a formal program of exercise fail and then get discouraged, says Dr. Heath. They do too much, get sore or injured, get bored by doing something they don't really like, or fall off the wagon, miss a few days, and never get started again.

"To become a habit, exercise has to be a priority in your life," says Dr. Heath. "Realize that this is a process that will take time."

122

Sharpen
Your Wits

Your brain is stupendous. Okay, read those words again. Think how easily you understand each word—and all of them together.

Now think about how you first learned to comprehend words. Years ago, you heard the word *your*, and it began to take on meaning. Later, you found out about *brain* and what it signifies—and that's something you have never forgotten. Later still, some teacher taught you how to read and pronounce *stupendous*, and you haven't had to look it up since.

That's just a small sampling of your nimble noggin at work. Multiply that kind of knowledge by millions, and you have a picture of your brain in action. In fact, in the powerhouse of your remarkable mind, you can store information equivalent to 20 million books the size of this one. A bookshelf holding all those books would be 631 miles long.

Not bad for a head that holds about three pounds of gray matter.

So how come the holding power of that incredible reservoir seems to start leaking at the seams as we age? Maybe it's too full (20 million volumes of information is a lot to hold). Maybe all that intake of information gets a little—well—old, and we just don't pay attention as well as we used to.

Or maybe—and here's the radical thought—memory loss doesn't have to happen at all. Based on what researchers are discovering about the human brain and how it works, there's a good chance that you can actually protect your brainpower simply by using your mind more. And when you do that, you can actually protect yourself from aging.

123

"Your brain is the most important piece of real estate that you own," says Paul Spiers, Ph.D., a clinical neuropsychologist and visiting scientist at the Massachusetts Institute of Technology in Cambridge. "You need to do all necessary maintenance to keep it functional. You don't have to use hammer and nails, of course, but you do need to keep your brain mentally and physically active to maintain its value."

If you have never thought of your brain as active, maybe it's time to try some mental situps. Preserving or enhancing your brainpower doesn't mean that you have to take up ancient Greek or even recall *pi* to the 27th decimal place. It does mean that you may need to spend a few minutes every day putting that brain of yours through the equivalent of some calisthenics. And you may need to implement some tactics related to your diet and your health, tactics that reinforce your other age protectors as well as your brainpower.

Keeping Your Brain Vigorous

The vast majority of us can maintain or even improve our mental vigor throughout our lives, according to K. Warner Schaie, Ph.D., director of the gerontology center at Pennsylvania State University in University Park. Maintaining a good diet and getting regular exercise can have a direct effect on the mind's ability to stay young, he notes. Many of the "natural" changes that are thought to occur with aging don't have to happen at all.

And if you want to put the mental brakes on aging, you need to regularly expose yourself to a wide range of mental challenges, from learning a new language or doing puzzles to writing, painting, or making music, according to Vernon Mark, M.D., a neurosurgeon in Newport, Rhode Island, and co-author of *Reversing Memory Loss.*

"There are people over 100 years old who are functioning very well mentally," Dr. Mark says. "One of the reasons for this is that they don't retire from life. They keep challenging themselves in new ways. That's important because the brain abhors boredom. You need to keep it stimulated."

Leo Tolstoy, the famed Russian novelist, had his first bicycle

How the Mind Stays Young

Inside your brain are billions of nerve cells that communicate with each other by releasing chemicals called neurotransmitters. These chemicals are released from a cell through axons and received by dendrites, both of which are rootlike structures that branch out and seek connections with adjoining cells. The more dendrites you have, the greater your brainpower, says Arnold Scheibel, M.D., professor of neurobiology and psychiatry and former director of the Brain Research Institute at the University of California, Los Angeles.

Some doctors have theorized that mental challenges cause new dendrites to grow. So it's possible that the more mentally active you are, the more dendrites you'll have. "Dendrites transmit messages at delicate points of connection called synapses," says Daniel Alkon, M.D., a neurologist and chief of the Laboratory of Adaptive Systems at the National Institute of Stroke and Neurological Disorders in Bethesda, Maryland. "As you stimulate your mind by learning about or participating in an activity, you may increase the relative strength of these connections."

lesson when he was 67. Queen Victoria started learning the Hindustani language when she was 68. Grandma Moses didn't begin painting until she was in her seventies.

At any age, new and challenging activities are the brain's best friend. "The most important ingredient for the brain is intellectual stimulation," Dr. Spiers says. "The more you can keep your brain doing things—reading, writing, traveling, learning new information—the more resistant your brain will be to the effects of aging."

Add Mental Rooms

In 1884, Sarah Winchester purchased an eight-bedroom farmhouse near San Jose, California. For the next 38 years—until her death in her early eighties—this very rich, very eccentric woman had carpenters working on the house 24 hours a day.

According to Winchester, a psychic had told her that a ceaseless building project would break a family death curse and help

125

The Sharpness Image

When people contemplate getting older, it isn't necessarily the prospect of physical illness that seems most frightening. In a survey of 800 Americans, nearly 4 out of 10 people said that staying mentally sharp is more important than avoiding physical disability or changes in physical appearance.

"The quality of life really does depend upon your brain functioning well," says Vernon Mark, M.D., a neurosurgeon in Newport, Rhode Island, and co-author of *Reversing Memory Loss*.

No question, aging does take some toll on the brain. For example, people in their late eighties are about 50 percent less adept at basic math than they were in their fifties, according to K. Warner Schaie, Ph.D., director of the gerontology center at Pennsylvania State University in University Park.

But even if it sometimes takes a bit longer to balance the checkbook than it used to or if you occasionally have trouble recalling a certain word, your thinking cap can still stay in top-notch shape for a lifetime, says Andrew Monjan, Ph.D., chief of neurobiology of the Aging Branch of the National Institute on Aging in Bethesda, Maryland. The key is to maintain a healthy lifestyle and continue to be intellectually challenged, he adds.

Dr. Schaie's research has shown that even people in their seventies and eighties can readily sharpen their mental skills. In one study, Dr. Schaie and his colleagues gave a group of healthy elderly volunteers five hours of tutoring on spatial orientation (the skills used when reading a road map) and simple reasoning. He found that two-thirds of the volunteers showed mental improvement after the sessions. More significantly, 40 percent of the people regained a level of mental acuity similar to what they had had 14 years earlier.

"Many of these people had retired or left stimulating jobs during those years. They just weren't exercising or using the mental abilities that they had once used on the job," says Sherry Willis, Ph.D., a gerontology researcher at Pennsylvania State University in University Park. "But when they were put back into a situation that demanded them to use those abilities, they were intellectually challenged again."

her achieve eternal life. By the time of her death in 1922, Winchester had constructed an additional 152 rooms at a cost of $5.5 million. She had also outspanned her short-lived forebears by nearly a lifetime.

126

Certainly a challenge was dreaming up strange and curious rooms as she did—rooms with trap doors, no doors, dozens of windows, extreme shapes and sizes. It so happened, Winchester had stumbled on a great way to break the family short-life curse. When she put her brain to work dreaming up all those rooms, Winchester harnessed a powerful age protector.

The human brain, like Winchester's curious house, is always a work in progress, according to Dr. Spiers. It requires constant stimulation—the addition of new "rooms," if you will—to stay strong and active. In fact, when you spend a few minutes a day pushing your mind beyond its usual boundaries, you sharpen your wits and thinking skills—not just today or next year, but for the rest of your life.

Even doing familiar tasks can enrich your mind—if you add new twists. "If you're right-handed and try to play tennis with your left hand, then you are using a totally different set of reflexes," says Arnold Scheibel, M.D., professor of neurobiology and psychiatry and former director of the Brain Research Institute at the University of California, Los Angeles. "Everything you're doing is essentially reversed, and that makes it the equivalent of a totally new experience."

The important point is that you don't have to take on enormously difficult challenges to make substantial improvements in how well your brain works. Doing anything new or different will help strengthen the brain and keep the mind sharp.

Makeover Minutes

To Sharpen Your Wits

"Mental calisthenics" are not only curious and challenging but also fun. When you consider the payoff, giving your brain a daily workout is eminently worthwhile. Using your extra reserves of brainpower is not just a sign of youth, it also makes you feel youthful.

Getting into mental shape can be as easy as doing a crossword

127

puzzle or doodling in a notebook. By spending a few Makeover Minutes every day, you not only build your mind power but also stimulate memory and quick thinking. So sharpen your pencil. Here are some tips that experts recommend when you're adding rooms to your mental mansion.

Tease your brain at the market. Here's an easy way to flex your mental muscles. The next time you go shopping, leave the list in the car, says Michael Chafetz, Ph.D., a clinical psychologist in New Orleans and author of *Smart for Life*. Take a minute to memorize six or eight items that you need.

Once you're in the store, get a cart and pick a starting point. Go get your first item, then return to the starting point. Then get the rest of the items, one at a time, returning to the starting point each time.

That's all. This simple exercise will help strengthen your memory while at the same time improving the mind's ability to create a mental map of where things are, says Dr. Chafetz. When you do this regularly, you'll find that you can remember more and more things—not only groceries but also tasks you need to do at work or home—at one time.

Turn off the telly. It's no accident that television became known as the boob tube. Researchers at Kansas State University, Manhattan, found that people who watched just 15 minutes of television had diminished brain-wave activity, an indication that their minds were turning off. "For the most part, the images on that screen just flow through you without enhancing your life," Dr. Chafetz says.

He recommends making at least one night a week a no-television night. You may be surprised at the number of mind-stimulating activities you'll come up with to fill the time.

Test with the tube. Although television is by nature a passive activity, there are ways to watch and still be mentally active, says Thomas Crook, Ph.D., director of Memory Assessment Clinics in Scottsdale, Arizona, and Gaithersburg, Maryland, and author of *How to Remember Names*. When watching TV, he says, jot down a few notes about facial expressions, clothing, or anything else that's happening on the screen. Set the notes aside. A day or two later, see how much you can recall. It's fun putting your mem-

128

A Drink to Help You Think

Moderate amounts of alcohol have been shown to help prevent heart disease, relieve stress, and possibly help people live longer. And some evidence suggests that alcohol may help people think more clearly, too.

In a 20-year study of 4,000 male twins, researchers at Indiana University School of Medicine in Indianapolis found that men who drank one to two alcoholic beverages a day had better learning and reasoning skills than those who drank less, says Joe Christian, M.D., Ph.D., lead author of the study and professor of medical and molecular genetics at Indiana University School of Medicine. It may be, he says, that having one to two drinks a day improves blood flow to the brain, helping it work more efficiently.

The study also showed that people who limited their alcohol intake to one to two drinks did better than those who drank more. Too much alcohol—more than one drink a day for women and more than two a day for men—may actually slow blood flow to the brain or damage nerve cells. In addition, too much alcohol can cause a decrease in magnesium, calcium, and potassium—minerals the brain needs to communicate, says Max A. Schneider, M.D., clinical professor of psychiatry and human behavior at the University of California, Irvine, College of Medicine.

Obviously, if you don't drink alcohol, the slight mental boost from a couple of drinks a day should not be a motivation to start. But for those who do drink, it's nice to know that having a drink or two a day may help the mental wheels turn a bit more smoothly.

ory to the test, and doing this for even a few minutes will help keep both your memory and powers of observation sharp, Dr. Crook says.

Tune in to pulp fiction. Why not pick up the latest best-seller and lose yourself in a thriller, mystery, or romance? Reading is a time-tested brain booster that helps improve language skills while keeping your memory strong, according to Dr. Chafetz.

You don't have to read Plato's *Republic* or Shakespeare's sonnets to exercise your mind. Even light reading can powerfully improve your word skills, says Dr. Chafetz. He recommends picking up a book or magazine daily and reading for at least 15 minutes.

Keep doing head counts. It wasn't so many years ago that most of us did math in our heads. These days, many clerks have a hard time making change unless the computer or calculator is telling them what to do. "If you use a calculator every time you have to add three numbers together, your mental abilities are going to suffer," Dr. Crook says.

Inscribe your thoughts. Few things clarify thoughts and improve memory and logic as well as writing does, says Alan S. Brown, Ph.D., professor of psychology at Southern Methodist University in Dallas and author of *How to Increase Your Memory Power*. Even if you don't fancy yourself a wordsmith, take a few minutes to write at least one letter a week to a friend or relative, he suggests. Or write a letter to the editor or a note evaluating a product you recently bought. Anytime you pick up a pen instead of the telephone, you help keep your mind sharp, says Dr. Brown.

Create a challenge. Put your mind to work with a simple puzzle that you can make at home, like the one Dr. Mark suggests below. The larger, the better—and if you want to repeat the puzzle, make some photocopies. Any set of random numbers and letters will do the trick, he says. The goal is to circle in pencil certain numbers and letters within a given time. For instance, try to circle every *2* and every *c* within 15 seconds.

```
k 3 f g 8 4 g 3 c s 0 1 n z d 8 2 f g h 6 0 1
j l 5 d 9 v b 7 3 3 2 a b 6 c n 4 b q d 3 4 4 d
p u 6 v 9 1 u 8 v a 0 m n 2 h g z w 6 r y t 7
c 1 1 e c b q p b 9 7 m 3 6 g u w 3 c 2 3 8 u
2 4 h t y l 5 3 8 n e a 9 2 9 k m z 7 y 3 m 9
p h 4 f d s a 3 2 8 v m r 0 4 b 6 1 1 c d l 8
```

Repeat the exercise again on a fresh copy, finding a different set of numbers and letters. Doing this once or twice a week is a good way to help improve your concentration and attention span, Dr. Mark says.

Tie up your tongue. Doing tongue twisters not only improves speech but also helps improve concentration by exercising speech and language circuits, Dr. Chafetz says. At least once a day, he says, take a minute to practice your favorite tongue twister—like "Fresh fried fish don't flip like fresh fish flip"—five times in a row.

130

Be punny. Puns and other types of humor spark creativity and encourage your mind to look at problems in new ways, Dr. Chafetz says. Take a moment to really think about words you hear and then see what odd twists you can come up with. For example, the word *illegal*—a sick eagle; *dumbbell*—a bell that's not too bright.

Cut it out. Take a few minutes to clip funny cartoons, photos, and stories from newspapers and magazines and put them up in your "humor gallery" in your home or office. Whether you're making your own humor or enjoying someone else's, you need to look at the world from odd angles. This change in perspective will help keep your mind active, Dr. Chafetz says.

Get cross with words. What's a five-letter word for cowboys and Indians? Could be *fight* or *movie*—or maybe it's *teams*—as in the Dallas Cowboys and the Cleveland Indians.

With clues like that, crossword puzzles are a great way to puzzle your mind. And embracing their twisted logic may be one of the best things you can do for your brain. Doing crosswords and other puzzles exercises the brain cells involved in word retrieval, vocabulary, and comprehension, says Dr. Chafetz.

"Crossword puzzles encourage people to look at things in less-than-obvious ways, and I think they help people stay mentally sharp," agrees Judy Weightman, Ph.D., senior variety editor at *Official Publications*, a puzzle magazine company in Ambler, Pennsylvania. If you have never done crossword puzzles before, Dr. Weightman has this advice:

■ Don't try to complete an entire category—Down or Across—at the same time. A better way is to do 1 Across, followed by 1, 2, and 3 Down.

■ Then begin moving around the puzzle clockwise, filling in as many clues as you can.

■ If you get stuck, go back up to the upper left corner and start moving down counterclockwise.

"This way you can fill in the puzzle in related clumps rather than as disconnected factoids," Dr. Weightman says. "You'll rarely get stuck in both directions if you do it that way."

know what?

It would take about 32 million years to count all the connections in the part of the brain that controls rational thought.

131

Toying with Rodents

True, we humans have come a long way in our evolution from rat-hood, but research has shown that rats, like us, definitely get a big charge out of novel situations.

In animal studies, Marian Diamond, Ph.D., a neuroanatomist at the University of California, Berkeley, to find out how caged rats would react when the toys in their cage were changed three or four times a week. In the young animals, the change of playthings stimulated brain development, her studies showed.

Not only that, new toys clicked with the oldsters, too. Rats that were more than 900 days old—the equivalent of 90 years in a human—demonstrated more development than rats that had no toys. "It shows that changes in the environment can positively affect the brain at any age," says Dr. Diamond.

What's the equivalent of "changing toys" in the world of an adult human who wants to protect brain cells from aging?

"Quite clearly, exposing yourself to new areas of work or challenge is the best tonic for the brain," says Arnold Scheibel, M.D., professor of neurobiology and psychiatry and former director of the Brain Research Institute at the University of California, Los Angeles. "If I decided to take up Russian, for instance, it would be a real challenge."

When your mind tackles challenges, your brain actually builds up its synapses, according to Dr. Schiebel. The synapses are those critical connections between nerve endings, where the "spark" of a message leaps from cell to cell—and the more the synapses get built up, the more quickly and efficiently your mind makes connections and solves problems.

Just imagine your braininess. With a technique called mental imagery—which you can practice in bed, in the shower, or in line at the store—you can readily improve your memory and powers of thinking, says Dennis Gersten, M.D., a psychiatrist in San Diego and author of *Are You Getting Enlightened or Losing Your Mind?*, who has studied ways in which American prisoners of war kept their minds active.

One of the simplest forms of mental imagery involves focusing on an image or situation, then using your imagination to embellish it with as much detail as you possibly can. "The pris-

132

oners of war in Vietnam who survived the best were the ones who created problems in their minds and worked on solving them," says Dr. Gersten. "One man built a two-story house in his head. He imagined the process in such great detail that he would actually discuss the color of the tile in the bathroom with his cellmate. When he was released, he built that house in a Midwestern state exactly the way that he had pictured it in his mind."

Here's an exercise that you may want to try. Picture a cube in your mind. Imagine that each side is a different color.

In your mind, turn the cube from side to side, memorizing the colors as they appear. Then, rotate the cube again and *predict* the colors before they appear. "There's a lot of mental effort involved in picturing a cube and consciously trying to rotate it," he says. "You're really forcing your mind to work in a very active way."

With a little practice, says Dr. Gersten, you'll soon find it's easy to predict which colors will appear next. You'll find that doing this simple exercise for five minutes twice a day will substantially improve your memory and help you think more clearly—not just while doing the exercise, but in all aspects of your life, he says.

Long-Term Tactics
For Brain Gain

Other favors you can do for your wits and memory may take longer, but they're worth trying for a lot of reasons. You not only will get the age-protector benefits from the following strategies but also may find talents that you never knew you had. And the only risk is that you might enjoy yourself so much that you'll never want to give up what you have started.

Take up an instrument. Playing music brings an enormous number of skills into play, from improving coordination and concentration to fostering your creative instincts. And you don't have to practice six hours a day to get the benefits. Playing an instrument 10 to 15 minutes a day will give your brain a good workout, Dr. Scheibel says.

133

Share your passion. From photography and pottery to Swedish and Swahili, we all have skills we can share with others—and the challenge of teaching those skills is very good for the mind, says Dr. Brown. It's not hard to find a classroom to teach in, he adds. Most community centers and civic organizations are eager for volunteers who can teach hobbies, languages, or other skills.

Do anything classy. Perhaps you're more comfortable being in the class rather than in front of it. Adult education, be it Spanish, accounting, calligraphy, or dancing, provides an excellent mental workout, Dr. Brown says. You'll discover stimulating ideas and people to discuss them with. Plus, studying for tests is a superb way to help improve your memory.

Add challenge to games. Chess, Scrabble, jigsaw puzzles, and other mind-stretching games are terrific challenges that help keep your mind clicking at a youthful tempo. But why not go a step further and give your brain an even tougher workout?

There are many ways to put a new twist on old games, says Dr. Chafetz. When playing Scrabble, for example, use some new rules. Require that each word have a minimum number of letters, or limit the allowable words to nouns or adjectives. When doing a jigsaw puzzle, put it together from the blank side.

And for chess aficionados, here's what Dr. Chafetz suggests that you do to reach the height of mental challenge: Pick a worthy opponent and blindfold yourself. Ask your opponent to call out the moves. See how long you can continue the game, just picturing the board in your mind. When you attempt this, you'll stimulate your imagination, focus your concentration, and put your logical skills to the test, says Dr. Chafetz.

Makeover Minutes

Getting Your Mind Foods

While mental workouts are great age protectors for your brain, don't forget that your brain also needs feeding.

What you eat, says Dr. Mark, can have a potent impact on how clearly you think. The brain uses nutrients such as choline,

134

vitamin B_{12}, thiamin, niacin, and folic acid to enhance brain function. The brain also needs minerals like copper, iron, and zinc, which are thought to influence the function of nerve endings. In addition, the brain uses electrolytes like sodium, potassium, calcium, and magnesium to transmit electrical signals between cells. For starters, see the advice under Stop-Time Tactic No. 1 on page 3—and check out the top 10 foods for protecting your brainpower on page 30. Here are some other things that you can do to help keep your mind focused and alert.

Concentrate on carbohydrates. In the snack department, look for high-carbohydrate foods—avoiding snacks that are high-fat. High-carb, low-fat snacks can help stimulate the production of serotonin, a chemical in the brain that helps control emotion and appetite, says Judith Wurtman, Ph.D., a research scientist at the Massachusetts Institute of Technology in Cambridge and author of *The Serotonin Solution*. She recommends eating about 1½ ounces of graham crackers, pretzels, or rice cakes in the afternoon. In addition, make your carbohydrate intake a major component of your dinner meal to help calm your mind and allow it to renew itself for the next day. For maximum effect, says Dr. Wurtman, try to eat high-carbohydrate main-course meals like rice-and-lentil stew or hearty potato soup.

Get the jump on protein. The brain needs protein in order to maintain its mental efforts, such as studying for an exam or learning a new task or hobby, says Dr. Wurtman. Protein-rich foods, like poultry, fish, and lean red meats, are important to include in meals that you eat during periods of the day or evening when you must mentally exert yourself. You don't need a lot of protein to get the benefits. For most people, five to six ounces of protein-rich foods a day is plenty, she suggests.

Fill up with fruit for the mind. Having two to four servings a day of fruits like bananas, cantaloupe, dried figs, and oranges will provide many of the nutrients that the brain needs to work efficiently, Dr. Mark says. By combining vitamin-rich fresh fruits and mineral-rich dried fruits, the brain will benefit from nutrients like potassium, calcium, vitamin C, zinc, and iron that are necessary for optimum operation, he says. Fruits are also high in complex carbohydrates, so they provide a burst of energy without the mental let-

135

Megafuel for Mental Racing

Even though having a well-balanced diet provides you with most of the nutrients that your body needs, your brain has a larger appetite. "I have found that even a balanced diet often doesn't contain enough water-soluble B vitamins to keep your brain working at its best," says Vernon Mark, M.D., a neurosurgeon in Newport, Rhode Island, and co-author of *Reversing Memory Loss*.

In your usual diet, you're probably not getting enough thiamin, for example. This is a nutrient that is vital to keeping the brain operating at peak levels, Dr. Mark says.

And if you follow a vegetarian diet, you may have trouble getting enough vitamin B_{12}, which is found in meat and in other animal products. Low levels of vitamin B_{12} may cause the brain to work more slowly, Dr. Mark adds.

Riboflavin is another B vitamin important for top brain performance. You would have to drink 24 cups of milk a day, for instance, to get what Dr. Mark considers the optimum amount of riboflavin in your diet.

Here are some of the main "mind nutrients," along with Dr. Mark's recommendations for getting optimal levels. But be aware that Dr. Mark's recommendations are definitely an "alternative route." The doses he recommends for thiamin, niacin, vitamin B_6, and zinc exceed most nutritional guidelines. And though the levels are safe, many experts believe that the most beneficial vitamins come from food sources—and that supplementation at these high doses is unnecessary.

down that often occurs after eating less-nutritious foods.

Mind the Bs and minerals. As we have noted, nonfat milk, cheese, and other dairy foods are excellent sources of B vitamins and minerals. They are also loaded with amino acids that the body needs to manufacture brain-arousing chemicals, Dr. Mark says. Getting two to three servings a day of these foods will help keep your mind in working trim, he says.

Skim the fat and spare the cells. While the brain needs some fat to coat nerve-cell membranes, eating fat can increase the

136

Vitamins and Minerals	Daily Value	Dr. Mark's Optimal Amount
Vitamin A	5,000 IU	10,000 IU
Vitamin D	400 IU	400 IU
Vitamin E	30 IU	100 IU
Vitamin C	60 mg.	1,000 mg.
Thiamin	1.5 mg.	20 mg.
Riboflavin	1.7 mg.	10 mg.
Niacin	20 mg.	250 mg.*
Vitamin B_5	10 mg.	20 mg.
Vitamin B_6	2 mg.	20 mg.
Folic acid	400 mcg.	400 mcg.
Vitamin B_{12}	6 mcg.	100 mcg.
Biotin	300 mcg.	300 mcg.
Choline	—	3 g.
Calcium	1,000 mg.	1,600 mg.
Phosphorus	1,000 mg.	1,600 mg.
Iodine	150 mcg.	150 mcg.
Iron	18 mg.	20 mg.
Magnesium	400 mg.	400 mg.
Copper	2 mg.	3 mg.
Zinc	15 mg.	25 mg.*

NOTE: The values listed are for adults and children 10 years and older who do not have allergies to specific foods containing these vitamins and for people who don't have diabetes or liver, thyroid, or kidney disease.

*This dose should only be taken under medical supervision.

time it takes for the stomach to empty itself, which in turn can cause a minor mental slowdown, Dr. Mark says. Overeating, in general, can make you lethargic, he adds. Experts advise limiting your fat intake to no more than 25 percent (preferably less) of the total number of calories you take in each day.

Sip away from confusion. Most people don't drink enough water, or they drink too much coffee, cola, or other caffeine-containing drinks, which causes the body to lose fluids. In either case, low fluid levels in the body may result in memory loss and confused thinking, Dr. Mark says. He recommends drinking at least six to eight eight-ounce glasses of water a day.

Rigors and Resting

The mind/body connection isn't a one-way street. Just as your thoughts and emotions play a role in how your body feels, how you treat your body clearly affects your mind, says Barry Gordon, M.D., Ph.D., a behavioral neurologist at the Johns Hopkins University School of Medicine in Baltimore and author of *Memory: Remembering and Forgetting in Everyday Life.*

Research has shown, in fact, that regular exercise isn't just good for your heart and lungs. It can also pump up your brainpower. In one study, researchers at Ohio State University in Columbus found that people who rode stationary bicycles three times a week for nine months were able to improve their attention span, concentration, and short-term memory. Other studies have shown that people who are active tend to have faster reflexes and think more quickly than those who aren't.

It doesn't take a lot of exercise to get the benefits, Dr. Gordon says. Simply doing some type of aerobic exercise, like walking, running, or swimming, for 20 minutes three times a week can make a significant difference.

Just as exercise is important for keeping the brain healthy, rest also plays an important role. Research has shown that while the body is largely still during sleep, the brain is surprisingly active. It needs this time to organize all the information you took in during the day—which is why it's often hard to keep track of things when you haven't been getting enough sleep, Dr. Chafetz says.

Everyone needs different amounts of sleep, of course. For most people, getting six to eight hours of sleep a night will give the brain time to recharge and begin fresh the next day, he says.

Being Upbeat

You are what you think. And if you happen to be a pessimist, researchers say, thinking can be dangerous to your wits.

"It's long been known that people behave a lot in terms of

138

Hints from an Idea Maven

It's barely seven in the morning, and Jerry Andrus is full of ideas. Again.

Andrus worked as a lineman for a power company before retiring at age 54, and he never got a college degree. He has spoken at scientific conferences, appeared on television, and had an exhibit of his magical illusions featured at a science museum in Vancouver, British Columbia. He also has thought of 10,000 song titles and developed more than 15 inventions, including a keyboard that allows his fingers to work more efficiently. Just for kicks, he writes poetry and makes up imaginary words like *interlectual*, *spleach*, and *joinuary*.

"I never want to retire my mind. I'm having too much fun thinking of new things," says Andrus, of Albany, Oregon, who is now in his eighties. "If a man had a wonderful machine, but he kept it locked up and didn't share it with the world, he'd be crazy. Well, that's what most of us do with our brains. We lock them away and don't use them. There is no reason why we all can't wake up in the morning and say, 'I have a wonderful mind, and I can think of some ideas today.'"

There are certainly plenty of ideas rumbling about in his mind. Every day he tape-records ideas whenever they pop up, then transcribes them into a computer. Between 1980 and 1996, he had recorded more than 112 hours' worth of ideas.

"I just keep inventing all the time. Other than time off for minor surgery, I haven't had a day of rest in 50 years," Andrus says. "If I'm not in absolute agony when I'm lying there dying, I'll probably say, 'Man alive, I've just thought of a terrific idea. I'm dying and won't have time to try it out. Quick, while I can, let me tell you about it so you can try it.'"

their self-perceptions," Dr. Schaie says. "Optimists tend to get involved in activities that stretch themselves, while pessimists may opt out and say, 'It's no use.' And if you stop doing things, your mental skills will eventually decline. It becomes a self-fulfilling prophecy."

When you're struggling with work, raising a family, and making enough money to pay the bills, it's not always easy to maintain an optimistic point of view. That's why Dr. Chafetz recommends that you keep a journal in which you jot down at least 20 good things that happened to you that day. Even small things count, like finding a dollar under the sofa. Doing this regularly will help you feel more positive about yourself and life in general. This in turn will make you more likely to take on new challenges, keeping your brain active.

It's also a good idea to push yourself in new directions, even if that means occasionally failing, says Jack Matson, Ph.D., director of the Leonard Innovation Center at Pennsylvania State University in University Park. "Taking a risk increases your passion because you have put your soul out there for all to see. Even if you fail, it generally forces you to think more deeply about the problem and brainstorm other possible ways to solve it."

Sleep More Soundly, Wake Refreshed

In India, there is a saying that sleep "nurses all living beings." And, not surprisingly, most cultures connect good sleep to health and longevity. Sleep is the balm, the relief, the renewal, and a commonsense prescription for mental and physical fatigue.

Sleep may be as important to your long-term health as exercising and eating right, says Dave Dinges, Ph.D., chief of the division of sleep and chronobiology in the department of psychiatry at the University of Pennsylvania School of Medicine in Philadelphia. And to look at the flip side, it's something we can't do without. "We don't know all the consequences of sleep loss, but it seems to exact a toll that builds up over time," he observes.

We spend nearly one-third of our lives in sleep, but we're only beginning to answer the big questions about this mysterious state: What is sleep? Why do we sleep? Is sleep for the brain or the body? But what's becoming clear from the research is that good sleep is essential for good health.

Researchers don't have all the answers to these questions, but they confirm what most of us know intuitively: Sleep well at night, and you'll feel sharper, think more clearly, and have more energy. You'll also have more spring in your step—and probably feel more youthful.

Not only that, getting an adequate amount of sleep can help prevent a whole range of health conditions that tend to age you fast. "If you have persistent sleep problems—anything that lasts two weeks or more—you are at greater risk for psy-

141

chiatric problems such as depression and anxiety and for medical problems like stroke, heart attack, and high blood pressure," says Steve Weber, Ph.D., director of the Sleep Disorder Center at the University of Wisconsin Hospital and Clinics in Madison.

Snoozing for Protection

That sleep restores you and helps you stay healthy is hardly breakthrough science. When you're rundown, stressed-out, and sleep-deprived, you are more likely to catch colds and infections and generally feel achy.

This health erosion occurs because sleep seems to be strongly linked to the immune system. When you lose a night's sleep or sleep less than you should, your immune system may be weakened, says Christian J. Gillin, M.D., professor of psychiatry at the University of California, San Diego.

Dr. Gillin and his colleague Michael Irwin, M.D., studied 10 men between the ages of 22 and 61. In a sleep laboratory, they allowed the men to snooze for a few hours, roused them at 3:00 A.M., and then kept them awake until morning. The hours between 3:00 and 6:00 A.M. are a time when you are sleepiest, that is, the period when your body is essentially programmed to sleep, says Dr. Gillin.

In blood tests of the sleep-deprived men, researchers found substantially reduced levels of T cells, or killer cells, a class of white blood cells that helps the body fight infections. So it appears that lack of sleep impairs the body's ability to defend itself against invaders—at least temporarily, says Dr. Gillin. Similar studies have found a reduction of killer cells in people who are going through bereavement and having sleep loss as a result, he adds.

"All of this gives us some clues that the body's defense mechanisms don't function as well without sleep," says Dr. Gillin. "This may have implications for people who chronically don't get enough sleep. One night is bad, but what if you are a shift worker who consistently gets less sleep than you should?"

142

Rat Reactions

In experiments with rats, researchers have found that when the animals are totally deprived of sleep, they are unable to regulate their body temperatures. They lose weight—despite trying to compensate by eating more food—and die after about three weeks. When allowed some sleep, but not enough to recover from sleep deprivation, the animals live somewhat longer than that, but no more than five weeks.

For obvious reasons, there are no human studies like this. But the results would probably be the same for people, says Dr. Dinges. The longest a person has gone without sleep in a study is about four days, he says. But some studies already point to a link between sleep and life span.

"If you sleep seven to eight hours a night, you tend to live longer than people whose sleep is longer or shorter," says Dr. Gillin. One study found that men who had slept just four hours per night were about three times more likely to have died within the study's six-year follow-up than men who had slept seven to eight hours per night.

Dr. Gillin cautions that there's more involved than just the sleep factor. In other words, some of the short-term sleepers could have been alcoholics, or they were driven type A people more prone to accidents and health problems. Their abbreviated sleep might have been just another symptom of a disease or behavior.

"But when you look broadly at these studies, you can make the general conclusion that if you get an optimal amount of quality sleep—which for most adults is in the range of seven to eight hours per night—you tend to live longer," he explains. "Sleep is part of a healthy lifestyle."

Dangers of Deprivation

If sleep is part of a healthy lifestyle, then many Americans may be endangering their health. The National Center on Sleep Disorders Research estimates that 70 million Americans have some sort of sleep problem. Many of us have sleep disorders that deny us the rest we need.

know what?

In a study of sleep patterns during the arctic summer—when it never gets dark—people slept about 10 hours per day. Maybe that's how much we need, researchers suggest.

143

Why do Americans have such a hard time getting their shut-eye? If you are a single mother who commutes to and from work, runs a household, and cares for young children, you may start the day at 5:30 A.M. by ironing clothes and end your day around midnight by putting the last load of dishes into the dishwasher. The nurse on rotating shifts, the sales representative with long evening appointments, or a caterer working until midnight all have jobs that reward feats of stamina. Even if you do have a chance to catch up during daytime hours, you may not be able to get more than a couple of long naps.

And sometimes, distractions seem to conspire to deprive us of sleep. After all, it's easy to stay awake when there's so much to do. You can shop at a 24-hour supermarket, surf three dozen TV channels, or log on to the Internet for an all-night chat with a pal in Singapore.

"The problem many of us have is that we can't push away these electronic socializers—VCRs, radios, and computers. They are tacking two to three hours onto our waking day," says Dr. Weber.

As a result, many of us may be going through the day in a state of "effortful wakefulness," says Dr. Dinges. You're not really awake unless you're downing several cups of coffee, doing something physical like mowing the lawn, or puffing on a cigarette once an hour.

When sleep-deprived, you need stimulation. And as soon as you sit passively to watch a movie, read the paper, or—heaven forbid—drive the car, you're ready to fall asleep.

"Some people think it's normal to be sleepy frequently off and on during the day. It's not. That's a sure sign of having a sleep deficit," says Dr. Dinges.

Finding Rest Stops

At the turn of the century, before electricity and when most people still lived on farms, people went to bed at sunset and got up when the rooster crowed. Back then, Americans slept 9 to 10 hours per night. By the time World War II came along, cities were lit up all night, shift workers were punching the time clock at every conceivable hour, well-lit nightclubs were open till the wee hours, and sleep time had dropped to about 8 hours per night.

Now, our sleep time is even more abbreviated than before. But even though we have drastically changed our sleep habits, we haven't changed the biological need for sleep that has evolved over thousands of years, says Donna Arand, Ph.D., clinical director of the Sleep Disorders Center at the Kettering Medical Center near Dayton, Ohio.

"Our lifestyles just don't value sleep. We don't have the time for it. We're all trying to cram more into our days," says Dr. Arand. And after we have used up the daylight hours, we carve out time from the night, she points out.

"If you need an alarm clock to get up during the week, then you aren't getting enough sleep," says Dr. Arand. In addition, here are some other clues that you're not getting enough sleep.

▎Are you so exhausted that you fall asleep the instant your head hits the pillow?

▎Do you sleep late on the weekends?

▎Do you fight sleepiness during the day?

▎Do you fall asleep at meetings, while reading, or while watching TV?

▎Do you find yourself nodding off right after supper?

Answer yes to any of these questions, and you're just not spending enough time in the Land of Nod, says Dr. Arand. Devote more hours to sleep, and you'll probably feel a lot more energetic and youthful.

Remaking Your Wake-Ups

Individual biology should determine how much sleep you need, not the TV schedule or the days of the week, says Dr. Arand.

If you want to wake up every morning without an alarm clock, an automatic buzzer, or the Sky Chopper's morning rush-hour report blaring in your ear, you can do it, says Dr. Arand. But, she adds, you have to follow a simple prescription: Get the

know what?

During sleep, nearly everyone has rapid eye movements (REM) when they dream. The longest period of dreaming recorded in a sleep lab was three hours, eight minutes.

145

Turning On Your Brights

Do you feel more vibrant and cheery on a sunny day? More awake and rarin' to go when sunlight floods the kitchen in the morning?

Sunlight is part of our natural makeup, and doctors have found that artificial light—bright enough to mimic sunlight—alters mood and has a profound effect on when we sleep and awaken. Bright light therapy is now being used to treat people with problems related to the phases of sleeping, says Stuart Menn, M.D., a sleep specialist at Pacific Sleep Medicine Services in La Jolla, California. These sleep disorders—called advanced-phase and delayed-phase syndromes—are extreme examples of "morning lark" or "night owl" tendencies.

Although most people's biological clocks don't automatically run on an exact 24-hour schedule, they can usu-ally set it themselves with the natural light/dark cycle and a regular routine of getting up at the same time every day.

If you're a morning lark (in advanced-phase syndrome), your biological clock forces you to bed early, and you're probably up prowling around before the birds are singing. It's no problem if you're a trout fisherman, but you're likely to nod off if you're at an evening basketball game or if you're trying to stay up late and play bridge with the neighbors.

If you're a night owl (in delayed-phase syndrome), you have the opposite dilemma. You don't rise until noon, and you're still going full speed when the party's breaking up. That's okay if you live in New York—the city that never sleeps—but otherwise, you may end up staring at a Godzilla movie at 3:00 A.M., while the rest of your town sleeps.

amount of sleep you need every night. That way, you won't need an alarm clock or any other type of external cue to wake you up.

"When you have a regular schedule of good sleep, your brain will pop you out of sleep when it's had enough," Dr. Arand says. "You'll wake up naturally."

Here's her advice for making sleep—and wake-ups—come more naturally.

Bed down earlier. Go to bed a half-hour earlier for a few nights. If you are still waking up to the alarm clock and not ready to get up, then move up your sleep time another half-

146

"People with phase syndromes are probably born with a kind of hard wiring that is difficult to change," says Dr. Menn. But sleep therapists and doctors see bright light therapy as a promising new treatment for advanced- and delayed-phase syndromes, he says.

Bright light therapy is also being used to treat depression-related sleeping problems as well as seasonal affective disorder, a depression brought on by the lack of natural day-light in winter.

Bright light therapy helps reset the biological clock. You usually sit, read, or work in front of a specialized box of bright lights for a few hours each day. You don't need to stare into the box for the light to enter the retina and go straight to the area of the brain that regulates your circadian rhythms, says Dr. Menn. "Light has the ability to push the clock in one direction or another, depending on when one is exposed to it."

Although light boxes are available for $250 to $525, Dr. Menn says that you should talk to your doctor before basking in the light of an artificial sun. "If you use it at the wrong time of day, you can make things worse—shift your-self the wrong way," he cautions. "We have only been doing light therapy for about 10 years, so there is still a lot to learn," he observes.

Exposure to bright light in late afternoon or early evening helps morning larks stay up later. If you happen to be a night owl, you can shift toward an earlier bedtime by getting light therapy early each morning. Sometimes, you can get the same ben-efit by going for an evening walk in summertime or sitting in front of an open window in the morning, says Dr. Menn.

hour. If your kids or schedule don't allow for an earlier sleep time, try taking a nap during the day to compensate.

Don't sleep in. Wake up at the same time every day, seven days a week. Don't use the weekends to make up for sleep loss. Anchor your sleep in a schedule.

"Just as your body prefers to eat at a certain time, it also prefers to sleep and be awake at a certain time," she explains. "The body responds to conditioning."

Conk out when your body tells you. Don't procrastinate going to bed when you are feeling sleepy. Drowsiness is a natural cue to

147

snooze. Follow it. When you delay getting your shut-eye, you throw the body out of whack.

Keeping the Beat with Circadian Rhythms

Sleeping and waking can work like clockwork because deep in your brain there is a chemical timepiece known as the circadian, or biological, clock. The word *circadian* simply means a period of about 24 hours. Throughout your body, many daily biological rhythms stay keyed to that circadian timepiece—secretion of hormones, proteins, and enzymes; fluctuations in blood pressure; and regulation of body temperature.

Sleep is hot-wired to the biological clock. That clock sets into motion a whole series of internal events, says Claudio Stampi, M.D., Ph.D., director of the Chronobiology Research Institute in Boston.

One of the most important of these biological rhythms is the secretion of the hormone melatonin. From what researchers have learned about melatonin, it appears to be the body's way of sending you off to dreamland. During the daylight hours, there is very little melatonin in your body, but the hormone builds up during the evening hours and contributes to feelings of drowsiness, says Dr. Stampi.

"The release of melatonin is on a very set schedule," says Dr. Stampi. The hormone essentially tells you when to bed down. That's why, when you cross several time zones flying to Japan from America, you're going to get jet lag. When you set down in Tokyo after soaring halfway around the world, your biological clock will be out of sync with your new locale. You may want to take a nice, long nap after a dinner of sushi and sake your first night in Tokyo, but your brain and body are still on Chicago, San Francisco, or New York time, ready to start the day with a coffee and a bagel. Sleep just won't come despite your attempts to woo it.

No matter how much you try to change the clock settings—by drinking caffeine or going to sleep or taking melatonin pills—you can't beat the clock entirely, says Dr. Stampi. If you're a jet-lagged Tokyo tourist, you had better accept the fact that

148

When Drowsy Spells Danger

It's no coincidence that auto accidents are more common among people with sleep apnea or narcolepsy. But even if you don't have to have a sleep disorder, you're likely to get groggy behind the wheel.

Frequency of auto accidents also reflects circadian rhythms, the cycles of the human internal time clock. Accidents peak twice a day, both of which are during the natural downtimes of circadian rhythms—early morning and midafternoon—according to research by the National Highway Traffic Safety Administration.

If you try to keep driving when your head is nodding, your drowsiness may be steering you to death's door, warns Dave Dinges, Ph.D., chief of the division of sleep and chronobiology in the department of psychiatry at the University of Pennsylvania School of Medicine in Philadelphia. Drowsiness behind the wheel accounts for 56,000 automobile accidents and more than 1,500 fatalities annually.

your circadian rhythms will be out of sync for a few days until your sleep/wake cycle resets itself for Tokyo time.

While most of us are familiar with jet lag—whether or not we have trekked to Tokyo—we are often unaware of the eccentricities of the biological clock. That clock constantly needs to be reset to keep our body's temperature, blood pressure, hormones, and sleep patterns cycling at regular intervals. Strangely enough, the internal clock actually runs faster than 24 hours. When volunteers have camped out in a cave without daylight hours to reset their biological clocks, they got tired earlier each night and woke up at a different time each day.

So the clock uses environmental cues to reset itself. The singing of the birds or the noise of your neighbor cranking up the lawnmower at 7:00 A.M. tells you it's morning time. Social behaviors like having lunch with friends or going for an evening walk in the neighborhood also anchor you in time. But your brain's most important cue for when to go to sleep and when to wake up is sunlight, says Dr. Stampi. When the sun is up—even if it's tucked behind clouds—the daylight reaching your brain through nerve endings in your eyes will tell you, "It's not time to sleep."

149

Linked to waking and sleeping is the rise and fall of body temperature. The difference between your high and low points may be less than 1°F, but that shift brings about a distinct response. When your body temperature dips to its lowest point between 3:00 and 6:00 A.M., sleep is urgent. "Your alertness wanes. You have lapses of attention, and if you're awake then, you may even feel chilled enough to put on a jacket," explains Dr. Weber.

Another low point occurs at midafternoon, during the siesta hours. Despite the daylight, you may find yourself looking for a place to take a nap or taking a couple of extra trips to the coffee machine to wake up, says Dr. Weber.

As you move past these drowsy periods, you go through an ascending phase, where body temperature rises, adrenaline flows, and alertness increases. That's why you may be able to stay up all night and then get a second wind in the morning that will carry you through to the afternoon.

Shifting Sleep

If you are a shift worker—or anyone who's on call in the early-morning hours—you are most at risk for drowsiness-related accidents and health problems associated with poor or insufficient sleep. Someone who has a job that demands alertness at 2:00 A.M. is pitted against the inexorable natural forces of the biological clock.

About 20 percent of shift workers fall asleep on the job, and many more probably have periods of "microsleep" or split-second lapses where the brain drifts into a state of near sleep, according to Donald Bliwise, Ph.D., director of the Sleep Disorders Center at Emory University School of Medicine in Atlanta. Shift workers are nearly always a little sleep deprived because they routinely get five to seven hours of sleep a week less than daytime workers.

If you work nights, you may find it hard to sleep in the day. You may be moody and irritable, suffer from stomach problems, and even have problems with depression. Some people—especially older workers—simply don't tolerate shift work well, says Dr. Weber.

Stop-Time Tactics

Night-Shift Adjustments

Today, one in four men and one in six women in the United States work the evening and night shifts. If you are one of them, here is what the experts recommend to help you improve your sleep.

Go bright. If you have to work at night, don't work in dim light. The brighter the light in your work environment, the better, says Dr. Bliwise. Bright lights mimic the intensity of sunlight and help keep you more alert.

Shade the day. Wear sunglasses on the drive home in the morning. If you're a passenger, cover up your eyes. Bright morning light can reset your biological clock and keep you awake, according to Dr. Weber.

Black it out. Make your bedroom as dark as you can—as pitch black as a photographic darkroom. Try to block out daytime sounds as well. You want your brain to think it's night so that your body will be lulled into the head-to-toe conviction that it's time to sleep.

"Unfortunately, your body doesn't take its cues from your work schedule," says Dr. Weber. The body responds to a day–night cycle. "So you have to try to shift the dark/light cycle around and fool your body into thinking that now you live on the other side of the world. Literally, you get up and go to sleep when the Japanese do."

Keep your schedule. Many shift workers revert back to a daytime schedule on their days off. It's natural to want to spend time with your family—and that means catching up with a spouse and children who are awake when you're asleep. But this flip-flopping just makes it harder for you. For your own sake, it's better to stay on your nighttime schedule, says Dr. Bliwise.

Enjoy the morning. Some nighttime workers sleep better when they delay their slumber until late morning or early afternoon, says Dr. Bliwise. That way, they take advantage of the body's natural inclination to nap in the afternoon.

151

Shanghaiing the Sandman

No matter if you work nights tending patients in an intensive care unit or spend your days seated on a tractor etching furrows in a cornfield, you'll have better luck falling asleep if you follow a routine, according to John Harsh, Ph.D., professor of experimental psychology at the University of Southern Mississippi in Hattiesburg.

Sleep onset, that period of time when drowsiness begins to set in, is mainly a process of letting go—physically and mentally. You relax your muscles, let your attention to the outside world lapse, and blank out your mind. Sometimes sleep comes without effort, and other times you have to make yourself turn off the TV and hit the hay, notes Dr. Harsh. Once there, you can push away your worries and the events of the day and get around to some serious shut-eye. Sleep onset should not take more than 30 minutes, he says.

"Most people who are healthy and getting enough sleep every day usually fall asleep in 5 to 10 minutes," says Dr. Harsh. "If you are asleep as soon as your head hits the pillow, you're probably sleep-deprived. If falling asleep takes more than 30 minutes, on the other hand, that's a clue that you might have insomnia."

Makeover Minutes

To Help You Nod Off

Having some trouble letting the sandman come? Here are some easy-to-try techniques that might make sleep come faster.

Wind down. Set aside the hour before bed for quiet activities. Relax by reading a book, listening to the radio, doing some light stretching exercises, or taking a warm bath, Dr. Harsh suggests. "Sleep onset starts before you get into bed," he says.

Shush up. Create a quiet, dark environment. Shut the bedroom door and turn down the TV in the other room. The bedroom should be your cocoon.

152

Put out the cat. Develop a bedtime ritual, suggest experts at the Mayo Sleep Disorders Center at the Mayo Clinic in Rochester, Minnesota. Check the doors, adjust the room temperature, and think pleasant, relaxing thoughts. Do things that comfort you and give you a sense of security.

Space out. Use self-hypnosis to relax. Imagine your muscles loosening, your limbs getting heavier, your body sinking into the bed, says Dr. Harsh. Start with your toes and move up the body. By the time you reach your head, you may be asleep.

Just imagine. If you find you just can't get the day's events out of your head, don't obsess, advises Dr. Harsh. Chant to yourself or picture a relaxing scene. Count sheep, if that works.

Missing Out on Shut-Eye?

What if you have tried everything, and you're still tossing and turning when you should be slipping into a state of slumber? It could be that you have a specific sleep disorder that needs attention.

A sleep disorder is a medical condition that interrupts normal sleep. If you have insomnia, which is really one kind of sleep disorder, you may have difficulty falling asleep or problems going back to sleep in the middle of the night. Or maybe you're bothered by repeated arm or leg movement during sleep, which actually has a clinical name, periodic limb movement disorder (PLMD). If so, you may be awakening hundreds of times a night, even though you're not aware of it. That's not exactly a prescription for deep and restful sleep.

There are more than 70 conditions that fall into the category of sleep disorders, according to the National Center on Sleep Disorders Research. Fortunately, most sleep disorders are curable or can be managed with the help of a sleep specialist, says Dr. Weber. Over the last 20 years, more than 2,000 sleep disorders clinics have popped up all over the country at universities and most major hospitals. There's probably one close to you.

"Sleep disorders have become recognized as a real medical problem," Dr. Weber notes. "We now know that what's happening with people at night often has a big effect on their health during the day."

153

Out Like a Light

You may remember your grandfather taking afternoon naps, and the tendency to nod off is certainly associated with aging. But for some people, those with narcolepsy, the problem of falling asleep at inappropriate moments, can worsen with age.

The person with narcolepsy simply has an irresistible urge to fall asleep. Sleep can come to a person at the most inappropriate of moments—while talking to the boss, on a ladder painting the house, or even in the middle of having sex, according to Meeta Goswami, Ph.D., assistant professor in the department of neurology at Albert Einstein College of Medicine and director of the Narcolepsy Institute at the Montefiore Medical Center, both located in Bronx, New York.

"Narcolepsy creates havoc in people's lives, partly because other people don't understand what is happening," says Dr. Goswami. "Your spouse thinks you're not listening. People believe you're lazy. You can't stay awake in class, and you probably can't hold a job."

About a quarter of a million Americans have narcolepsy. The number of men and women who get it are about equal. The condition runs in families.

Though the problem may start in a person's teen years, by the time a person is 20, he may have daytime drowsiness. The effects may worsen with age in some cases, until the urge to nap becomes impossible to resist, says Dr. Goswami.

Those who suffer from narcolepsy often have problems with nighttime sleep as well. Just as they are falling asleep, they may have vivid dreams, known as hypnagogic hallucinations, sometimes about the very situation

Relief for Your Bedmate

A sleep disorder may be a problem for you, but it's also an aggravation for the person who shares your bed. Imagine trying to sleep through snoring that reminds you of a freight train.

"Sleep disorders can really be a couple's disease. The partner may have been suffering for a long time," explains Rochelle Zak, M.D., a neurologist at the Sleep/Wake Disorders Center of the New York Hospital–Cornell Medical Center at

154

and people they are with at the moment of sleep.

"People with narcolepsy sometimes can't tell what is real and what is a dream," Dr. Goswami explains. "It can be very frightening."

Individuals with narcolepsy often experience sleep paralysis, a sensation of not being able to move when they fall asleep or awaken. Many people have that feeling occasionally, but narcolepsy is also associated with bouts of cataplexy, the loss of all muscle tone in response to emotional events.

"When they are excited, very happy, or angry, they may just collapse and fall to the ground. It's a much more severe form of feeling weak at the knees," says Dr. Goswami.

Narcolepsy was identified as a sleep disorder only a few decades ago. Because they have uncontrolled sleeping episodes, many narcoleptics were labeled as lazy, epileptic, or mentally ill. Even today, patients may go for 10 to 15 years dealing with the problem before they're diagnosed and treated, says Dr. Goswami.

While there's no known cure, the symptoms can be managed with drugs and counseling. Once you understand the condition, you can plan for the moments when you will fall asleep, says Dr. Goswami. "The symptoms of narcolepsy vary from mild to severe. People with mild or moderate symptoms can function almost normally with appropriate medications and counseling."

"We stress good diets, scheduled naps, regular nightly sleeping habits, and taking medications at the same time every day. All of this makes the episodes of sleep more manageable," she says.

Westchester. "We like to speak to the partners because they may provide the best description of what's happening. The partner or family member really helps in the diagnosis of a sleep disorder."

If your kids or spouse claim that you snore like an outboard motor, listen up. By itself, snoring is not a sleep disorder, but it can call for medical attention, says John Galgon, M.D., medical director of the Sleep Disorders Clinic at the Lehigh Valley Hospital in Allentown, Pennsylvania.

You snore when air moving toward your lungs vibrates the

155

Exorcizing the Sleep Devil

According to Terry Ryan's husband, sleeping with Terry was like bedding down with something from *The Exorcist*. She flopped around in bed, mumbled out loud, bit her cheeks, and uttered garbled cries as if she had swallowed her tongue. Down the hall, Terry's three children complained that her snoring literally rattled the walls.

Terry, a housewife in her early forties from Croton-on-Hudson, New York, had upper airway resistance syndrome, a mild version of obstructive sleep apnea. Because of this sleep disorder, she had labored breathing and woke up frequently.

Sleep apnea is often associated with overweight since excess fatty tissue in the neck can actually inter-fere with airflow. By the time Terry was diagnosed, she weighed more than 300 pounds.

Though she sometimes remembered her noisy, troubled sleep of the night before, what bothered her most was the wasted, bone-tired feeling she had during the day. She could take naps nearly anywhere, anytime.

"I was very frustrated. I never looked forward to going to bed," she says. "My husband was always tired, too, because I was keeping him awake."

Terry's husband urged her to go to the Sleep/Wake Disorders Center of the New York Hospital–Cornell Medical Center at Westchester. There, Terry was given a full checkup, exam-

soft tissues in your throat. Muscle tone keeps the airway open during the day, but at night when your muscles relax, the airway narrows. The more effort you make to pull air past the smaller opening, the louder you snore. If the airway closes completely, you have what's called obstructive sleep apnea, according to Dr. Galgon.

We all snore on occasion, says Dr. Galgon, but snoring usually occurs when we're very tired and our throat muscles are relaxed. You're also likely to saw logs when you sleep on your back, giving your tongue the opportunity to slip down and nar-

156

ined for polyps in her nose and excess tissue in the throat, and wired up for a night's sleep-over.

The diagnosis came quickly, according to Rochelle Zak, M.D., a neurologist at the Center.

To remedy the nightly gasping-for-air, Dr. Zak prescribed a procedure called nasal continuous positive airway pressure (CPAP) that Terry could do at home.

At night, Terry put on a CPAP mask that covered her nose. The mask was hooked up to a machine that keeps up constant air pressure, pushing air down the throat and preventing the collapse of the airway. With CPAP, Terry began sleeping through the night.

"Terry's not your typical sleep apnea patient because sleep apnea is more common in overweight, middle-aged men," says Dr. Zak. "However, women are susceptible and should be evaluated, particularly if they have chronic, unrefreshing sleep and snore loudly."

In addition to using the nasal CPAP, Terry started a weight-loss program that included a low-fat diet and walking. If she could lose 50 pounds, her doctor told her, it was likely her apnea problem would go away.

"I had never heard of apnea before," Terry recalls, "and I never imagined I had a sleep disorder." And, of course, she had no idea that the noises she made while sleeping were like a scene from *The Exorcist*. "I think more people out there have the problem but don't realize it."

row your airway. That's why, if you're a snorer, the sound effects will usually stop if someone gives you a good nudge and tells you to turn on your side.

Other factors can also tilt the scales toward a snore-filled night. Smoking cigarettes, being overweight, and drinking alcohol in the evening can all lead to snoring.

But sometimes the cause is as plain as the nose on your face. "Most people we see have nose problems," says Dr. Galgon.

Often people come in with nasal congestion and postnasal drip due to untreated allergies, says Dr. Galgon. Or the snorer

157

has a deviated septum, that is, an abnormality in the fibrous portion between the nostrils that causes obstructions in breathing and drainage. Occasionally, the sleep problem is caused by polyps, growths in the nasal cavity.

If you have a dry mouth when you wake up, a deviated septum or nasal polyps may be your problem, says Dr. Galgon. "Because your nose is all blocked up, you spend the night breathing through your mouth," he explains. "Sometimes, all we do is send people home with a nasal steroid, a prescription spray such as fluticasone propionate (Flonase), which reduces inflammation, clears the nasal passages, and usually fixes the problem."

The Wrath of Apnea

Apnea, related to a Greek word for "without breath," occurs when your airway becomes so narrow that it partially or completely closes during sleep. Your tongue may flop back to cover your throat, or your airway muscles may become so relaxed that the airway closes and you stop breathing. You may stop breathing for a period of 10 to 60 seconds, says Dr. Galgon.

Eventually, your slumbering brain recognizes the problem and is awakened long enough for your throat to open and your breathing to recover with a snort or gasp.

Your bed partner may hear you struggle for breath, but you're probably unaware that anything was wrong. Someone who's having this problem throughout the night may be having 200 to 500 apneas every time they sleep, according to Dr. Galgon.

"It may seem like you're sleeping through them, but each apnea wakes up the brain, and the brain fixes the problem before you are fully conscious," Dr. Galgon says. "When you have these continual awakenings, your brain can't get the kind of deep sleep it needs. The next day, you feel really tired and sleepy."

Daytime sleepiness is only one consequence of sleep apnea. Years of this nightly strain and struggle may damage your heart, contribute to high blood pressure, increase the risk of stroke, and even lead to premature death.

According to the National Center on Sleep Disorders, 20 million Americans have sleep apnea. Most are middle-aged or

158

elderly men. Many have a long history of snoring. Frequently, the men who snore and have apnea are those who are over-weight, according to Dr. Galgon.

Snoring often develops into full-blown apnea. As you age and gain weight, your throat tissues lose their tone and the ac-cumulated fat in your throat narrows the upper airway. Apnea sufferers tend to have thick necks (size 17 or greater), and many are cigarette smokers, says Dr. Galgon.

If you suspect sleep apnea, talk to your doctor who may refer you to a sleep disorders center. If your case is severe, the sleep specialist may prescribe a continuous positive airway pres-sure (CPAP) device. If you wear a CPAP mask at night, you place it over your nose for when you're sleeping, and a jet of air blows into the mask. The pressure inside the mask forces the upper airway to remain open and should stop snoring and apnea, says Dr. Galgon.

Long-Term Tactics

To Tone Down Apnea

Though obstructive sleep apnea requires diagnosis and medical attention, there are strategies you can take to help the condition. While the changes may take some work, you'll reap the benefits in sounder sleep and more alertness when you are awake. Here are some suggestions from Dr. Galgon.

Cut the suds. Don't drink in the evening. Alcohol relaxes all of your muscles, even throat tissues. Relaxed muscles allow the airway to collapse more easily.

Slim down. If you have mild apnea, just a 10 percent drop in weight can make a difference. By making gradual changes in diet and exercise—and using Stop-Time Tactics No. 1 and No. 2 on pages 3 and 36—you should be able to keep off the excess weight.

Get enough sleep. Lack of sleep can actually cause sleep apnea. That's because sleep-deprived people tend to sleep more

159

deeply and their throat tissues tend to relax more at night. So once you start to sleep better, don't cheat yourself by staying up for those late-night shows.

Crush all cartons. Smoking irritates the tissues in the nose and throat, makes them swell, and narrows the airway. If you go on a no-smoking program to kick the habit, you might ditch the apnea, too.

Roll over. If your snoring occurs mostly when you are on your back, you can sew pockets in the back of a T-shirt and place tennis balls in the pockets. You'll be prodded by the lumpy balls every time you start to lie on your back. That will force you to sleep on your side.

See the dentist. Not all apnea is related to fat in the throat. The natural position of your jaw may be a problem—and, if so, your dentist can fit you for a mouth device that brings your jaw forward and keeps your throat open. So be sure to tell your dentist if you have been wakened at night with snoring or apnea.

Kicking the Kicking Habit

If your nights are restless even though you're breathing easily, maybe some late-night kicking is the hurdle to sound sleep. If your bed partner announces that he feels like the grapes at the bottom of a barrel—stomped through the night—you know your legs have been running wild.

Periodic limb movement disorder is actually a condition that can involve the arms as well as the legs. The kicks or twitches come in bursts, usually 20 to 40 seconds apart for up to one hour at a time, and are followed by quiet periods, according to Katherine Albert, M.D., director of the Sleep/Wake Disorders Center of the New York Hospital–Cornell Medical Center, Manhattan Division.

These repeated field-goal attempts aren't just a problem for your partner, they can rouse you from sleep—up to 200 times in one night. But it's unlikely that you'll ever be aware of these awakenings, says Dr. Albert.

"With PLMD, you're probably awake less than 10 seconds per movement. You have to be awake 30 seconds to two minutes

160

to regain consciousness," says Dr. Albert. "You'll fall back asleep and never know you were awake." You'll feel sleepy the next day, and excessive daytime sleepiness is a symptom that you have this disorder.

But the surest sign of PLMD is another related condition called restless legs syndrome, says Dr. Albert. People describe it as a creepy, tingling sensation in their legs that can be relieved temporarily by shifting positions or walking around. Restless legs symptoms usually occur when you are sitting still or lying in bed. Because the condition gets worse around bedtime, restless legs may prevent you from falling asleep.

"If you have restless legs syndrome, you almost certainly have PLMD, too," says Dr. Albert.

The causes of restless legs and PLMD aren't known, but both may be caused by chemical reactions within the brain. The evidence: Some people are less likely to kick up a nightly storm when they're treated with the prescription drug levodopa (Dopar), a medication sometimes used to treat the tremors caused by Parkinson's disease. And levodopa has a direct effect on brain chemistry.

But there's also a hereditary link. If your father or mother had it, you may develop PLMD later in life, too, according to Dr. Albert.

Periodic limb movement disorder also may be a symptom of a circulation, kidney, or spinal problem. Or possibly it's just a symptom of not getting enough sleep every night. "When you treat these other conditions, the movements may disappear," says Dr. Albert.

know what?

The average person between ages 19 and 30 gets 8 hours of sleep per night. For people over age 50, the average is 5½ hours per night.

Beating Insomnia

You don't hear many teenagers or twenty-somethings complaining about sleep loss, unless it's self-induced by staying up all night. But as the years edge upward, many of us find ourselves tossing and turning quite a while before sleep catches up with us.

Those most likely to experience insomnia are older people and women, says Peter Hauri, Ph.D., administrative director of

161

Let Sleeping Pills Lie

Twenty years ago, when you went to your family physician complaining of insomnia, the doctor probably dashed off a prescription for sleeping pills. You gulped down a couple of capsules, and they knocked you out cold.

But these days, doctors who are tuned in to the research on sleeping pills are apt to give you a warning before they start scrawling.

Whether of the prescription or the over-the-counter variety, sleeping pills are no magic bullets for good sleep. They can leave you hungover in the morning, and if you use them repeatedly, their effectiveness wears off. You may even become psychologically dependent on them, according to Donald Bliwise, Ph.D., director of the

Sleep Disorders Center at Emory University School of Medicine in Atlanta.

If you have jet lag or are going through a stressful period, such as marital problems or bereavement, then the pills can give you some relief, suggests Dr. Bliwise. But he warns, "Sleeping pills should only be taken occasionally. You shouldn't need them to sleep. If you have chronic sleep problems, you should seek out professional help."

The fact is, doctors say most insomnia can't be solved with sleeping pills. And if other conditions are causing sleep loss, such as depression, stress, or an underlying disease, then these are the conditions that ought to be treated first.

the Sleep Disorders Center at the Mayo Clinic in Rochester, Minnesota. Older people probably have more insomnia because they have other medical conditions that affect their sleep, he says.

Insomnia is a general term for sleep loss. It can mean that you have a hard time going to sleep, difficulty in going back to sleep after awakening, or a problem with waking early in the morning. The causes of insomnia are almost endless, says Dr. Hauri.

You may be anxious or depressed by a bad marriage, the death of a friend, or a work situation. You may smoke, drink, or nap too much during the day. You may not get enough exercise. Or you could have a sleep disorder like an off-kilter biological clock (a phenomenon called delayed-phase syndrome) that keeps you up late at night. Serious illness may hurt your sleep, and so can medication.

162

"Sometimes the cause of insomnia is insomnia itself. You become so anxious about your sleep that you can't get to sleep," says Dr. Hauri.

Often, the best way to cure insomnia is to treat your underlying condition, which may be stress or depression. And some doctors help people with insomnia by addressing their "sleep hygiene" habits. For instance, you may be drinking too much caffeine-laden soda in the evening or sleeping too much during the day, says Dr. Hauri.

"You can't take sleep for granted. You have to make it happen," says Dr. Hauri. "The more sleep problems you have, the more you have to be regular about everything you do. Go to bed at the same time. Get up at the same time."

Some older people have insomnia related to the life changes that come with retirement. No longer anchored to a work schedule and responsibilities, they may fall into irregular habits, staying in bed much too long, napping a lot during the day, replacing work with television, and keeping an erratic sleep schedule, says Dr. Hauri.

"If you're going to retire, then retire into something. Don't just sit around doing nothing. Boredom is bad for sleep," says Dr. Hauri. "If you sit around and watch TV all day, every day, you'll have trouble sleeping."

Makeover Minutes

To Sleep Off Insomnia

Even if you aren't too sure what's keeping you awake—or rousing you at unwanted hours—you can try some easy tactics and see if they help. Here are some commonsense guidelines recommended by Dr. Hauri to combat insomnia.

Sneak a small snack. Hunger interferes with sleep. Have an apple, some crackers and cheese, or that old-fashioned elixir of milk before going to bed. "But keep the snack light. A full stomach is liable to keep you awake," says Dr. Hauri.

163

Throw out the clock. You probably wake up and immediately look at your clock. If you have insomnia, you may watch it all night and then worry that you only have a few hours left to sleep. The solution is to send that time-reminder into exile.

"If you're afraid you won't get up, have someone else wake you up or put the alarm clock into the dresser drawer, where you'll hear it but not see it," says Dr. Hauri.

Don't force it. If you can't go to sleep, read some magazines or listen to some soft music. Whether you should do this in bed or out of bed is debatable. Try it both ways and see which works for you.

Be moderate. Too much food, alcohol, and coffee can interfere with sleep. Most important, do not drink caffeine in the evening. Even avoid it in the afternoon if you are especially sensitive to caffeine's stimulating effects.

Exercise. Exercise in the late afternoon and make it vigorous. Walk briskly, jog, do aerobics, or do some hard physical work. After that, your body will welcome sleep. But don't exercise any later than three hours before bedtime.

Don't stretch out your naps. A short nap of 15 to 30 minutes is okay, but taking longer naps or more than one nap a day can set you up for a sleepless night. Why would your body want to sleep if it has been asleep half the day?

Getting the Stages You Need

We're all looking for that deep, restful sleep that makes us feel like leaping tall buildings, digging out the rosebushes, or spending the day on a hiking trail.

To get proper rest and restoration, you need hours of uninterrupted slumber so that you can go through what are called the stages of sleep, says Dr. Gillin.

All sleep is not the same. During the night, most normal sleepers cycle through four stages of sleep. Stage 1 is a transitional phase between wakefulness and actual sleep. Stage 2 sleep, known as REM (rapid eye movement) sleep, is the stage that takes up 50 to 60 percent of total sleep time. Stages 3 and 4 are a time of deep sleep when brain waves slow down dramati-

164

cally and the body releases substances—such as growth hormone—that help restore muscles and tissues.

During stage 2, or REM sleep, you dream. REM is the brain's way of cleaning up, filing, and organizing emotions, memories, and learning.

You usually don't reach stages 3 and 4 during a short nap, so you need a full night of sleep to get the greatest benefit, says Dr. Gillin. The body likes deep sleep. If you're extremely tired from physical work or fatigued from staying up late, your body will automatically give you more deep sleep. "You will literally sleep like a log," he says.

The problem is that you begin to lose your capacity for deep sleep in your early twenties, and by age 50 or 60, you may experience no stage 4 sleep at all.

Doctors really don't know if that is a problem, however. Maybe older adults just don't need as much deep sleep, Dr. Bliwise suggests. But if that's the case, why do some adults continue to reach the deep-sleep stage even as they are aging, while others of the same age may never be able to sleep very soundly?

Dr. Hauri thinks that waking activities have a lot to do with sleep procedures. "You can never sleep as well as you did when you were 10 years old, but your sleep does not have to deteriorate greatly as you age," he says. "By keeping active and using your body and mind vigorously, you can slow down the decline."

As you age, your biological clock is less precise about keeping time, and without a regular schedule of waking, sleeping, and activity, it's hard to keep it on a 24-hour cycle. "The whole sleep system is a little weaker in the elderly," says Dr. Hauri.

When you're older, the difference between your high and low body temperatures may be less pronounced. This indicates that the wake/sleep rhythms are weaker, and you may go through the day in an in-between state—half-awake and half-asleep.

An easy way to create a greater temperature difference is with vigorous exercise—a bike ride or brisk walk—which can boost body temperature for up to five hours. If you exercise in late afternoon, your temperature will fall during the evening hours and coincide with bedtime, and that will help you sleep.

know what?

Your metabolism—the rate at which your body burns energy—falls as much as 15 percent when you're sleeping.

165

"Exercise regulates the body temperature and makes you feel a little more tired. And it reinforces the natural circadian rhythm," says Dr. Hauri.

Catching Up with Napping

If you're nagged by insomnia, some sleep specialists will immediately ask about your napping patterns. If you're hitting the couch a couple of times a day for a snooze, your napping may be interfering with nighttime sleep.

Not that naps are bad. A brief daily nap may actually be beneficial to your health and daytime alertness—especially in your adult years, says Dr. Dinges.

"A lot of people find that when they are over 40, if they just close their eyes and drift into a light sleep for a few minutes, they feel really refreshed afterward," says Dr. Dinges. "A short nap each day is probably good for you."

Napping is an entirely natural part of your sleep patterns. Animals nap regularly, as do the elderly and young children. In many warm-climate cultures, the afternoon siesta is taken for granted: Put your feet up, take a snooze, and come back refreshed. But north of the border, we sort of frown on the practice, says Dr. Stampi.

"Still, if you're getting less sleep than you should, napping is a way to make up the deficit. A simple cure for sleepiness is sleep," says Dr. Stampi. "Taking naps is one way to catch up and recharge your batteries." But before you nod off, consider this advice from Dr. Stampi.

Get into the habit. Some folks have a hard time napping, even though a little catnap could do them a world of good. Napping can be a learned habit. You just have to make it part of your routine.

Keep it short. Usually, 15 to 30 minutes of rest is long enough to restore you. If you sleep too long, you're bound to feel

166

groggy. "The beauty of a nap is that it can be brief and still do you a lot of good," says Dr. Stampi. If you extend your sleep to an hour, you'll probably wake up from a period of deep sleep, so you'll still feel groggy after your nap, he adds. To take advantage of normal sleep cycles, a nap should be less than 30 minutes or at least 1½ hours.

Get comfortable. Loosen your shoes, lie on a couch, or just relax in an easy chair. If you need a nap while you're driving, just pull over to a rest area and lock the doors, tilt back the seat, and pull down the sunshades. You'll go to sleep quicker if you make the environment feel right.

Ease into everyday action. Don't just get up and rush back to what you were doing—especially if you have just been driving. Spend a few minutes overcoming what doctors call sleep inertia. Have a cup of coffee, make a phone call, or stand in the bright sunshine to ease off the effects of a nap. When you feel alert again, you can resume what you were doing.

167

Shrug Off
Stress

The show: *I Love Lucy*. The episode: Lucy and Ethel are working in a chocolate factory. Their job is to wrap chocolates that are moving down the conveyor belt.

At first, the belt moves slowly, and Lucy and Ethel easily keep pace. As the belt speeds up, chocolates start whizzing by. Desperately, Lucy and Ethel begin stuffing chocolates into their uniforms, their hats—even their mouths—in a hilarious attempt to keep up. A very sweet job has turned into a rampant, full-steam-ahead stress producer.

Sound familiar?

We all love the sweet things in life, but when the pace becomes too hectic, we discover to our distress that we can't pack it all in. And then along come the not-so-sweet surprises: a stack of unpaid bills, a bad review at work, or news that an ailing parent has taken a turn for the worse. The stress inducers are all around us.

Bodily Harm

When stress starts sizzling, your body bites back. First, it releases stress hormones, such as epinephrine and norepinephrine, which make your heart rate rise, your metabolism speed up, your muscles tense, and your breathing become faster and more shallow. These reactions stem from the fight-or-flight response, the body's involuntary, split-second reaction to danger.

Since the body can't tell the difference between a physical threat and a mental one, it can sound the fight-or-flight alarm

168

Fighting Fight-or-Flight

It sounds simple, but just learning how to breathe correctly can help defend your body from the age-inducing influences of chronic stress.

The body's automatic response to stress is the fight-or-flight response. This response sends heart rate and blood pressure soaring and can eventually damage your heart and blood vessels if it occurs too often. Breathing from your diaphragm—the large, dome-shaped sheet of muscle under your lungs—instead of from your chest can interrupt the fight-or-flight response, says Phil Nuernberger, Ph.D., author of *The Quest for Personal Power: Transforming Stress into Strength*.

Learning diaphragmatic breathing takes practice, says Dr. Nuernberger, who is also the president of Mind Resource Technologies in Honesdale, Pennsylvania. "But if you can control your breathing, you can control your emotions," he says. "And if you can control your emotions, you can control your stress."

Here's how to do the breathing according to Dr. Nuernberger.

1. Put your right hand over your stomach with your little finger over your belly button and your other fingers spread as widely as possible.
2. Put your left hand on your upper chest.
3. Breathe "through your belly." Instead of moving your chest and shoulders up and down, move your stomach out and in. Imagine you're filling a small balloon in your stomach. If you're doing it right, your right hand will rise as you inhale and fall as you exhale, while your left hand won't move at all. The lower part of your chest should move slightly, but your upper chest should stay still.

Practice diaphragmatic breathing for 10 to 15 minutes twice a day—before you get up in the morning and then before you go to sleep at night, advises Dr. Nuernberger. Eventually, as this antidote to stress becomes second nature, you'll automatically "breathe diaphragmatically" every time your heart starts pounding and your palms get sweaty.

dozens of times a day, regardless of whether the reaction is caused by your boss's yelling or a Mack truck bearing down on you at 80 miles per hour. Prompted by the run-amok proliferation of that response, your body can go into a chronic state of vigilance. Ultimately, all the ongoing everyday signals can damage your heart, blood vessels, and brain.

When your stress is constant and severe, you can feel robbed of your energy and drive—and often, your youth.

But youth-robbery doesn't have to steal up on you that way. You can master stress. As strange as it may seem, the key is to stop fighting it.

"Stress hits when you feel like you're not in control," says Paul J. Rosch, M.D., clinical professor of medicine and psychiatry at New York Medical College in Valhalla and president of the American Institute of Stress in Yonkers, New York.

To master stress, then, you need to distinguish between the things you can do something about and the things you can't. Once you learn to change your mindset, you can get a reprieve from many of stress's youth-sapping consequences.

Once you start winning the stress battle, it's almost a sure thing that you'll stay healthier. "Stress accelerates the onset of age-related diseases," says Allen J. Elkin, Ph.D., director of the Stress Management and Counseling Center in New York City. "There's virtually no part of the body that escapes the ravages of stress."

When you are stressed-out, your body produces more free radicals, which are unstable oxygen molecules that attack and damage cells. Since free radicals add to the wear on your body's systems, those marauders make your body old before its time. "Free radicals are responsible for most signs of aging, including cataracts, gray hair, dry skin and wrinkles, and even some cancers," says Dr. Rosch.

How It Robs Years

Stress also unleashes a flood of stress hormones into your bloodstream. With chronic stress, your blood pressure can shoot up and stay high. High blood pressure increases your risk of developing hardening of the arteries (atherosclerosis) and sets the stage for a heart attack or stroke.

In one study of 591 men, ages 42 to 60, researchers at the Public Health Institute in Berkeley, California, found that men

170

with high blood pressure caused by job stress developed atherosclerosis faster than men with less-demanding jobs. Another study involving 33,000 men, conducted by researchers at Harvard University, found that the more anxious the men were, the more likely they were to die unexpectedly of heart attacks.

There's even evidence that your immune system may be overtaxed when you are highly stressed, allowing cancer cells to thrive. When researchers from the University of California studied the relationship between stressful life events and the development of colorectal cancer in 1,000 men, they found that those who had a history of severe, work-related problems were five times more likely to develop the cancer than calmer men.

Mastering stress can also help you break habits that age you, like chain-smoking, drinking too much, and overeating. "All of these habits can damage your body and make you look and feel older than you really are," says Dr. Elkin.

But you don't have to wait years to reap the physical and mental benefits of serenity. Your rewards come right away. Stress-related "darn nuisance" complaints that make you feel older than your years—like headaches, back pain, digestive problems, and lack of sexual desire—are likely to become less severe or disappear completely as you begin winning stress battles. Insomnia, too, may end—and with it, the fatigue that can make you feel like you have aged a decade.

Brain Gains

Learning to manage stress isn't just good for your body. It keeps your mind and spirit more youthful, too.

With fewer worries to tax your brain, don't be surprised if your noggin becomes more nimble. Under highly stressful conditions, it's simply harder to remember things and to concentrate. When stress hits high gear, you may be unable to retain a sentence that you have just read or remember someone you met minutes before.

Some evidence even shows that high levels of stress may shrink the part of the brain that governs learning and memory. Scientists who studied the brains of people with severe depres-

know what?
Stress can weaken your resistance to viruses. In fact, chronic anxiety can increase your susceptibility to colds by up to 90 percent.

171

know
what?

Maybe you
should
consider
some stress-
relieving
laughter to
accompany
your next
workout.
According
to humor
researcher
William Fry,
laughing 100
times is the
aerobic equiv-
alent of 10
minutes on
a rowing
machine.

sion and post-traumatic stress disorder found that one part of the brain, called the hippocampus, actually became smaller when high-level stress kicked in. Some researchers speculate that the shrinkage could result from raised levels of stress hormones called glucocorticords.

When stress declines, you are more likely to stretch your physical and mental boundaries, suggests Phil Nuernberger, Ph.D., president of Mind Resources Technologies in Honesdale, Pennsylvania, and author of *The Quest for Personal Power: Transforming Stress into Strength.* Less worry means more energy to take on new challenges or reconnect with the things that are meaningful to you, such as taking up a sport you like or renewing old friendships. This kind of reaching out is itself an age protector because studies have shown that people with strong spiritual beliefs and social support live longer, healthier lives.

Angling for a Carefree Outlook

The question is how do you reduce the stress in your life? After all, tranquillity doesn't come easily when you have a job that makes you frantic with worry and a "to do" list that is as long as a Russian novel.

While we can't escape stress, we can learn to withstand it without feeling as if we were a million years old, says Dr. Elkin. Admittedly, it sounds odd to say that reducing stress takes effort, but according to Dr. Elkin, it's true. Counter-stress work pays off in the end, he says. So it is worth taking a couple of basic steps to ensure that you don't let stress get the upper hand.

First, build stress breaks into your schedule. "You need to spend time relaxing every single day," says Herbert Benson, M.D., president of the Mind/Body Medical Institute and director of behavioral medicine at Beth Israel Deaconess Medical Center East, affiliated with the Harvard Medical School in Boston. "In fact, my recommendation is a 10- to 20-minute session twice a day." The stress breaks written into your appointment book should be inscribed in ink.

Second, customize your stress-management routine. The more time you devote to things you enjoy—birdwatching, doing

172

jigsaw puzzles, sitting down to an hour of needlework—the less time you waste stewing about things you can't control.

Rule of thumb? Do something positive, and do it regularly. "That's the key to managing stress successfully," says Dr. Elkin.

You Gotta Laugh

Stress may not be a laughing matter to you. But maybe it should be. Humor is one of the most powerful stress-reducing tools there is.

"Just as studies have shown the negative effects of stress on the body, we're now finding that humor has positive effects," says Karyn Buxman, R.N., editor of *Therapeutic Humor*, the journal of the National Association for Therapeutic Humor.

When you laugh, your heart rate and blood pressure rise— giving your cardiovascular system a mini–aerobic workout— then temporarily dip lower than they were before. Your immune system makes more immune cells. Tight, tense muscles relax. Even your brain gets a workout: The thought processes involved in understanding a joke force us to use our entire brain, which makes it more agile.

A big chuckle reduces stress because it helps us cope. George Vaillant, M.D., former professor of psychiatry at Harvard Medical School, has been quoted as saying, "Humor is one of the truly elegant defenses in the human repertoire." Dr. Vaillant identified humor as one of five positive defense mechanisms healthy people depend on to survive hard times.

How else could we turn less-than-amusing episodes in our lives into funny stories? If your long-awaited Caribbean vacation is smashed to pieces by Hurricane Betty, you really have two choices: laugh or cry. Go the laugh route, and you'll at least get a vacation from the stress of the experience.

As we grow older, a sense of humor becomes a vital stress-management tool, says Christian Hageseth III, M.D., a psychiatrist in private practice in Fort Collins, Colorado. So older people with strong funny bones stay younger longer? "They sure seem to," he says.

Humor may indeed have an effect on longevity. When re-

173

searchers at the University of Akron in Ohio studied a group of older people, ages 66 to 101, who had outlived their brothers or sisters by an average of seven years, one personality characteristic stood out. The long-lived sibling had a better sense of humor. Laughing their way around life's obstacles added not only color to their lives but also years.

Makeover Minutes

Getting Your Chuckles

You don't have to remember complicated jokes or lead the conga line at every wedding to rejuvenate yourself with humor. Spend a few Makeover Minutes every day laughing and acting like a child, and chances are, you will be a more relaxed—and youthful—grown-up.

Make a face. We make faces at babies to make them laugh. Why not mug in front of a mirror for your own benefit? "Your face is constantly giving feedback to your brain about how you feel," says Dr. Hageseth. "Making faces may convince your brain that you are more lighthearted than you thought."

Treat yourself to toys. Dr. Hageseth calls them props. We call them toys—the classic phony-nose-and-glasses disguise, yo-yos, squirt guns—and they are extremely potent stress reducers. He suggests keeping a stash of props at home, in your car (for when you are stuck in traffic), and at the office. "Props give you a break during which you can mentally escape from stressful situations," he says. "You can break up an otherwise difficult moment by bringing out your prop when the going seems tense."

Go "Looney Tunes." If it has been years since you watched Bugs Bunny outwit Elmer Fudd, Dr. Elkin thinks it's a fine idea to tune in to an all-cartoon channel and see if 10 minutes of giggling at Daffy, Bugs, and Yosemite Sam can soothe your frazzled nerves. "Actually, some of my patients watch cartoons," he says.

174

Just for Fun

While you don't have to be a natural-born comedian to reap the benefits of humor, you may need time to build your humor "muscles." Here are some aerobics for your funny bone.

Develop a playlist. On an index card, list five things that you find relaxing or that make you laugh, suggests Buxman. Make sure that they're activities you can accomplish easily, virtually anywhere.

Remember to carry the card with you. The next time you're feeling anxious, pull out your card, choose an activity, and do it. "Even if you don't want to," says Buxman. "Tell yourself, 'I will feel better afterward.'"

Tape some tickles. Assemble a humor library of books, audiobooks, and videos that make you laugh, suggests Dr. Hageseth. You might designate one shelf of your entertainment center for this purpose. Search out new material and keep adding to your collection. Eventually, you'll automatically turn to "Humor Central" when you're feeling tense.

Hone some goofy skills. Our society is so intent on setting, reaching, and surpassing goals that we sometimes think results are all that counts. But anyone who takes the time to learn to play the kazoo or whistle "The Flight of the Bumblebee" with crackers in his mouth has a guaranteed reprieve from the rigors of life.

To help you master such oddball, stress-reducing tricks, contact the Institute of Totally Useless Skills, which encourages its members to "learn everything you'll never need to know." You can even earn a "practitioner of uselessness" degree. For more information, write to the Institute at P.O. Box 181, Temple, NH 03084.

Fake it till you make it. If you're not normally a belly laugher, try this 15-minute laughing meditation, recommended by Dr. Elkin. For the first 5 minutes, simply stretch. Yawn if you can. Warm up by making funny faces.

In the second 5 minutes, slowly smile and begin to laugh until you're laughing from deep in your belly (rather than from

175

your throat). In the last minute of this stage, close your eyes as you continue to laugh.

During the third 5 minutes, stop laughing—suddenly—and keep your eyes closed. Stay completely still. Let your mind drift. People who perform the laughing meditation regularly have reported feeling deeply relaxed, as if a burden had been lifted from their shoulders.

Makeover Minutes

For Some Mellow Moments

Learning a few simple relaxation techniques is another way to master stress. From deep breathing to meditation to visualization, these exercises are based on the premise that calming the mind helps calm the body as well.

Many stress-management techniques utilize the power of the relaxation response, a physiological state proven to short-circuit the fight-or-flight response. Your metabolism and breathing slow, your blood pressure drops, and your muscles relax. Even brain activity changes: Your gray matter stops making the faster beta waves and produces slower alpha, theta, and delta waves, which are associated with a more relaxed state.

You don't have to become a Zen master to master relaxation techniques—some can defuse stress within minutes. Try these fast-acting mental stress-busters.

Do the dishes. You can transform any task, even washing the dinner dishes, into a calming ritual using a mental technique called mindfulness, writes Jon Kabat-Zinn, Ph.D., in his book *Full Catastrophe Living.* As described by Dr. Kabat-Zinn, mindfulness is the ability to focus intensely on what you are doing.

Concentrate on each plate, glass, and fork as you wash it. Notice how your fingers, hands, and body move as you hold, scrub, and rinse. Think of nothing but those dishes, as though you could wash them with the intensity of your focus. Learning to live in the moment has many benefits, writes Dr. Kabat-Zinn.

176

"De-Feet" Stress with Reflexology

Tranquillity is just a foot rub away when you learn the basics of reflexology.

"Massaging the feet can soothe the nerves," says Laura Norman, a nationally certified reflexologist; owner of Laura Norman and Associates, a reflexology treatment and training center in New York City; and author of *Feet First: A Guide to Foot Reflexology*. Reflexologists believe that certain spots on your feet connect with other parts of your body that get balanced when you apply pressure to the foot properly. With the foot sessions of reflexology, they say, you can aid a wide variety of health conditions, including stress.

To get relief in specific areas of your body, you might want to make an appointment with a reflexologist. In the meantime, here's how to get a foothold on one stress-relieving procedure that you can do at home. Norman calls it thumb- and finger-walking.

1. Sitting comfortably in a quiet room, lift your right ankle to your left knee. Hold your right foot firmly in your right hand—gripping it by the heel and ankle or by the toes. Place the thumb of your left hand on the sole of your right foot.

2. Applying steady, even pressure with the outside edge of the ball of your left thumb, press one spot, move your thumb forward a bit, then press again.

3. Continue up the foot until you reach your toes.

4. Go back to your heel, pick a new spot, and repeat the progression.

5. When you have worked the entire bottom of your right foot, do the same on the top of the same foot, but using all your fingers instead of just your thumb.

6. Change your position and do the same procedure with the left foot.

For maximum relaxation, dim the lights and put on soft music while you're doing this, suggests Norman. "You might also massage your feet with aromatherapy oils, such as chamomile or lavender, added into a cream," she suggests. "If you have the type of stress that leaves you exhausted, use energizing oils, like mint or cinnamon."

You can do a bare-bones reflexology session virtually anywhere—in the car during a long trip, for example. If you want to do it in the office, "just slip off your shoes under your desk," says Norman. Her personal favorite is in the bathtub. "I work on my feet in the tub every night," she says.

"Cultivating mindfulness can lead to the discovery of deep realms of relaxation, calmness, and insight within yourself."

Take some doze-off. Who has time to go on a vacation? You do, when you use the mental technique known as visualization.

Close your eyes and think of a peaceful place you have been. Inhale deeply through your nose and exhale through your mouth as you mentally relive a perfect afternoon at the lake or in the woods. Chances are, you'll feel more relaxed in less than a minute, says Michael A. Tarrant, Ph.D., professor of forest recreation at the University of Georgia, who has studied the psycho-physiological effects of imagining past nature experiences.

Dr. Tarrant and his colleagues found that after people recalled these experiences, they reported feeling more relaxed. "Some people's mental state improved after only one minute of visualizing," he says.

Repeat yourself. Relaxation is a skill that can be developed to help with stress, says Jon Seskevich, R.N., who teaches stress-reduction techniques to seriously ill people and their families at Duke University Medical Center in Chapel Hill, North Carolina. Repeating a phrase silently to oneself over and over also has a calming effect. When the mind wanders, simply return again and again to the phrase.

Try repeating "The Lord is my shepherd," inhaling on "The Lord" and exhaling on "is my shepherd." Or try "easy does it," breathing in on "easy" and exhaling on "does it," says Seskevich. As you concentrate on the phrase and your breathing, your stress will begin to fade.

Get some R and R. Rapid relaxation, that is. This 30-second technique "is a simple way to let go of tension—to become sort of like a limp rag," says Dr. Elkin.

It's simple to do. When you feel yourself getting stressed, Dr. Elkin says, touch your thumb to any finger on the same hand and press them together, hard. As you do this, take a deep breath through your nose.

Hold that breath for about five seconds or so. Then, part your lips slightly and exhale. Release your fingers as you imagine a wave of relaxation spreading from the top of your head to the tips of your toes.

178

Make like Pavlov's dogs. Take a few minutes to pinpoint which everyday occurrences regularly make you tense. For most people, the stress inducers are things like sitting down to pay bills, answering your phone at work, or trying to zoom through intersections before the yellow light turns red. Mentally link these "stress signals" to a relaxation exercise. "Hearing your office phone ring might be your cue to take five seconds to stretch or breathe deeply before you pick up," suggests Dr. Elkin. "Or an adhesive dot stuck to your steering wheel reminds you to do a mental exercise like rapid relaxation when you hit a string of red lights or a traffic jam. These prompts can really help take the edge off your stress."

Burst some bubbles. When nothing else works to relieve tension, bubble wrap comes in mighty handy. Popping these sealed air capsules reduces stress, according to a study conducted by Kathleen Dillon, Ph.D., a psychologist and professor of psychology at Western New England College in Springfield, Massachusetts.

It's a throwback to the classic worry bead, a smooth stone the ancient Greeks carried with them and rubbed between their fingers to release tension. "Playing with the poppers seems to have the same effect as a lot of nervous habits, but there are no side effects," says Dr. Dillon. "It's a lot better than smoking cigarettes."

Long-Term Tactics
For Easy Bliss'ning

Stress-management exercises are like situps: The more often you do them, the more you benefit. But to get really good at them, you need to practice. Here are some stress blasters worth learning.

Breathe with your bellows. Most people breathe using the muscles in their chests. But chest breathing actually perpetuates stress and makes the heart and lungs work up to 50 percent harder than they should, according to Dr. Nuernberger. He

179

Coping with Caregiver Stress

When Donna Baldwin's mother, Laura, had a stroke in 1986, Donna knew that she wanted to care for her at home. But wishing and doing are two different things. Donna wasn't so sure that she would be able to cope with all the day-to-day stress of day care for a parent. "I remember thinking, 'Will I ever be able to get out and have a normal life?'"

That was before the speedboat ride.

Donna had been caring for her mother for two years when friends of the Baldwins invited the family out for a ride in their new speedboat. Donna's oldest son, Michael, was supposed to stay home with his grandmother but got called into work. "I told Michael, 'Go. I'll stay home with Mom,'" says Donna.

Then Laura spoke up. Although the stroke had impeded her speech, the question came out as clear as a bell: "Why can't I go?"

Donna's response was, "Well, why *not*?"

"So we got her on the boat," Donna recalls, "and she had a little scarf around her head and sunglasses on. We strapped her into her seat. Then the boat took off, and I heard my mother say, 'Oh, my God.' And I said, 'What have I done?'"

They had a great day. "My mother really seemed to enjoy herself," recalls Donna. "We went down the river and had wine and cheese, and my mother had her medication. I thought, 'Just because I'm taking care of Mom doesn't mean that we—and she— can't have some fun.'"

notes that many mental disciplines, including yoga, get people to practice nonstressful breathing methods to relax the body and focus the mind.

Instead of overworking those chest muscles, breathe using your diaphragm, the dome-shaped muscle under your lungs, advises Dr. Nuernberger. Using that muscle like a big expanding bellows, you actually pull air into the blood-rich lower lobes of the lungs. This allows the lungs to work more efficiently than when you are chest breathing. (For more information on the

180

Stop-Time Tactics

After that outing, it seemed as if the sky was the limit. Donna took her mother to her son's baseball and soccer games. Later, Laura came to her grandsons' high school and college graduations. When Michael got married, his grandmother was there. Even when Laura could no longer stand or walk unassisted, Donna continued to take her to church.

Finding out that her mother could do all these things was quite an eye-opener to Donna—and it gave her a fresh lease on her own life. Donna discovered that caregivers need to balance their own needs, the needs of their families, and the needs of the parent. "That's how you survive," says Donna.

"If I had let this situation take over my life," Donna reflects, "then I would have spent these past 11 years at home with my mother, the way the doctors said it would be." Instead, Laura goes to adult day care three times a week, while Donna does many of the day-to-day things that she just has to get done.

And Donna has made sure to protect her marriage from the added stress of having a dependent parent: She and her husband make sure that they regularly go out for dinner or long drives. Also, Donna is active in Children for Aging Parents (CAPS), a support group that she has attended since Laura had her stroke.

"I wouldn't be human if I didn't get stressed," says Donna. But she adds, "Every time I get through another adventure with my mother, I think, 'Well, we got through that, now we can move on.'"

steps to mastering this technique, see "Fighting Fight-or-Flight" on page 169.)

Make your ratio two to one. While breathing with your diaphragm, try the two-to-one breathing technique to relieve stress. If you exhale twice as long as you inhale, these drawn-out exhalations help relax and quiet the body, according to Dr. Nuernberger.

Learn to meditate. Meditation, which triggers the relaxation response, is a proven stress reducer that's also good for your heart. It lowers blood pressure and cholesterol levels and may even help people with heart problems live longer, healthier lives. Researchers from the State University of New York at Buffalo and the Maharishi University of Management in Fairfield, Iowa, taught a small group of men with heart disease how to meditate. After eight months, these men were able to exercise 14 percent longer and 12 percent harder than a group of nonmeditators.

Nurtured Body, Calmer Mind

If you're having a bout with stress, count on it that your eating habits are likely to go haywire. For some people, it's famine time: You're too tense to eat. For others, it's feast: You eat everything in the refrigerator except the condiments. And if you're just too busy to eat well, these are the times when some people live on Butterfingers and Chinese takeout.

But consuming a diet high in sugar, salt, and fat doesn't just lead to a less-than-trim figure; it can also contribute to age-related maladies like heart disease, high blood pressure, and cancer. Such haphazard eating habits can also rob you of the nutrients you need to withstand stress's attack on your body and brain.

On the other hand, a low-fat diet that includes lots of fresh fruits, vegetables, and whole grains helps you reach your physical and mental peak and stay there, no matter how much stress you are under.

Makeover Minutes

Finding the Soothing Foods

With supermarkets full of low-fat yogurt, whole-grain bagels, and pre-cut vegetables, following a healthy diet can be as simple as steering a grocery cart down aisle A and skipping aisles B, C, and D.

"If you have just 60 seconds, you have time to eat nutritiously," writes Evelyn Tribole, R.D., in *Eating on the Run*. You just have to make the right choices. Here's what to feed your body when you are feeling frantic.

Pop off tension. Stress depletes the brain's level of serotonin, the feel-good brain chemical that promotes feelings of relaxation. You can help combat stress's effects on the brain by eating foods high in complex carbohydrates which generally stimulate the production of serotonin. Eat some air-popped popcorn, whole-grain bagels, or a plate of pasta, and you'll help replenish the brain's level of this chemical, for quicker relaxation, says Tribole.

Water your brain. Deprive yourself of liquids, and your brain can become thirsty enough to cause conditions in your body like fatigue and headache. "The brain is 75 percent water by weight and is the first organ to be affected by dehydration," says Dr. Rosch. You need to drink at least eight eight-ounce glasses of liquids a day to stay hydrated. If you keep a bottle of water at your desk, that will remind you to keep sipping throughout the day.

Lunch on a "tranquillity sandwich." When the morning's events threaten to give you the heebie-jeebies, rescue your body with a calm-down lunch: Use whole-grain bread instead of white for your sandwich. Whole-grain has at least three grams of fiber in every pair of slices (white has only one or two grams), so the whole-grain takes longer to digest. Slower digestion means that your body won't transform the food to instant blood sugar. That's important. Because when you're under stress, your blood contains more sugar than usual, and you don't need any extra helpings.

Long-Term Tactics

For Less-Edgy Eating

While it isn't easy to start eating nutritiously after years of fueling your body with coffee, chocolate, and cheese puffs, you still can make the shift with some gradual changes. These simple strategies can help you eat to beat stress, one step at a time.

Decaffeinate your workplace. For some reason, the more tense we are at work, the more we seem to tank up on caf-

183

feinated drinks like coffee and cola. That's not a good idea because caffeine causes your body to make more stress hormones, according to a study conducted at Duke University Medical Center in Durham, North Carolina.

The Duke study showed that people who drank two to three cups of coffee had 37 percent more of the stress hormone epinephrine in their urine than when they drank no coffee at all. "What's more, work stress seems to increase the amount of coffee people drink, further intensifying their response to stress," says James D. Lane, Ph.D., associate research professor in psychiatry and behavioral sciences at Duke.

Eat with eating in mind. The more stress you are under, the less you heed what and how much you eat. So make a point of becoming conscious of what you eat. You'll end up eating carelessly if you try to read, work, or watch TV while you munch.

Microwaving a sausage-egg-and-cheese biscuit gives you a quick breakfast that you can munch during the ride to work—but it's second-rate nutrition. Instead, eat at the table. Zap the TV. And, of course, you're better off with a bowl of whole-grain cereal than a grab-and-go high-fat breakfast, says Tribole.

Similarly, if you normally review reports while wolfing a burger at your desk, stop shuffling papers long enough to get to a lunch table. Enjoy that meal—even if it's brief. And again, while you're at it, make that meal nutritionally appetizing—a small can of water-packed tuna on whole-grain crackers along with a piece of fruit, for instance, says Tribole.

Makeover Minutes

Getting Your Kicks In

In China, people in middle and old age can be seen in public parks, practicing tai chi. A gentle kind of martial art, tai chi is "moving meditation" that tones the muscles while it calms the mind.

Research has shown that gentle exercise, like tai chi, is an antidote for stress, but it is not the only one. Even a short walk

184

Unwind with a Furry Friend

Dashing after dogs and chatting with cats is fine—but what about picking fur off your clothing or sponging accident evidence out of the living room rug? Surely there's some way to share your love for animals without dealing with their untamed habits.

"Yes, you can get the stress-relieving benefits of animals without actually owning one," says Alan M. Beck, Sc.D., professor of ecology at Purdue University in West Lafayette, Indiana, and co-author of *Between Pets and People: The Importance of Animal Companionship*. Here's what he suggests.

Walk on the wild side. Going to the zoo is a great way to reduce stress, says Dr. Beck, because being around a few elephants, zebras, and waddling penguins brings out the best in people. "Studies show people see each other more positively when they are in the presence of animals," he says.

Feed the birds. Hang a bird feeder in your backyard or outside your window, and a little bit of fluttering nature will come to you. Feeding birds gives you what Dr. Beck calls the helper's high, a feeling of nurturing another life.

Borrow a dog. Ask friends if they will let you walk their dogs on a regular basis. Taking a stroll with a four-footed friend can help dispel the lingering angst of a bad day at work. The outdoor exercise will help you unwind, and in all likelihood the pet's owner will thank you profusely for giving the family pet a bonus stroll.

Go fish. You don't need to buy rare, expensive fish. Low-maintenance fish, like goldfish, will do just fine, says Dr. Beck. Watch them and feed them. It's just one more connection with nature that can help relieve stress.

helps burn off stress hormones lingering in the blood and helps release endorphins, brain chemicals that give you a feeling of well-being.

"Walking or other moderate exercise produces a holistic pattern of change—what I call general body arousal," says Robert Thayer, Ph.D., professor of psychology at California State University, Long Beach. "Your heart rate and metabolism increase. The tension in your muscles goes down. And there are changes in hormones and in brain neurotransmitters, which have a significant effect on thinking and mood."

When it comes to beating stress with exercise, every move counts. These 5- to 15-minute moves are proven stress busters.

For 10,000
yen (about
$80), you
can take your
turn in Yoshi
Ogusawara's
ceramic-
smashing
room near the
foot of Mt.
Fuji, where
you can
hurl ceramic
antique repro-
ductions
against a
wall while
shouting,
"Take that!"
in Japanese.

Give yourself some rope. Just a few minutes of jumping rope can help reduce stress, says Daniel M. Landers, Ph.D., a researcher at the Arizona State University Exercise and Sports Research Institute in Tempe. Since it's an aerobic activity, jumping rope gets your heart pumping, which moves stress hormones out of your system. You can even jump rope at work. If you have an office with a solid door, put on your sneakers and skip away tension in privacy.

Stretch out your neck. Taking a minute to stretch will loosen the muscles in your neck and shoulders, which tend to knot up when you spend hours staring at a computer monitor or sitting at a desk. Here are two ways, recommended by Dr. Landers, to help stretch your neck muscles.

▌ Take a deep breath, drawing your shoulders up toward your ears. As you exhale, bring your shoulders down and back.
▌ Take a deep breath and, as you exhale, turn your head as far to one side as you can. Hold for 10 to 15 seconds, while continuing to breathe out evenly. Repeat, turning your head to the other side with the next exhalation.

Take your brain for a stroll. Forget speed-walking around the mall. Instead, take a meditation walk: a slow, comfortable stroll. Research has shown that a meditation walk can reduce anxicty as well as a brisk walk does.

In a meditation walk, pay attention to your footsteps, counting "one, two, one, two." If you find your thoughts drifting, think, "Oh, well," and return to counting your footsteps. A group of people who practiced this technique over a 16-week period reported feeling less anxious and more positive about themselves.

Long-Term Tactics
More Mellowing Moves

If just a few minutes of moving and stretching can melt away tension, imagine what a regular workout can do. Any work-

Solutions for Life's Little Stresses

It's actually amazing how little stresses can drain your mental and physical energy. Take anything that bothers you—hunting for your car keys, watching your spouse channel-surf, spending precious after-work time in a supermarket checkout line—and it can start to add up to a big headache, or worse. The result is just the kind of wear and tear you don't need. So you are better off resolving a few of life's little irritants. Here's how to beat the small stressors.

Losing car keys. Put a hook near the front door and make it a habit to hang up your keys as soon as you come in, suggests Dr. Rosch.

Losing glasses. If you tend to misplace your glasses, buy two sets—one for work and one for home, says Dr. Rosch.

Commuter crunch. If you're on a schedule such that you hit rush-hour traffic every morning, talk to your boss about changing your schedule, suggests Dr. Rosch. Maybe you can adjust your hours so that you come in earlier and leave earlier—or come in later and leave later.

Overcoming "closetphobia." "I cleaned one of my closets recently, and I felt as if my life had turned around," says Carol Venolia, an architect and author of *Healing Environments: Your Guide to Indoor Well-Being.* "I felt good every time I walked past it." No big deal—right? But putting it off can aggravate stress more than you realize.

Waiting in line. If waiting in line at the grocery store sends you over the edge, grab a tabloid or celebrity magazine from the rack, says Dr. Rosch. Whether you buy it or not, just browsing can pass the time. Remember: the line won't move any faster just because your blood pressure's rising.

out, like running, that gets your heart pumping and your blood moving can be a powerful stress buster, says Dr. Landers. But if you have been there, done that, you might want to consider a more unconventional workout. Here are a couple.

Box with your tootsies. Kickboxing, a martial art like karate or judo, definitely helps to melt pent-up stress. (It also melts fat. The sport can burn up to 900 calories an hour.)

Want to vent some hostility? To locate a kickboxing class, look under "martial arts" in the yellow pages. Or rent a kickboxing tape before you commit to a class.

187

March with the volks. If you prefer a more leisurely workout to let off steam, consider joining a volksmarch club. A volksmarch, which means "a walk for the people," is a 6.2-mile noncompetitive group walk that combines three stress reducers: exercise, companionship, and nature. Volksmarching, which originated in Germany and started here 20 years ago, is one of several group events collectively called volkssporting.

"A lot of folks tell us how much they love volksmarching," says David Stewart, executive director of the American Volkssport Association (AVA). "We've all walked together somewhere in the world, and we're all friends. When we have our convention every two years, it's like a family reunion." Over 30 percent of the AVA's 422,000 members are over the age of 55, and 20 percent are retired. There are over 500 volksmarching clubs and 1,100 AVA trails in the United States. To find or form a volksmarch club in your area, write to the AVA at 1001 Pat Booker Road, Suite 101, Universal City, TX 78148.

Home, Stress-Free Home

If coming home from work isn't any more soothing than actually being at work, your home may not be the haven it could be. "Most people don't realize how profoundly their home environment affects them," says Carol Venolia, an architect and author of *Healing Environments: Your Guide to Indoor Well-Being.* And she's not just talking about decor. "Sometimes they don't think about how things like light, sound, and air quality can affect them," observes Venolia.

One of the simplest ways to make your home a more soothing place is to welcome in natural light. Spending too much time in artificial light can disrupt your body's daily rhythms, which can cause stress and fatigue, research shows. Natural light is not only, well, more *natural*, it also conveys real information about time and weather, and that's information your body needs to maintain its natural rhythms.

To get more natural light every day, you might rearrange your kitchen so that the breakfast nook is against a sunny window. Or you might need to change your sleeping arrangements so that

188

your bedroom gets morning sun. While it might seem odd at first to convert your study into your bedroom, you may also feel more energetic once you're getting the natural light your body needs.

Makeover Minutes

Nesting Made Easy

In addition to getting more light in your life, there are other things you can do to stress-proof your home. Some take just minutes to accomplish. Try these quick home improvements.

Take off your shoes. In Japan, people exchange their shoes for slippers as soon as they get home. Buy a cushy pair of slippers and keep them right inside your front door. The simple shoe-swapping ritual can help you make the transition between the stress "out there" and the serenity of home.

Brew a cup of tea. "There are few hours in life more agreeable than the hour dedicated to the ceremony known as afternoon tea," wrote Henry James in *Portrait of a Lady*. So unpack Grandmother's china tea set, brew a cup of tea (decaffeinated or herbal), and spend a few minutes savoring its flavor, aroma, and soothing steaminess. "Little touches like this are extremely important," says Venolia.

Broaden the spectrum. It may be energy efficient, but fluorescent lighting is not what you would call soothing. "Most fluorescent lights are the old-fashioned kind that hum and flicker and turn your skin a sickly color," says Venolia. But she points out that we now have newer fluorescent lighting that provides illumination much closer to natural light. Full-spectrum fluorescent lights, as they are called, actually mimic the full-spectrum light of the midday sun.

Light a single candle. You don't have to reserve candlelight for romantic dinners. "This kind of warm, low-level light is soothing because it's primal," says Venolia. "It still touches a place in us. You get a similar feeling from this kind of light that you do from watching the sun set."

189

Spotlight for atmosphere. Keep general lighting levels lower. But if you want to read or do needlework, use a small, brighter task light, like a clip-on lamp, Venolia suggests.

Pick up the scent of serenity. Research shows that pleasant aromas encourage relaxation. In studies at the Royal Berkshire and Battle Hospitals in Reading, England, researchers found that critically ill people treated to the scent of lavender oil felt more positive and less anxious. Lavender, apparently, seems to increase the brain's production of alpha waves, a tangible measurement of relaxation. To reap those soothing benefits, look for naturally scented soaps, oil, and candles that can lend a benign, soothing fragrance to your home environment.

Long-Term Tactics
For Creature Comfort

Other ways to stress-proof your home take more time, but the rewards can be worth it. Consider these suggestions.

Clean out the sniffle-makers. Constantly being sick can be stressful, says Venolia—and that's how you may feel if you are allergic to something in your house. Before Venolia found out that she was allergic to mold and took measures to control it, she recalls having constant colds and respiratory problems.

After Venolia's doctor determined that she was allergic to mold, she cleaned out hidden mold sources in the closets, bathroom, and bedding. The problems subsided—and stress diminished.

If allergies are making you tense and exhausted, be sure to get tested by an allergist. If you do turn out to have an allergy, you may end up cleaning more often. But it's a small price to pay for less stress, more vigor, and a more welcoming home.

Bring the outdoors in. Think of how peaceful you feel when you listen to the patter of raindrops on leaves or see a mother duck drift across a pond with her ducklings. "Feeling connected to living things reduces stress," says Alan M. Beck,

190

Sc.D., professor of ecology at Purdue University in West Lafayette, Indiana.

One way to connect with nature is by bringing plants into your home. "I have two or three bookshelves that are filled just with plants," says Venolia. "I believe that seeing plants is healthy, and caring for them certainly feels good."

Noise-proof your home. If there is street noise outside your window, it can filter through, adding to your stress more than you realize. Investing in double- or triple-pane windows, weather stripping, and thermal insulation can reduce outside noise, says Venolia. You can also reduce reverberation inside your house with fabric wall coverings, cushy furniture, and carpeting. "All of these absorb noise," she notes.

Go to some land Down Under. Some grade-school teachers set aside one corner of their classrooms as a sort of stress-free zone, says Venolia. "Kids who need time out can retreat to this corner. It might have a pile of soft pillows to lie on, books to look at, and tapes of nature sounds to listen to. There might even be a little bowl of potpourri." This corner is called Australia or Antarctica—a land far, far away from the stresses of the classroom.

To create a mini-Antarctica for yourself, set up one room—or even one corner of a room—as your private place to sip a cup of tea, suggests Venolia. Use that retreat to practice stress-reduction exercises or perhaps just browse through a favorite magazine. "It may give you some much-needed peace," she says.

Put Work Stress in Your Out Box

The hours are long and the pay is lousy. Your boss doesn't listen to you. Nobody appreciates what you do. The copy machine is always jammed, and your voice-mail light is always blinking. In other words, you have no control.

Yes, you do, says Jeanie Marshall, an empowerment consultant and founder of Marshall House, a Santa Monica, California, company that trains people and organizations to be more effective. To beat stress at work, says Marshall, you have to move from feeling beleaguered to feeling empowered.

know what?

Two movies to avoid when you're under stress: *Falling Down* (1993): Nerdy Michael Douglas loses it on the Los Angeles Freeway, amasses weapons, and goes on an ire-induced rampage. *Network* (1976): TV newsman goes postal. First use of the phrase, "I'm mad as hell, and I'm not going to take it anymore!"

Be a Player at Work

The prescription for work stress isn't a desk drawer full of aspirin and Tums. More likely, it's yo-yos and Silly Putty, according to Howard Papush, founder of Let's Play Again, a Los Angeles–based company that has helped workers from a wide range of organizations—the U.S. Postal Service to Walt Disney—rediscover the pleasures of play.

"The more stress you're under, the more you need to play," says Papush, who prefers to be called Dr. Play. "When we were kids, we went to our job—which was school—every day. School was stressful, too. But at some point during the day, we got recess. It was a chance to let off steam." What Papush is recommending for adults is really just another form of recess.

Here's the mental exercise that Papush suggests, so you can take recess without ever leaving your desk.

1. Close your eyes and try to remember how you played when you were a kid.
2. See yourself coming home from school, changing into play clothes, then beginning to play.
3. Imagine the scene exactly. Are you in the backyard? On the front stoop? Roller-skating down the street? Walking in the woods? Playing with Barbie dolls?
4. Remember the faces of the kids around you—kids you perhaps haven't thought about in 20, 30, or even 40 years.
5. Now see your own face. Are you happy? Smiling? Having a good time?
6. Stay with the scene until you can actually feel stress drain out of your body.

"This mental recess lowers stress levels and gives you the energy you need to work productively," says Papush.

Another way to play is to bring toys to work—ideally, the toys that you loved as a child. "I have a set of wooden blocks," says Papush. "When I work, I make a point of taking a break and playing with my blocks. Then I can go back to being a grown-up."

Prefer crayons? Keep a set in your desk. Anytime you pull them out, you can return to a time in your life when skies were green, cows were purple, and stress was the shocking discovery that you had no cookies in your lunch bag.

192

"Empowerment isn't power that somebody gives you," says Marshall. "You already have it." But the first step is knowing what you can change and what you can't. Being aware of what's beyond your control actually makes you feel less helpless. You'll also become more efficient and productive, says Marshall, because you won't waste time trying to fix the unfixable.

Take This Job and Love It

While empowerment may seem like an imposing challenge, small changes can count for a lot. Here are some instant actions that can help define your area of control—and help take the stress out of work.

Ask the right question. When you feel powerless in some conflict with a co-worker or you're feeling helpless in the face of a looming deadline, ask yourself how you can get some control over the situation. If it's a co-worker issue, the answer might be to talk over the problem with your colleague. If it's a deadline that's giving you the jitters, why not break the project into easy-to-handle parts and focus on one part at a time?

What's the benefit of approaching problems this way? "A sense of control," says Marshall.

Make a "priority card." Write your priorities on an index card, keep the card in your desk, and glance at it frequently. For instance, your priorities might be "learn something new every day," "find out what customers really want," and "think innovation." No matter how many tasks and obligations you have on your daily schedule, having this card in front of you helps put things in focus. "It can be a helpful tool in the first few weeks and months if you forget what your priorities are," says Marshall. But at some point, the card will become irrelevant, and you won't need to remind yourself anymore. "Then you know you've internalized your priorities," she says.

Have a two-minute vent. Ranting to a trusted co-worker about

193

a botched project definitely reduces stress. The problem is, most of us don't know when to quit. "Vent for five minutes, then be done with it and move on," says Marshall. That way, venting becomes a conscious decision instead of an unconscious reaction that fuels stress.

Make a different kind of list. Many time-management experts advise making a "to do" list and checking off each item as you do it. But this technique doesn't work for everyone, says Marshall. "A lot of people find list-making very frustrating because they still don't get things done."

Another approach? Write down what you have accomplished, suggests Marshall. By allowing yourself to feel good about your accomplishments, you will find that such a list pushes you to move on to doing other things so that you can add them to the "done" list rather than the "to do" list. "I suggest people try this when they feel overwhelmed with things to do," says Marshall. "They usually come alive because they realize that they really have accomplished a lot."

Long-Term Tactics

For Taming Job Stress

In addition to the quick fixes that can help rein in job stress, you might need to adopt some customizing practices and make them a habit. Here are the places to begin.

Just say it. Learning to say no—to committees, projects, even requests for help—is one of the simplest ways to stay calm on the job, says Marshall. Of course, you don't want to refuse every task, every colleague, and certainly not your boss. But if you're not sure when to say no, check your priority card. If the task doesn't match one of your priorities, nix it if you can.

Don't give your all. It's important to work at a capacity that replenishes us, rather than depletes us, advises Marshall. "If we work at 80 to 95 percent capacity on a regular basis, we tend to feel exhilarated at the end of a day rather than exhausted. And

194

then when we are required to give more than 100 percent, we find the extra reserves are available."

Make excellence good enough. Perfectionists often work harder and less effectively because they can't let go of one project to attend to others. Also, they may procrastinate, which adds to their stress. "When priority one bumps up against priority two, which bumps up against priority three, we need to decide when—and what—we're willing to let go," says Marshall. If you go for excellence rather than perfection, there may be a few bugs in a project, but it gets done. If you're trying to eliminate every last flaw, a single project can take forever.

Do many things, focus on one. "Working on one project while worrying about the other that just hit your desk not only makes you tense, it makes you less effective," Marshall says. So give your full attention to one thing at a time, no matter how busy you are, she advises.

Don't sweat the mess. Many people think that if their office is neat and their files are alphabetized, they'll automatically become more productive. Again, the self-inflicted pressure to get organized may actually work against you, especially if you're the creative type. So if your desk and filing system seem disorganized, but you know where everything is, "let go of feeling guilty about the mess," says Marshall.

195

Find a Good Challenge to Turn Back the Clock

In his midfifties, Andrew Dworkis signed up for Outward Bound's eight-day sailing trip in the Florida Keys. Looking around as he stepped aboard, he realized that many of his fellow voyagers were in their midtwenties. He knew right then—if he hadn't known before—that he was in for an adventure.

The biggest challenge came at the end of the trip, when participants did a mile-long swim. "I like to swim in a pool, where I can get to the side as fast as possible, where I can touch the bottom, and where there are no waves," says Dr. Dworkis, a veterinarian. "This swim involved everything I don't like."

It took him longer than anyone else to finish the course across choppy, windblown salt water—a distance equal to the length of 72 Olympic-size swimming pools. But the accomplishment was worth every aching stroke and flailing kick. "It was incredible, such a stretch," Dr. Dworkis says. "When I finished, I thought, 'If I can do that, I can do a lot of other things, too.' "

Bound for New Adventures

To the organizers of Outward Bound adventures, it's no surprise that Dr. Dworkis discovered a whole realm of expanded possibilities when he swam his way into Stop-Time Tactic No. 8.

"While people come and experience some wonderful ad-

196

Outward Bound for Adventure

Nearly every teenager gets a yen for adventure, but you don't always have the chance or resources to fulfill those fantasies when you're younger. With the help of some organizations, however, you can swing back the hands of the clock and enjoy some of the challenges you may have missed.

Providing folks with the opportunity to surpass their expectations is the essence of Outward Bound, a non-profit educational adventure group that teaches skills like sailing, white-water rafting, and rock climbing. But there's always more on the agenda than learning to sail a boat or rappel off a cliff.

In fact, most people who sign on for Outward Bound treks choose not to play it safe, often in a big way. People who are afraid of heights frequently choose the climbing courses. Aquaphobes go for water courses.

If cliff-hanging isn't quite your cup of tea, however, there's another organization that might serve you better—especially if you go for educational classes or leisurely pursuits. An organization called Elderhostel offers classes at universities, museums, national parks, science centers, wildlife preserves, temples, and other locales throughout the United States and abroad. The "Elder" in this title should be interpreted broadly. Elderhostel courses are actually open to anyone who is age 55 and older.

Typical Elderhostel programs run five days to three weeks and combine instruction with related activities and travel. You can find classes on virtually any subject. Study the Islamic Koran. Take a course in Woody Allen's comedies. Study nature photography in the shifting light of the Sierra Nevadas.

Whichever way your tastes run, you can join in an Outward Bound or Elderhostel program almost any time of year. To contact Outward Bound, write to R.D. 2, Box 280, Garrison, NY 10524. For Elderhostel, write to P.O. Box 1959, Wakefield, MA 01880.

ventures in spectacular environments, the most important thing they learn is that they have greater capabilities than they thought they did, that their limitations are quite often self-imposed," says Barry S. Rosen, vice president of Outward Bound. "Our instructors ensure that you're going to be safe, which

197

makes it possible for people who haven't been risk-takers to try new things and overcome their fears."

If you've gotten into a routine that's comfortable and familiar, you might find it hard to imagine that difficult new challenges can actually make you feel years younger. Whether you swim a mile, travel a distance, or stretch your mind, you have a lot to gain by taking some risks and reaping the age-protection rewards.

Seeking new adventures is an important way to protect both your mind and your body from aging. "It's thought that withdrawing from the strenuous world of activity and challenge is what leads to people deteriorating as they get older," says Salvatore Maddi, Ph.D., professor of psychology at the University of California, Irvine, and president of the Hardiness Institute in Newport Beach. "Without challenge, you can't have growth. If you don't have to deal with anything new, you stagnate."

Trouble is, adventure doesn't just appear at your front door and invite itself in. You have to "push yourself a bit," Dr. Maddi notes. That means seeking new adventures wherever they can be found. And, of course, adventure means different things to different people. For some, it is an exercise program at the YMCA, while for others, it is a visit to a foreign country that seems to hold a special welcome.

know what?

Seeking a little travel in his later years, Major Will Lacy of Great Britain traveled by plane to the North Pole at age 82. Two years later, at age 84, he flew over the South Pole.

Reap the Benefits

Not only do new challenges help you stay vital and vigorous, they also keep you mentally sharp. Research has shown that people who engage in a variety of challenging activities often have better problem-solving skills, according to Allen Neuringer, Ph.D., professor of psychology at Reed College in Portland, Oregon.

When you take on a challenge, there's some sort of problem attached to it. Even if you're simply finding your way through an unfamiliar part of town, you have to use your problem-solving skills to reach your destination. More adventuresome folks get more practice dealing with changing situations, and as you might expect, this usually means they stay sharper. Fill your life with challenges, and it stands to reason that your mind will be more active as well.

198

Youth in Them Thar Hills

Dick Secord Jr., never knows when he will strike gold. An intrepid miner—flourishing in his second career—Secord owns an entire network of tunnels under the foothills of Oregon's snow-capped Cascade Mountains. There, he mines for gold daily—with the youthful enthusiasm of an irrepressible adventurer.

A mechanic with 20 years' experience under his tool belt, Secord knew zero about mining when he bought the mine in 1994. But he felt age creeping up on him and felt things turning stale. "I'd been doing the same thing for so long, I was going stagnant. I needed something different," says Secord, who was in his midforties when he made the switch. "This is definitely different."

The site he chose for his treasure hunting had opened at the turn of the century and was shut down in the 1950s. Secord suspected it still harbored gold, and when the mine went on the market, he and his father bought it.

He works the mine spring through fall. In winter, when heavy rain and seeping water make mining dangerous, he takes the ore from the mine to the local quartz mill and mills it, looking for gold.

Risky? You bet, agrees Secord. The tunnels through Secord's mine are not only pitch black but also wet and slippery. Old supporting timbers sag ominously. Then there are the economic risks—the mine has yet to pay off financially. Secord, his wife, and their daughter are living off savings.

But in many ways, Secord says, he's already hit the jackpot. Life is more of an adventure these days. It's a lot more exciting than it was before he started digging for gold. Reopening the mine has given him a sense of accomplishment. And he's in better shape—mentally and physically—than he has been in a long time.

There's another benefit you'll get from challenge seeking—some protection from the wear and tear wrought by stress. Challenge seeking is a key characteristic among business executives who tend to stay healthy under pressure, according to Dr. Maddi and his colleague Suzanne C. Ouellette, Ph.D., who conducted a study on the subject at the University of Chicago.

199

Other factors—like feelings of commitment and control—also played a role in the executives' health profiles. But generally, the researchers concluded, executives who sought challenge and who felt that they had control were less likely to get sick than their equally hard-driving counterparts who lacked these characteristics.

In addition, the emotional benefits of challenge seeking can help you feel a lot more youthful. Adventure and challenge trigger the release of endorphins and other brain chemicals that lift your mood, explains Bernard Vittone, M.D., a psychiatrist and director of the National Center for the Treatment of Phobias, Anxiety, and Depression in Washington, D.C. Along with a sense of rejuvenation come greater feelings of fulfillment. A study at Rutgers, the State University of New Jersey, in Kilmer found that people who did a variety of things that allowed them to express different aspects of themselves were the most satisfied with their lives.

But that doesn't mean that you should pile up more challenges than you can handle. "You should be mixing time spent doing comforting, familiar things with time spent sprinkling in challenging new things," says Powell Lawton, Ph.D., senior research scientist at the Polisher Institute of the Philadelphia Geriatric Center. "It doesn't take a whole lot of zestful sprinklings to make life interesting."

Those sprinklings of challenge need to continue through every phase of maturity—even into retirement. "People of middle age at the end of the twentieth century may be looking at another three or four decades of life," says Daniel Perry, executive director of the Alliance for Aging Research in Washington, D.C. "Deciding to learn Italian or take up the piano or get another degree at age 50 is a wise investment toward the decades of life ahead."

Why We Get in Ruts

If challenge and adventure are so rejuvenating, why don't we seek them out more often?

Truth is, getting in a rut—and staying there—can feel pretty

200

comfortable. "A rut sometimes appears to be the easiest route to what we want, but it may not be the ideal route," says David Abramis, Ph.D., an organizational psychologist and chairman of the department of management and human resource management in the College of Business Administration at California State University, Long Beach.

Sometimes it makes sense to do things the same old way—like when you have attempted all the other ways and happened on the best one.

But sometimes we do the same thing over and over again because we have simply stopped trying out other ways. "The longer one is in a particular position or lifestyle, the more likely it is that the lifestyle or position will become habit. And once something is habitual, it's harder to change," says Dr. Abramis.

If you're wondering whether you are spending too much time in a rut, ask yourself what you have done the last five Saturday nights, suggests Sidney B. Simon, Ed.D., professor emeritus of psychological education at the University of Massachusetts, Amherst, and author of *Getting Unstuck: Breaking through Your Barriers to Change.* If you can't remember, or if you did the same thing each of the five, odds are that you're running an adventure deficit.

Unless you have an unusually high tolerance for sameness, you need more excitement, says Dr. Simon. Break out of the rut, and you'll feel more vigorous and vital.

Get Physical

Anyone who tries to meet new physical challenges is getting a good dose of age protection. If you can get a half-hour of aerobic exercise like walking, cycling, swimming, or jogging at least three or four times a week, your cardiovascular fitness level will begin to resemble that of a younger person. You'll have more stamina, and your muscle tone is likely to improve, according to Dan Hamner, M.D., a physiatrist in New York City and author of *Peak Energy.*

You have probably guessed the moral of this story: It's never too late to take up an athletic challenge—to learn a new sport

know what?

An avid swimmer, Bertram Clifford Batt of Australia plunged in and swam 21 miles across the English Channel at age 67.

or become active for the first time. Suppose you want to do weight training, for instance. In a study at Tufts University, researchers taught a group of out-of-shape volunteers the basics of weight training and saw impressive results. For eight weeks, the volunteers followed a high-intensity, resistance-training regimen. By the end of the program, some had achieved three- and fourfold increases in strength. Not bad, considering that they were all in their nineties.

Taking on the challenge of learning a new sport offers another set of dividends. Exercising is more interesting when you have more than one activity to choose from. The athletic skills you hone in one pursuit can improve your performance in another. And if you get injured, a second, third, or fourth sport can keep you off the bench.

If you're the competitive type, there is a good chance that you need the challenge of beating the elements or scoring over an opponent to keep those youthful feelings. To give yourself a winning edge—and a fresh set of challenges—consider adventure sports like whitewater rafting, mountain biking, kayaking, and skiing, suggests Mike Logsdon, director of Adventuresports at the Adventuresports Institute at Garett Community College in McHenry, Maryland.

Adventure sports pit you against some wily force of nature— the force of a current, the pull of gravity on a slippery ski slope. Take kayaking, for instance. "If you're paddling down a river, you have to figure out how to use the force of the river to help you maneuver. This is what the best paddlers do," Logsdon says. Whether or not you can challenge top kayakers, you'll meet plenty of challenge every time you descend a new river or shoot a different set of rapids.

"There's always a challenge, no matter your sport or your level," says Tracy Grilli, a swimmer and executive secretary of U.S. Masters Swimming. "If you're just learning to swim, your goal is to swim a length without stopping. Once you can do that, you aim for two, then three, then four lengths. When you have built up your endurance, then you want to see how fast you can swim. And once you're past that point, you start fine-tuning your stroke. Proper technique is important and should be worked on

202

continuously for two reasons: so that you become more efficient in the water and so that you don't repeat bad swimming habits."

Makeover Minutes

To Start Up in Sports

You probably already know that you should check with your doctor before starting a new sport or exercise program. "You can learn new sports at almost any age as long as there aren't any medical complications," advises Michael Kaplan, M.D., Ph.D., medical director of the Rehabilitation Team in Catonsville, Maryland. Beyond getting a checkup, there's some additional advice to keep in mind.

When you first start a new sport, take it slow, Dr. Kaplan says. "That's the best way to avoid overdoing it and getting hurt." Going slow will also help you avoid frustration and burnout. Starting a new sport correctly will increase your chance of staying with that sport, he notes.

Keeping caution in mind, here are three things that you can do immediately to start stretching your exercise routine. Just make a phone call or two, and you'll soon be on your way.

Get the info. Fortunately, there are programs that cater to athletes of every age and ability. Call your local parks and recreation department, university sports program, chamber of commerce, or local YMCA for the U.S.A. Masters Track and Field Committee in your area, or write to their national office at 1 RCA Dome, Suite 140, Indianapolis, IN 46225, suggests Barbara Kousky, chairman of the U.S.A. Masters Track and Field Committee. To reach the U.S. National Senior Sports Organization, which organizes the senior Olympics and state and local Senior Games, write the organization at 1307 Washington Avenue, Suite 706, St. Louis, MO 63103.

If you are involved in friendly competition, you have a goal—and having a goal makes it more likely that you will continue exercising, Dr. Kaplan says. "Without a goal, people tend

203

to flounder more. They'll say, 'I'm tired today' or 'The weather's bad,'" he adds.

Find a tutor. If you're interested in taking up weight lifting or an adventure sport, it's a good idea to get some instruction. That way, you'll learn to do it right, avoid injury, and see better results, Logsdon says.

If you're interested in an adventure sport, contact a professional instructors association, like the Professional Ski Instructors of America, suggests Logsdon. You can find these groups in the *Encyclopedia of Associations*, which is located in the reference section of your library.

Explore the gym. Most gyms have instructors on staff who can teach you the basics of weight lifting, swimming, and other sports that the gym is equipped for. They are a good place to go to work out or play when the weather's rotten. Before you join a gym, tour it and make sure that you are comfortable there.

Go for the Limits

There's always the chance that your adventure will turn into a misadventure. Your first time on the dance floor, you may step sideways when you should be stepping back. Your plan to hike Mount Monument may turn into a soggy slog if the day turns out to be mucky. Let's face it: Challenges and chance are closely related.

"When you try something new, you have to be willing to fail," says Dean Keith Simonton, Ph.D., professor of psychology at the University of California, Davis. "I decided in my late forties to start learning languages again, and it's very frustrating. When you start learning a new language, you say things incorrectly; people who know the language are in stitches when you talk."

Fortunately, most of us are fairly adept at measuring risk by midlife, says Dr. Maddi. When in doubt, ask yourself, "What's the worst that can happen, and is that something I'm willing to tolerate?" he suggests. "If you're going downhill skiing for the first time at age 75, the worst can be substantial."

204

Burning Rubber: Better with Age

It may come as a surprise to you that some skills are much improved with age. Take race car driving, for instance.

While the racetrack is probably the last place you would expect 50-plus types to outpace younger ones, they often do. At more than 20 road-racing circuits across the country, including Lime Rock Park racetrack in Lakeville, Connecticut, low-slung Skip Barber formula cars are piloted at speeds of more than 125 miles an hour by older men—and women—who often finish the nonstop 30-minute races in first place.

"Guys in their forties, fifties, and early sixties often outperform the 18-year-olds because they're generally more disciplined about driving a race car," says Rick Roso, public relations manager for the Skip Barber Racing School, headquartered near Lime Rock Park. "It's not just experience, although that counts for a lot. Counter to common belief, being a good racing driver is not about bravery; it is about analytical thinking, anticipation, and a disciplined work ethic. Think about it. Where are you more likely to find those attributes? In an impatient, 'immortal' teenager, or a successful 47-year-old businessman who has been around the block? You have to want to get better, to make yourself improve your braking and cornering techniques every time you get in the car. Mature people do that."

Sometimes it's easy to calculate the risks of a challenging, new undertaking. Do some homework. Read up on whitewater rafting; find out when it's safe to try your paddles on a Class III river. "Check with other people," says Dr. Simon, who wisely sought the advice of experienced cyclists before taking his first motorcycling trip through Europe at age 50.

And be realistic about your tolerance level. While a public-speaking class may push the limits of your willingness to take risk, your neighbor might take to it like a filibustering politician. Why the difference?

Upbringing seems to play a major role, says Dr. Simon. If your parents taught you that tree climbing invariably leads to broken necks and that even the friendliest-looking dog is secretly rabid, you are probably less inclined to take risks than the next guy.

205

And there's absolutely nothing wrong with that. The idea isn't to risk everything, says Dr. Lawton. "You just need to go a bit further than is totally comfortable," he says.

Practice Risk

With practice, risk taking can get easier. In a now-classic study, Stanford University psychology professor Albert Bandura, Ph.D., and colleagues recruited seven men and 26 women who were terrified of snakes. The researchers divided the volunteers into three groups. Those in the first group watched a therapist handle a boa constrictor, then handled the snake themselves. The second group merely watched the therapist with the snake. And people in the third group did nothing whatsoever to confront their fear of snakes.

The researchers found that the folks who watched and handled the snake—those who confronted their fear and took a risk—made the most significant gains. More important, after the experiment these brave souls were far more confident about their ability to cope with other risky situations as well.

Once you have determined to try something, find people who will support you in your efforts—with information, experience, or just the encouragement of moral support. And avoid the naysayers, Dr. Simon advises. They believe that they have your best interest in mind, but only you can tell them what's really in your best interest. "Tell them, 'I can see why you might not want to do that, but for my own well-being and esteem, I have to,'" he recommends.

Seek Smarts

Eunice Wardwell retired from her job as a biology teacher and went right back to school—this time as a student. Since she retired, Wardwell has taken a dozen or so courses, often trekking far from her home base in Seattle. She has studied ecology on canoe trips through the Adirondacks and on Utah's Green River, learned about geology while trekking the Grand Canyon, acquainted herself with glaciers while dogsledding and cross-coun-

206

try skiing in Alaska. "I've learned a lot, met interesting people, and had wonderful adventures," says Wardwell, who has discovered her own fountain of youth in travel and education.

Intellectual adventures are particularly rewarding when you share them with other people, says Dr. Neuringer. "When you read a poem, you interpret it the way you're used to interpreting poetry," he explains. "But others interpret it differently. Hearing their views can be eye-opening."

Next time you hear about adult-education classes—usually advertised in the local newspaper—take a closer look. Unlike traditional day classes, adult-education classes are designed with busy adults in mind. Many colleges and universities welcome older students by providing flexible schedules, part-time programs, and night and weekend classes. Some schools don't wait for you to come to them. They offer their classes off campus, at satellite sites like high schools or senior centers.

"I teach students ranging in age from 18 to 70," says Dr. Abramis. "And the older students are so much better. Why? Because they know more, they know how to learn, and they know why they're here."

"Nontraditional students now fill one in four seats," says Drew Allbritten, Ed.D., executive director of the American Association for Adult and Continuing Education in Washington, D.C.

Adventures in the Arts

If Bea Wattenberg hadn't risen to the challenge and danced with a folding chair, she might never have become a professional dancer or toured the country with the Liz Lerman Dance Exchange, an intergenerational dance troupe.

But she did. And this is how it happened: Thinking that a local dance troupe called Dancers of the Third Age was an amateur ballroom dance group, Wattenberg went to the troupe's open house, planning to spend the day cha-chaing and fox-trotting. Instead of a partner, though, troupe members gave her a folding chair and asked her to improvise. She improvised so well that Third Age's founder offered her a job shortly after with the touring troupe, the Liz Lerman Dance Exchange.

know what?

In 1995, nearly half of all adults between the ages of 25 and 54 took an adult education class or course.

The ABCs of Ambitious Cooking

At La Cucina al Focolare in a small town outside Florence, Italy, you can study traditional Tuscan cooking. At the Oriental Food Market and Cooking School in Chicago, you can learn to cook Chinese. At Manhattan's New School, you can sign up for a culinary arts course where you'll learn everything you could possibly need to know about chocolate desserts.

And this is only a small sampling of the cooking classes that are available throughout the United States and abroad. In fact, there are more than 600 cooking schools, vocational schools, community colleges, and cookshops offering cooking classes worldwide.

Many cooking schools, trade schools and community colleges offer both long and short courses for professional, would-be professional, and amateur cooks. Amateur courses are both culinary and social affairs—you get together with a group of people with a shared interest in food and pass the time cooking, talking, and eating.

Programs that run more than a day or so often combine classes with travel.

At La Cucina al Focolare, for instance, a weeklong course includes five half-day cooking classes (one for each of the courses in a traditional Tuscan meal); wine tastings with expert sommeliers; a visit with an opera-singing bread baker; tours of wineries, outdoor markets, cheese makers, an herb farm, and medieval villages; and expeditions to nearby San Gimignano, Florence, and Sienna.

"We try to let people step into the lifestyle, to experience what it's like to live, eat, and cook in Tuscany for a week," explains Peggy Markel, La Cucina's director.

For information about schools like La Cucina, check your library for *The Guide to Cooking Schools*. The directory includes information on course location, difficulty, focus, length, and cost. (If you can't find the book at the library, ask your librarian to order it through interlibrary loan.

"If I could do it, anyone can," says Wattenberg, who lives in Washington, D.C., and had no dance training before she began her professional career at age 62.

In our culture, we tend to believe that only certain people can dance, paint, sing, or write poetry, says Dr. Simonton. We also tend to believe that even those lucky and creative few see their creativity wane as they get older. But neither is true.

"One of the great myths in our country is that creativity is something special, that only some people have it," he says. In places like Bali, by contrast, everyone's assumed to have artistic abilities.

Research suggests that everyone, to one degree or another, does. "Studies show that the main difference between people with talent and those without is that those *with* have spent time developing that talent," Dr. Simonton says.

Studies also show that creativity doesn't wane as time goes by. In fact, many people get more creative as they grow older. The Greek playwright Sophocles wrote *Oedipus Rex* at 70 and dashed out *Electra* when he was somewhat more mature—at age 90. Opera composer Giuseppe Verdi composed *Otello* at 72. The revered German poet Johann von Goethe finished his great epic *Faust* when he was 82.

"There are a lot of people out there who have a lot of creativity that they're not utilizing at all," Dr. Simonton says. That's regrettable because research finds that people who express their creativity in one way or another find greater satisfaction and meaning in life than those who never explore it. And the extra charge of creative energy is a prime age protector.

Of course, there are all sorts of venues for expressing creativity, not just the creative arts. You can put creative problem-solving to work to resolve problems in relationships or at contentious meetings of the city council. But there's something special to be gained from expressing your creativity in poetry, dance, painting, music, and theater, says Sylvia Riggs Liroff, coordinator of the National Center on Arts and the Aging.

"I think that painting or making a pot offers a kind of satisfaction that's hard to put into words," Liroff says. "When you're doing something like this that's so creative and deeply absorbing, that's when you're most fully alive. You're participating in our culture; you're not isolated. And by making a work of art— whether it's carving decoys or doing fabric arts—you're making something that not only expresses but transcends yourself. You're making something that can stand on its own after you're gone, perhaps a legacy to your own children or someone you've never met."

For Launching Your Art

Here's how to get started, whether you want to write some verses, play the tuba, or sculpt in clay.

Play with poetry. Anyone who can wield a pencil or plink on a word processor can write a poem. Check your daily newspaper, and you're sure to find out about creative-writing classes or poetry-writing workshops.

Call the teach. Charlie "Yardbird" Parker may have taught himself the sax, but most of us could do with a little instruction at the beginning—whether we want to study music, painting, or drama. But how do you get an instructor you'll like?

Talk to prospective teachers before signing up, suggests Angela Franklin, a visual artist and art teacher in Baltimore. "Find out their philosophies of teaching," Franklin says. "If they're teaching because their objective is to train professional artists who go on to grad school, maybe that's not your class. If they're teaching because they think art is a basic human experience everyone should have, that's probably a better fit."

Long-Term Tactics
For Creativity

Once you have tiptoed into the waters of creativity, you might find yourself wondering whether or not to stick with it. After all, it isn't always easy—and sometimes you may need to take risks. Here are three reminders to help you stick with it.

Give yourself time. It takes time to learn to play the French horn or master the art of figure drawing. Remember that. "Students will show up for my classes the first day and say, 'I can't draw,'" as if they should know how even before the first class, says Franklin. "I tell them, 'No one shows up for Spanish class the first day and says I can't speak Spanish.' Be patient."

210

Go with the flow. Over time, you may find that you want to shift gears. If you're not happy with your progress, though, don't throw in the towel, Franklin says. Instead, try a different medium. If you're taking art classes, you might try sculpting with clay instead of drawing with pen and ink. If you're exploring music, maybe you would rather play clarinet instead of violin. Different arts require different abilities, Franklin points out, but you need to be open to change.

Show off. You can learn a lot by showing your work to other people, says Franklin, who suggests that you participate in group critiques that are part of most art classes. Constructive criticism can help you identify and shore up weaknesses. By the same token, take advantage of opportunities to read your work aloud in writing classes and perform at music and dance recitals.

Your Ticket to Travel

After 50 years on solid ground, Catherine and Tom Pacheco traded their home for a 37 foot sailboat and set sail for nowhere in particular.

Newly retired, the couple spent almost a decade traveling where whim and wind carried them. The scenery, the weather, the cuisine, and the official language at port side, changed constantly. There were many moments of bliss—anchoring on sun-dappled Caribbean waters, sipping daiquiris, and eating conch. And just as many moments of challenge and danger when they rode out the night on storm-tossed seas.

The challenge of adjusting to whatever came along was rejuvenating, says Catherine Pacheco, author of *Breaking Patterns*, a book about her experiences on ship and the value of challenge seeking in midlife and beyond. "It keeps you younger and healthier," she says.

Travel can be truly revitalizing, largely because it forces you to be more flexible, says Charles Garfield, Ph.D., clinical professor of psychology at the University of California School of Medicine, San Francisco, and author of *Peak Performers*. When you're not on your own turf, you have to be more accommo-

211

dating. That's often easier on the road than it might be back home. When everything around you is different, it's easier to break out of old patterns.

"When you travel, the change of context allows you to re-think assumptions about what's possible and what's not," Dr. Garfield notes.

Makeover Minutes

Launch Your Wanderings

Travel adventure is easily combined with all sorts of other adventures—incorporating food, education, sports—depending on your interest. There are planned adventure-travel trips for almost every pursuit, from skiing and cycling to sailing and diving.

"There's no age barrier," says Jerry Mallett, president of the Adventure Travel Society in Englewood, Colorado. Let your interests guide you, not your perceived limits. "A woman in her seventies or eighties might be able to do a lot of trekking in Nepal. I know of a woman who, at 51, hand-pulled a sled weighing 129 pounds for 29 days to the Arctic Circle."

While adventures like those are certainly ambitious, often a single conversation or glimpse of a travel brochure can get you started. Here are four things that you can do to get in the mood for moving.

Start at the library. To find places that are off the beaten path, read up on the city, region, or country you plan to visit. A good guidebook will tell you about climate, costs, don't-miss attractions, and getting around on your own. Libraries may also have travel essays on your chosen destination.

You can write to travel bureaus for additional information, suggests Catherine Pacheco. And if you're planning to travel abroad, she says, it's also a good idea to learn a bit of the language and try the cuisine before you leave.

Call for adventure-travel combos. If your feet are itching for

212

Adventures in Good Reading

Turning the pages of Bram Stoker's classic novel, *Dracula*, you might well wonder, "What would Freud say about all this?" Well, if you belong to a book club, you can talk about it at your next meeting.

"People join book clubs for different reasons," says Ellen Slezak, editor of *The Book Group Book*, a collection of essays singing the praises of book clubs. "Some people join because they want to be motivated to read more or to read books they wouldn't try on their own. Others read plenty on their own but want to talk about what they have read with other people who have read the same thing."

Since book groups are enjoying a surge in popularity, there are many to choose from. Some read only the classics, while others go for new literary works or bestsellers. Most groups meet once a month or so at members' homes, libraries, restaurants, bookstores, or the cafeteria at work.

There's a good chance that a bookstore near you is sponsoring a book group, Slezak says. Many libraries do the same. And most have open-door policies. Just read the book and show up—and you can drop out any time you like. "You haven't made a commitment to someone whose living room you're sitting in," Slezak says.

While armchair adventures aren't quite like the real thing, your imagination is a powerful tool—and with the stimulus of fresh reading, you can travel far.

the Inca trail or some other adventure-travel destination, simply pick up your phone and call a travel agent for the names of tours that leave from cities near you, Mallet says. Or you can sign onto the Internet and type the key words "adventure" and "travel" for more options.

When discussing a trip with a tour operator, be sure to specify how much daily walking you want to do, whether you want to backpack or climb, and whether you want to camp out or spend nights in hotels, Mallett says. Tours should be able to take care of special dietary needs. If you want to make your own itinerary for adventure traveling, he suggests you consult the "Lonely Planet" tour guidebooks, your best bet for solo adventure traveling.

Keep your passport up-to-date. Seems like a minor detail—

but having your passport up-to-date is a reminder that you can travel abroad anytime you want to. It's a sign of your freedom to get up and go. Passports are good for 10 years. When they expire, you can usually renew them at the city or town hall or at the post office.

Negotiate with intransigent partners. What if your partner, like Bulgarian wine, doesn't travel well? "I suggest you negotiate," says Dr. Simon. Offer to stay home for the next vacation if he agrees to go traveling this time around. If that doesn't work, set off on a solo expedition, he says.

214

Work Smart to Stay Young

A job is just a job. You go to it, do it, come home. But work you love, even crave, is different. When you feel that you would *choose* to do what you do rather than any other job in the world, a passion seeps deep into your soul and becomes a vital part of your being, says Maynard Brusman, Ph.D., a psychologist and president of Working Resources, a personal and organizational development firm in San Francisco.

You can hear it in the voice of a waitress who once told oral historian Studs Terkel, "I'd get intoxicated with giving service...to be a waitress, it's an art. I feel like a ballerina..."

You can imagine it in the New York bus driver recalled by business consultant Ann McGee-Cooper, Ed.D. "When people got on his bus, he always had something cheerful to say to them. By the time they got off, they were in a totally different frame of mind." It was the driver's attitude that made the difference. "He had decided long ago that being a bus driver wasn't much," Dr. McGee-Cooper says, "but he could change people's lives. So he made it his job to leave people feeling better than when they got on his bus."

You can sense it in the measured tones of 87-year-old Milt Hinton, a jazz legend who has been playing bass for most of his life. "Jazz has always been my life," Hinton says. "I can't think of anything else I would want to do. I've never considered it a job. I'd do it even if I didn't make a dime at it. I feel like the happiest person in the world. I'm almost certain my passion for what I do is keeping me alive."

215

America's Best Listener Won't Quit

After nearly six decades of searching for his niche, Studs Terkel is still fully engaged in a work in progress.

"Work is as essential to life as love," says Terkel, famed author of oral histories including *Working* and *Coming of Age*. "I have no doubt in my mind that without work I probably wouldn't be alive today."

In his late eighties, Terkel continues to host a daily radio talk show in Chicago and compile interviews for his books chronicling how Americans feel about war, poverty, work, and aging. "I've had a lot of jobs, but I finally found what was right for me," he says. "I look forward to it every day."

But getting to that point wasn't easy. New York–born Terkel spent his childhood in a working-class neighborhood in Chicago, where his mother ran a rooming house. His first career ambition was to be a lawyer.

Though Terkel went to law school at the University of Chicago and even passed the bar exam, he found that he was unhappy in his first profession. "I thought I'd be Clarence Darrow, attorney for the underdog," Terkel told gerontologist Lydia Brontë, Ph.D., in 1992. "And I get to law school, and I get things like 'Contracts' and 'Real Property.' It drove me out of my mind."

Next, he went to Washington, determined to become a civil servant. He got a job at the Treasury Department stuffing envelopes with bonus coupons for World War I veterans. According to Terkel, it drove him nuts. He had to get out.

Back in Chicago once again, Terkel changed tactics. Instead of planning his career, he decided to take whatever job he could find and see how it worked out. He drifted into acting, and it turned out his gravely voice was perfect for gangster roles on radio soap operas like *The Guiding Light*. He also tried his hand as a disc jockey, sportscaster, and finally, commentator—but in that role, his blunt opinions worked against him during the McCarthy era. He was blacklisted in the early 1950s and had trouble finding work. Eventually, he was hired by WFMT to host a radio talk show. More than 45 years later, he's still doing it.

"I couldn't conceive of retiring from what I'm doing. Others dream of it, but I don't," Terkel says. "This is my job, this is my work, this is my life."

Even if you think of your work as just "an office job" or "being a homemaker," you can have as much passion as this waitress, bus driver, or musician. And that's important—because researchers are discovering that having a passion for work can strengthen the immune system, fend off heart attacks, and, yes, possibly even slow down the aging process.

"Passion for work keeps you excited about what you are doing, and being excited about work helps keep you feeling vibrant," says Mildred Culp, Ph.D., a Seattle workplace consultant and syndicated columnist. "As most people get older, they have to fight getting stale on the job. If they don't, the child within them may disappear. But if you create something in your work that causes passion, then you will always be alive."

The Fuel of Enthusiasm

Whatever you call it—bliss, satisfaction, passion—enthusiasm for what you do is essential if you want to feel younger and more fully alive, says Richard Bolles, author of *What Color Is Your Parachute?*

"Enthusiasm for work fuels the psyche and the spirit," Bolles says. "It is the feeling that you're eager to wake up in the morning and greet the day. It is the foundation for defining your purpose in life. Many people who retire die prematurely because they have no worthwhile definition of why they are still here on Earth."

A few decades ago, many doctors might have considered this concept far-fetched. But as researchers compile more and more supportive evidence, it's becoming clear that a passion for work can have a powerful impact on mental and physical health, says Larry Dossey, M.D., author of *Healing Words*.

Such observations are borne out by the supportive evidence of Lawrence LeShan, Ph.D., a psychologist in private practice in New York City. Learning that many of his cancer patients were deeply unhappy in their work, Dr. LeShan counseled them individually to help them find out what type of work they really wanted to do. Combining this search with ongoing therapy, Dr. LeShan was able to achieve a 50 percent long-term remission rate in people with terminal cancer, says Lydia Brontë, Ph.D., gerontologist and author of *The Longevity Factor*. "LeShan's research indicates that doing work that you love is not just good for your day-to-day happiness, it is good for your health," Dr.

know what?

Average number of hours a year worked by an adult peasant in thirteenth-century England: 1,620. Average number of hours worked a year by a typical American worker in 1850: 3,650. Average number of hours worked each year by a typical American worker in the late twentieth century: 1,949.

217

Brontë reports. "The message is clear: If you don't like what you're doing now, don't just sit there. Get busy and find something you like better."

Enjoying your work also may fend off heart disease, Dr. Dossey says. A few years ago, researchers began noticing that people were more apt to have heart attacks at about 9:00 A.M. on a Monday than any other time of the week. Surprisingly, the top risk factor for this problem—called Black Monday syndrome—wasn't smoking, high blood pressure, elevated cholesterol, or other physical woes. It was job dissatisfaction.

"Your attitude toward your work is critical. If you hate your job, you're going to be at much greater risk for Black Monday syndrome," Dr. Dossey says. "It's a huge predictor of heart disease."

Dodging the Doldrums

Men and women who do hectic, monotonous jobs—the ones most likely to breed discontent—have almost twice the risk of developing heart disease as people who have more control over their work environment, according to researchers at University College London Medical School, who did a five-year study of 10,308 British civil servants, ages 35 to 55. Other researchers have concluded that people who have stressful, inflexible jobs—like waiters and garment workers—are five times more likely to develop lethal symptoms of heart disease than people who have less-stressful jobs, like architects or telephone linemen.

"Jobs that require lots of skill, experience, and judgment, but aren't particularly psychologically stressful, are the fountain-of-youth jobs. They just don't seem to produce as many cases of heart disease," says Robert Karasek, Ph.D., professor of work environment at the University of Massachusetts in Lowell and author of *Healthy Work*.

While it's unclear how job dissatisfaction influences disease, some researchers speculate that a gung-ho attitude on the job triggers the brain to release endorphins, natural body chemicals that boost the immune system, relieve pain, and may help suppress tumor growth.

218

Are You Burning Out?

Job burnout doesn't happen overnight. Apathy, helplessness, chronic fatigue, frustration, boredom, and other symptoms often take months or even years to appear. But when you do get those symptoms, the message is clear: The thrill is gone, and you have to do something.

Recognizing that you have a problem is the first step to recovery, says Dennis Jaffe, Ph.D., an organizational consultant and psychologist in San Francisco.

To find out if you're on a collision course with job burnout, take a couple of moments to answer the following questions developed by Dr. Jaffe and Cynthia Scott, Ph.D., co-authors of *Take This Job and Love It*. Count the number of questions to which you answer yes. That will be your burnout score.

1. Do you feel generally more fatigued and less energetic?
2. Do you feel less of a sense of satisfaction about your job performance?
3. Are you working harder and harder, but accomplishing less and less?
4. Do you feel more cynical and disenchanted with your work and the people at work?
5. Are you getting more irritable, angry, and short-tempered with people around you?
6. Are you seeing close friends and family members less frequently?
7. Are you having more than your share of physical complaints like body aches, pains, headaches, colds, or the flu?
8. Do you feel that you just don't have anything more to give to people?

If you answered yes to more than five of these questions, you are in the early stages of job burnout, and you'll want to use Makeover Minutes and Long-Term Tactics to start climbing out of the rut. More than two yes answers indicates that you should watch yourself—you may be starting the burnout process, advises Dr. Jaffe.

A passion for your work may also focus your concentration, helping you to lose track of time and feel less stressed, says Stephan Rechtschaffen, M.D., founder of the Omega Institute for Holistic Studies in Rhinebeck, New York. Excessive stress triggers your body to produce cortisol and adrenaline, a pair of hormones that in combination can constrict the blood vessels,

219

raise blood pressure, and place additional strain on the heart, according to Dr. Rechtschaffen.

Humming Instead of Humdrum

Even if you're positive that work enjoyment is a terrific age protector, how do you inject zest into work that's gotten humdrum? The truth is that no matter whether you wake up enthusiastic about your workday or with feelings of dread, there are plenty of ways that you can help cultivate and sustain more passion for your career, Dr. Brusman says. According to the experts, here are some of the best ways to quickly revive your working zeal.

Inquire within. Take a few moments to think about your life, suggests Tom Welch, a career counselor in Stuart, Florida, and author of *Work Happy, Live Healthy*. Then write a mission statement that summarizes what you think your purpose is in life, what you want to achieve in your career, and what skills you enjoy using on the job. Also, write some phrases describing what you take pride in and who benefits from what you do.

Carry the statement with you and read it every day, Welch says. That will help you focus on the parts of the job that are meaningful to you beyond the paycheck. "What you think about, you become," he says. "So if you continuously think about that mission statement, you're much more likely to rediscover your passion."

Update this statement every four to six months, Welch suggests.

Fill in the blanks. When someone is absent from work, ask your boss if you can cover that person's area of responsibility for the day, suggests John Sena, Ph.D., chief operating officer of Healthcare Research Systems in Columbus, Ohio, and author of *Work Is Not a Four-Letter Word*. Spending time doing another person's job may be the perfect antidote for boredom or complacency.

Color outside the lines. Volunteer to take on new tasks or extra assignments that will help you learn and grow, suggests Dr. Sena. Be on the lookout for problems on your job that aren't being addressed and suggest ways to solve them. Reaching beyond your grasp for new challenges provides excitement, interest, and even passion in a job, Dr. Sena has observed.

Dump the drudgery. Take a few minutes each week to review your upcoming schedule. If it's clogged with tedious meetings, phone calls, and paperwork, figure out what you can delegate to others, then delegate. Ridding yourself of monotonous tasks can reinvigorate your interest in your work, Dr. Sena says.

Dive into the office pool. If you can't delegate mundane tasks like stuffing envelopes, try to arrange your schedule so that you can do these kinds of tasks with co-workers, Dr. Sena suggests. If you're working with others even on routine tasks, time passes more quickly, and the task may seem more enjoyable.

Shuffle the deck. At least once a month, experiment with change, says Dr. Sena. If possible, work at home or in a different part of your office for a few hours. When you drive to work, try out some new routes. Rearrange your desk every once in a while. Change the order in which you do your job. Finding fresh and innovative ways to work will help keep you motivated.

See how the other half lives. Offer to serve on committees or projects involving people from other departments, Dr. Sena suggests. Arrange brown-bag lunches in which colleagues from various parts of the company can discuss their common concerns. Not only will you get to know more people, you may develop a deeper appreciation for the importance of what you do.

Take a knowing look. Knowledge is power. Devote at least 30 minutes a day to reading magazines, professional journals, books, and other work-related materials that will help keep you on the cutting edge of your industry. The more you know, the more you'll be valued on the job, Dr. Sena says. And that can boost your passion for doing it well.

Let the good times roll. Feed on a constant diet of work, and you're sure to starve passion. So have some fun, Dr. Sena says.

know what?

Number of paid vacation days an average U.S. worker received in 1987: 12.17. Number of vacation days in 1997: 11.37. Average number of days an employee needed to work to earn one vacation day in 1987: 22.4. In 1997: 23.9.

221

Write Your Own Happy Ending

Each day, let go of bad memories, hold on to the good, and your passion for work will be rejuvenated, says Richard Bolles, author of *What Color Is Your Parachute?*

"Our memory tends to concentrate on the things we didn't like in a day— a way of the self saying to the self, 'avoid these things at all cost in the future.' This habit focuses us in the wrong direction," Bolles says. But with a little practice, you can train yourself to focus on life's shining moments instead.

How do you do it? Bolles suggests a visualization technique developed by Jack Schwarz, founder and president of the Aletheia Psycho-Physical Institute in Mendocino, California, and author of more than seven books on mind/spirit/body healing. "I think it is a brilliant technique for changing memory," says Bolles.

Just before you go to bed, sit in a quiet room facing a blank wall. In your mind's eye, project all the day's activities and thoughts onto an imaginary movie screen. (Most people find it easier to do this exercise if they close their eyes.) Begin with your first waking moment and let your day roll by on the screen.

When you observe an event and judge it to be negative, stop the film. Look at this frozen moment in time. Study this single image and make an effort to see its positive side. Remember that every time a problem is born, its solution is created, too, Schwarz writes in *Voluntary Controls: Exercises for Creative Meditation*. See the solution to the problem on the screen. Try to move beyond your initial judgment of it and embrace an understanding of both its positive and negative aspects. Weed out guilt you have implanted in yourself as a result of your self-condemnation. Acknowledge what you have learned from this situation and your reaction to it, and forgive yourself. Then roll the film again and complete the picture of the day. Viewing this movie of your day should take no more than three to five minutes, Schwarz says.

"As you watch this movie, you notice what turned you on and what things you enjoyed the most," Bolles adds. "You also ask yourself, what did I learn today that will be valuable to me in charting my tomorrows? Thus, you are able to change your memory so that it notices what things fill you with passion."

222

Keep a file folder full of cartoons, jokes, and other humorous material. Take a few moments each day to flip through that material and find something that makes you laugh. Develop hobbies like acting or skiing that can give you a different sense of excitement and accomplishment than what you get from work. Without play, it's difficult to recharge your batteries and stay motivated, he observes.

Celebrate discoveries, not deeds. Take a moment at the end of each workday to reflect on at least one new thing you learned, suggests Bolles. "If you are measuring your success by accomplishments, like writing 15 business letters that day, that isn't going to be very satisfying. But if you measure it by the fact that you learned something new, played a bit, and used your best skills in a way that you love, then every day will be so much more gratifying."

Get Off the Work-Go-Round

John Henry, according to the classic folk song, could out-work any man on the railroad. So when a machine came along that could do his job, he swore he could outperform steam power any day. In the contest, John Henry did beat the machine, but then he immediately collapsed and died.

While John Henry is the stuff of which legends are made, many of us still believe that if you work faster, harder, and longer than the next person, you will be rewarded. In reality, the ultimate reward for workaholism is physical and mental exhaustion, ruptured friendships, shattered families, and premature aging, says Leonard Felder, Ph.D., a psychologist in Los Angeles and author of *The 10 Challenges*.

Why do so many of us work so hard? Part of the answer is simple: We get rewarded. "You get a lot of encouragement, you get a lot of status, you get a lot of money," Dr. Felder points out. "So working hard serves a whole bunch of needs. But if you keep focusing on just one part of yourself—your work—that self not only gets overused, but the other parts of your personality will be hungry and will scream for attention. So people who are workaholics often get depressed or turn to drugs and alcohol. And if

223

you're in that situation, you can start to feel real old really fast."

You are a workaholic, he says, if:

- You're irritated with people you love because they are asking for more of your time.
- You're unable to stop and be satisfied or enjoy successes because you are too focused on the next project.
- You constantly think about work even when you are trying to relax or are on vacation.
- You notice yourself complaining or bragging that all you do is work, work, work.

Long-Term Tactics
Slaving Less and Enjoying Work More

Breaking the workaholic pattern can be a tough proposition. Whether you're trying to break away or to prevent workaholism in the first place, here are some tactics based on what Dr. Felder calls your rights.

Just say no. You owe it to your employer, peers, family, and yourself to refuse tasks that you can't do well because of competing demands on your time, Dr. Felder says. If possible, negotiate a more flexible working arrangement. Instead of traveling on business, suggest to your boss that you can accomplish the same amount of work by phone conferencing or e-mail. That way, you can spend more time with your family.

Farm it out. People who are workaholics believe that no one can do a task as well as they can, Dr. Felder says. The trick is to let go of perfectionism and trust someone else to do a job for you. You may be surprised by how good the results are. It will also give you time to relax and restore your creativity.

Schedule mellow time. People with workaholism cling to work obligations, but they're willing to sacrifice personal plans, Dr. Felder says. Make your commitments for relaxation and fun, then take those commitments as seriously as work obligations. Avoid canceling vacations, lunches, or exercise.

224

Listen to your body. If you are a workaholic, your body is probably already giving you some good clues that you should slow down. "I always encourage people to find at least one role model who dropped dead because of workaholism. Think about that person every time you're tempted not to listen to your body," Dr. Felder says.

Schedule downtime into your workday. Set aside 15 to 20 minutes a day for a short rest, a relaxing walk, or quiet meditation, Dr. Felder suggests. Make it an appointment you can't break.

Separate home from work. You have to draw a line that can't be crossed, Dr. Felder says. Imagine that you're making love—but you stop as soon as the phone rings to take a business call. Do you want that to happen? Of course not.

Then broaden that image to figure out what you will and won't do. Will you let a client interrupt your meals? Do you want work to interfere with time you spend with your children?

If you make a list of all the times you don't want your private life interrupted, you will soon be able to create a home space. And you'll begin to see yourself as someone who is not just a 24-hour-a-day worker bee, says Dr. Felder.

Don't Dream It, Be It

Sometimes—let's admit it—a job or career gets stale. Once the passion is gone, and there is little hope of getting it back, it's time for a change. Not only can a career change renew your passion for work, it also can boost your energy and give you a refreshing sense of youthful commitment and purpose, Dr. Brusman says.

"Work should be fun and satisfying. You should enjoy what you do, feel turned on and delighted by it," Dr. Sena says. "When you reach the point where you are no longer having fun, when the job becomes deadening, routine, and boring, that's a good sign that you have outgrown the work and should look for a new challenge."

Each year, about 1 in every 10 working people plunge into new careers. Some take courageous leaps, diving into new jobs that require dramatically different expertise. But the vast ma-

225

jority who change pursuits do it gradually rather than suddenly, according to Bolles.

They are like the Englishman who discovered it was illegal for him to tear down his house and build a new one. Rather than defy the law, he "repaired" his home by replacing it one floor at a time.

According to Bolles, building a new career is often more like the floor-by-floor reconstruction rather than wholesale demolition and rebuilding. It isn't a leap, observes Bolles. "You just change one part of your life at a time until, one day, you can look back and say, 'Oh, my goodness, I'm in a new career.'"

Often, it isn't necessary to make a complete career change. Welch, for example, recalls a dentist who hated his work but felt trapped because he had a mortgage and many other financial obligations. After discussing his interests with Welch, the dentist discovered he had a passion for public speaking. So he joined an amateur speaking club until he became proficient enough to become a professional speaker.

"Eventually, he was able to shut down about a third of his dental practice and make up the income with public speaking," Welch says. "He got so excited about this new part of his life that dentistry, the other two-thirds of his work, didn't seem nearly as dreary anymore. Making a small change like that really enhanced his life. So you don't have to jump overboard to make a positive change. You can make compromises."

Long-Term Tactics

To Manage a Job Move

Whether you're eager to make a clean break from your past or you simply want to modify the career you have established, planning, patience, and persistence are essential. Here's what the experts recommend to help you make that turnaround.

Look before you take a leap. Some career changes will require months or even years of effort, Dr. Brusman says. So

226

don't be in a rush. Seriously consider the rewards and draw-backs to each new career option before diving in. Otherwise, you could be tempted to make an impulsive decision that you might regret.

Go solo. Arrange one or two getaway weekends by yourself so that you can contemplate your future without the pressures and distractions of family and friends, Dr. Brusman advises. Choose a location within two hours' driving time of your home. That makes it far enough away that you won't be disturbed, yet not so far that you'll be stressed-out from traveling. Avoid sightseeing and other recreational activities. Instead, use the time to read, write, and take reflective walks that will help you reevaluate your skills and focus on what you really want to do.

Assess your assets. The best clues to your next career are often found in your past, Bolles says. Take a look at your ac-complishments in both your personal life and your professional life. Then ask yourself the following questions:

- Which tasks energized you? Which ones exhausted you?
- What skills, talents, and abilities did you use in doing those tasks that energized you?
- Which ones did you enjoy using the most? Why?
- What have been your hobbies? Do you wish to transform any of these into a career?
- What problem in the world would you most like to eradicate or help fix? How could you use your favorite skills to do that?

In short, Bolles concludes, you can help yourself make the career change by deciding what turns you on and what you want out of life.

Assign the time. According to Bolles, you shouldn't worry if it takes you several weeks to figure out your answers. Pick one night a week, then spend one or two hours considering answers to the questions you're asking yourself. When you're done, try to summarize your career goal in a one-sentence statement. For example, you might conclude, "I want a position as _____ in a leading organization in which my passion, knowledge, and ex-perience in _____ can be fully utilized." Carry that statement with you and read it at least once a day, advises Bolles.

know what?

Need job ideas? When Oprah Winfrey featured "the best jobs in the world" on her show, guests included: a party-going champagne promoter, a taster for Godiva chocolates, a cosmetic de-veloper who dreams up new names for lipsticks, a consumer spy who stays at luxury hotels, a professor who selects the top 10 beaches in the world, and a designer of futuristic cars.

227

Finding a Calling

It can be a tough call—trying to figure out the job that's just right for you. And you probably know some people who have made a career change in midlife or later.

Here's a sampling of some celebrities' pasts. Who would have guessed that:

- Bandleader Desi Arnaz once was a birdcage cleaner.
- Former president Gerald Ford earned a few bucks as a male model.
- Comedian Bob Hope was a boxer before he entered show-biz.
- Marilyn Monroe was a factory worker.
- Character actor Boris Karloff sold real estate.
- Singer Madonna punched the clock at a Dunkin' Donuts in Times Square.
- *Top Gun* star Tom Cruise studied for a year in a Franciscan monastery.

Look for your reflection. Another good way to narrow your career choices is to think to yourself, "Whose job would I most like to have in all of the world?" Bolles suggests.

Look at everyone you know, everyone you have read about or have seen on television. Whose life would you like to mirror? Make a first, second, and third choice. Then do the following.

1. On three separate sheets of paper, jot down what each of these people does.
2. On each paper, break down their jobs into parts. What is it about the job that attracts you? List as many things as possible.
3. Review all three sheets of paper and choose the job that is of greatest interest to you.

With that goal clearly in mind, you can now try to figure out how you could get such a job.

Dodge the misery makers. Though it may sound contradictory, you can also motivate yourself by listing all the reasons that you're disenchanted with your present job or career and why a change will make you happier. Carry the list with you. Whenever fear or procrastination bogs you down, look at the reasons that

228

you are unhappy, and it will keep you moving in the right direction, Welch says.

Get a reality check. Talk to as many people as you can who are in the profession you are interested in, Bolles suggests. What do they like and dislike about the work? What kind of special training do you need to do this work? Ask if you can spend a day following someone who actually does the job. This all-day visit is critical, he says, because many jobs that look exciting are actually less so when you get an opportunity to see what really is required.

Go for a test drive. Once you have talked to others and seen the job done, ask if you can try it out yourself. Start small. If you're interested in boat repair, for instance, offer to do a minor repair job for free, Dr. Brusman says. Doing a small job well will build your confidence, inspire you to do more, and impress a potential employer.

Plan an alternative route. Have a written backup strategy laid out before you start your new career, Bolles suggests. That way, if your original idea doesn't work out, you'll save valuable time because you'll know exactly what you'll be doing next.

Manage
Your Time

Before there were hours, minutes, or seconds, time literally flew. In fact, for most of human existence, migrating birds were one of the only reliable measures of time. Their departure just as the leaves began turning meant the beginning of the long descent into winter. Their return in the spring signaled the start of the growing season. For century after century, that's about as accurate as time got.

People lived and worked at a much slower pace than we do now. Craftsmen in the Middle Ages often took several hours off in the middle of the workday to visit friends, do chores, or visit the local tavern. In some European countries, there were as many as 115 holidays a year.

Then in the fourteenth century, the clock arrived, and time became our captor, regulating every aspect of our lives. Suddenly, time was money. Time was fleeting. Time was the enemy. So for nearly 700 years we have been trying to squeeze more out of time.

But now, researchers are discovering that time is probably squeezing more out of us.

"Certainly, an overwhelming sense of time urgency can age you and cause premature death," says Logan Wright, Ph.D., a psychologist and professor emeritus at the University of Oklahoma College of Medicine in Oklahoma City. Time urgency speeds up the digestive tract. It causes the heart to beat faster. It raises blood pressure. It lowers the effectiveness of the immune system so that you are more susceptible to the flu, colds, and other respiratory ailments. It just puts more wear and tear on the whole body.

Are You Feeling the Crunch?

In 1991, the Hilton Hotel Corporation commissioned a national survey of time values. Researchers found that at least one in three Americans feel "time-crunched," meaning they "always feel rushed to get things done." To find out how time pressure is affecting your life, take this quiz used in the Hilton Time Study. If you agree with more than three of the following statements, consider yourself time-crunched.

1. I often feel under stress when I don't have enough time.
2. When I need more time, I tend to cut back on my sleep.
3. At the end of the day, I often feel that I haven't accomplished what I set out to do.
4. I worry that I don't spend enough time with my family or friends.
5. I feel that I'm constantly under stress—trying to accomplish more than I can handle.
6. I feel trapped in a daily routine.
7. When I'm working long hours, I often feel guilty that I'm not at home.
8. I consider myself a workaholic.
9. I just don't have time for fun anymore.
10. Sometimes I feel that my spouse doesn't know who I am anymore.

Where Did the Hours Fly?

No matter how we try to stretch it, there is only so much time. Each week you have 168 hours, 10,080 minutes, or 604,800 seconds to work and play. But more than likely, you spent the better part of your time rushing, dashing, and scurrying. It was not supposed to be this way. In the mid–twentieth century, futurists predicted that computers and other labor-saving devices would free up time and transform America into the most leisurely society in history. But exactly the opposite happened.

As we enter the next millennium, 45 percent of all Americans say that the amount of time available to them in their daily lives is shrinking and that they are putting in more hours at work than did their parents. What went wrong?

We're suffering from an epidemic of speed inflation, says Ralph Keyes, author of *Timelock: How Life Got So Hectic and What You Can Do about It.*

know what?

Percentage of Americans under age 65 surveyed in 1965 who said they always felt rushed: 24. Percentage who always felt rushed in 1992: 38.

"The harder we try to beat time, the more time beats us up," says Keyes. "How many times have you stood in front of your microwave watching the timer count down thinking to yourself, 'Come on, come on, what's taking so long?'

"Just a few years ago, we would have thought, 'Wow, 30 seconds to reheat a muffin, that's amazing.' Now we're standing there going, '25...24...23...come on, cook already.' That's speed inflation. Your tempo accelerates to match the speed of a new convenience, and your expectations go up," he adds.

Of course, you don't have to be a helpless victim of this across-the-board speed-up of living. When it comes to "modern conveniences," you're the boss. But before you decide to accept the new pace or take control over it, you need to look at what's eating up time—and how.

The Hidden Cost of "Saving" Time

Housecleaning is a prime example of the effects of speed inflation. In 1920, an average housewife put in about 51 hours a week keeping her house spotless. Nearly 80 years later, the amount of time devoted to housework has not significantly changed. Despite widespread use of vacuum cleaners, washing machines, dryers, and microwave ovens, women still spend about 49 hours a week cooking and cleaning, according to Juliet Schor, Ph.D., associate professor of economics at Harvard University and author of the *Overworked American: The Unexpected Decline of Leisure.*

In fact, women who own so-called labor-saving devices spend virtually the same amount of time on specific housework chores as those who don't, says John P. Robinson, Ph.D., professor of sociology at the University of Maryland in College Park and director of the Americans' Use of Time Project.

A typical American woman, between ages 18 and 50, spends about 57 minutes a day cooking. Women who have microwaves spend a mere 4 minutes less time on this chore than women who don't own one, Dr. Robinson says. Women with automatic dishwashers spend barely a minute less cleaning up after meals than those who don't have this appliance. As for laundry, those

232

women who have washing machines spend almost twice as much time cleaning dirty clothes than those who don't.

The reason? "I call it the convenience catch," Keyes says. "It's a paradox that once you can do a job more easily with mechanical or electronic help, you tend to do that job more often. When we didn't have washing machines, a person didn't feel as if he had to wash every piece of clothing that had a tiny speck on it. Now, of course, we feel that everything has to be washed constantly to meet our higher standard of cleanliness. So laundry has gone from being a once-a-week chore to being a once-a-day necessity. And that takes up a lot of time that you could be using for more enjoyable things."

Even something as basic as yard work has been affected by speed inflation. Barely a century ago, for instance, most lawns were far more scruffy than they are now. That's because few homeowners were willing to endure hours of backbreaking labor trimming their yards by hand with scythes and sickles. But once power mowers became common, cutting the grass once a week or more became the norm. As a result, the lawn mower has ended up costing far more time than it has saved, Keyes says.

The Info Age in Overload Mode

In the time it takes a person to ask a simple question like "What are you talking about?" two computers can exchange more words than the sum total of all the words exchanged since human beings first appeared on Earth 2 million or 3 million years ago, according to Jeremy Rifkin, author of *Time Wars: The Primary Conflict in Human History.* But instead of freeing us from tedium, the computer's vast ability to store and instantaneously transfer information has actually increased workloads. As of April 1997, for instance, Americans were exchanging an estimated 10 million America Online e-mail messages via computers each day. But the increase in e-mail hasn't been offset by a corresponding decrease in conventional mail volume. From 1992 to 1996, the volume of mail processed by the U.S. Postal Service increased from 166 million pieces to 183 million pieces annually.

know what?
Number of hours of "free" time the average American reports having each week: less than 20. Number of hours the average American reports watching television each week: 21.

233

What the Tortoise Can Teach Us

Nearly 3,000 years before the first traffic jams, assembly lines, and jet lags, Aesop knew that faster wasn't necessarily better. In his fable "The Hare and the Tortoise" this sixth-century B.C. storyteller and slave created a classic confrontation that still teaches a powerful lesson.

"No matter how many times you tell the story, the tortoise always wins. To me, the lesson is clear: When you take your time, you'll actually be more productive, and odds are you'll finish first," says Jacqueline Valdez, a meditation instructor and intuitive counselor in Encinitas, California.

Although it may not seem possible in this frantic era, you can still make like a tortoise and get everything done, Valdez says. Meditation—an intense form of concentration that allows you to focus on the here and now—helps slow down the mind so that tasks become more enjoyable and you feel under less time pressure, she says.

Simple forms of meditation, such as deep breathing, can be done while washing dishes, taking a shower, or waiting in line, Valdez suggests. "When I teach people how to meditate, I tell them that breath and thought are one and the same. If you are anxious, your breathing is anxious. If you're peaceful, then your breathing is peaceful," she says. "So if you can slow your breathing, you can stop your mind from racing."

Not only that, "Taking the time to meditate is a part of productivity," she adds. "It's a part of taking care of the tasks. It's a part of taking care of yourself."

To get some meditation practice, Valdez suggests, start like this: Lift your tongue to the roof of your mouth and gently press it up against your front teeth. Begin to breathe a little more deeply. Each time you inhale, repeat a phrase like, "Cool, calm mind." When you exhale, think, "peaceful, relaxed body." Whenever your mind begins to wander and you start to worry about things like deadlines, schedules, and urgent errands, refocus your attention on your breathing.

Repeat this simple meditation exercise a couple of minutes several times a day, Valdez suggests. It can be done anywhere. You can meditate while you're washing your hair, eating a meal, or getting ready for bed.

"You don't have to think about it as something separate from your daily routine," Valdez observes. "While you're standing in the shower, for instance, use that space to purify the mind, purify the heart, and purify the body all at the same time."

In addition, other forms of instant communication in the computer age like voice mail, fax machines, and cellular phones have made it even harder for you to get away from it all and enjoy some downtime.

"It used to be that you got on an airplane and could relax," Keyes says. "You could say to yourself, 'Nobody can reach me here, and I don't have the tools I need to work anyway, so I'll just sit back and enjoy the trip.' Now you have a phone in the seat back in front of you. You might have a laptop computer or a tape recorder so that you can do work and not 'waste' time while you're on the go. We simply have fewer and fewer sanctuaries from the busy world."

Microtechnology also has all but eradicated simple tasks like winding your watch or changing paper in the typewriter that created natural breaks in the relentless pace of your day, Keyes says.

"We've become a breathless society," Keyes says. "We're always rushing to do something because our so-called timesaving devices don't give us a moment to stop so that we can catch our breath."

How Haste Harms Your Health

A few years ago during a simple test studying commuter stress, two commuters were asked to drive the same section of highway at rush hour. One was told to drive as fast as he could. The other was merely told to keep pace with traffic, recalls Stephan Rechtschaffen, M.D., founder of the Omega Institute for Holistic Studies in Rhinebeck, New York, and author of *Timeshifting: Creating More Time to Enjoy Your Life*. The speeder arrived at the destination five minutes before the slow driver. But while the slow driver arrived relaxed and serene, the speeder was frazzled.

"(The fast driver) had saved five minutes but endured enough stress to take those five minutes, or more, off his life," Dr. Rechtschaffen says. "Clearly, we are paying a very significant price in terms of stress and illness in our lives that are a direct result of living at an extremely rapid pace."

Some doctors believe time, or hurry, sickness—a chronic sense of urgency—may be as prevalent as the common cold and

know what?

Percentage of Americans who feel they devote enough, if not too much, time to their jobs: 85.

what?

Average
amount of
time a typical
visitor to the
National
Zoo in
Washington,
D.C., spends
looking at
an animal
exhibit: 5 to
10 seconds.

as harmful to the body as chronic stress, says Larry Dossey, M.D., an expert on mind/body medicine, who lives in Santa Fe, New Mexico. In fact, feeling time-crunched produces many, if not all, of the symptoms of stress, including increased heart rate and blood pressure elevation, insomnia, anxiety attacks, muscle tension, and lingering anger.

"Our perceptions of speeding clocks and vanishing time cause our own biological clocks to speed," Dr. Dossey writes in his book, *Space, Time, and Medicine.* "The end result is frequently some form of 'hurry sickness.'"

Needless to say, all these time-crunch responses age you faster than the ticking of the biological clock. In fact, some researchers suspect that the body's response to these time crunches can:

▋ Break your heart. Researchers at the Meyer Friedman Institute in San Francisco have found that type A people—time-obsessed, unusually ambitious, and chronically angry people—are up to twice as likely to suffer heart attacks as men and women who are relaxed and less time-driven.

▋ A chronic sense of time urgency elevates production of hormones such as adrenaline that can increase muscle tension and raise blood levels of cholesterol and other artery-clogging substances that contribute to heart disease, according to Dr. Dossey.

▋ Jumble your diet. Living on the run usually means eating on the run, too. And when you are in a rush, you're more apt to reach for sweets, snacks, and fast food like hamburgers, which are loaded with artery-clogging fat and cholesterol.

▋ Weaken your immune system. For some people, living at a hectic pace may be a way of suppressing anger and other negative emotions, Dr. Rechtschaffen says. But the more we repress these negative thoughts, the more impact they have on the immune system, he speculates. If the immune system is weakened, it's easier for bacteria, viruses, and other "invaders" to have their way.

▋ Rattle your joints. Meat cutters, supermarket checkout clerks, and others who do jobs that require rapid, repetitive movements are at greater risk for carpal tunnel syndrome and other

236

types of repetitive motion disorders, says Robert Markison, M.D., a hand surgeon and associate clinical professor of surgery at the University of California, San Francisco, School of Medicine. Time pressures and the incessant nature of assembly line work can provoke muscle tension and reduce blood flow to the hands and wrists, making these parts more vulnerable to injury, he says.

"Doing something repetitively at a fast pace can accelerate aging of the joints. It pushes the warranties on all of our moving parts," Dr. Markison says.

Makeover Minutes

To Find More Time

Although a long, relaxing vacation may seem like the best cure for feeling time-crunched, it is actually only a temporary solution. After all, the time pressures you left behind will probably still be there once you return. In reality, the best solutions are the ones that you can fit into your daily life, Dr. Rechtschaffen says. Here's a look at a few quick but powerful antidotes.

Wrench off your wristwatch. Stop wearing a watch at least one day a week, Keyes suggests. Reduce the number of clocks in your home. Keyes had 23 before he banished most of them. If you must have a clock in your home, get one that has a small dial and place it in an out-of-the-way location so that it is accessible without being obtrusive, he suggests.

Trust your natural rhythms. Once you have eliminated the majority of clocks from your life, do what our prehistoric ancestors did—rely on natural phenomena like shadows, sunrises, or the position of the stars to keep track of your day, Keyes suggests.

"It's actually a lot more fun to tell time that way," Keyes says. "With practice, you can get to be fairly accurate."

Keyes, for instance, has a banana every morning at 11:30. How does he know that? Using a clock, he began eating a banana about that time of day until gradually he didn't need to rely on the clock anymore. "Now when I get hungry, I know it is 11:30 and it's time for my banana," he says.

Take the pause that refreshes. Tape recorders have pause buttons, and so should you, Dr. Rechtschaffen says. When you feel time closing in on you, take a moment to wind down. Whenever the telephone rings, for instance, instead of snatching it off the hook, let it be a reminder to stop and take a deep breath. You'll find yourself slowing down and living more in the present. And when you're living in the here and now, time pressure evaporates, Dr. Rechtschaffen says.

Shift gears. Plan to end your workday with your easiest, least deadline-oriented tasks, suggests Barbara Mackoff, Ed.D., a psychologist in Seattle and author of *The Art of Self-Renewal*. It will help you wind down from a fast-paced day and shed any sense of time urgency before you head for home. Spend the last 30 minutes at the office reading professional magazines, cleaning off your desk, or returning phone calls, she advises.

Take a quick trip. Dr. Mackoff suggests taking a vacation in your imagination. It could be to Tahiti or Mount Rainier or Paris. Wherever it is, close your eyes and picture yourself enjoying the vivid sights, sounds, and sensations of the vista. Even if you only stay in this spot for a couple of minutes, you will feel refreshed and less time-pressured, she says.

Leave your track shoes at the door. Take a few moments when you get home each day to slow down. Simply sit in the car for a few minutes, walk the dog, play with your children, or take a warm shower to wash off the day, Dr. Rechtschaffen suggests. Developing rituals like these will help you shift gears.

Don't surf the channels. Television is probably one of the worst choices for winding down, says Jeff Davidson, executive director of the Breathing Space Institute in Chapel Hill, North Carolina. Channel surfing and other habits you develop while watching television actually can make it harder for you shift into a slower time frame, he says.

"Television is an extremely fast paced medium. It's just one quick scene after another as producers try to squeeze as much as possible out of every millisecond," Keyes says. "I know that when I watch it, it gets my heart racing and my skin gets tense."

Stop-Time Tactics

A Go-Getter Stops Going

For years, time was Tony Alessandra's enemy. A marketing consultant and professional speaker, Alessandra was constantly trying to squeeze 30 hours of professional and personal life into every 24-hour day.

He would think nothing of flying to Boston on a Thursday evening, giving a speech on a Friday morning, dashing home to San Diego for his son's soccer game on a Saturday afternoon, then rushing to the airport to catch a plane so that he could be in Orlando for a convention on a Sunday. In all, he was on the road more than 150 days a year, working 12 to 15 hours a day. In addition, he was writing a book and recording a self-help audiocassette each year.

His cellular phone was always in hand, his pager constantly beeping, and his briefcase was perpetually bulging. "The pace of my life was aging me," says Alessandra, who is now in his fifties. "I didn't have enough time to exercise, eat right, or even sleep well. I was completely frazzled."

One day in 1990, it dawned on him that he had spent nearly half of his eight-year-old daughter's life away from home. "I realized I was getting older, and I didn't want to live this way anymore. I didn't want to wait until retirement to start enjoying life. I decided I wanted to live for the now," Alessandra says.

For starters, he accepted fewer speaking engagements and consulting jobs. "Learning to say no has given me a lot more downtime. I feel much more human these days," he says.

He devotes less time to writing—producing a new book every two years instead of annually. He seldom carries work on planes with him anymore. Instead, he now prefers to sleep or read newspapers, magazines, or books. Although he still spends up to 120 days a year on the road, his wife, Sue, travels with him at least once a month. And instead of flying all night to see his children briefly on a weekend, he blocks out more lengthy time on his schedule for family events like long summer vacations.

"I feel much better about myself, and I feel much healthier than I did when I was in a rush all of the time," Alessandra says. "I look younger, I act younger, and I feel younger than I have in many, many years."

Outfox Time-Eaters

One way to free yourself from a frenetic pace is by cultivating slow-paced hobbies such as coin collecting, gardening, or playing word games. In addition, here are some everyday changes in your work and home environment that can help you cool your heels more.

Stop juggling. The more tasks you attempt to do at once, the more time pressure you will feel. Try to stay focused on one task—it will help make you less aware of time, Dr. Rechtschaffen says.

Always clear your work area of papers and tools that are not essential to do the job at hand, Davidson suggests.

Prune your commitments. A polite but firm no is one of your best defenses against feeling time-crunched, Davidson says. Look at your schedule for the next month. Is there anything you really don't want to do? Cancel it, and don't accept anything that would fill the unscheduled time. Consider it "found" time that you can use as you please.

Make time a friend. At the beginning of each week, take a moment to write down what is the most precious thing you want to accomplish in the next seven days. That way, if you accomplish nothing else, you can feel good about yourself because you did that one precious thing. You'll also be less apt to see time as an enemy and get upset that you didn't complete everything you set out to do, says Meyer Friedman, M.D., a pioneering researcher who developed the concept of type A behavior and its relation to coronary artery disease.

"Almost nothing that we do in any given week will be memorable. So why treat these events as if they are a matter of life or death?" Dr. Friedman says.

Meet with John Q. Phantom. Take at least 15 to 20 minutes daily just for yourself, urges Leonard Felder, Ph.D., a psychologist in Los Angeles and author of *The 10 Challenges*. If necessary, schedule a phantom client into your daily calendar as a reminder. Treat that time like an appointment you can't break. Then take a nap, walk, read a pleasurable book, or simply meditate.

240

Make it a family affair. Regardless of the difficult logistics, insist that your family eat dinner together every night, says John Sena, Ph.D., author of *Work Is Not a Four-Letter Word.*

"If you're on a tight time schedule, odds are your family is, too," Dr. Sena says. "So it's easy to lose contact with one another. Shared activities will lessen your sense of time pressure and isolation." In addition to dinners together, commit yourself to regular family outings like picnics or afternoons at the beach that have no particular agenda, he suggests.

Get swept away. Use a routine task like sweeping the floor to practice focusing on the present, Dr. Rechtschaffen suggests.

If you're sweeping the kitchen floor, for instance, bask in the moment instead of rushing through it, Dr. Rechtschaffen suggests. Bring your full attention to the interaction of your body and the broom. Try to feel each muscle as it moves. Listen carefully to the sound of the broom against the floor. Allow yourself to get swept up in the rhythm of the moment.

You can do the same with other household tasks like washing dishes or filing papers. Time pressure only exists if you're feeling regrets about the past or worrying about the future, Dr. Rechtschaffen observes. So if you can learn to focus on the here and now, you'll be less apt to feel time-crunched.

Clear the smoke screen. Nicotine is a stimulant that can heighten your sense of time urgency, Dr. Markison says. In addition, smoking slashes blood flow to the hands and wrists by up to 60 percent, increasing your risk of repetitive strain injuries. So if you haven't stopped smoking yet, do it now.

what?

The first clocks had no dials. They merely rang on the hour. The hour hand first appeared in the 1500s, the minute hand was introduced a century later, and the second hand was added in the early 1700s.

Stay in Touch with Your Youthful Emotions

Poised at the very edge of a 225-foot drop-off, Gary Kyriazi smiles and leans back in his seat.

Suddenly, the seat lurches forward, and plummets.

And Kyriazi howls with delight. "Who-o-o-o-o-a-a-a-a-ahhh!"

A passenger on the Desperado, a gigantic steel roller coaster in State Line, Nevada, Kyriazi is whisked down, through a hole in the ground, back to the Earth's surface, then in and out of a series of rapid rises and drops that leaves him momentarily airborne.

Still a roller-coaster fanatic at the age of 40-plus, Kyriazi has been on the Desperado plenty of times previously. He has been on numerous other coasters, too. But every ride is a thrill, he says.

"I like the speed, the freedom, the feeling of flight—it's an incredibly fun experience," says Kyriazi, who works as an independent consultant for the amusement industry in New River, Arizona, and happily drives four hours north to State Line for an 80-mile-per-hour spin on the Desperado.

The author of *The Great American Amusement Park*, Kyriazi has been riding roller coasters since he was two years old. (His first fling was on a pint-size kiddie coaster.) He rides as often as possible.

"Riding roller coasters makes me feel happy," says Kyriazi. "By nature I'm young at heart, and riding roller coasters is a way of expressing it—and it's part of my job."

242

Coast Back to Childlike

The truth is, riding roller coasters can help *you* stay young at heart, too. So can reveling in all sorts of other experiences that cultivate childlike qualities—like playfulness, spontaneity, joyousness, flexibility, and optimism.

It's a worthwhile investment of time and energy. Why? These kidlike qualities confer substantial age-protecting benefits. Studies find that people who are optimistic and playful live longer, healthier, and happier lives.

"We're not talking about being childish," says Joel Goodman, Ed.D., director of the Humor Project in Saratoga Springs, New York, and co-author of *Chicken Soup for the Laughing Soul.* "It's important to distinguish between being childlike—being spontaneous and flexible and so forth—and being childish. Being childish is being irresponsible and immature. But being childlike can be a very mature way of coping with and enjoying life."

But what if you weren't particularly spontaneous or flexible as a kid? Well, you can still cultivate these kidlike qualities as an adult. It's just a matter of knowing how.

One of the benefits of growing up and becoming an adult is that you can change, says Bonnie Jacobson, Ph.D., a clinical psychologist and director of the New York Institute for Psychological Change in Manhattan, and author of *If Only You Would Listen* and *Love Triangles.* You can cultivate these qualities now even if you didn't have them then.

"When you're a child, you just *are*, but when you're an adult, you have the ability to choose how you want to be," says Dr. Jacobson. "You can develop strategies to change."

M a k e o v e r   M i n u t e s

For Wholehearted Laughter

This very moment, you can start making the kind of changes that cultivate kidlike qualities. All you have to do is revel in assorted kidlike pleasures. So get ready, get set, and...

243

Playing for a Living

When adults asked her what she wanted to be when she grew up, Francie Berger always told them that she wanted to be an architect.

"But I'd only say that because I *knew* you couldn't get a job building things out of Lego bricks, which is what I really wanted to do," recalls Berger.

Shortly after graduating from architectural school, Berger got a job that was literally a wish come true. She got to build things out of Lego bricks.

By the time she was in her thirties, Berger was a model-designs supervisor with Lego Systems, where she builds giant Lego models for children's museums and toy stores. Every model is made from thousands and thousands of the same tiny plastic Lego bricks that so many kids play with. Over the years, Berger has designed all manner of Lego constructions—from two-foot-tall Lego scuba divers and a three-foot-long Lego checker cab to Lego jungle animals, and two-foot-tall Lego dragons.

"I love my work," says Berger, who works in the company's U.S. headquarters in Enfield, Connecticut. "It's perfect for me. I never stopped being a kid; I can't imagine working anywhere else."

If you can't play at your job, find another time to play, says Berger. She's given Lego sets to many of her adult friends, a subtle hint to join in the good times. "Play," she says, "makes life much more enjoyable."

Laugh your head off. A sense of humor offers bona fide age-protecting benefits. Studies suggest it can lengthen and improve the quality of your life. Among other things, humor seems to help insulate you from stress. In a series of studies, women executives who scored high on tests designed to measure sense of humor felt less stressed-out, had fewer stress-related health problems, were less likely to get burned out, and had higher self-esteems than those who scored low.

In other studies, humor has been shown to improve problem solving and creativity. And humor often goes hand in hand

244

with other age-protecting attributes like resilience, says Irene Deitch, Ph.D., professor of psychology and chairman of "Options," a college study program for older adults at the College of Staten Island in New York City.

"People who are resilient often have a good sense of humor," says Dr. Deitch, "When the going gets tough, they use humor to cope."

If your sense of humor is getting a little dull around the edges, just seek out things that amuse you, says Ruth Hamilton, founder and executive director of the Carolina Health and Humor Association (a.k.a. Carolina Ha Ha), a nonprofit organization that promotes the therapeutic use of humor.

"Humor is cumulative—the more you use your sense of humor, the more things seem funny to you," she says.

Remember your Uncle Milty. What makes one person laugh may leave another cold. A sense of humor is a very individual thing. If you aren't sure what might amuse you, think back to your childhood, Hamilton suggests.

"Ask yourself who was the funniest person in your family," she says. "Then ask yourself why they were funny." Or skip the relatives if they were sourpusses and try to recall who was the funniest person in the world when you were a kid. You may still find that person and his style of humor funny today, she says.

One way to become more playful and emotionally open is to play games such as charades with friends. "Humor is social and interactive. Lighten up and do it with others," says Carolyn Saarni, Ph.D., a developmental psychologist and professor in the graduate department of counseling at Sonoma State University in Rohnert Park, California. Other possibilities are picnicking with friends and family or renting a funny video.

Carry a fake nose. Once you know what your humor preferences are, Hamilton suggests that you assemble your own portable "humor first-aid kit" and carry it with you for regular sense-of-humor workouts.

"Get a big bag and start filling it with stuff that makes you laugh," she says. Throw in a few of your favorite comic books. Add amusing articles from newspapers and magazines. If fake noses with bushy eyebrows make you chortle, include one. Toss

245

in a funny video. In Hamilton's bag, for instance, you'll find assorted hand puppets, giant drinking straws that wrap around
your eyes like glasses, assorted jars of bubbles and bubble wands,
a book of cartoons, and Mr. Potato Head.

Find free-form fun. Before adults teach them to play to win,
most kids play simply to have fun.

"Children take pleasure in playing for the sake of playing,"
says Dr. Saarni. "They do it for the sensory and experiential
value; they don't have to achieve and win all the time."

Unfortunately, many of us grow less playful and more pre-
occupied with winning as we grow older. To reclaim that playfulness you enjoyed as a kid, Dr. Saarni suggests that you try
some new recreational pursuit. "Learn to do something sensory
and enjoyable—just for the sake of doing it, not so you can
excel at it," she says. "When I was in my midforties, I decided to
learn to scuba dive. I decided that I wasn't going to push myself
but simply enjoy the process of doing it. And it gives me great
pleasure."

If you're the hard-driving, competitive type, Dr. Saarni suggests that you tell yourself—repeatedly, if necessary—that your
attempt at noncompetitive play is simply an experiment. Remind yourself that you don't have to stop competing in all areas
of your life. Only this one. That should make it easier to simply
play for fun.

"Pencil in" playtime. It was easy to find time to play when you
were a kid. At school, you had recess every day. At home, there
was usually someone telling you to "go out and play" so that they
could "get something done around here."

The problem is, you don't get recess on the job. And you're
probably too busy getting things done around the house after
work and on weekends to find time to play then.

Which is why you have to make time for play, says Walt
Schafer, Ph.D., professor of sociology at California State University, Chico, and author of *Stress Management for Wellness.*

Dr. Schafer suggests that you write playtime into your schedule. At least once a week, set aside time to play. You can usually
find at least a few hours to spare, hours you might otherwise
spend watching television.

246

Self-Confidence: Not Kid Stuff

"Without self-confidence we are as babes in the cradle," wrote Virginia Woolf, the British novelist.

Most babes in the cradle would agree—if they knew how. "Confidence comes from knowing we can handle whatever life hands us," says Susan Jeffers, Ph.D., author of *End the Struggle and Dance with Life*. In other words, self-confidence is something we develop as we grow older and grow up. It comes from encountering difficult situations and handling them well.

But what if your confidence is shaky? You can build self-confidence, Dr. Jeffers says, and she suggests that you start with the following simple steps.

Be afraid. It's only natural to feel scared when you hit a rough patch. But it's a mistake to assume that because you're afraid, you're also incapable. Even the most capable, self-confident folks feel scared in difficult situations, Dr. Jeffers says. "They feel the fear and go forward anyway," she says.

Silence the chatterbox. Perhaps you have a nagging voice of doubt in your head, the one that pipes up whenever there's a challenge afoot. If that voice warns you that you don't stand much of a chance, there's only one appropriate response, says Dr. Jeffers. You need to out-talk that voice, using positive words.

Give yourself pep talks. "Tell yourself, 'I'm a strong person,' and 'I'll handle it,'" says Dr. Jeffers. "The more you repeat these positive affirmations, the more you start to believe them."

Help out. Helping someone in need makes you feel good about yourself. "It's confidence-building," says Dr. Jeffers. You can directly contact any organization you would like to help—or call the United Way chapter in your area to find out who is looking for volunteers. Also, your local newspaper might list ways to volunteer in your community.

Stop blaming. If you always blame other people for what's wrong in your life, you'll end up feeling pretty powerless. A better choice is to stop thinking about what the other person did and ask yourself, "What can *I* do to change the situation?" Dr. Jeffers says. Then do it.

Play makes you more resilient, he notes. And playing with other people improves your relationships with them.

Go exploring. A psychologist in Chicago, Jonathan Smith, Ph.D., has spent more than a decade studying what he calls R-states. The R stands for relaxation, Dr. Smith explains. Aptly

247

Trust in the Ha-Has

Open wide and...laugh out loud.

Humor, it seems, is just what the doctor ordered. Not only can it help reduce stress and open channels of communication between people, research suggests humor can help ease pain, facilitate recovery, help problem solving and decision making, and help you maintain your balance and your positive outlook.

"Humor isn't a substitute for health care, but it can be a powerful and fun adjunct," says Joel Goodman, Ed.D., director of the Humor Project, an organization in Saratoga Springs, New York, that offers seminars, conferences, and publications on the therapeutic use of humor, and co-author of *Chicken Soup for the Laughing Soul.*

Turns out that mirth has a number of salubrious effects. Laughter stimulates the production of hormones called catecholamines, which may in turn trigger the release of endorphins, brain chemicals that ease pain and foster a sense of well-being. Some evidence suggests laughter can improve immunity by impeding production of hormones that suppress immune cell activity. Laugh heartily, studies find, and your heart rate, blood pressure, and muscle tension drop to below normal levels, leaving you very relaxed.

"The whole body relaxes, which is why people sometimes fall down when laughing," says Ruth Hamilton, founder and executive director of the Carolina Health and Humor Associa-

so, since R-states are characterized by feeling physically limp, distant, and at ease. When you're experiencing R-states, you also have feelings like optimism, hope, joy, and awe.

"R-states can rejuvenate and renew us," says Dr. Smith, professor of psychology at Roosevelt University and founder and director of the Roosevelt University Stress Institute in Chicago.

While kids seem to experience awe fairly regularly—in the course of discovering seemingly mundane things like birds' nests—we adults experience it less often, says Dan Gottlieb, Ph.D., a family therapist in Cherry Hill, New Jersey, and author of *Family Matters: Healing in the Heart of the Family.*

If that weren't bad enough, some of us become less optimistic and less hopeful as we grow older, says Christopher Peterson, Ph.D., professor of psychology at the University of Michigan in Ann Arbor.

tion, a nonprofit organization that promotes the therapeutic use of humor.

"Carolina Ha Ha," Hamilton's association, supplies hospitals with Laugh Mobiles, carts stocked with rubber chickens, funny video- and audiotapes, Groucho glasses, joke books, and the like. Increasingly, health care workers are incorporating humor into treatment, Hamilton says.

The relief is welcomed by many patients—and endorsed by therapists. "In some situations, the anxiety can be overwhelming, so you need something to reduce the tension," says Irene Deitch, Ph.D., a psychotherapist and professor of psychology at the College of Staten Island in New York City, who uses humor in her practice. Because it makes people feel better, humor makes them more receptive and better able to view difficult situations from different perspectives. "Humor can help people step back and gain insight," she says.

For more information on the therapeutic value of humor, contact the Humor Project at 110 Spring Street, Saratoga Springs, NY 12866 or Carolina Ha Ha at 5223 Revere Road, Durham, NC 27713. There's no humor specialty in the field of psychotherapy, so if you're looking for a therapist who uses humor, interview prospective therapists and see if they have a sense of humor that matches your own, Dr. Deitch suggests.

But we can recapture those special feelings and experience R-states, Dr. Smith says. For example, first do something relaxing, he advises. Then do something simple and fun.

"I'd say that being young at heart means being able to cultivate and savor R-states," Dr. Smith observes. To get in the right frame of mind to experience an R-state, you must relax first, he says. A number of powerful relaxation techniques, including massage by a professional therapist, are good for cultivating different R-states. A professional massage, for instance, might make you feel physically relaxed and calm, while yoga might make you feel refreshed and awake. And meditation may make you feel prayerful and spiritual. All of these techniques can help still your mind and prepare you for an R-state.

Yoga stretching is probably the easiest to do on your own, according to Dr. Smith. One simple yoga stretch is to sit upright

249

in a comfortable chair. Slowly raise both arms, lifting them like the wings of a bird, and reach for the ceiling. Feel the stretch along your entire body. Then slowly release the stretch and let yourself begin to bow over. Bend forward from the waist all the way so that your hands point toward the floor. Finally, return to a comfortable, upright position. This is one of several thousand invigorating yoga stretches.

Once you have done yoga stretching or another relaxation technique, follow up with the simple and pleasurable activity of your choice, Dr. Smith says. If you don't want to explore the woods, try gardening or go for a bike ride.

Enjoy your ice cream. True, kids are capable of throwing blood-curdling tantrums when they don't get what they want. But, by and large, they're flexible.

"Children are oriented toward the present. They don't dwell on past wrongs or fixate on the future, so they often accept what's in front of them," says Dr. Saarni.

Fortunately, you can develop flexibility, no matter what your age. The trick is catching yourself when you start getting rigid, reminding yourself that you can make allowances, then following through.

Let's say that you have vowed to eat better, but you have broken down and bought yourself an ice cream cone with sprinkles. The rigid response would be to berate yourself so mercilessly that you can't possibly enjoy the ice cream. The more mature response would be to enjoy half of the cone and throw the other half away.

"Don't tell yourself, 'Oh, God, here I go. I'm going to be fat again, like I was five years ago,'" Dr. Saarni says. "Just go ahead and enjoy the flavor and the texture. Be present-oriented. Accept what's in the here and now."

Take a nap. Of course, life isn't all ice cream cones and walks in the park. Even when you were a kid, there were math classes to sit through and lawns to mow. Odds are, you made the best of these unpleasantries by taking strategic breaks.

Do the same, and you'll enjoy greater resilience. If you have been working on your taxes for two hours straight, take a break. Take a nap. Or take a walk around the block.

"Do any of those little things that give you immediate pleasure. You're entitled to a 10-minute snooze," says Dr. Saarni. "You'll feel better. You'll feel rejuvenated."

Get curiouser and curiouser. Ever notice how many questions kids ask? Did you? Ever? Huh?

Kids are full of curiosity, another of those attributes that makes life more vibrant.

"The payoff of curiosity is that your world becomes bigger," Dr. Saarni says. "If you're curious, your horizon keeps getting pushed back."

When we grow up, many of us grow less willing to ask questions and to try things we don't know how to do. We worry that our questions will be dumb. We think we should already be experts in everything.

Again, the solution is to try something new and tell yourself that it's okay to be a novice, says Dr. Saarni. Then jump in and get wet behind the ears. Tune in to a radio call-in show and ask some questions. Sign up for that wine-tasting class at the local vineyard.

If you're a hard-driving type who finds the novice role terrifying, remind yourself that the alternative to being curious is being bored. "Tell yourself, 'If I don't try out new things, I'll have a very small, little world,' " suggests Dr. Saarni.

Indulge in fantasy. Life's hard knocks can put serious dents in youth's optimism—and rob you of its age-protecting benefits.

When it comes to health and well-being, optimism is optimal. Research finds that people who score high on tests of optimism find greater pleasure in life, feel less hassled and stressed by everyday demands, report fewer health problems, and even recover more quickly from major surgery, than those who get low scores.

You don't have to be a dreamer to be an optimist. But it helps, says Dr. Jacobson.

One way to cultivate optimism is to pay attention to your daydreams and fantasies. But not all daydreams are created equal. "Either we're having positive fantasies or negative ones," says Dr. Jacobson. Tuning in to images of yourself winning the monthly sales award or finishing a 25-K race can brighten your outlook, she says.

Under stress, optimists are more likely to ask family and friends for support than pessimists are. Optimists are also more likely to expect personal growth, or some other dividend, from stressful events.

251

Youthful Expressions

Childhood has its lingo. Whether you grew up in the Bronx or Batavia, odds are, you spoke kid-speak. Can you still translate? Just for fun, try the quiz below to see if you can match the kid word to the adult-speak definition. (Answers, at bottom.)

1. Monkey's uncle
2. "No taxes"
3. Fungo
4. Jinxing
5. "For fair"
6. Aggies
7. Enders
8. "Chips"
9. Butterfingers
10. Short line

A. The task of holding the jump rope in group jumping games.
B. Decree, made by the owner of a piece of sports equipment, to the effect that he will be reimbursed the cost of the equipment if it's lost in the course of play.
C. Words to seal the deal in a wager; translation: "No backing out."
D. Marbles.
E. Edict that specifies that all marbles will be returned to their original owners after a game—the opposite of "for keeps."
F. Putting one hand on the pavement, for balance, while picking up a token in hopscotch. Players may declare "no butterfingers" at the start of a game, ruling out the practice.
G. The ball, once it's been thrown in the air by the batter, in games in which the batter also acts as pitcher, like punchball.
H. Line where the ball is served from in handball—which is 16 feet from the wall.
I. The loser in a game.
J. Attempts to distract, or otherwise undermine, the performance of another player in a competitive game.

(Answers: 1, I; 2, C; 3, G; 4, J; 5, E; 6, D; 7, A; 8, B; 9, F; 10, H.)

Surprisingly, you can also reap some benefits by tuning in to negative fantasies as well, according to Dr. Jacobson. If you really start paying attention to your negative fantasies—rather than letting them drone along in the background of your consciousness like a television someone's forgotten to shut off—you'll start to see the flaws in them, she says.

Let's say that you find yourself fantasizing about the speech you have to give to the marketing department. In the fantasy,

252

you flub the speech. What you need to do is examine the fantasy and compare it with your usual real-life performance at past marketing department meetings. You don't flub those, right? So your fantasy doesn't appear to be particularly accurate.

"Eventually, negative fantasies begin to seem ridiculous to you," Dr. Jacobson says. "You get tired of them. And, automatically, they start to change."

Listen to your buddies. Chances are, you had a best friend when you were a kid. You were inseparable and told each other everything.

That kind of sharing is essential to forming and keeping close friendships, says Dr. Jacobson. Close relationships foster emotional health and contribute to physical well-being as well. Various studies find that people with close relationships report greater satisfaction in life. If your close friends are optimistic and fun loving, all the better. Friends like these make us more resilient, she says.

To make close friends, you have to spend time listening to people talk, especially about themselves, she says. The more you let another person talk about himself, the more likely it is that you will find common ground, which is the basis for close friendships.

Many of us don't put in enough time listening to one another, so our conversations linger on a fairly superficial level, as do our friendships, Dr. Jacobson says.

"If you're talking to someone you'd like to get close to, and they tell you they were just in Rome and loved it, let them talk a long time about Rome," she suggests. "Let them talk long enough that you really get a sense of what they liked so much, so you really have something to talk about."

And practice what's known as active listening, says Marlene F. Watson, Ph.D., a couple and family therapist and director of graduate programs in couple and family therapy at Allegheny University of the Health Sciences in Philadelphia.

After the other person has finished speaking, paraphrase what he has just said. This reassures the other person that you're really listening.

"Sometimes the speaker's intent isn't clear to the listener," says Dr. Watson. "If the listener can say back to the speaker what

253

he has heard, that provides an opportunity to clear up any misunderstanding."

When you paraphrase, start your sentences with "My understanding of what you just said is..." or "As I understand it, you're saying...," Dr. Watson suggests. This way, it's clear that you're giving your interpretation of what the other person is trying to express. If there's a potential misunderstanding brewing, your phrasing will help ensure that the other person doesn't get defensive. "Saying, 'You just said...' can put the other person on the defensive," she notes.

Long-Term Tactics
The Oh in Wows and Gee in Whizzes

Some kidlike pleasures make you feel young at heart right away. Others pay dividends after a longer investment. Here's how to invest your time and energy for maximum age-protecting results.

Remember the Boy Scout creed. Particularly the part about being trustworthy.

Life's rough spots can wear away trust and leave us cynical. And that's truly unfortunate. Living is a lot more stressful and less enjoyable when you don't trust. Not surprisingly, studies find that cynics have significantly more health problems than trusting types.

The thing about trust, though, is that you have to be trustworthy if you're going to trust others, says Dr. Saarni. "Trust is paradoxical," she says. "The way to rebuild trust in others is to put yourself in a position where people trust you."

If you're more cynical than you'd like to be, consider volunteering at a local school or at a respite center for mentally disabled adults, she suggests. "Like kids, mentally disabled folks tend to be trusting and inspire trust," Dr. Saarni says.

Savor your successes. Teach a five-year-old the lyrics to "Old MacDonald's Farm," and she will happily croon it until the cows

254

come home. Kids get a lot of satisfaction from everyday accomplishments. And that's a good thing since savoring your successes builds optimism, says Dr. Peterson.

"If you want to be more optimistic, one of the things you can do is define success in terms of things you can achieve," he says. "If you define success in such a way that you'll only feel successful if you earn a million dollars a year, you're setting yourself up for disappointment. If you tell yourself you'll be a success if you can enjoy your work and put food on the table, you'll feel better about life and feel more optimistic."

Optimism is often self-fulfilling. Deriving satisfaction from one task can help you succeed at the next. "Research suggests that optimists are more successful at school and at work and tend to have more and better relationships," he adds. It only makes sense. Because optimists expect things to work out eventually, they're persistent. Because they're persistent, things work out for them.

Make new friends. It's tough to be the new kid in town. And it's not much easier to be the new adult. But it happens. A lot. According to the Census Bureau, the average American moves 11 times in a lifetime.

In a culture this mobile, it helps to know how to make new friends. Spend some time watching kids play together, and you'll pick up some pointers, says Dr. Saarni.

"Watch kids who successfully negotiate what we call peer entry, and you'll see that they all do certain things," says Dr. Saarni. "These kids observe what's going on and try to join in the activity. They don't try to draw attention to themselves or try to take control or be in charge. They don't go up to other kids on the slide and say, 'Look, let me show you the best way to go down that slide.' If they did, they'd be rejected."

If you want to make new friends, your best bet is to join a group that's doing something you like. Love gardening? Go to a garden club meeting. When you get there, look around, see what everyone else is doing, and join in. If the group is repotting mums for the upcoming plant sale, do the same. Whatever you do, don't be bossy, try to take control, or hog all the attention.

255

Hop To!

Remember how much fun it was to jump rope when you were a kid? Try it again. These ballads and chants will help get your feet moving.

I'm a little Dutch girl dressed in blue.
These are the things I like to do.
Salute to the captain, curtsy to the queen,
And turn my back on the mean old king.

Apples, peaches, pears, and plums,
Tell me when our birthday comes.
(Chant the months until your birthday,
and then the days until your birthday.)

Mabel, Mabel
Set the table
Close the door when you are able
Ten, Twenty, Thirty (etc.)

Forgive the bullies. Spend time watching kids, especially little kids, and you'll also pick up pointers on cultivating another talent—forgiving.

"Forgiveness seems to be easier for children," says Gerald G. Jampolsky, M.D., a psychiatrist for children and adults and the founder of the Center for Attitudinal Healing in Sausalito, California. "A five-year-old can get into a fight with a friend who's taken one of his toys and, five minutes later, forgive his friend and start playing with her again. But when adults fight, they may not speak to each other for years."

What happens? As we get bigger, so do our egos, says Dr. Jampolsky. We become more judgmental. "The more judgments we make, the more unforgiving we are, and the stronger the ego feels," Dr. Jampolsky explains.

Unfortunately, though, there is a trade-off. Withholding forgiveness inflates your ego but undermines your peace of mind. Ironically, by refusing to forgive someone you actually give that person considerable power over you and your well-being, he says.

But how can you really forgive someone who has done you wrong?

Assume that the person is afraid, Dr. Jampolsky says. It's a safe assumption since most wrongdoing stems from fear. Consider the colleague who took credit for your idea for the Waldenstein account. Odds are, he did it out of fear of not look-

256

ing good. Once you realize he is afraid, it's easier to feel some compassion for the guy.

Keep in mind that forgiving doesn't mean condoning. You don't have to convince yourself that it was okay for your office-mate to steal your idea. And you don't have to continue sharing your ideas with him. In fact, you may be better off if you don't. But if you remind yourself that he's probably filched your idea out of fear, eventually you can sympathize, forgive, and feel better. Research finds that forgiveness is often followed by a letup in anger, depression, anxiety, and related emotions.

Plan for surprises. When you have to juggle multiple obligations—such as a job, relationships, car maintenance—you have to schedule your time. Schedule every moment, though, and there's too little room for discovery or surprise.

Kids tend to have an innate appreciation for spontaneity, says Dr. Gottlieb. Not surprisingly, they have a knack for discovering all sorts of surprises, even amidst the ordinary, he says.

"One afternoon, I had a young friend, a three-year-old, dropped off at my house," Dr. Gottlieb recalls. "I'd been working frantically on about four different projects, like we all do. When she arrived, I said, 'What shall we do this afternoon?' And she said, 'I don't know.' Anytime I asked her a question that had a time reference, she gave me a monosyllabic answer. So I decided that she, I, and the dog would go for a walk. Well, along the way she found an anthill, and she pulled me over to see it, and we watched that anthill for about 20 minutes. It was fascinating. We gave each of the ants a name and a role. And we talked about all sorts of ideas and feelings. We had a wonderful time."

Get creative. Give a kid a crayon, and he won't waste time berating his erstwhile Muse or worrying what the critics will think. He'll color.

Kids are a lot less likely to edit their creative urges than we adults are, says Carolyn Adams-Price, Ph.D., associate professor of psychology and chairman of the gerontology program at Mississippi State University in Mississippi State, and author of *Creativity and Successful Aging*.

We adults, however, tend to have a lot more creative potential than kids do.

257

"I'd say that creativity is being able to produce something that is meaningful or inspiring, something other people can relate to or attach meaning to," Dr. Adams-Price says. "And adults are better able to do that."

If you have concluded that you're not creative because you didn't do well in art class, think again. There are innumerable ways to be creative—and most of us have talent for at least some of them, says Dr. Adams-Price.

So try your hand at quilting, photography, papier-mâché, or sculpting with odd bits of wire and other found objects.

Research suggests that creative expression fosters openness, flexibility, playfulness, humor, and resilience—all boons to mental health.

Tell tales. As any teacher who has ever inquired about a missing homework assignment can tell you, kids are good at telling stories—and not just when they have to either. Kids make up stories for the sheer pleasure of telling them.

Storytelling is just one more way of being creative. Try it and, odds are, you'll find you're better at it now than you were as a kid, says Dr. Adams-Price. As we get older, we get better at expressing ourselves and at judging the interests of our audiences, she says.

Try telling or writing stories about your experiences, she suggests. Recall some significant event in your life and write about it, or tell someone about it. (If you're feeling shy, tell your story to a kid.) Tell your story even if you're not sure what it means, Dr. Adams-Price says. In telling and retelling these stories, she notes, we discover new meaning in our lives.

Celebrate your birthday. Kids enjoy birthday parties because they know what birthday parties are about. Birthday parties aren't about worrying that you're a year older. They are about having a good time with people you love.

Birthdays are times to celebrate the pleasure of being alive, says Dr. Deitch. So take the opportunity to celebrate. Throw a party. Invite your favorite people. Pop some corks.

Stay young forever. The best way to experience the world as a magical, wondrous, awe-inspiring place is to spend time with a kid, says Dr. Gottlieb. You don't have to be a parent to do this,

258

of course. You can be a scoutmaster or a Big Sister or a volunteer at the local elementary school, he says.

"Spend time with children, and not only will it show you the world through their eyes, I guarantee it will contribute to your sense of purpose," says Dr. Gottlieb.

When you're with kids, remember to pay attention. Listen to them. Ask them questions about their thoughts. Ask about spiritual issues, Dr. Gottlieb suggests.

"Children have a kind of spirituality, a kind of awe at the world, a sense of the godliness of the world that we have literally forgotten," he says. "It would behoove us to become their students."

Keep the Faith to Add Years to Your Life

Should we pray for youth? The very notion conjures up images of laying on of hands. Of visitations to the sites of miracles. Of faith healers who promise to pluck out tumors and restore sight to the blind.

But a new group of professionals are now looking closely at the power of faith, prayer, and healing—a group that has no religious ax to grind and no investment in miracle waters. Physicians, psychologists, and cardiologists, including medical doctors and teachers from some of the nation's most prestigious medical schools, are coming to similar conclusions about the positive powers of faith.

Their findings might not prompt you to buy a round-trip ticket to Lourdes, the Vatican, Mecca, or the Wailing Wall. But based on their research, you might want to consider praying a bit more than you have in the past. Or perhaps you will consider attending religious services—if you aren't already—or will contemplate trying out some of the experiences that are described as "living your faith."

The reason? Faith, as it turns out, is a protective factor that can help brighten your outlook, calm your nerves, ward off health problems, and lengthen your life. Obviously, these are all factors that contribute to feelings of youth that go far beyond the spiritual. That's what makes the practice of faith, whether by praying, singing, or seeking fellowship, such an age protector.

"There are at least 250 studies showing that people who follow some type of religious practice in their lives—and that almost always includes prayer—are healthier across-the-board compared to people who don't," says Larry Dossey, M.D., the Santa Fe, New Mexico–based author of *Prayer Is Good Medicine* as well as six other books on the healing aspects of prayer and religious involvement. "They go to the doctor less. They consume fewer health care dollars. They get sick less often."

The single most common issue that those 250 studies deal with is mental and psychological health, notes Dr. Dossey. Based upon those studies, many researchers have concluded that "people who pray don't suffer from stress as much as those who don't pray," he says.

For over two decades, scientists have been studying the effects that prayer or quiet meditation has on the human body. "It's a relaxation response," says Dr. Dossey. "When people enter a prayerful state of mind, when they meditate or relax in other ways, the body loves it. The blood pressure drops. The heart rate falls. The body's requirement for oxygen and the production of carbon dioxide diminish. Even cholesterol levels fall over time."

In some respects, then, having faith is a potent preventive medicine. "It appears from the research done that having some sort of regular religious involvement or spiritual practice such as prayer is beneficial," says Dr. Dossey. "Just as we know that smoking and type A behavior are risk factors of disease, the lack of spiritual involvement seems to be a risk factor for lots of things...including stress."

People with faith do seem to experience less stress than those without, reports Dave Larson, M.D., a research epidemiologist formerly at the National Institutes of Health who now heads the privately funded National Institute for Healthcare Research in Rockville, Maryland. That's probably related to the fact that people with faith appear to have a larger network of social support and a world view that allows them to keep their problems in perspective. In general, they seem more likely to feel comfortable handling the various stresses that life throws their way, he says.

So will going to church or temple once a week prevent you from feeling stressed? Maybe. Religious people tend to suffer from stress less often than those who don't attend services as often, according to Dr. Larson. "But even when people have

know what?

Twenty percent of Americans say that they have had a revelation from God in the last year; 13 percent say that they have seen an angel or sensed its presence.

261

equal levels of stress, studies show that churchgoers tend to cope better and have fewer psychiatric disorders than people who attend church infrequently." Although most of the published studies done to date have focused on religious commitment, as opposed to prayer, "we do know that when people are trying to relax, many turn to ritual prayers like the Lord's Prayer, Hail Mary, and the Shema as their mantras."

Praying for Healing

But faith and prayer do more than relieve stress. Many studies are leading to the conclusion that faith can actually help speed recovery if you have an existing health condition. "Faith is clearly a beneficial factor in healing," according to Harold Koenig, M.D., director of the Center for the Study of Religion/Spirituality and Health at Duke University Medical Center in Durham, North Carolina. "I've reviewed hundreds of studies conducted since 1980 on various aspects of the issue, and most of them confirm its effect."

Among the studies that support these conclusions are the following:

▌In a survey of nearly 92,000 Maryland residents that was based on census statistics, researchers found that people who attended church more than once a week were far less likely to get certain diseases than those who attended infrequently. Over a five-year period, the death rate from heart disease was twice as high among those who didn't go to church very often as it was for the frequent attenders. Similarly, during a three-year period, the infrequent attenders were twice as likely to die of emphysema and four times as likely to die of cirrhosis of the liver as were the frequent attenders.

▌A study of 232 older men and women who had just had cardiac surgery at the Dartmouth-Hitchcock Medical Center in Hanover, New Hampshire, found that those who said that they received strength and comfort from practicing their faith were three times more likely to survive than those who didn't.

262

In a six-year study of nearly 3,000 men and women over age 65, researchers found that people who attended church every week were half as likely to have strokes as were those who never or almost never attended services.

A study of 393 men and women admitted to the cardiac care unit at San Francisco General Hospital found that patients were far more likely to recover and go home if their families and friends prayed for them. And those on the receiving end of prayer were less likely to require antibiotics.

"Faith is a powerful instrument," concludes Louis Lussier, M.D., former professor of sports medicine at the University of Illinois and now a priest and doctor in Milwaukee's hospital-based Order of St. Camillus. He points out that doctors need to be aware of the element of faith involved in a patient's recovery. "The physician's technical skills account for about 15 percent of healing," he says. "That means there's a large area in which we don't know how healing happens. I think that's the area in which faith works. It's the area in which physician, God, and patient meet."

Today's doctors may hesitate to write a prescription for prayer, but they are beginning to talk about ways that faith can be used in treatment, notes Dr. Dossey. In fact, 11 of the top medical schools in the United States have added courses in prayer and healing to their curricula to help the next generation of doctors figure it all out.

Exploring the Heart of the Matter

Some researchers have focused on prayer and meditation to help explore the connection between physical changes and some little-explored aspects of human intelligence that relate to stress and its effects on the body. One such study was undertaken by Herbert Benson, M.D., president of the Mind/Body Medical Institute; director of behavioral medicine at Beth Israel Deaconess Medical Center East in Boston, affiliated with the Harvard Medical School; and author of *Timeless Healing*.

263

A Line to Faith Online

Near a high stone ridge in the New Mexican desert, standing amid a cluster of simple buildings and stucco huts, a visitor can hear the sound of Gregorian chants rising on the desert wind.

This is Christ in the Desert, a Benedictine monastery where cowled monks gather for prayer seven times a day—and run an online prayer service that's available all around the world through the Internet.

Traditionally, an older monk, called a porter, used to greet visitors at the monastery door. But in the Internet Age, monastery visitors are greeted by "Brother URL" (Uniform Resource Locator, in cybertalk) at the monastery's Web site. The "Brother" can then lead you to other sites that explain the monks' communal life and traditions.

At some of these sites, you have an opportunity to actually "participate" in monastic life. For example, Brother URL can guide you to the Chant page where you can listen to an "angel" sing (if your computer has a sound system). He can drop you off at the chapel where you can pray, and even ask the desert monks to pray with you. Or he can guide you to the Desert Fathers page where you can read stories of the men and women who first lived in this monastic desert community.

The address of the monastery's web site is http://www.christdesert.org.

Visiting a Tibetan monastery where he could study the effects of prayer and meditation on the body, Dr. Benson found that people have the ability to lower their blood pressure levels, heart rates, breathing rates, and metabolic rates simply by closing their eyes and focusing on a single word or phrase for 20 minutes or so.

Among people who use this meditation or prayer technique, the words that they choose invariably are related to their faith. The healing chemicals humans generate in response to words of faith may indicate that we are in a very profound, physical way "wired for God," Dr. Benson suggests. So the act of meditating or praying goes beyond stress relief, though that certainly is a factor. By meditating, you actually become more open to a discovery of faith.

Of course, we can't all join a monastery or devote our lives to religious practices. But there are other less drastic ways to make faith a part of our day-to-day lives.

Makeover Minutes

Prime Time for Praying

While many faith-related activities appear to be associated with health and longevity, prayer is one of the most powerful. There are many forms of prayer—from the chanting of public prayers in an urban temple to wordless expressions of intentions.

"I pray by breathing," says Dr. Dossey. "I don't ask for anything special. I just have the intention that the best thing should happen." This type of prayer is what he calls nondirected prayer—meaning, it never dictates what God (or some other higher power) should do for someone who is sick or injured.

But there are many other types of prayer apart from the nondirected kind. In directed prayer—also called prayers of petition or prayers of intercession—you're asking God to do something for you or someone else. Other prayers are for confession or for lamentation. There are also prayers in which you simply praise God (prayers of adoration) or offer gratitude (prayers of thanksgiving).

If you haven't tried praying in a while, here are some ways to make that quick ritual a part of your regular daily life.

Heal at meals. "Probably the most natural way for people to get started in prayer—especially for people who haven't done it—is to give thanks, as opposed to asking for something or trying to change the world," says Dr. Dossey. "One of the best ways to do that is at meals. If you feel gratitude for the food you're eating, you can silently give thanks—that's prayer."

Count your blessings. So you made it through another day? That's more than some other folks. "One practice of mine is every morning when I wake up, I say, 'Boy, I made it to another one. Thanks, I'm grateful for seeing another day,'" says Dr. Dossey.

265

You might consider giving the same kind of thanks for all the other blessings in your life: having friends and family who are healthy, being employed, owning a home. Just acknowledging these blessings is a form of prayer, Dr. Dossey points out. "And after you become used to this natural approach, you can expand your prayer life in other directions."

Go to group worship. Quiet prayer is fine, but you'll likely reap more benefits if you do it in a house of worship. When you go to a church or temple, you're surrounded by other people—and that carries its own benefits. "It's been well-documented that any social involvement is probably good for overall well-being," says Dr. Dossey.

But a place of worship is a cut above the average bowling club get-together or town meeting in other respects. "Besides allowing you to be with other people, it gives you positive emotions, faith, and beliefs that encourage good-health behaviors. These are things that you can't necessarily get being around other people at a PTA meeting," Dr. Dossey points out.

Get back to nature. Just going out into nature is a great way to connect with a higher being, says Dr. Dossey. "Many people find that exposure to nature is one of the best ways of getting involved with prayer. It feels right to be quiet and sit down."

Searching for Centering

Just as there are many forms of prayer, there are also many methods—and some require more concentrated attention than others.

One of the oldest methods of communicating with God is "centering prayer," which is practiced among people of all faiths. Based on a fourteenth-century book called *The Cloud of Unknowing*, centering prayer is taught in workshops around the country. Here are the four-step guidelines to centering prayer, as taught by Father Thomas Keating, former abbot of the Trappist Monastery of St. Joseph's Abbey in Spencer, Massachusetts, and author of *Open Mind, Open Heart*.

1. Choose a sacred word as the symbol of your intention to consent to God's presence and action within.

2. Sitting comfortably and with eyes closed, settle briefly, then silently introduce the sacred word as the symbol of your consent to God's presence and action within.

3. When you become aware of thoughts, return ever-so-gently to the sacred word.

4. At the end of the prayer period, remain in silence with eyes closed for a couple of minutes.

The sacred word can be any word that comes to you during a brief period of prayer, Father Keating says, and it should be a word that is especially suitable to you, providing personal inspiration. For one person this might be a word such as *Lord, Jesus, Abba,* or *Maria*—while someone else might be inspired by a word such as *love, peace, mercy, calm, trust, shalom,* or *amen.* Once you have chosen the sacred word, be sure to stay with it throughout the prayer.

Taking a comfortable position with your eyes closed does not mean falling asleep, Father Keating notes. He advises that you choose a sitting position with your back straight and close your eyes "to let go of what is going on around and within" you.

"Introduce the sacred word inwardly," Father Keating adds, "and as gently as laying a feather on a piece of absorbent cotton."

Step 3 of the guidelines, "Return ever-so-gently to the sacred word," means that you keep coming back to the word with a minimum of effort. You are sure to have other thoughts while you are praying, such as sense perceptions, feelings, images, memories, reflections, and commentaries, but the activity of returning to the sacred word helps you stay focused on centering prayer.

The minimum time for centering prayer is 20 minutes—and Father Keating recommends two periods each day, one session first thing in the morning and one in the afternoon or early evening. During the prayer, you may have some physical symptoms—some pains, itching, or restlessness or some heaviness or lightness in your arms, hands, legs, and feet. "In either case, we pay no attention, or we allow the mind to rest briefly in the sensation," he says. "Then return to the sacred word."

what?

Ninety-six percent of all Americans say that they believe in God or some form of universal consciousness; 72 percent believe in angels; 65 percent believe in the devil.

267

Long-Term Tactics

For Keeping the Faith

Although prayer is a powerful way to encourage health and longevity, it's not the only way. People who actively practice their faith make it a habit to attend services and participate in social activities with members of their congregation. That kind of participation plays an important part in healing—not only in the physical sense of being healed from illness but also in a spiritual way.

"From a Jewish perspective, healing *begins* in community," says Rabbi Simkha Y. Weintraub, rabbinic director of the National Center for Jewish Healing in New York City.

Of course, not everyone is a member of a congregation. If you have never belonged to a church or temple—or if you once did but haven't been attending—you might not feel comfortable diving directly into the mainstream of religious life. So where do you start?

When you visit a church, synagogue, or any place of worship, you'll probably want to see what kind of atmosphere it has. To some people, the pastor or rabbi is important, and you might want to talk to that person first. And of course, you will want to attend a service to find out what it's like. In addition, here are some other steps you can take.

Begin with books. Before you can choose a faith community, you need to explore your own spirituality and gain a sense of what you believe, says Barry Holtz, Ph.D., associate professor of Jewish education at the Jewish Theological Seminary of America in New York City. Books on religion, which you can find at a library or a bookstore, can help you do that. They provide an entry point into almost every faith.

Get a tour guide. If you want someone to give you guidance, you might want to call someone who teaches religion at a local school or college, or drop by to see a local rabbi or priest, says Dr. Holtz. Any one of them will be more than happy to discuss various faith communities in your area, listen to your views, and help you decide where you might feel most comfortable. Every

268

Rise Up Singing

No matter what the timbre of your voice, you can enjoy the fellowship and spiritual participation of singing with others. Singing allows you to express your faith and emotions, share your values, and strengthen the supportive bonds of a faith community, notes Harold Koenig, M.D., director of the Center for the Study of Religion/Spirituality and Health at Duke University Medical Center in Durham, North Carolina.

Marietta Quinby, a member of the Religious Society of Friends (Quaker), who teaches troubled youths in Sellersville, Pennsylvania, discovered the power of song. Invited to a sing at a neighboring Quaker meeting, she overcame her initial reluctance and decided to go. "I can't carry a tune," says Quinby. "But I walked into the house where the party was held, and the sense of warmth, bonding, and joy was overwhelming."

After that experience, Quinby decided she would periodically hold a sing in her home. She invites members of her own and another Quaker meeting to join her family. The gatherings usually take place in the evening after dinner. Quinby borrows songbooks from a local meeting (the title of the songbook she uses is *Rise Up Singing!*), and she asks some volunteers to bring dessert.

"Usually, we sing for an hour, then take a break to eat," says Quinby. "Then we sing for another hour. We close with a moment of silence as we stand in a circle and hold hands."

If you enjoy lifting your voice in song and want to participate regularly in music for worship, you could join a choir or become a cantor in a temple. But for many people, just singing with a congregation provides a spiritual reward that can have a positive effect on your health, says Dr. Koenig.

faith has so many different traditions to choose from that it's not a bad idea to look for a tour guide to help you sort out some of the options, he says.

Look for programs that please. Many of the larger Protestant churches today have adopted a full-service approach to fit a variety of needs, says the Reverend Keith A. Brown, co-pastor of the 3,000-member First Presbyterian Church in Bethlehem, Pennsylvania. For example, you might find multiple programs such as marriage encounters, divorce support groups, parenting seminars, social activism ministries, and inner-city work camps.

269

Even though the congregation may be large, you're likely to feel more at home if you attend one of these smaller groups. It's a way to maintain the warm person-to-person connection and sense of community.

Tune in. Not all of us are emotionally or physically able to attend worship services or participate in the discussions and activities of a congregation. But surprisingly, even watching religious programming on television seems to encourage health and healing, says Dr. Larson. And if you want to be more actively involved, you can generally call the toll-free numbers that these programs often provide to request prayers, talk to a pastoral counselor, or order religious literature.

part 2

Whole-Body Protection

Protect Yourself
from Arthritis

Murphy Huston felt like he had it all. He loved his job as an announcer at WISN radio in Milwaukee. He was raising four energetic kids and still finding time to pursue his passion for sports, particularly softball, basketball, and football. At 30, he felt strong, fit, and in the prime of life.

Then everything changed. Halfway through a weekend softball tournament, his shoulders and knees started screaming with pain. Huston could barely swing a bat or walk to first base.

For four days he toughed it out. Then he hobbled in to see his doctor, and what he learned surprised him: He had rheumatoid arthritis.

Even though arthritis is often believed to be a disease of the elderly, it usually begins fairly early in life, says John Thompson, M.D., professor of medicine at the University of Western Ontario Medical School and author of *Arthritis: Everything You Need to Know about Arthritis.* "Most people who get rheumatoid arthritis develop it in their thirties, forties, or fifties," he explains. Another form of arthritis, called osteoarthritis, may occur in younger folks, although it is generally associated with aging. Virtually everyone over age 50 has it to some degree, he says, but many of those people are without symptoms.

But no matter what kind of arthritis comes along—and there are more varieties of arthritis than Baskin-Robbins has flavors—there are just as many strategies for keeping the pain and stiffness under control. What's more, doctors know some very effective techniques for stopping osteoarthritis even before it strikes.

273

Two Kinds of Pain

Your body is a virtual Lego structure assembled with connecting joints, which are simply the places where pairs of bones meet. The ends of each bone are covered with cartilage, a tough, slippery material that allows bones to glide smoothly back and forth. To make movement even easier, each joint is covered with a cushiony membrane that's filled with lubricating liquid, called synovial fluid, which helps to keep the joints nearly friction-free.

That's what's supposed to happen. When you get arthritis, however, the joint's natural movements get rough and creaky. Lubrication declines, and the cartilage gradually wears away. Instead of sliding smoothly, the bones begin to grate. This is what causes pain, stiffness, inflammation, and other arthritis symptoms.

Although there are more than 100 kinds of arthritis, the two most common varieties are osteoarthritis and rheumatoid arthritis. If you haven't seen a doctor, it's difficult to tell them apart since they cause many of the same symptoms. But for either type of arthritis, you need to take positive action; otherwise, your joints will gradually get worse. And as anyone with arthritis will tell you, the pain and stiffness can really cramp your style, making you feel much older than your years.

While there isn't a cure for arthritis, you can do a lot to manage or even eliminate the discomfort. "I take care of myself," Huston says. "I work out, and I make sure I get enough rest. I don't let it get me down."

Help for Wear and Tear

Osteoarthritis, which affects almost 16 million Americans, is so common that if you had x-rays taken today, you would probably show some signs of it. The telltale indicators are a little wear in the bony joints in your neck and spine, for example, or some roughness on the bony surfaces in your hips, knees, toes, or fingers.

This "wear-and-tear arthritis" is largely the result of cartilage

274

Walking Away from Surgery

Leo Caito had put a lot of hard miles on his knees by the time he limped into a hospital waiting room in the fall of 1991. A former football halfback, Caito had played with the University of Notre Dame and the University of Nebraska. During his athletic career, he had torn his right knee on the field and his left knee while playing touch football.

Over the years the pain in both knees had become progressively worse. "I figured I had osteoarthritis," says Caito, an insurance executive in Chardon, Ohio. As he soon found out, however, there wasn't an easy fix.

"The doctor looked at x-rays of my knees and, after about 15 seconds, told me that I needed to have both knees replaced," Caito recalls. "I said to myself, 'There has to be something other than this.' "

There was. Caito found an arthritis specialist who was willing to give his knees a second chance. First, Caito began taking medications to ease the pain and inflammation. Then he started seeing a physical therapist who taught him exactly how to take care of his aching joints.

"They showed me how to exercise, and they had me lose some weight," says Caito, who is in his fifties. And that was just the start. Today, Caito regularly walks, golfs, and swims—all joint-friendly activities that help keep his knees limber and strong. When the pain returns, as it does from time to time, he knows it is time to ice his knees or slip into a hot tub. "Now, I know what to do about it," he says.

wearing out and bones rubbing against each other. It's most common in places where there is a lot of pressure. A good example: Baseball umpires, who spend their careers squatting, are particularly vulnerable to osteoarthritis in the knees, says Alan Lichtbroun, M.D., assistant professor of rheumatology and internal medicine director of the alternative medicine department at the Robert Wood Johnson Medical School in New Brunswick, New Jersey.

"Your hips, knees, toes, fingers, neck, and lower back are particularly susceptible to osteoarthritis because so many activi-

275

ties put stress on these joints," adds Doyt Conn, M.D., a rheumatologist and senior vice president for medical affairs at the Arthritis Foundation.

Makeover Minutes

To Ease the Pain

Because osteoarthritis usually occurs slowly, you may not even know you have it—until one day your fingers hurt when you are opening a can, or your knees are so stiff that you have trouble getting up from a chair. When that starts to happen, you'll want relief. Here are some things that you can do every day—in just a few minutes—to help keep your joints strong and healthy.

Apply heat. Nothing is more soothing than a hot bath when you're feeling sore and achy since heat relaxes muscles and improves blood flow to the area. But you don't have to fill the tub to get fast relief. According to the Arthritis Foundation, you can wrap a heating pad or hot pack in a towel and just lay it on top of the sore area. Try to keep the heat on that area for 20 minutes—and repeat the treatment three times a day. The heat will help relax the muscles surrounding the joint, increase circulation, and get the joint moving smoothly again.

Put on some cold. Since arthritis pain is often caused by inflammation, the Arthritis Foundation recommends that you chill the joint when you have a sudden flare-up. (Reserve heat for the times when you're feeling sore and achy.) Chilling the joint helps constrict blood vessels.

The best way to get relief? You can immerse the sore spot in cold water—using the sink or bathtub. But it's probably more convenient to just apply a cold pack or ice bag to the area for about 20 minutes. You can make an ice pack by putting ice cubes in a plastic bag, or you can use and reuse a large bag of frozen peas. But you don't want ice on your bare skin since it can damage nerves right under the surface, says Donna Os-

276

baugh, a physical therapist with the Colorado Physical Therapy Services in Denver. Wrap the cold pack in a pillowcase, and after you have applied it for about 20 minutes, wait at least 45 minutes before you put it on again.

Apply a salve. A number of over-the-counter creams contain capsaicin, the same compound that gives chili peppers their bite. This spicy substance appears to deprive nerve endings of a compound that is known as substance P, which is responsible for sending pain signals to the brain. The cream doesn't work for everyone, Dr. Lichtbroun says, but it can often provide significant relief.

Get the most from over-the-counter drugs. Many common medications like aspirin, ibuprofen, and acetaminophen work very quickly to relieve pain in tender joints. Acetaminophen is often the best choice because it rarely causes stomach upset or other side effects, says Dr. Lichtbroun.

The problem with acetaminophen is that it doesn't work against inflammation, which often occurs during osteoarthritis flare-ups. Aspirin and ibuprofen, however, along with a variety of anti-inflammatory drugs, can be very effective, says Dr. Thompson. Since these medications sometimes cause stomach upset, your doctor might prescribe an additional medication that will help counteract the nausea.

Since everyone responds differently to anti-inflammatory drugs, be sure to tell your doctor if you're not getting relief, Dr. Lichtbroun says. There are more than a dozen kinds to choose from. When one drug doesn't work, another possibly will.

Perfect your posture. Bad posture puts a lot of pressure on various joints, causing bone and cartilage to wear away in certain spots—just as poor alignment in your car can cause tires to wear unevenly. It can also cause a lot of pain. So check yourself to make sure that you're sitting or standing straight. As you read this book, for example, are you slumped in your chair with your head tilted forward? If so, you are putting unnecessary pressure on your neck and lower back, which could lead to problems later on, says Dr. Lichtbroun.

The idea is to sit and stand in such a way that your bones are evenly balanced, rather than veering off at odd angles. Seek out

know what?

Gardeners and on-your-knees floor scrubbers, beware! People who spend a lot of time kneeling have three times the risk of developing osteoarthritis of the knees than folks who spend more of their time upright.

277

Get a Grip

Left to your own devices, you can make life easier on your joints. The trick, of course, is choosing the right devices.

Manufacturers have created a variety of everyday tools that are designed to reduce painful stress on the fingers, knees, and other joints, says Donna Osbaugh, a physical therapist with the Colorado Physical Therapy Services in Denver.

Long-handled shoehorns, for example, allow you to get dressed without bending your back very much. You can buy "grabbers" that will remove lightweight items from high places or hard-to-reach places, like off the floor. Next time you buy a suitcase, get the kind with wheels that will spare your shoulders a lot of grief when you travel.

Even some of the tools we take for granted, like hammers or garden tools, are now being offered with big grips. This makes them a lot easier to hold and use than their narrow-handled counterparts. "A lot of these things you can find at drugstores and hardware stores," says Osbaugh.

If you don't feel like spending extra money, there are ways to make it easier to use the tools you already own. Get some pipe insulation from a hardware store, and you can tape it around rake handles, screwdriver handles, or even pencils. The insulation is thick, soft, and spongy, and if your joints tend to be stiff, it makes any tool much easier to use, Osbaugh says. For smaller objects such as pencils, she also suggests using the foam from sponge hair curlers.

a chair that has a firm seat and straight back for support. And when you are seated, hold your head and upper back straight, keeping your knees level with your hips and your feet flat on the floor, Dr. Lichtbroun advises. When you are standing, keep your shoulders in line with your hips and your hips in line with your knees and feet. You don't need to stand at attention. The idea is simply to keep your body relaxed and straight with your weight evenly distributed. This one simple trick will take a lot of stress off your joints, he says.

The way you walk can be as good—or bad—for you as the way you stand. If you walk with your back hunched over or your ankles turned out, you could be putting a lot of pressure on vulnerable joints, says Dr. Lichtbroun. "If people had their gait

278

evaluated by a doctor and changed it so that they walked better, it would help save their knees and hips in the long run."

Ease the burden. There is a good reason that you don't carry a backpack with your little finger. Smaller joints aren't as strong as bigger ones, and giving them too much of a load can cause pain and stiffness later on. That's why doctors advise doing any job with the biggest joint that you can.

When you are carrying groceries, for example, don't walk all the way to the door holding the bags by your fingers. Instead, shift the weight to your arms, which have longer joints and are better able to support the load, Osbaugh says. Similarly, if you tote a purse, get one with a shoulder strap instead of a handle, or better yet, get a fanny pack. The weight that might cramp your fingers is barely a flyweight for the stronger joints in the shoulder.

Eat some protection. The Arthritis Foundation's suggestions for diet are simple: Eat a balanced diet based on plenty of vegetables, fruits, and grains and take in only moderate amounts of sugar, salt, fat, cholesterol, and alcohol. Some researchers believe, however, that specific supplements may relieve the symptoms of arthritis. Even though osteoarthritis is mainly caused by mechanical wear-and-tear on the joints, there is some evidence that free radicals—harmful oxygen molecules that damage tissues throughout the body—may play some role in causing joint damage, says Neal Barnard, M.D., president of the Physicians Committee for Responsible Medicine and author of *Eat Right, Live Longer*. To combat the free radicals, it is important to get more of the antioxidant nutrients, such as vitamins C and E, in your diet.

In one study, for example, Massachusetts researchers found that people with higher amounts of vitamins C and E in their diets had less pain or cartilage loss in their knees than people getting small amounts of these nutrients.

It's very easy to get plenty of vitamin C from food since generous amounts of this vitamin are in a variety of fruits and vegetables, such as broccoli, peppers, strawberries, and citrus fruits. Vitamin E, however, is somewhat trickier to get. It's in seeds and whole grains, but the main source is vegetable cooking oils,

know what?
The slippery synovial fluid that lubricates your joints has the consistency of egg white.

279

which are all fat. To get the benefits of vitamin E without the excess calories, you may want to take daily supplements. According to Dr. Lichtbroun, 400 international units of vitamin E is a good daily dose.

Sleep naturally. Even though we are accustomed to propping ourselves up with pillows when we sleep, this can put unnecessary stress on a variety of joints, Osbaugh says. To give your joints some relief, she recommends sleeping in a neutral position. This means lying on your back or side and keeping your neck in line with your back, with your arms and legs in a soft, relaxed position and your elbows, wrists, knees, and ankles bent very slightly. This position generally puts the least possible stress on the joints and can be very soothing when arthritis flares.

Put electricity to work. Another way to get quick relief from the pain is with a procedure called transcutaneous electrical nerve stimulation, or TENS. The principle is simple. Electrodes are attached to the skin over the painful joint. The electrodes deliver mild electrical impulses into the nerves, which can quickly ease the pain. "Only a certain amount of electrical activity can go through your spinal cord to your brain at one time," Dr. Lichtbroun explains. "If you have this continuous pulse from the TENS machine, pain impulses from your joint don't get through to your brain."

With a doctor's prescription, you can buy or rent a TENS machine from a medical supply store. A small machine is about the size of a pager—and can be worn on your belt—while the larger-size machines need to be set up and used at home. But all require a doctor's prescription, according to Dr. Lichtbroun.

Long-Term Tactics
To Tame Arthritis

The human body is designed for movement—and move we do, virtually every minute of every day. This means our joints, over time, invariably begin showing signs of wear. But it doesn't mean that osteoarthritis—or the pain, stiffness, and swelling that may accompany it—can't be prevented. Far from it. By keeping your muscles strong and limber and by doing everything you can to reduce pressure on your joints, you can stay flexible and pain-free for the rest of your life. Here's what experts advise.

Keep your muscles strong. Although we think of osteoarthritis as being a bone problem, it often begins in the muscles. If your muscles aren't strong, joints tend to slip out of alignment, causing hot spots, where the pressure is greatest, says Dr. Lichtbroun. But when you exercise regularly, you build up muscle strength. This helps keep the joints stable and makes them more flexible—and less likely to show signs of wear.

Some of the best exercises for controlling and preventing osteoarthritis are those that are low-impact, like swimming and walking, which don't put a lot of stress on your joints, says Dr. Lichtbroun. Swimming is particularly good, he adds, since the water helps support your weight so that your joints don't have to.

No matter what kind of exercise you do, it's extremely important to spend some time doing what experts call range-of-motion exercises, Osbaugh says. (For more information, see "Staying Limber" on page 284.) If you do a combination of these exercises, you'll move your joints in all possible directions, keeping them strong and flexible. In addition, you might want to try many of the flexibility, aerobic, and strengthening exercises in Stop-Time Tactic No. 4 on page 87. But before you start any exercise program, check with your doctor or physical therapist and have him tailor a routine for you, Osbaugh advises.

Begin moderately. Once you have made the commitment to regular exercise, it's tempting to give it everything you have—right away. Slow down, Osbaugh says. It's important to start workouts slowly to give blood time to flow to the muscles. This will make you more flexible, which in turn makes it possible to get the most benefits from the exercise with less risk of getting hurt.

Warmups don't have to be fancy, she adds. When you're walking, for example, simply walk slowly for the first 5 to 10 minutes, then gradually pick up the pace. The same goes for using

know what?

The ancient Greeks believed that arthritis was caused by an excess of humours— bodily substances that flowed from the brain through the joints. The word *rheumatism*, in fact, is from the Greek word meaning "flow."

281

exercise equipment, like cycles or treadmills. Start slowly and with low resistance, then gradually increase the difficulty as your muscles and joints get warm and limber.

Keep an eye on your weight. Shedding extra pounds is one of the best ways both to prevent and relieve osteoarthritis in the knees and hips, says Dr. Lichtbroun. After all, your joints work hard carrying you around. The more of you there is, the harder they work—and the more likely you are to have problems with pain and stiffness.

The keys to losing weight, of course, are getting more exercise and taking in fewer calories. For a complete weight-loss program, see Stop-Time Tactic No. 2 on page 36.

Know about needling. For years, Eastern doctors have been treating osteoarthritis with acupuncture, the procedure where very tiny needles are painlessly inserted in critical parts of the body. No one is sure why acupuncture seems to help, although research suggests that it may cause the body to release chemicals that help relieve pain.

If you do give acupuncture a try, don't expect instant results, says Dr. Lichtbroun, also a certified acupuncturist who studied the procedure in China. "One treatment is not enough," he says. "You usually begin with two treatments a week for a couple of weeks, then once a week for a few weeks. Give it 8 to 10 treatments to see if there is an improvement."

People with mild osteoarthritis may benefit the most from acupuncture, Dr. Conn adds.

Ask about surgery. Sometimes the joints afflicted with osteoarthritis are so worn that surgery is needed to repair the damage. Though most people with osteoarthritis won't need joint replacement, some may need to have their damaged joints replaced with metal, ceramic, or plastic replacements. For those who have the procedure, joint replacement can make a tremendous difference, says Dr. Conn.

Hip-replacement surgery, for example, can relieve pain and restore flexibility in 98 to 99 percent of cases, says Gerald Eisenberg, M.D., president of Advocate Medical Group in Park Ridge, Illinois, and former director of rheumatology at Lutheran General Hospital in Chicago. Knee surgery also works very well, he

282

says, but results in replacing other joints is less predictable. If you're in a lot of pain, the best thing is to talk to your doctor about the potential benefits and drawbacks of having replacement surgery, says Dr. Conn.

Relief from Inflammation

We think of arthritis as hurting only the joints, but one kind of arthritis—and one of the most serious—is more wide-ranging. "Rheumatoid arthritis can cause inflammation throughout the body, which is why people with this condition often don't feel well in general," says Dr. Eisenberg.

Unlike osteoarthritis, which comes on gradually, rheumatoid arthritis often appears all at once. It explains why Murphy Huston could barely drag himself off the field by the end of his softball tournament—even though he started the tournament in fighting trim.

Doctors still don't know what triggers the inflammation. But they have observed that people with a family history of the disease are three times more likely to get it than those who don't have it in the family; so heredity may play a role. There is also a gender bias to the disease—because it's three times more common in women than in men. In addition, evidence suggests that diet may play a role in some cases, says Dr. Barnard.

If you have rheumatoid arthritis, your body's immune system begins attacking the membranes lining the joints. This inflammation can spread to cartilage, tendons, ligaments, bones, and even internal organs. Sometimes rheumatoid arthritis can suddenly subside—for weeks, months, or even years. Eventually, it usually comes back, causing painful, fatiguing flare-ups that can make a movement as simple as buttoning a shirt seem impossibly difficult.

Since no one knows for sure what causes rheumatoid arthritis, there's no sure way to prevent it. "But experts say that a combination of exercise, medications, and perhaps even changes in your diet do make the affliction easier to live with," says Dr. Eisenberg.

what?

When a joint is under pressure, the lubricating fluid is forced from the cartilage, seeping back in like water to a sponge when the pressure is relieved. This process is called weeping lubrication.

283

Staying Limber

Joints are made to move, and unless you move them regularly, they'll start flunking their flexibility tests. That's why range-of-motion exercises, in which you move your joints to their fullest potential, are so important.

When doing range-of-motion exercises, always start with 5 to 10 minutes of gentle exercise—walking a few blocks, for example, or riding an exercise bike slowly—to give your joints time to warm up, says Donna Osbaugh, a physical therapist with the Colorado Physical Therapy Services in Denver. Once you start doing the exercises, pay attention to how you feel, she adds. If your joints are hurting today, you obviously won't move them as far as you did yesterday or the day before. Just move them gently as far as you can. Most of the time, however, you'll find that your range of motion will improve, while pain and stiffness will lessen.

The Arthritis Foundation cautions that you should do these exercises slowly, without any bouncing movements—and, of course, stop exercising if you have severe pain. Do 3 to 10 repetitions of each of these eight exercises and repeat once or twice a day. Be sure that you don't hold your breath. In fact, you will help your pacing and breathing if you count out loud.

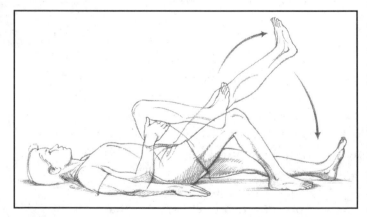

1. Knee and Hip

◄ Lie on your back with one knee bent and the other straight in front of you. Clasp your hands behind the knee of the straight leg and slowly pull the knee to your chest, then hold for a second. Straighten the leg into the air, then gradually lower the leg to the floor. Then repeat with the other leg. If you feel pain in your knee, don't straighten it into the air. Just lower your leg to the floor.

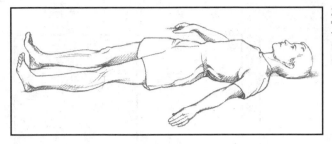

2. Hip

◄ Lie on your back with your legs straight and about six inches apart.

► Keeping your toes pointed up, slide (don't lift) one leg out to the side, then return to the starting position. Then repeat with the other leg. *Caution:* Don't do this exercise if you have had hip-replacement surgery or if you have lower back problems or osteoporosis.

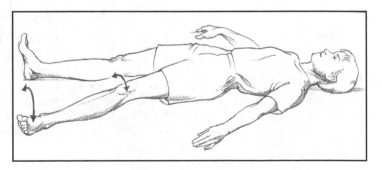

3. Shoulder

◄ Lie on your back with your arms at your sides. Keeping your elbow straight, slowly raise one arm over your head until your biceps muscle is close to your ear. Slowly lower the arm back to your side, then repeat with the other arm.

4. Hip and Knee

► Lie on your back with your legs straight and about six inches apart, with your toes pointed up. Using your hips only, roll both your legs in and then out, keeping your knees straight.

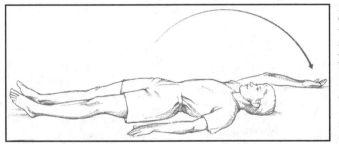

285

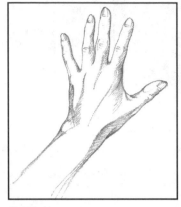

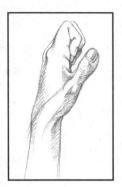

5. Fingers

▲ Open your hand so that your fingers are straight and spread apart.

▲ Curl your fingers until your fingertips touch the top of your palm.

▲ Reach your thumb across your palm until it touches the joint of your little finger as shown, then stretch it out. Repeat with the other hand.

6. Chin and Neck

◀ Looking straight ahead, pull your chin back—it will look like you have a double chin. Do this without looking down, keeping your head erect and continuing to look straight ahead. Hold for three seconds.

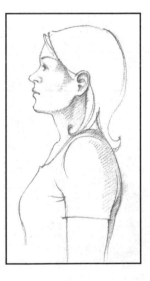

▶ Then raise your neck as though someone were pulling you up by your hair.

Whole-Body Protection

7. Back

◀ Reach one palm over your shoulder as though you were patting yourself on the back. At the same time, place the back of your other hand on your lower back and slide your hands toward each other as if you were trying to bring your fingertips together. (Most people can't do it—it's too much of a stretch.) Then switch the position of each arm and do it again.

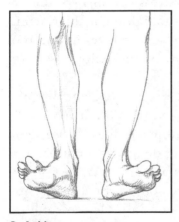

8. Ankles

▲ Sit with your heels on the floor, and bend your ankles so that you lift your toes as high as possible.

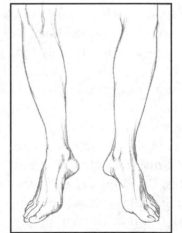

▲ Then drop your toes to the floor and lift your heels as high as possible.

Protect Yourself from Arthritis

To Help Soothe Rheumatoid Arthritis

Many of the same strategies that can help you get the upper hand with osteoarthritis—like stretching and regular aerobic and strengthening exercises—also work with rheumatoid arthritis. But rheumatoid arthritis is really an entirely different condition, which means that you can control it in different ways. Here are some tactical hints.

Give yourself a break. Even when it's mild, rheumatoid arthritis can make you feel surprisingly tired. Listen to your body, Osbaugh recommends. Set aside regular rest breaks so that you can recoup your strength. During flare-ups, for example, a 15-minute break every hour will help you feel stronger and more energetic. In fact, you may find that you get more done by allowing for pauses than by attempting to work straight through.

Breathe easy to conquer stress. There's simply no way to eliminate stress from your life. What you can do is keep it under control. This is important because stress can disrupt the immune system as well as cause muscles to tighten, making arthritis flare-ups even worse. Though everyone relaxes in different ways, here is an easy strategy that many find helpful, says Dr. Eisenberg.

Sit in a comfortable chair, close your eyes, and breathe deeply, making sure that your stomach rises when you inhale and falls when you exhale. If your stomach doesn't rise when you breathe in, you're not breathing deeply enough. Do this once or twice a day for 15 minutes at a time. While you are doing this, Dr. Eisenberg suggests that you try visualization. You can visualize pleasant scenes from your past. Or you could visualize the pain or stress in your body symbolically. Then focus on the symbol and try to make it disappear, taking your stress and pain with it.

Tense different parts. Another relaxation technique is called progressive relaxation, says Dr. Eisenberg. Here's how it works: Lie down and breathe deeply for a minute or two. Then slowly

288

tense the muscles in your feet and calves, hold for several seconds, then relax. Progress upward to the next group of muscles—those in your thighs, buttocks, stomach, arms, hands, and shoulders—tensing and relaxing them in turn. By the time you have covered your whole body, you'll find that you are feeling surprisingly calm and in control. Do this once or twice a day for 15 minutes at a time, Dr. Eisenberg recommends.

Chow Choices for Grief Relief

Most people find that the best way to control rheumatoid arthritis is with prescription or over-the-counter medications. In fact, aspirin or ibuprofen are often all it takes to dramatically relieve the pain, says Dr. Eisenberg. (Acetaminophen usually does not work as well because it has little effect on inflammation.) In addition to those medications, there are more than a dozen prescription drugs that are very effective at fighting inflammation, says Dr. Lichtbroun. But paying attention to what you eat may also help some people who have rheumatoid arthritis.

According to the American College of Rheumatology, diet does not have an important role in the nutritional treatment for most patients. But studies suggest that there are two ways that foods could affect arthritis. For a small number of people, food allergies could worsen the symptoms—and certain diets seem to affect the inflammation. Furthermore, evidence suggests that certain foods can aggravate rheumatoid arthritis, at least in some people, says Dr. Barnard.

Everyone reacts to different foods differently, but some common offenders include animal fat, corn and safflower oils, milk, eggs, wheat, citrus fruits, caffeine, tomatoes, and chocolate. "In some cases, if you get rid of the offending food, all symptoms disappear," he says.

It's not always easy to discover what foods you may be sensitive to. For starters, ask your doctor for a complete list of foods that have been linked with arthritis flare-ups. Try eliminating all of the more common offenders for about four

289

Reclaiming Lost and Youthful Cartilage

In the future, it may be possible for doctors to repair the cartilage damaged by osteoarthritis. In the meantime, researchers have been studying substances the body uses to make cartilage, and they have come up with some intriguing results.

Studies have shown that when people take supplements containing glucosamine and chondroitin sulfate—synthetic versions of compounds the body produces naturally—they may have some improvement in arthritis symptoms. "Studies suggest that these substances can help control pain and, more important, may result in actual structural improvements in damaged cartilage," says Alan Lichtbroun, M.D., assistant professor of rheumatology and internal medicine director of the alternative medicine department at the Robert Wood Johnson Medical School in New Brunswick, New Jersey.

Italian researchers compared chondroitin sulfate to a nonsteroidal anti-inflammatory drug (NSAID) to see which best reduced the symptoms of osteoarthritis of the knee. The NSAID offered prompt relief, but symptoms returned when the medication was stopped. Chondroitin took longer to bring about relief, but the benefits lasted up to three months after the medication was stopped.

While early studies have shown promise, it's too early to say whether or not these substances will prove to be effective. Larger, longer studies are needed to determine if they are safe and effective.

---

weeks. If that strategy doesn't work, Dr. Barnard recommends a more strict elimination diet—cutting back to very slim meals and then gradually adding a new food every day. This allows you to easily pinpoint the problem food. But other doctors warn about the dangers of malnutrition on a very strict elimination diet, so you should never try it without a doctor's supervision.

There's also debate about the role of fat as it relates to arthritis. Research suggests that omega-3 fatty acids, which are found in cold-water fish, canola oil, and flaxseed, can slow the body's production of immune cells that cause joint inflammation. Researchers from Brigham and Women's Hospital in Boston analyzed 10 studies on the role of omega-3 fatty acids and rheumatoid arthritis. They found that taking fish oil supplements for three months resulted in modest but measurable improvements in joint tenderness and morning stiffness. At the University of Washington in Seattle, researchers found that women eating two servings a week of baked or broiled fish had about half the risk of joint pain from rheumatoid arthritis as women who ate less than one serving per week. The effective dose appears to be three to five grams of omega-3s a day, or five to eight ounces of salmon or tuna steak.

Protect Yourself from Cancer

Cancer is sneaky. It can quietly develop cell by cell, often taking years to cause problems. So it's easy for a person who feels youthful and healthy to become complacent about important lifestyle habits, like eating well, that can help stave off the disease. Not too surprisingly, age-protector tactics often take on new urgency only after the C-word pops up.

"After I was diagnosed, I wanted to do everything I could to be healthy for the rest of my life," says Shaun Hughes, the founder of Sun Precautions, a Seattle clothing manufacturer in his forties who survived melanoma—skin cancer—when he was 26. "I think every cancer survivor's dream is to go on with life and either die in your sleep or after getting hit by a school bus while you're walking across the street at age 93."

While it may seem as though the news about cancer has risen dramatically in recent years, it's actually been with us for a very long time. Dinosaurs may have had it. Five-thousand-year-old Egyptian mummies show signs of it. And written descriptions of cancer date back nearly 3,500 years. Even plants can get it.

Just a couple of generations ago, the odds of living a long life after cancer weren't great. As recently as the 1970s, melanoma, the aggressive form of skin cancer Hughes had, was rarely treated successfully. Testicular cancer, the most common cancer among men ages 15 to 35, was almost always fatal. And among women, recovery from cervical cancer was considered unlikely, according to Tim Byers, M.D., professor of preventive medicine at the University of Colorado Health Sciences Center in Denver.

292

Benefits from Breakthroughs

Once as mysterious as it was frightening, cancer is now far better understood by scientists—which is a boon to us all. "It has been a black box, and we have learned to pry open the lid. It's beginning to be, if not illuminated, dimly lit," said Richard Klausner, M.D., director of the National Cancer Institute in Bethesda, Maryland, in a speech marking the 25th anniversary of the National Cancer Act.

Advances in prevention, screening, and treatment have helped prolong and save numerous lives. Since 1973, survival rates for testicular cancer have soared 66 percent, Hodgkin's disease survival is up 57 percent, and colorectal cancer survival has improved 17 percent.

Around 1990, death rates from cancer started to level off—and began to fall—after a century of relentlessly increasing. By the year 2000, advances in cancer prevention, detection, and treatment will save an additional 27,500 lives per year, says Robert C. Young, M.D., an oncologist and president of Fox Chase Cancer Center in Philadelphia. By 2040, that figure will rise to 137,500 lives annually.

"The recent drop in the cancer death rate marks a turning point from the steady increase that we have seen throughout the century," Dr. Klausner said in a National Cancer Institute announcement of the decline. "The 1990s will be remembered as the decade when we measurably turned the tide against cancer."

Better Chances to Cancel Cancers

Since the 1970s, researchers have discovered many more ways to prevent cancer and survive it. They have also uncovered many ways to protect yourself from a recurrence. Certainly, cancer is still a very long way from being treated like the common cold, and we don't want to discount the damage that cancer can do to your body and spirit. But cancer survival, once considered a rarity, is much more commonplace.

And progress continues. By the mid–twenty-first century, researchers suspect they can corral most cancers. They hope to transform the affliction from a common killer into a troublesome disease that can frequently be cured if not prevented.

"There is no theoretical reason why we can't get to that

293

What's Wrong with These Cells Anyway?

Life certainly would be a lot easier if science could develop a pill to prevent or banish cancer. But don't count on it. For one thing, cancer isn't a single disease, says Robert C. Young, M.D., an oncologist and president of Fox Chase Cancer Center in Philadelphia.

Cancer is a complex set of diseases—perhaps more than 100—caused by abnormal cells that develop and divide uncontrollably. So a lung cancer cell, for example, is slightly different than a prostate cancer cell, which is slightly different from a breast cancer cell. Because of that, it is unlikely that a single treatment will be effective against all of them.

"We are finding solutions to this disease," says Dr. Young, "but cancer is a far more complex problem than most people imagine."

Why cancer develops in the first place may have a lot to do with your age and your body's natural defenses, according to Paul Engstrom, M.D., a medical oncologist and senior vice president of population science at Fox Chase Cancer Center. Normally, cells divide and replicate themselves perfectly without a problem. But once in about every million cell divisions something goes wrong, and the process produces an abnormal cell.

Usually, these abnormal cells are quickly detected and destroyed by your body's immune system. But if the cell isn't destroyed, there is a possibility that it can lead to cancer.

As you get older, the body might begin producing more abnormal cells, and perhaps the immune system becomes less efficient, Dr. Engstrom says. That may be why two of every three cancers occur in people older than 65. The immune system reacts very much like a computer spell-checker that discovers too many misspellings in a word-processing document. The system can be overwhelmed by the sheer numbers of abnormal cells.

By adapting strategies for cancer prevention, we essentially help to keep the immune system—the body's spell-checker—in tip-top shape, says Dr. Engstrom. "By choosing what we eat and how we live, we can help take some of the burden off of the body's spell-checking system."

point," says Robert C. Young, an oncologist and president of Fox Chase Cancer Center in Philadelphia. "We can't get there yet, but we are moving in that direction. We have actually learned more about cancer in the past 10 years than we did in the previous 100."

294

"Forty years ago, it was argued whether cancer was theoretically curable," noted Richard Klausner, M.D., director of the National Cancer Institute in Bethesda, Maryland, in a speech marking the 25th anniversary of the National Cancer Act. "And now cancers have been cured. The proof is there."

Survival rates are constantly improving. More than half of all Americans who develop cancer are still alive five years after they have been diagnosed, according to the National Cancer Institute.

Among women, there's similar good news: With early detection of cervical cancer, 91 out of every 100 women live at least five years after treatment. And at least 97 out of every 100 will live five years or longer after breast cancer treatment. For both sexes, 95 out of 100 have a five-year survival rate from melanoma, while the five-year survival rate for colorectal cancer is 91 out of 100. (But researchers emphasize that the chances of survival are only this good when the cancer is detected early.)

Get Protection Before You Need It

As researchers peel away the mysteries behind this disease, they are finding that you can take some steps—anytime in life— to help protect yourself from certain kinds of cancer. And considering cancer's nasty track record, every one of those protective measures is worth serious consideration. Just take those measures to heart, and you are arming yourself with powerful weapons against a disease that could rob you of youthful vim and vigor.

Many scientists agree about cancer-related factors in our habits and our environment—and the warnings are going out. In the past 20 years, scientists have found that many types of cancer are linked to diet and smoking, and quite a few others may be linked to lack of exercise, sun exposure, and being overweight.

Not so long ago, it was considered a revolutionary notion that some types of cancer may be largely preventable. "In the 1960s, when I was in medical school, nobody seemed to be asking why a particular person got cancer," recalls Walter Willett,

Mammograms: 40 Is the Time to Start

When should a woman start to have x-ray screenings for breast cancer? The whole subject of mammograms—and when to have them—has sparked a controversy that has led to contradictory recommendations.

Not long ago, the National Cancer Institute had concluded that there was no evidence that the screenings significantly reduced the number of deaths in women under 50. But after reviewing more recent evidence, they concluded that women in their forties, who are at average risk for cancer, should get a mammogram every one to two years.

"Deciding when to begin getting mammograms should be a no-brainer," says Stephen Feig, M.D., professor of radiology at Jefferson Medical College and director of breast imaging at Thomas Jefferson University Hospital in Philadelphia. "The vast majority of doctors working in the real world still believe that women should be getting annual mammograms beginning at age 40. The number of lives we could save is certainly worth it."

Breast cancer is the leading cause of cancer deaths for women in their forties to midfifties. But mammograms may often make it possible to spot a small cancer about one year or more before a women in her forties or her doctor could detect it with a manual exam, Dr. Feig says.

That's important because when breast cancer is detected and treated early enough, it's curable in about 97 percent of all cases. Swedish researchers have found that regular mammograms beginning at age 39 can lower a woman's risk of dying from the disease by up to 44 percent.

Early detection also increases the likelihood that cancer will be limited to one small well-defined lump, which can be successfully treated without removing the breast.

So if you are 40 and have no family history of breast cancer before menopause, begin scheduling annual mammograms now, Dr. Feig urges. If your mother or sister had breast cancer before menopause, begin scheduling annual mammograms at age 35 and at least 5 to 10 years before the age at which your relative's cancer was diagnosed, suggests Dr. Feig.

M.D., Dr.P.H., professor of epidemiology and nutrition at the Harvard School of Public Health. "It was just assumed to be an act of God. Even in the 1970s, when it was mentioned that diet might be responsible for the cause and prevention of a lot of cancers, it struck me as a very strange idea. So for us to even conceptualize that cancer is, to a large extent, preventable is an enormous step forward."

And the keys to prevention are in a healthy lifestyle—which means adopting many of the Stop-Time Tactics in Part 1 of this book. In fact, doctors now believe that simply adopting a healthy lifestyle may slash your cancer risk in half, Dr. Willett says. And those effects are likely to begin almost immediately.

"If somebody starts exercising and eating fruits and vegetables, loses weight, stops eating a high-fat diet, and stops smoking, my hunch is that a month later their risk of cancer would be reduced," Dr. Young says. "I can't prove it, but I'd be willing to bet your risk starts going down just as soon as you change your behavior."

Target the Likeliest

One of the nastiest characteristics of cancer is the way it shows more preference for some families than others. But when you think about prevention, that factor can actually work for you as a warning. It's like a flashing railroad-crossing signal—telling you what to watch out for.

Between 5 and 10 percent of all cancers show up in some families more than others, research shows. The family tendency is written in the genes, the cell's coding device that carries the potential for certain kinds of cancer from one generation to the next. But in some families, lifestyle factors are far more significant since traits like smoking, overeating, or eating an unhealthy diet set the stage for certain kinds of cancer.

If you want to know which cancer could be the first to come calling, gather as much information as you can about the health of your parents, grandparents, aunts, uncles, siblings, and cousins, suggests Moshe Shike, M.D., director of the Memorial Sloan-Kettering Cancer Prevention and Wellness program in New York City and co-author of *Cancer Free*. That goes for the next generation, too. If your children have had cancer, it may mean that you are at a higher risk for the disease as well.

know what?

In 1775, British surgeon Sir Percival Pott was the first to recognize that cancer could be caused by an external substance. He noted that chimney sweeps had a high incidence of cancer of the scrotum and speculated that it was linked to the soot in flues.

297

Share this family information with your doctor, who can help you decide at the outset whether you need certain screening tests or genetic counseling, Dr. Shike says. If your family history calls for it, you might need to be screened more frequently than the next person for certain kinds of cancer.

Your doctor can help you set up a screening program that can detect cancer early, suggests Dr. Shike. Once you're on a program, be sure to follow through religiously with your regularly scheduled cancer screenings. The earlier the cancer is found, the more likely it can be successfully treated, he says.

But whether or not your family history puts you at risk of certain kinds of cancer, there are many kinds of potent weapons you can choose to carry in your arsenal. It's just a matter of making those weapons part of your everyday life. Here's a look at the best things that you can do to lessen your chances of getting cancer.

Eat Meat Less Often

Scientists estimate that as many as 30 percent of cancers are linked to diet.

For instance, men who eat beef, pork, or lamb as a main dish 5 to 6 times a week are 2½ times more likely to develop colon cancer than men who eat red meat less than once a week, according to Dr. Willett. Colon cancer is infrequent in countries where meat is rarely eaten and less frequent among Americans who eat a vegetarian diet, he says.

Eating a diet that limits total fat to 20 percent of calories reduces the development of precancerous skin growths and helps prevent skin cancer, according to researchers at Baylor College of Medicine and the Veterans Affairs Medical Center, both in Houston. In their studies, researchers found that people who ate a low-fat diet developed three times fewer precancerous lesions called actinic keratosis than those who ate the typical American diet.

According to the National Cancer Institute, limiting fat in your diet is certainly one key toward warding off some kinds of

Eating Right to Raid the Radicals

Eating a diet loaded with red meat and other fatty foods creates free radicals, unstable molecules that can damage cells and tissues. Inside your body, these rogue molecules cause cholesterol to cling to artery walls and clog them up. But they also can disrupt cell structure and make cells more prone to cancer, according to Paul Engstrom, M.D., a medical oncologist and senior vice president of population science at Fox Chase Cancer Center in Philadelphia.

Eating at least five daily servings of fruits and vegetables, which are good sources of antioxidants like vitamin C, can help destroy free radicals and possibly reverse damage to cells before it leads to cancer, Dr. Engstrom says.

Fruits, vegetables, and grains like whole-wheat bread are also good sources of insoluble fiber, an indigestible substance that helps food zip through your gut. And that rapid movement is important because it reduces the amount of time potential carcinogens in your food will have to damage cells in the digestive tract. Eating more fiber also will push fat and excess calories out of your diet and may help protect you against cancers of the prostate, uterus, and breast. Dr. Engstrom suggests that you get 20 grams of fiber daily.

cancer—and the institute recommends that you stick to a diet of less than 30 percent calories from fat. Naturally, if you do that, you will probably have to start eating no-fat or low-fat fruits, grains, and vegetables instead of high-fat meat, oils, and baked goods. And that's a good switch. As we noted in Stop-Time Tactic No. 1, eating more fruits and vegetables slashes your risk. A study of 976 men and women in California, for instance, showed that those who ate the most fruits, vegetables, and grains were less likely to develop precancerous colon polyps as were those who ate the least of these foods, according to research conducted at Kaiser Permanente Medical Center in Los Angeles. European researchers who investigated the dietary habits of 2,112 men in Wales over a 13-year period came to similar conclusions. They found that regularly eating fruits and vegetables may slash the risk of dying from cancer.

Little wonder, then, that modifying your eating habits tops

299

Selenium Supplements to the Micro-Rescue

Supplementing your diet with a small amount of the trace mineral selenium may make a huge dent in your cancer risk, according to Arizona researchers.

In a 10-year study of 1,312 men and women, those taking selenium supplements had 37 percent lower incidence of cancer than those who took a placebo, a look-alike pill that has no effects, says Larry C. Clark, Ph.D., lead author of the study and associate professor of epidemiology at the Arizona Cancer Center at the University of Arizona College of Medicine in Tucson. The supplements appeared to have a big impact on prostate cancer, cutting incidence of the disease by 63 percent. Those who took selenium also had 58 percent fewer colon cancers and 46 percent fewer lung cancers than those taking the placebo.

Dr. Clark suspects selenium may encourage abnormal cells and small, undetected tumors to self-destruct before they can cause trouble.

While these promising results must be confirmed by further study, the findings are generating enthusiasm among medical professionals. "It's probably the most exciting study that has been done in many years," says Tim Byers, M.D., professor of preventive medicine at the University of Colorado Health Sciences Center in Denver. "It's certainly hard to dismiss."

Selenium is found in fish, shellfish, meats, whole-grain cereals, milk, cheese, and other dairy foods. The recommended Daily Value for selenium is 70 micrograms. People in Dr. Clark's study took 200 micrograms daily. Check with your doctor, however, before you start taking this much selenium.

Even if you adhere to a diet based on the basic food pyramid, you wouldn't necessarily get enough selenium, Dr. Clark points out. Meat provides selenium, but if you eat more meat, you're also likely to overload on dietary fat. "That's why at this point a supplement is probably your best choice for enhancing your dietary selenium levels," says Dr. Clark.

our list of cancer-preventing strategies. To find out how to fit the top 10 cancer-preventive foods into your diet and help cut the fat, see the recommendations in Stop-Time Tactic No. 1 on page 3 and Stop-Time Tactic No. 2 on page 36.

Toss Tobacco Out of Your Life

Thanks to cigarettes, Patrick Reynolds' grandfather, who was the founder of the R. J. Reynolds Tobacco Company, created a vast financial empire that has kept his descendants living in luxury.

But tobacco ruined the Reynolds family that it enriched. Patrick's aunt died of lung cancer, and his father died of smoking-related emphysema. As tobacco took its ruthless toll on his family members, Reynolds began to ask himself the inevitable question: Am I next?

Rather than wait for the answer, he took steps to halt smoking. In 1985, he quit his 17-year pack-a-day habit, divested himself of all Reynolds Tobacco stock, and founded the Foundation for a Smoke-Free America.

Today, Reynolds has no traces of emphysema in his lungs. And he breathes a lot easier knowing that his risk of lung cancer is now virtually the same as for someone who has never smoked.

"I've aged incredibly well," Reynolds says. "I maintain a low-calorie diet, exercise regularly, take vitamins, keep my stress level under control, and, of course, don't smoke."

If you smoke, you probably can recite from memory all of the nasty things you do to your body when you puff away. Cigarette smoking is linked to 30 percent of cancer deaths—add in cigars and pipes, and that rate increases to 42 percent of male cancer deaths.

Other statistics speak just as clearly: Men who smoke are 2,000 times more likely to develop lung cancer, and women who smoke are 1,200 times more susceptible to this disease. Tobacco smoke contains 60 cancer-causing substances, and the risk goes far beyond lung cancer. Smoking substantially elevates your risk of cancers of the larynx, esophagus, mouth, bladder, kidneys, and pancreas.

Anyone who has tried to quit smoking has experienced first-hand the magnetic effect of the prime ingredient in tobacco. Once you are in the grasp of nicotine, which is one of the most addictive drugs known, it takes a determined effort to break free

know what?

Millions of Americans are trying to kick the smoking habit and nicotine dependency. When smoking-cessation products such as Nicorette and Nico-Derm CQ became available over the counter, sales rose from $710,000 to more than $460 million.

301

Snuff Out Those Stogies

David Letterman does it, so does Arnold Schwarzenegger and Bill Cosby. Even actress Demi Moore and President Bill Clinton have been known to light one up.

But don't be fooled. Despite its chic image, the cigar is not a safe alternative to cigarettes, says Robert C. Young, M.D., an oncologist and president of Fox Chase Cancer Center in Philadelphia.

Even if you don't inhale cigar smoke, you are still at three times greater risk of developing lung cancer than a nonsmoker is. Plus, puffing on stogies can actually increase your risk of many disfiguring cancers of the head and neck that can ruin your youthful appearance and destroy your social life, he says.

"Head, neck, lip, and tongue cancers can really only be dealt with through very mutilating forms of surgery and radiation therapy. Knowing that, it just boggles my mind that some people think that cigar smoking is cool," Dr. Young says.

Yet, since the mid-1990s, more than 100 swank cigar lounges have opened nationwide. From 1991 to the end of 1996, the number of premium cigars imported to the United States more than tripled from 100 million to more than 300 million, according to *Cigar Aficionado* magazine. Enthusiasts, such as Robert Langsam, founder and chief smoking officer of the International Association of Cigar Clubs, say that cigars are a symbol of success, and the resurgence is an inevitable backlash against antismoking campaigns.

Dr. Young acknowledges this resurgence but fears that it will have tragic consequences. "When you see supermodel Linda Evangelista on the cover of *Cigar Aficionado* magazine, just imagine what she is going to look like when she has to have half of her jaw surgically removed because she has cancer," Dr. Young says. "Cigar smoking is a disgusting, self-destructive behavior. I don't understand how anyone could think it is sophisticated and cool."

from it, particularly if you have been smoking for many years. Reynolds, for instance, tried to quit 11 times before he was successful.

But the point is, he did it. And if he can do it, Reynolds says, so can you. Even if you have smoked for decades, it is never too late to quit, he emphasizes.

Research shows that you get some cancer-prevention benefits no matter when you quit. By quitting now, you may be putting the brakes on genetic changes so that cells don't develop into a cancer months or even years later, Dr. Young says.

Within a year of quitting, for example, your risk of lung cancer dips considerably, and 10 years after you swear off cigarettes, your risk of the disease is not much greater than that of someone who has never taken a puff. The risk of developing many other cancers—including those affecting the mouth, kidneys, and pancreas—also begins to diminish as soon as you quit, Dr. Young says.

To get you started on the road to cancer protection, here are some recommended ways to steer yourself toward a smoke-free life.

Make a clean break. Most people find it easier to quit cold turkey, says Gary DeNelsky, Ph.D., director of the smoking-cessation program at the Cleveland Clinic in Cleveland. Cutting back gradually can prolong withdrawal symptoms like insomnia and irritability and actually make it more difficult to quit.

Set a quit date, preferably within the next two weeks, and stick to it, Dr. DeNelsky suggests.

Weed out the trouble spots. Many smokers are prone to light up in specific situations—when stuck in a traffic jam, for instance, or while talking on the telephone. Even before your quit date, stop smoking when you are in two or three of the most common of these situations to turn off that automatic, conditioned response, Dr. DeNelsky suggests. Then, when you do quit cold turkey, you have prepared yourself to deal with cravings in these tough situations, and you will be less tempted to reach for a smoke.

Chuck every carton. On your quit date, throw out every cigarette in the house—and every cigar and pipe, too, if you're a multiple smoker. Don't hold back. If you have any hidden in places like sweaters, pockets, and glove compartments, ferret

303

any hidden packs and give them the heave-ho as well. Be sure to get rid of lighters, matches, and ashtrays, too.

"Getting tobacco products out of your life is extremely important," Dr. DeNelsky says. "If the closest cigarette is in your pocket, you only have two seconds to stop yourself from lighting up. But if you have a craving and the nearest cigarette is 10 minutes away at a convenience store, that gives you 10 minutes to really think about what you're doing before you make that purchase."

Count to 3,000. By the time he made his 12th attempt to quit smoking, Reynolds had learned something extremely important from his 11 prior failures. He learned that long after the urge to smoke had quieted down, anytime from 1 to 24 months after his quit date, he would be overcome with an unexpected, nearly out-of-control desire for a cigarette. These surprise attacks would come in moments of stress—negative or positive—such as at a dinner or during vacation. He learned that if he could just hang on for five minutes, the urge would pass, and he would still be a nonsmoker.

Making it through the first minute was the worst, he recalls. After that: "As I wrestled with myself, suddenly I remembered that relief was now four minutes away. "Still dying for a smoke— now three minutes to hold on for. And sure enough at the end of five minutes, the urge was gone, and I was quite proud of myself. It's the best secret I can share with people who are trying to quit."

Consider patching up. If you use a transdermal nicotine patch, you can increase your chance of quitting successfully.

Researchers at Duke University in Durham, North Carolina, found that the ability to abstain the first day while wearing a nicotine patch most accurately predicted who would be smoke-free six months later. People who abstained on the first day were 10 times more likely to quit than those who gave in and smoked.

Nicotine patches don't require a prescription and are available in most drugstores. Just follow the manufacturer's instructions. When you wear one of these patches on your skin, it releases tiny amounts of nicotine into the bloodstream for up to

Whole-Body Protection

24 hours. That eases withdrawal symptoms and makes it easier for you to quit. When you are using these patches, gradually reduce the dose to wean yourself off the nicotine, Dr. DeNelsky advises.

Stop it, by gum. Nicotine gum, another form of nicotine replacement that's available in drugstores, also has helped many people quit. Both the patch and gum are readily available over-the-counter, but be sure to check with your doctor to see if either would be appropriate for you, Dr. DeNelsky says. A number of health conditions including angina, high blood pressure, diabetes, and stomach ulcers may be aggravated if you use these products.

Though both the transdermal patch and nicotine gum can help you resist the nicotine craving, these products are only a temporary solution, Dr. DeNelsky reminds smokers.

"I think the patch and gum are both helpful," Dr. DeNelsky says, "but that doesn't mean that a person who uses one of these methods to quit will never have a craving to smoke again. They will. What it takes beyond the patch or gum is commitment, persistence, and an ability to use any and all coping strategies to fend off cravings."

Shed That Weight

Between her teen years and the age of 50, a typical American woman gains about 17 pounds. The average man, on the other hand, adds about 23 pounds of extra baggage during that same life period.

These unappealing extra pounds do more than rob us of our youthful appearance. Being 20 to 35 percent over your ideal body weight can up your cancer risk considerably. How much? Well, consider these findings.

▪ After following 5,600 women up to age 74 for 10 years, researchers at the National Cancer Institute concluded that those who had gained 50 to 60 pounds since age 25 were 2½ times more prone to postmenopausal breast cancer than women who gained 25 pounds or less.

305

■ Studies have shown that very heavy women with more upper-body fat—the so-called apple-shaped body—have five to six times greater risk of breast cancer, according to David Schapira, M.D., senior associate dean of the University of Nevada School of Medicine in Las Vegas. Studies also indicate that these women are 15 times more likely to get endometrial cancer than are women who are slender.

■ Men in their sixties who are 20 percent over their recommended healthy weight are at three times greater risk of developing one type of cancer of the esophagus than are men who tip the scales at an ideal "healthy" weight, according to researchers at National Cancer Institute.

■ In a six-year follow-up study of 47,723 male dentists, pharmacists, and other health professionals, Harvard University researchers found that men who had waist circumferences of 43 inches or more were 2½ times more likely to develop colon cancer than were those whose waists were less than 35 inches.

■ In a 13-year study of 750,000 men and women, American Cancer Society researchers concluded that those people with weights 40 percent higher than average have a 33 to 55 percent greater risk of dying of cancer than those who are trim. The same study found that overweight men are more prone to cancers of the colon and prostate, and overweight women are more susceptible to cancers of the gallbladder, breasts, cervix, endometrium, uterus, and ovaries.

It's not clear why weight is so closely allied with cancer risk, but researchers are making some educated guesses. Some researchers suspect that eating too many calories triggers reproduction of cells. The more cells your body makes, the greater the chance that one or more will become cancerous, observes Susan Mayne, Ph.D., director of the cancer prevention and control program at the Yale Comprehensive Cancer Center in New Haven, Connecticut. Dr. Mayne and others also believe that excessive body fat increases the production of sex hormones such as estrogen. And since estrogen sparks excessive cell production, it is quite possibly one of the culprits that helps cancer get a foothold.

Whole-Body Protection

And there's another phenomenon that goes along with high amounts of body fat. When you have a lot of fat, you have less of a protein that binds to sex hormones and deactivates them. So more sex hormones are in circulation, resulting in a greater risk of developing cancer, Dr. Schapira says.

"The more body fat you have, the more estrogen you have. Being overweight is almost like self-medicating yourself with estrogen," Dr. Schapira says. "That's why overweight women have high rates of endometrial cancer. They have high levels of estrogen, and estrogen drives cell proliferation in certain areas of the body, including the endometrium."

To lose those extra pounds, you can start by using Stop-Time Tactic No. 2 on page 36. If you get your weight in line with healthy weight standards, you can reduce your risk of these cancers significantly, Dr. Schapira suggests. Losing 10 to 15 pounds, for instance, may drive a woman's risk of breast cancer down by as much as 45 percent, he says.

"Clearly, from a number of perspectives, including prevention of heart disease, high blood pressure, diabetes, and some cancers, losing weight can have dramatic beneficial effects," Dr. Schapira says.

Sun No More

Like many of us, Paul Engstrom, M.D., a medical oncologist and senior vice president of population science at Fox Chase Cancer Center in Philadelphia, grew up enjoying working and playing in the sun. He only learned later in life about the toll the sun takes on the skin.

"I have a very definite precancerous lesion right here," says Dr. Engstrom, pointing to an area under his right eye. "It's sun-related. So I make sure it is covered and coated every time I go out into the sun because I don't want it to become cancer."

More than 900,000 new cases of skin cancer are diagnosed in the United States each year—and one in every five Americans will be diagnosed with skin cancer.

Much of this could be prevented. Skin cancer, wrinkles, and liver spots could be drastically reduced if excessive sun exposure

307

Skin Cancer Survivor Invents Sun-Protective Clothing

Growing up near Seattle in the 1970s, Shaun Hughes impatiently endured the monotonous drizzle of the region's long, rainy winter. So when the bright summer sun finally arrived, he was always first among the eager youngsters who wanted to transform his pale skin into a golden brown.

"We all thought sun tanning was the right thing to do. We didn't know how dangerous it was," says Hughes, now in his forties. "I used to put cocoa butter and baby oil on my skin in search of the perfect tan."

Attending college in southern California, Hughes reveled in being able to lounge by a pool, basking in the sun while he studied. That was before 1983 when, during a vacation trip to Philadelphia, a friend noticed an unusual mole on Hughes's back. Frightened, Hughes had it checked out at Memorial Sloan-Kettering Cancer Center in New York City.

The mole was benign, but another one nearby wasn't. It was malignant melanoma, an aggressive and dangerous form of skin cancer. Hughes was 26.

"Naturally, when you're diagnosed with any potentially lethal cancer, it throws you into a tailspin. But I felt like I was a lucky guy," Hughes says. "I'm an absolute living tribute to early detection and expert advice."

After Hughes recovered, he followed his doctor's advice and began wearing

were avoided, says Pearon G. Lang, M.D., professor of dermatology at the Medical University of South Carolina in Charleston. Doctors believe that skin cancers develop because the ultraviolet light in the sun's rays damages DNA, the chain of message-units inside your cells that pass along the genetic code whenever cells reproduce. When the DNA in the proliferating cells in the skin are damaged, there is an increased likelihood that cancerous cells will form. At the same time, the ultraviolet rays suppress the immune system, which allows those cancerous cells to survive and proliferate. The more deeply penetrating ultraviolet rays also damage the elastin and collagen fibers in the skin, which results in wrinkles.

To get an idea of how this damage accumulates, imagine that you can measure sun exposure on a 100-point scale, starting with zero points. On the day you're born, your exposure is

sunscreen, sunglasses, long-sleeved shirts, and hats. But soon, Hughes found that wasn't enough.

"I used to find that even when I put on sunscreen I would still be tan at the end of the day, and through a typical T-shirt, I'd have slight redness at the end of the day. I knew both of those things had to be too much," Hughes says.

In 1989, with the help of doctors, Hughes decided to find a medically accepted sun-protection solution. The result is a company called Sun Precautions and a line of sun-protective clothing called Solumbra. Solumbra is constructed of a patented fabric that provides all-day protection from ultraviolet A and B rays. The clothing provides a sun protection factor of 30-plus. That means it will protect your skin in the sun for more than 30 times longer than if you don't wear it. Even when wet, it is at least 6 times more effective at blocking the sun's rays than a T-shirt, according to Hughes.

"For people who are extremely sensitive to the sun, this type of clothing is certainly worth investigating. It does seem to work well for those people who are high risk for getting burned," says Craig Eichler, M.D., a dermatologist at the Cleveland Clinic Florida in Fort Lauderdale.

For a free catalog, write Sun Precautions, 2815 Wetmore Avenue, Everett, WA 98201.

literally zero, notes Michael Kaminer, M.D., assistant professor of dermatology at Tufts University School of Medicine in Boston. That baby-soft skin has never known an instant of ultraviolet zapping.

But suppose, at 100 points, you get skin cancer, Dr. Kaminer speculates. How long can you spend in the sun before you use up all your points?

Add up those carefree days of summer when you ran on the beach or basked in a lawn chair. Now assume that every time you exposed your unprotected skin to sun, it damaged the skin a bit, and you added on points, Dr. Kaminer says. Sometimes, a lot. Just one bad sunburn in your teens, for instance, might add 20 points to your lifetime total. Even tanning, which is really part of the skin's defense mechanism, is a sign that harm has been done and more points are piling up.

309

If your lifetime sun exposure score has been high, it's just as if you're moving along in years at an accelerated rate, says Dr. Kaminer. But you may be able to halt the process right now, using some of the strategies in Stop-Time Tactic No. 3 on page 56, such as wearing sunscreen. Such tactics may stop you from getting those last few points that would push you irreversibly toward skin cancer, he says.

The problem is, it can be difficult to determine where you are on that imaginary scale. You can look perfectly fine but could be getting close to topping 100 points and developing a skin cancer. That's why it's so important to start taking sun precautions right now, Dr. Kaminer says.

The precautions don't have to be draconian. "I don't tell people that they have to go live in a cave," says James Spencer, M.D., professor of dermatology at the University of Miami School of Medicine. "You can enjoy the sun, but you have to be smart about it. Just wearing a hat and covering yourself with sunscreen will save you a ton of trouble later in life."

Sweat Your Risk Away

Keep moving, and certain cancers will have a harder time catching up with you.

Go for an afternoon bike ride. Swim a few laps in the neighborhood pool. Go for a brisk stroll the next time you have 20 minutes to spare. These and other kinds of aerobic exercise not only renew youthful vigor but also can help you literally run away from colon and breast cancers, says Leslie Bernstein, Ph.D., professor of preventive medicine at the University of Southern California School of Medicine in Los Angeles.

Summarizing studies on the cause of cancer, the "Harvard Report on Cancer Prevention" estimates that a sedentary lifestyle contributes to about 5 percent of all cancers. If your activity level is way down near the zero level, doctors warn that you escalate your risk of developing colon cancer—no small matter since this is a disease that affects more than 100,000 Americans annually.

Men who exercise the most have half the risk of colon cancer as those who are more sedentary, concluded researchers at Harvard University and Brigham and Women's Hospital in Boston, after studying 47,723 male health care professionals, ages 40 to 75. Nearly 40 other studies have suggested similar conclusions, says I-Min Lee, M.D., Ph.D., assistant professor of epidemiology at the Harvard School of Public Health.

Dr. Lee suspects there's a direct connection between regular aerobic exercise and the rate at which you digest food. Exercise speeds digestion, she says, so potential carcinogens spend less time in the intestinal tract. Regular workouts may also strengthen immunity. "If you started exercising now, within the next 15 to 30 minutes, you would see a boost in immune cell activity," she says. "Within a couple of hours, that activity seems to go back down."

But some of the benefits of improved immunity may linger even after you stop, Dr. Lee notes. "We know, for instance, that athletes, even when they are resting, have higher levels of immunity than people who never exercise," she observes.

Two to four hours of exercise a week can also reduce the risk of premenopausal breast cancer, says Dr. Bernstein. When she compared the lifetime exercise habits of 545 women who had breast cancer with 545 women who didn't, Dr. Bernstein found that those who consistently averaged four or more hours a week reduced their risks by as much as 58 percent. This was especially true if women began exercising as teenagers, but women who started substantial exercise later also were protected.

Exercise probably diminishes the breast's exposure to cancer-promoting hormones, especially estrogen. Women might get these benefits because exercise changes the length of the menstrual cycle. Or perhaps regular exercise helps to reduce the high production of hormones at peak times, so there is less hormone activity in the system.

Based on these studies, Dr. Bernstein suggests that women should feel strongly motivated to include a regular exercise program of 30 to 40 minutes a day as part of their lifestyles. "You don't have to be a marathon runner to get these benefits. We're talking moderate exercise," she adds.

311

The Price of Remission

Wendy Pannier believes in her dreams. So she felt it more than just a little foreboding when she dreamed that she had cancer. Shaken, she tried to push the vision out of her mind, but it haunted her even though regular visits to her gynecologist showed nothing. Then 14 months after her dream, at age 45, she was diagnosed with an advanced and aggressive form of endometrial cancer.

"In the 1970s, my diagnosis would have been a death sentence," says Pannier, a Philadelphia-based medical and business writer. "Instead, today, I am alive and in re-mission because of advances in cancer research."

After Pannier had a hysterectomy, her doctors at Fox Chase Cancer Center in Philadelphia urged her to participate in an experimental treatment to check the cancer's spread. The treatment consisted of unusually high doses of chemotherapy drugs supported by peripheral blood, the source of stem cells.

Stem cells are raw material needed to make new blood cells. Without stem cells—and most are destroyed during high-dose chemotherapy—it takes longer to produce healthy blood cells, which are critically needed to facilitate recovery. When the cancer is severe, as Pannier's was, transplanta-tion of healthy stem cells after high-dose chemotherapy may mean the difference between life and death, says Russell Schilder, M.D., a medical oncologist at Fox Chase Cancer Center.

But first she decided to explore other options. After alternative medicine practitioners told her that there was little they could do for her late-stage cancer, she contacted the Cancer Information Service, a telephone referral center funded by the National Cancer Institute. The service sent Pannier information about ongoing clinical trials at cancer centers nationwide.

Dr. Bernstein uses her own exercise program as an example. "I have a treadmill at home," she notes, "and I'm just trying to build up to walking more than two miles in about 30 minutes a day."

You can find tips on how to get started on an exercise pro-gram in Stop-Time Tactic No. 4 on page 87. Any exercise you do appears to be a cancer-risk deterrent.

312

"When you have cancer, you feel like many aspects of your life are out of control. The Cancer Information Service helped me feel as if I still had a hand in my own destiny. It's truly a fabulous service," Pannier says.

Reassured by her research, she went back to Fox Chase and began the recommended treatment. "The protocol, while it had its unpleasant moments, was nowhere near as horrible as I thought it would be," Pannier says. "Clinical trials are invaluable. They are cutting-edge research. I strongly recommend that anyone with a cancer explore what clinical trials might be appropriate for them."

She also looked for other ways to heal her mind, body, and spirit. During the treatment, she worked with a naturopathic physician and used nutritional and herbal supplements. After her experimental treatment at Fox Chase successfully ended, she again consulted alternative medical practitioners. They recommended homeopathic remedies to detoxify her body and acupuncture to increase her energy levels.

She began taking daily doses of high-potency vitamins and minerals like zinc and selenium. She also began doing strength training and aerobic exercise like walking and bicycling 30 to 45 minutes a day, five times a week. In addition, she started teaching dream interpretation workshops to help others cope with the disease. Now she says that she feels better than she has in years and believes her holistic approach is helping to fend off a recurrence.

"Cancer gives you the opportunity to reevaluate your whole life and to heal whatever parts of it you need to," Pannier says. "For those of us who are survivors, healing the other parts of our lives allows us the gift of living life more fully."

The toll-free phone number of the Cancer Information Service is (800) 4CANCER.

The Pollution Portion

Every day, it seems, the headlines announce more bad news about environmental damage that may be contributing to cancer. But despite the public alarms, statistics show that the vast majority of cancers are not caused by chemicals, pollution, and electronic gadgetry.

313

Only about 10 percent of all cancers are related to household use of pesticides, glues, paints, and other products containing potentially carcinogenic substances, estimates Philip Landrigan, M.D., director of environmental and occupational medicine at the Mount Sinai School of Medicine of the City University of New York in New York City and co-author of *Raising Children Toxic-Free*. And the "Harvard Report on Cancer Prevention" puts the risk of cancer related to environmental pollution even lower—at 2 percent.

That's in contrast to the percentage of cancers that are linked to smoking or poor eating habits—somewhere in the range of 60 percent, according to most estimates.

"It makes no sense to take environmental precautions if you're overweight, if you're drinking excessive amounts of alcohol, if you're sedentary, and if you smoke," observes David Bouda, M.D., clinical associate professor of oncology at the University of Nebraska School of Medicine and the chief medical officer of Alegent Health Systems, both in Omaha. "Why would you worry about the environment if you are not taking care of the behaviors that are far more risky?" he asks. "Sure, the environment does have a role in cancer risk. But the primary risks come from lifestyle factors that you can control."

For example, about 1 percent of all lung cancers in the United States are attributable to air pollution, according to Harvard University researchers. As for the dangers attributed to pesticides in your food and around your home, Dr. Shike believes the risks to be overrated. "The risk from household pesticides is real, but small," he says. "The benefits in terms of the cancer-preventing compounds you get from eating fruits and vegetables far outweighs the risk of getting cancer from pesticides."

Environmental hazards often get caught in the limelight of publicity. Between 1979 and 1996, for instance, more than 500 studies were conducted to confirm or deny that the electromagnetic fields (EMFs) produced by power lines could be linked to childhood leukemias and other cancers. When a National Research Council advisory panel reviewed all these studies, no link was found. "Research has not shown in any convincing way that electromagnetic fields common in homes can cause

314

health problems, and extensive laboratory tests have not shown that EMFs can damage the cell in a way that is harmful to human health," concluded Charles F. Stevens, M.D., Ph.D., a neurobiologist at the Salk Institute in La Jolla, California, and chairman of the National Research Council committee that investigated the issue.

Makeover Minutes

Dodging and Ditching the Hazards

Given the low impact of other environmental factors—and the big effect of eating and other habits—it only makes sense to watch your lifestyle habits in your campaign to protect your youth by warding off cancer. Eating more fruits and vegetables, getting more exercise, keeping your weight under control, and living a smoke-free lifestyle should rank as your top priorities, Dr. Bouda suggests.

Once you have these key lifestyle factors under control, however, then it might be worthwhile to consider changes in your household environment that could drive your chances of getting cancer even lower. Here are ways you can get started.

Bathe your munchies. Carefully wash all fruits and vegetables in clean running water to eliminate any pesticide residue that is lingering on the skin, Dr. Landrigan advises. Better yet, peel any fruit before you eat it.

Put the chimneys outdoors. If you're around chronic smokers, ask them to go outdoors when they want to light up, Dr. Bouda suggests. Alternatively, if you are living with a smoker who doesn't like being banished to the great outdoors, designate a well-ventilated room in your home as the smoking room—and warn others to stay away. Ask your guests who smoke to restrict their smoking to that room.

Nonsmokers who live or work with people who do smoke have a 30 to 50 percent higher risk of lung cancer, according to the National Cancer Institute. Breathing secondhand smoke

315

also is linked to an estimated 3,000 to 6,000 lung cancer deaths among nonsmokers annually.

Don't tamper with toxicity. Leave pesticides on the shelf. Look for nontoxic, organic products that can be used instead of the pesticide. Even if you can't come up with an alternative, you may be better off tolerating the pest than risking your health by handling the toxic product.

Eyeball those labels. If you must use pesticides, read the directions on the containers. Then read them again just before you use the product and observe the safety precautions. If the directions on a pesticide call for rubber gloves, masks, protective clothing, or goggles, you're probably eyeing a poison that ought to be used by a certified expert, Dr. Landrigan says.

Craft wisely. If you're doing a project like painting or glazing, read labels and make sure that the most dangerous toxic chemicals aren't in the products you are handling, Dr. Landrigan says. Avoid using products containing known or suspected carcinogens, such as benzene, carbon tetrachloride, trichloroethylene, or dioxane.

Leave asbestos removal to the pros. If you live in a home built prior to 1970, you may notice deteriorating asbestos insulation. If so, the Environmental Protection Agency suggests that you call a qualified asbestos removal professional.

Asbestos is an extremely potent carcinogen linked to cancers of the lungs, throat, larynx, and digestive tract. Though it's no longer used in new housing construction in the United States, it was sometimes used as fire-retardant insulation in homes that were built a few decades ago. As long as the insulation remains intact, asbestos can't harm you. But if it isn't removed properly, asbestos fiber can flake off the insulation, lodge in your lungs, and possibly trigger a cancer.

Be a fussy fueler. When pouring gas in a lawn mower, snow blower, or other gasoline-powered tool, wear rubber gloves and a face mask. Gasoline contains benzene, a chemical that is a proven cause of leukemia. Even if you don't inhale benzene, it can be easily absorbed through the skin, especially if you have nicks and cuts on your hands, Dr. Landrigan says.

Protect Yourself from Depression

Ahhh, the golden years. The time of your life when you can retire, sell your home, and move down to Florida. The kids are gone, and you don't have to worry about the daily grind. You and the mister (or missus) can just sit back, relax, and enjoy life. Right?

This popular image of frolicking, carefree retirement isn't always the happy ending some people get as they approach their older years. The changes that come with getting older can send some people into a blue funk, or even into a more dangerous clinical depression.

If you're generally an upbeat, active person, you know how occasional spells of the blues can make you feel like you're not yourself. Such spells can be triggered by external events like a death in the family or severe pressure at work.

Depression can make you feel day after day like you are under some kind of black cloud. When you're that depressed, anything in your life can feel negative. And you may start feeling a lot older than you actually are.

That's why you may need to take some active steps to help protect yourself from depression. By preparing for the changes that the years may bring, you can increase your chances of saving yourself from the more serious woes and lows that could be on the horizon. "The most effective weapon against depression is to take proactive steps to plan your life. You know that there will be change, and it is important that you start thinking now about how you are going to deal with that change," advises Michael S. Broder, Ph.D., a clinical psychologist in Philadelphia

317

and creator of the audio series, *Overcoming Your Depression in the Shortest Possible Period of Time.*

Beating Retirement Blues

Consider the impact of that classic blues-trigger, retirement. Even if your retirement seems far off right now, that phase of life is worth some preparation. A major life change like retirement may bring out depression in some people, says William Leber, Ph.D., associate professor of psychiatry and behavioral sciences at the University of Oklahoma College of Medicine and director of neuropsychology at the Veterans Administration Medical Center in Oklahoma City. If you are prone to depression because of your body chemistry or genetic makeup, such a change can trigger the dormant mood. But even if you're not predisposed to biological depression, you may get that sinking feeling as a response to change. Even a happy occasion can bring out feelings of worthlessness, hopelessness, and a loss of purpose.

"Retirement is the single biggest example," says Dr. Leber. "People literally just vegetate. Some haven't the slightest clue what to do with themselves. They find themselves cut off from their daily routine and their social circle. If they defined themselves by their work and the people they work with, when retirement comes, they are cut off from their identity."

A study performed by researchers at Georgia State University and the University of North Carolina at Chapel Hill bears out this correlation between retirement and depression. Researchers interviewed 737 men and women ages 58 to 64. Those who kept working scored high for self-esteem, while retirees who had high levels of education and those in poor health showed an increase in depression.

Taking the Menace out of Menopause

For women, there's another potential trigger for depression—the experience of menopause. The change in hormonal activity can initiate other changes that may lead to depression.

Beyond the hormonal effects, menopause has a change-of-

318

life message, reminding women that they aren't as young as they used to be. And it often coincides with children leaving the nest. Both these feelings could send women into a period of sadness. "It's change. And change—like having children grow up and go away to college—may start a mother's depression," Dr. Leber says. "But some people can prevent depression by being prepared for different life events."

You know in advance that the life changes of menopause or retirement—or both—are going to happen. Instead of letting these changes take the life out of you, you can plan ahead. Or if these events have already occurred, you can make some changes now to deal with these events.

And you do want to protect yourself from depression if you can because it's a downer that robs people of their will and spirit. At its worst, depression can turn into a thief that steals—but it steals youthfulness, vitality, and health.

A study at the Johns Hopkins School of Hygiene and Public Health in Baltimore found that people who had depression were four times more likely to have heart attacks than those who were not depressed. And there's other evidence that feelings of doom and gloom do a number on your normal health. Researchers at the Centers for Disease Control and Prevention in Atlanta found that having an episode of depression can predict the later development of high blood pressure.

For women, depression may also increase the chances of developing osteoporosis. Researchers at the National Institute of Mental Health in Bethesda, Maryland, studied the bone density in 24 women with depression and 24 without it. The researchers found that the women with depression had, on average, an 11 percent lower bone density than women who didn't suffer from depression.

Working Out the Doldrums

While many prescription drugs are now being used to help fight depression, it's important to remember that your body has its own defenses as well. Mood-altering chemicals are constantly flowing through your body, affecting your emotions and your

know what?
American author and Pulitzer Prize winner William Styron described depression as "a wimp of a word for a howling tempest in the brain."

319

health. So one way to attack depression is by getting your body to produce some chemicals that do you good.

When you exercise, for instance, your brain starts producing endorphins, neurotransmitters that can improve your mood and even quell pain. Exercise a lot, and you'll produce enough endorphins to produce a natural high.

These endorphins can be powerful mood changers that go right to the head—in a positive way—to combat moods like sadness. Evidence from several studies has shown that even low-intensity exercise is as effective as psychotherapy and antidepressant drugs in treating mild to moderate depression. "Exercise can do what the antidepressants do; it may even be a little bit more reliable," says Howard J. Rankin, Ph.D., a clinical psychologist and director of the Carolina Wellness Retreat in Hilton Head, South Carolina.

But it's more than brain chemicals that make you feel better when you're exercising. Stroll a dozen blocks every day, and you'll improve your body and health, which can also increase your self-esteem and self-image. Working out can also increase your energy—something a lot of people with depression don't have. Plus, exercise can reduce stress, a potential trigger for depressive episodes. "A lot of the symptoms of depression really have to do with a lack of energy. Exercise helps create energy, and it is the best stress manager," Dr. Rankin says.

Starting an exercise program now may help ward off depression later. When researchers in Finland interviewed about 1,600 people between the ages of 65 to 84, they found that those who did not exercise had a higher prevalence of depression than those who worked out. People who exercised regularly reported a better quality of life as well as better general health.

Long-Term Tactics

For Blowing the Blues Away

Developing an exercise regimen doesn't mean that you have to join a gym and wear yourself out every day. Research

320

has shown that exercise as simple as walking can help brush the blues aside. Start with some of the following suggestions, and you'll find yourself beating the blues before they beat you. But it's important to keep up the activities if you want to reap long-term blues-fighting benefits.

Do what you enjoy. Pick walking, biking, rowing, or any other pursuit, but make sure the exercise is fun for you. If you force yourself to do some activity you basically don't like, you probably won't do it in the long run. "It should be something enjoyable—otherwise, you won't stick with it," says Victoria Hendrick, M.D., assistant professor of clinical psychiatry at the University of California, Los Angeles.

Walk the blues away. "Walking is the easiest form of exercise," Dr. Rankin says. If you are really down, try starting with a walk around the block. Just getting out and moving around may help you feel better. Of course, if you would like to do more, you can go for a brisk walk for about 30 minutes at least three to five times a week, he says.

When you feel a bad mood descending, let walking come to the rescue. Get out the door and let your feet do the rest. "You will not feel as bad as you did before you left," Dr. Rankin says.

Whether it's the endorphin effect or the fact that walking makes you look and feel better, there's nothing like a good walk to improve how you feel about yourself. In a study at Northeast Louisiana University in Monroe, researchers studied the effects that walking had on 27 women ages 29 to 50. Those who walked regularly during the eight-week program showed significant improvement in their self-esteem.

Take in the view. While you are walking—or while you are doing any exercise for that matter—don't dwell on the fact that you're depressed. Depression can be a vicious cycle—the more you think about being depressed, the more depressed you get, says Michael Addis, Ph.D., assistant professor of psychology at Clark University in Worcester, Massachusetts. Think of pleasurable things or just enjoy the scenery around you. But this is not to say that a person can just snap out of depression. It takes hard work and often the help of a professional to make some of the necessary changes. Still, Dr. Addis adds, people can help themselves by paying attention to their moods and making small

321

When to Get Help

When B.B. King sings the blues, we're likely to hear his soulful sounds with more pleasure than pain. But if gloom begins after the music fades, take note: A constant feeling of being low might be a danger sign.

"When you just have the blues—rather than full-scale clinical depression—the symptoms don't persist every day, nor do they last for several weeks," observes David Dunner, M.D., professor of psychiatry and co-director of the Center for Anxiety and Depression at the University of Washington in Seattle. The blues are temporary, but in clinical depression the symptoms persist no matter how seemingly successful your life may be, he says.

Being diagnosed with depression doesn't sentence you to a life of misery. In fact, with the proper treatment, most people can expect a full recovery from depression, he adds. But if you do have clinical depression, Dr. Dunner urges you to seek a medical evaluation and treatment with either psychotherapy or antidepressants.

How can you tell the difference between being blue and being depressed? According to the American Psychiatric Association, if you have at least five of the following symptoms for two weeks or more, you may have depression and should see your doctor as soon as possible.

- Depressed mood most of the time
- Lack of interest in pleasure or all activities
- Unintentional 5 percent change in weight over a month or a significant increase or decrease in appetite
- Insomnia or oversleeping nearly every day
- Obvious agitation or an obvious slowing-down
- Constant fatigue and loss of energy
- Feelings of worthlessness or excessive or inappropriate guilt
- Lack of ability to think or concentrate
- Recurrent thoughts of death or suicide

Reprinted with permission from the Diagnostic and Statistical Manual of Mental Disorders, Fourth Edition. Copyright © 1994 by the American Psychiatric Association.

changes when they start to feel down.

Try some heavy stuff. You can lift your spirits by lifting weights, according to two different studies. At Tufts University in Boston, researchers assigned 32 men and women ages 60 to

322

84 to either a resistance-training program or a health education program; all of the participants had mild to moderate depression. The resistance-training participants used weight machines three days per week, gradually increasing the amount of weight at each session. All participants lifted between 45 to 87 percent of their maximum weight.

By the end of the 10-week program, 82 percent of the people who were weight training no longer showed signs of depression. Only 40 percent of the people in the health education class showed similar improvement.

Weight training has even been shown to out perform aerobic exercise when it comes to improving mood. Researchers at Northeast Louisiana University in Monroe studied the effects of aerobic exercise, weight training, and a combination of both to find out the optimal program. When the alternatives were tried out on 45 people with signs of depression, the weight-training program produced the most significant decrease in depressive symptoms, researchers found.

Enlist a friend. If motivation is your problem, get yourself an exercise partner. A friend can keep you on track. Often, the power of someone else saying, "Let's go!" can overcome any excuses you can dream up.

Put it on your schedule. In today's hectic world, people usually don't do anything if it is not logged in their date books. Consider exercise as important as a meeting and respect the "appointment" as much as any other event in your date book. "Plan it out in advance and then really force yourself to stick to that schedule," Dr. Leber says.

know what?

Throughout history, the condition known as depression has been described in scores of unflattering ways— including "melancholia," "spleen," "a damn'd melange of fretfulness and melancholy," a "dulness and thickness of brain," and a "shattered mode of thinking."

Get Out and About

When you retire from your job, sometimes your social life takes an instant nosedive. If you have enjoyed going to company parties and picnics, meeting with co-workers for drinks after work, or getting together with colleagues on weekends, the sudden dearth of invitations can feel pretty awful.

And when you're cut off from your normal social circle, it is

323

easy to withdraw into the depths of your home. As people lose their social outlets, they may intentionally distance themselves from friends and family, Dr. Leber says. "They need to grasp the importance of not closing the world out."

The depressive cycle works this way: Suppose you stay home because you feel depressed. It won't be long before you begin worrying that you aren't out enjoying life. Then you get depressed thinking about how you are depressed.

When someone is depressed about being depressed, they're likely to stay in and avoid social contact. Then the cycle starts all over again. "They have to get out of the house and do pleasurable things. One of the worst things that you can do with depression is stay inside," Dr. Hendrick says.

Actions to Exorcise Gloom

Getting out of the house may sound like a simple prescription, but there's a lot to be said for refusing to be housebound. It's never too early to develop some exercise habits and social connections that get you out and about. Find activities that you enjoy, and they'll help revive your spirits, Dr. Leber says. Here are some ways to raise your percentage of new friends and new activities.

Play participation sports. Group sports give you the benefits of exercise and the bonus of being around others. Sports like golf or even soccer can get you active both physically and socially, says Fred Penzel, Ph.D., a psychologist and executive director of Western Suffolk Psychological Services in Huntington, New York. Prior to starting a new exercise routine, it's a good idea to consult with your physician.

Take a yoga class. Here's another exercise activity that puts you in a group setting. If you sign up for yoga classes, you'll mingle with others on a regular basis, Dr. Penzel says. Beginner

324

Keeping Track of the Antidepressants

By the late 1990s, six million Americans had taken the antidepressant drug Prozac. That's more than double the populations of Montana, North Dakota, South Dakota, Wyoming, and Idaho combined.

Despite these numbers, antidepressant therapy isn't given to everyone, and it isn't meant for everyone, says Stan Kutcher, M.D., head of the department of psychiatry at the Dalhousie University Faculty of Medicine in Halifax, Nova Scotia. Whether a person needs antidepressants or cognitive therapy is decided on a case-by-case basis, he says. Doctors consider the patient's medical condition, severity of the depression, the person's response to previous treatment, the patient's family history of depression, and the patient's wants before prescribing drugs, he says. Drug treatment has about a 70 percent effectiveness rate.

Prozac is one of the newer antidepressants—called SSRIs, for selective serotonin reuptake inhibitors—which produce more brain serotonin, a neurotransmitter known to alter mood.

More serotonin doesn't exactly make a depressed person happier, says Francis Mondimore, M.D., a psychiatrist at the Carolinas Medical Center in Charlotte, North Carolina. But that chemical does interact with other neurotransmitters that contribute to the disease—or, conversely, it blocks such interactions. Whatever serotonin's exact effect, if you don't have enough, the other neurotransmitters may go haywire, possibly causing depression, he says.

Antidepressants developed in the SSRI class of new drugs have gained popularity because they produce fewer side effects than the older drugs, the tricyclic antidepressants. The now-outdated generation of tricyclics often stirred up a whole range of side effects, including weight gain, heart and circulatory problems, vision problems, and sexual dysfunction.

Although better than their predecessors, the new antidepressants do have side effects. The accompanying table shows just some of the possible side effects for frequently prescribed antidepressants.

Medication	Potential Side Effects
Effexor	Anxiety, anorexia, insomnia
Paxil	Dry mouth, fatigue
Prozac	Insomnia, extreme weight loss, nervousness
Serzone	Headache, fatigue, dry mouth
Zoloft	Loose stools, diarrhea

know
what?

Depression is
estimated to
affect about
10 percent of
all Americans
in any given
year. Over a
lifetime, about
17 percent
of all Ameri-
cans will
experience
an episode
of major
depression.

classes are easy, and you'll benefit from the relaxation and meditation as well as social interaction.

Go to a movie. Getting out and about doesn't have to be a
major event. Something as simple as going to a movie can help
lift your spirits, Dr. Addis says. "Sometimes it only takes small
changes to improve mood," he observes.

Ask someone out to lunch. When you're really feeling low,
you may get stuck with the idea that no one likes you, no one
cares about you, and no one wants to be around you. To put that
erroneous theory to the test, Dr. Leber tells people to ask someone out to lunch or for coffee. "Try striking up a conversation
and see if someone wants to go out for lunch," he says. When
the person accepts, you'll realize that people do want to be in
your company.

Keep a "social" list nearby. Sometimes when a person is depressed, everything seems impossible—even thinking, says Dr.
Addis. That's why he suggests that people make a list of pleasurable things to do and keep it with them at all times. List your
favorite music or films. Jot down all the things you like to do.
With that list at hand, you'll have an easy reference guide readily available, he says. Then, when you're feeling blue, just pick
an activity.

Plan Your Purpose Now

Some people wait their whole lives for the farewell luncheon
and the gold watch signaling the last day on the job. The day
they can walk out of work, knowing they'll never have to go
back, is like a dream of salvation.

But when the day finally comes, many discover that they're
more miserable than they could have imagined. Suppose
that for the last 40-plus years, you have defined yourself by
your job. When that's gone, you may find yourself wondering
what your role is and what you're supposed to do with all your
spare time. These feelings can lead you straight down the road
to depression, Dr. Broder says.

Similarly, if you have been anticipating the day when the last
child leaves the nest, you may be in for a shock. "You really have

to realize that you could have a whole different reaction to this than you may have anticipated," says Dr. Broder. "It is not at all easy to adjust to retirement or not having your children around."

But who says you stop having a reason for living when you stop working or when your kids fly the coop? Retirement and freedom from parenting open you up to a whole new world of opportunities.

"You have to start thinking now, 'What other contributions do I want to make?' But it has to be something more than just keeping busy. They have to be things that you value, things that you enjoy doing, and things that you would do whether you were being paid for them or not," Dr. Broder says.

Long-Term Tactics

Opening New Doors

You don't have to wait for retirement to start the ball rolling with some new activities. Years before you retire, you can start to experiment with things you'll have more time for when you get older.

As you start to plan ahead, here are some actions to keep you traveling in the youth lane.

Volunteer for Meals on Wheels. When you get out and do volunteer work that has a purpose, it's like being re-employed—in a very pleasurable way. When you contribute your time and services to Meals on Wheels, you are delivering food directly to people who need it—in their own homes. "Volunteering gives people a feeling of mastery over their lives again," Dr. Penzel says.

When you're volunteering, you quickly realize how much you are needed by others. "When you ask a person down in the doldrums, 'I need help. Would you do this for me?' then all of a sudden they feel important. That makes them feel much more worthwhile," says Clancy D. McKenzie, M.D., a psychiatrist and director of Philadelphia Psychiatric Consultation Service in Pennsylvania.

If you need some volunteering ideas, contact the Points of Light Foundation, a nonprofit, nonpartisan organization in Washington, D.C., that maintains a national database of volunteer needs. To find out about the nearest volunteering agency, write to the foundation at 1400 I Street N.W., Ninth Floor, Washington, D.C. 20005. The foundation also has a toll-free phone number.

Find a new career. As some people reach the end of their careers, they look back with disappointment at how their jobs have turned out. Perhaps they didn't accomplish what they set out to do, or they're unhappy with where they ended up in the corporate chain of command. "You can really get down on yourself at these times," Dr. Broder says.

Don't wait until you retire to figure out that you don't like your career. If you feel that you're not heading down a fulfilling path, start looking in another direction, Dr. Addis suggests. Find out what other careers interest you and pursue them.

Keep working. Who said that you have to retire? Even if you can't stay at your current job, there are plenty of part-time or even full-time jobs that you can do. "For some people, the solution to retirement depression turned out to be another job," says Dr. Penzel. "Some people like work better than anything because they need to stay active. There are plenty of people who work into their seventies and eighties who are quite happy. Working makes them feel needed and gives them a purpose."

Watch somebody else's kids. For some parents, having children move away is their retirement from the jobs of "mom" and "dad." But if that's what you love to do, there's no reason you can't use your well-honed parenting skills in another way. Dr. Penzel recalls one couple that adopted children and became foster parents when their own children moved out. Understandably, you might not be ready to start all over again. But maybe you could volunteer at a day care to help children learn how to read. Or you might volunteer to watch your grandchildren or your neighbor's kids.

328

When Feeling Depressed Isn't Bad

A lot of people confuse depression with another feeling—grief. Even the definitions are alike: Grief, according to *American Heritage Dictionary* is a source of deep mental anguish. Depression, the same source says, is the condition of feeling sad and despondent.

"After the loss of a loved one or any loss, it is normal to experience grief. But grief can be so similar to depression," says Michael Addis, Ph.D., assistant professor of psychology at Clark University in Worcester, Massachusetts. In fact, the two emotions are so close that after the death of a spouse or close relative, a clinical diagnosis of depression can't be made for at least two months, he says.

Life events like losing a loved one, getting divorced, or losing a job naturally bring out feelings of depression and loss of hope. Tragic events that are beyond our control—such as tornadoes, floods, and fires—can also send you into a dark mood for long periods of time, says Fred Penzel, Ph.D., a psychologist and executive director of Western Suffolk Psychological Services in Huntington, New York.

The difference between actually being depressed and just feeling low or blue is how you react to the problem. "Even when faced with these problems, a nondepressed person is able to find a response and come up with alternatives. They're able to solve the problems in an active way. You can be sad at the death of a loved one, but you don't stop going to work. You don't stop functioning," Dr. Penzel says.

On the other hand, grief can actually mask depression in some cases. The loss acts as a trigger in some people and brings out a depressive episode. "If the feeling persists after six months, and you have other signs such as having trouble sleeping and lack of concentration—and you're unable to feel any joy at all—then you probably need help," Dr. Addis says. Many therapists and counselors specialize in depression, and your family doctor should be able to refer you to one.

Get a pet. Maybe taking on some more children isn't what you were looking forward to in your later years, but you would still like to have someone to look after and care about. Then take a walk over to the pet store or the animal shelter. "Having to take care of a pet is like having to take care of a person. That pet needs you, and you have a purpose in taking care of it," Dr. McKenzie says.

Have a hobby. A hobby isn't just something you do to take up time. It can be a creative outlet and a passion, Dr. McKenzie says. Whether it be woodworking, stamp collecting, or painting, he suggests finding hobbies that allow you to be creative and expressive. "You have to be productive and not focus on yourself," he says.

Develop your spiritual side. Religion or any kind of spiritual activity, for that matter, can give a person a sense of purpose as well as a place to seek comfort and hope. "Religion is a very strong force in people's lives and can be a source of support. One should definitely not underestimate the power of faith," Dr. Penzel says.

Makeover Minutes

Avoiding Triggers

Part of winning the battle against the blues is to know your enemy very, very well. If you look closely at your own life, you may be able to see a pattern to your episodes of depression. Do you get in a funk every time you visit your in-laws? Do you know you're probably going to feel depressed after you talk to your boss at work?

Once you have learned the whens, whys, and hows of your blues, you can be on the offensive, Dr. Penzel says. By figuring out what sets you off, you can avoid those triggers—or at least tread cautiously when you see a high-risk situation looming on the horizon. You can also learn some techniques to change your own thinking and make your environment more friendly—just to make it less likely that you'll react to the trigger situation with the kind of nosedive that you have experienced before.

By learning how to recognize what put you in a bad mood, you'll be able to stop it before it happens. Here are some actions that you can take immediately if you feel a bout of the blues coming on.

Whole-Body Protection

Look for proof. Many depression triggers come from your own thinking. When you're criticized or something doesn't go the way you planned, the brain goes into overdrive with thoughts like, "I'm the worst worker ever" or "I'm a terrible parent." You convince yourself of your faults and fall right into depression, Dr. Penzel says.

One way to get out of this negative-thinking rut is to ask yourself for proof. Stop and ask yourself to back up your own statements with evidence, Dr. Penzel suggests. "Where does it say I'm a loser, a failure in life? If we dispute the ideas, then we see that they aren't true," he observes.

Write it down. Dr. Penzel has patients write down their negative thoughts. Then they can study their thinking patterns and work on challenging and changing them. "We use worksheets so we can see our thinking as a step-by-step process. After you do it over and over on paper, you're able to do it in your head," he says.

Writing a journal can also help you realize when bouts of the blues are coming. Sometimes, the low feelings creep up on you, but with a journal you can analyze what you're feeling and compare it to other times when you have felt low. "Keeping a journal helps people put their feelings in black and white rather than allowing them to explain away their feelings and not pay any attention to them," says Francis Mondimore, M.D., a psychiatrist at the Carolinas Medical Center in Charlotte, North Carolina.

Get aggressive. Feelings of guilt—especially those poured on by family and friends—can send some people into a period of sadness. To work around the guilt traps without falling in, learn how to say no, Dr. Hendrick recommends.

You don't need to feel as though you're a terrible person for taking such a stand, she adds. "So many people tell me that when they say no, they feel guilty. If you learn assertiveness techniques, you learn how to express your needs and how to react to such comments without feeling guilty."

Brighten things up. Although a dreary environment doesn't bring on depression, it's not going to help either. "Sitting in a gloomy room is not going to make you feel better," Dr. Penzel says. Decorate in bright colors and surround yourself with attractive and interesting things such as pictures or mementos that can lift your mood, he suggests.

Strike up the band. Another way of cheering up is to play some music. "Music has long been used in the treatment of mood states," says Stan Kutcher, M.D., head of the department of psychiatry at the Dalhousie University Faculty of Medicine in Halifax, Nova Scotia. Listen to what you enjoy and what makes you feel better. Better yet, if you play an instrument, get it out and regale yourself with some tuneful melodies. Just avoid playing songs in minor, weepy keys.

"And don't listen to depressing music when you are depressed," Dr. Addis adds. Research shows that repeated attempts to get in touch with our feelings when we are depressed can keep us depressed. While it can be helpful to spend some time trying to solve specific problems, ruminating about why we are feeling what we are feeling is not helpful.

Avoid drugs, alcohol, and caffeine. Drugs and alcohol can bring on depression or make it worse if it's already there, says John Altrocchi, Ph.D., professor of behavioral sciences at the University of Nevada School of Medicine in Reno. And if you use caffeine to climb back to a high after you have experienced the lows of drugs and alcohol, you're likely to mess up your health and sleep patterns. "You start to drink alcohol to get to sleep. Then you start to rely on caffeine to get you up. This can emphasize depressive symptoms," he says. With those ups and downs, you'll probably feel more lethargic and potentially depressed and possibly anxious, adds Dr. Altrocchi.

332

Protect Yourself
from Diabetes

Before he joined the Diabetes Prevention program, Joe Martinelli wasn't exactly a poster boy—make that a poster septuagenarian—for a healthy lifestyle.

"I was never one to count fat grams or exercise," says Martinelli, who lives in the suburbs of Pittsburgh. But with a family history of Type II (or non-insulin-dependent) diabetes, the most common form of the disease, he finally decided to get serious about his health. So when researchers began recruiting for a national study to examine ways to prevent or delay Type II diabetes, Martinelli signed up.

What he learned was troubling. The results of his oral glucose tolerance test, which measures the amount of sugar in the blood, was 199 milligrams of sugar per deciliter of blood. Since diabetes is present if the test shows blood sugar levels greater than 200 milligrams per deciliter, Martinelli was within a hairsbreadth of clinical diabetes.

"There was diabetes on my dad's side of the family, so I've seen what diabetes can do. My dad had a leg amputated and eventually went blind. My aunt, too," says Martinelli. "So I wanted to do whatever I could to protect my quality of life. I also wanted to set an example for my kids."

So began Martinelli's fight to ensure that the disease that killed his father—the fourth-leading cause of death by disease in this country—wouldn't claim him, too. He now owns a fat-gram counter, a book listing the grams of fat in many common foods, and knows how to use it. ("My God, I used to eat a quarter of a jar of dry-roasted peanuts at a time. You know how much

333

fat they have?") He takes a brisk, 30-minute walk four times a week. When we last talked to Martinelli, he had lost 10 pounds and was aiming to lose another 6.

"I feel real lucky that I did not get diabetes in my fifties or sixties," says Martinelli. "But I'm also lucky that I found out about my high blood sugar." As far as Martinelli is concerned, the discovery came "just in time."

Age Doesn't Matter

Diabetes is a disease that strikes about 625,000 new victims every year, and most of its new recruits are over the age of 55. So diabetes is one of the all-too-clear signals that you are aging—and probably a lot faster than you would like to. Well, maybe you *don't* have to join the diabetes club around the time that you draw your first pension check. Your risk of developing diabetes is often the result of many lifestyle factors, researchers say, and they are discovering those factors that you need to adjust to help reduce your risk at any age. Researchers now know that a high-fiber, low-fat diet; regular exercise; and maintenance of a healthy weight can play an important role in preventing the disease. Stick to a prevention program, they say, and you can mount a good defense against the onset of the disease.

"At least 75 percent of all new cases of Type II diabetes can be prevented," says JoAnn Manson, M.D., an epidemiologist and endocrinologist at Harvard Medical School.

To take just one example, obesity (defined as being 20 percent over your ideal weight) is a major risk factor for Type II diabetes. Dropping even a few pounds, studies show, can dramatically reduce that risk, even if diabetes runs in your family. Researchers at the University of Pittsburgh who studied 157 obese people with a family history of Type II diabetes found that those who lost just 10 pounds slashed their risk of developing diabetes by 31 percent.

There's even more good news. Some doctors, like Zeno L. Charles-Marcel, M.D., medical director of the Lifestyle Center of America, a preventive health care center in Sulphur, Oklahoma, believe that a healthy, active lifestyle may prevent or even

334

reverse impaired glucose tolerance (IGT), a precursor to diabetes that affects an estimated 20 million Americans. Like Martinelli, these Americans with IGT have high levels of blood sugar even though the levels aren't quite high enough to be considered diabetes. "Can catching IGT in time prevent it from progressing to diabetes? It's a reasonable hypothesis. We certainly believe it's possible," says Dr. Charles-Marcel.

The Body's Fuel Shortage

Joe Martinelli watched diabetes drain his father's youth and vigor, which is why he has attacked the enemy head-on. But even if diabetes doesn't run in your family, you need to know Martinelli's enemy—because his enemy could be yours.

People with diabetes have trouble getting blood sugar, or glucose (the body's main source of fuel) from the blood into the cells. Glucose is produced as we digest food. Normally, after digestion, glucose pours into the blood and is carried to cells throughout the body. But glucose can't make it into the hungry cells without a hormone called insulin. People with Type I diabetes, which usually occurs during childhood or adolescence, produce little or no insulin and need daily injections of the hormone. People with the more common Type II diabetes produce insulin, often lots of it, but their bodies don't respond to it. This inability to use insulin effectively is called insulin resistance.

In both forms of diabetes, the characteristics are the same: Without insulin or the ability to use it properly, glucose stays in the blood, building to 3, 4, or even 10 times the normal amount. This glucose overload finally spills into the urine unused and then is excreted. That means the cells don't get the fuel they need for growth and energy. What's more, all that sugar in the blood over time can damage the heart and blood vessels, eyes, nerves, and kidneys. But it does not have to happen.

The Perks of Prevention

In the majority of cases, Type II diabetes doesn't have to strike at all. If you can outwit this thief, you can add years to

335

what?

Between
50 and 60
percent of
men over
age 50 with
diabetes
become
impotent—
and men with
diabetes
develop
impotence
10 to 15
years earlier
than men
without it.

your life. And even if you just delay its onset, you'll help avoid problems like heart disease, stroke, kidney failure, and sight loss.

For instance, you'll protect your cardiovascular system. People with diabetes are two to four times as likely to get heart disease as people without it, and up to five times more likely to have a stroke. Diabetes seems to speed up the process of atherosclerosis (hardening of the arteries) because it changes the chemical makeup of some of the substances in the blood. These changes can clog or completely block blood vessels, setting the stage for a heart attack or stroke. People with diabetes also tend to have abnormal levels of blood cholesterol and lipids, which make them even more vulnerable to cardiovascular problems.

By taking measures to prevent diabetes, you may also safeguard your brain. Studies show that diabetes can affect memory and other brain functions, perhaps caused by the brain not getting enough "fuel"—that is, blood sugar. When researchers from India compared the cognitive skills of people with diabetes to those of people without the disease, the people with diabetes scored lower in tests of attention (60 percent low scores versus 21 percent), repetitive tasks (32 percent versus 7 percent), and short-term memory (43 percent versus 14 percent).

And then there's sex. Men, you could do your sex life a big favor if you protect yourself from diabetes. The disease can damage the blood vessels, reducing blood flow to the penis. Diabetes can also damage the nerves that send some important signals to the penis. Between 50 and 60 percent of men over age 50 with diabetes become impotent—and men with diabetes develop impotence 10 to 15 years earlier than men without it.

Diabetes can dampen a woman's sexual pleasure, too. The same nerve damage or circulatory problems that cause impotence in men can reduce sensation in a woman's genital area and can hinder her ability to reach orgasm. Chronically high blood sugar levels can also trigger yeast infections.

By warding off diabetes, you'll also safeguard your eyesight. Because Type II diabetes often goes undiagnosed for years, the eye damage caused by diabetes is often "silent." From 10 to 20 percent of people with Type II already have eye disease at the

336

time they are diagnosed. In fact, diabetes is the most common cause of adult blindness in the United States.

The best way to prevent these and other complications is to eat a low-fat diet, exercise, and lose weight, if necessary. But you might also want to get a blood test for elevated blood sugar levels, especially if you are over 40, are overweight, or have a family history of diabetes.

"There are around 16 million people in this country who have diabetes, and half of them don't know it," says David J. DeRose, M.D., a physician at the Lifestyle Center of America. "So you can make a case for knowing not only your cholesterol level and blood pressure but also your blood sugar level."

Chew the Fiber, Not the Fat

While genetics is an important factor in who does and does not get diabetes, it's by no means the only one. "A family history of diabetes is like a loaded gun—it isn't necessarily going to hurt you," says John A. Goley, Dr.PH., a health educator specialist at the Lifestyle Center of America. "It's our lifestyle that pulls the trigger." One bullet in that lethal weapon is the typical high-fat, low-fiber American diet, which plays a significant role in the development of Type II diabetes.

Your first step in reducing risk is to eat less fat. A high-fat diet reduces cells' sensitivity to insulin, especially if your usual meals and snacks are high in saturated fat, which is found in animal foods like meat, eggs, and cheese. A high-fat diet also sets the stage for obesity, that other major risk factor for diabetes. "Fat gets into muscle cells and basically slows down glycolysis, the process of changing glucose into energy," explains Dr. Goley. "That means the glucose in the blood has a more difficult time getting into the cells, even if insulin is doing its job."

You'll also want to increase the amount of fiber in your diet. "Without a doubt, consuming more fiber can help prevent diabetes," says Jorge Salmeron, M.D., Ph.D., investigator with the epidemiological investigations unit, health services division of the Social Security Institute of Mexico City. Dr. Salmeron and researchers from the Harvard School of Public Health, who ex-

know what?
Even animals can get diabetes. Cats and dogs, for example, are treated with insulin injections, just like humans.

337

amined the diets of 65,173 women, found that those who ate the least amount of fiber, especially cereal fiber, developed diabetes at more than twice the rate of women who ate the most.

The more fiber you eat, the less fat you tend to consume, says Dr. Goley. If you consume a high-fiber diet, you'll automatically fill up on complex carbohydrates, the "good" carbohydrates found in fruits, vegetables, and whole grains. And you'll eat fewer simple carbohydrates, the "bad" carbohydrates found in refined foods like cakes, cookies, and pastries.

Even if you're eating the low-fat variety of simple-carbohydrate foods, you're tempting diabetic fate. "Eating too many simple carbohydrates can elevate blood sugar, triggering increased insulin levels that may eventually lead to diabetes," says Dr. Salmeron. In the Harvard study, women who ate the most simple carbohydrates also had a higher risk of diabetes than those who consumed the least.

Finally, consume more fruits and vegetables. They are rich in antioxidants, nutrients that protect cells from destructive molecules called free radicals. People with diabetes have a shortage of antioxidants, especially vitamins C and E, in their blood. When there is a shortfall, people are more susceptible to the complications of diabetes, including blindness and heart disease, some researchers believe. And some studies even suggest that these nutrients may keep IGT from progressing to diabetes.

Makeover Minutes

At Home Plate

You can take steps to diabetes-proof your diet right now. These quick tips can help.

Choose cheeseless. Want to pare fat from a meal in a hurry? Lose the cheese from sandwiches, burgers, casseroles, and pasta dishes. Top a sandwich with lettuce, tomato, and a spicy brown mustard instead of one slice American cheese, for example, and you'll save 6.6 grams of fat.

Eat one less low-fat sweet. If you're hooked on low-fat cookies and pastries, consider substituting one of your daily treats for a piece of fresh fruit. You'll get more fiber. Compare: One brand of low-fat toaster pastries contains only 1 gram of fiber, while a pear contains 3.9 grams. Also, you'll replace the pastry's simple carbohydrates with the complex variety found in fruit. Finally, you'll save a substantial number of calories. The pastry packs 190 calories, while the pear contains 98.

Make a meal of cereal. The American Diabetes Association recommends consuming from 20 to 35 grams of fiber a day. To boost your fiber intake quickly and easily, have a bowl of high-fiber, whole-grain breakfast cereal every day, recommends Dr. Salmeron. "Choose a low-fat variety that contains at least 10 grams of fiber per serving," he advises. Many brands with the word *bran* in their names are good choices. But read the nutrition labels, too, if you want to find the cereals that have more than 10 grams of fiber per serving. One-half cup Fiber One, for example, contains 13 grams of fiber, while the same amount of All-Bran contains 10.1 grams.

Bean yourself up. Dried beans contain a mother lode of fiber; many varieties contain as much as 5 grams per half-cup. But canned beans are just as high in fiber as the dried variety, with the built-in advantage that you don't have to spend hours cleaning, soaking, and boiling. Even convenience foods made with beans—such as canned chili—are good sources of fiber.

In fact, your supermarket probably has a lot of bean-rich offerings. Many supermarkets carry premade containers of hummus, a Middle Eastern dip made with mashed chick-peas and seasoned with lemon juice and garlic; two-thirds cup packs 8.2 grams of fiber. If you buy canned beans, read the label for fiber, fat, and sodium information. Choose low-fat, low-sodium products because canned foods tend to be high in fat and sodium.

Go with the whole grain. Another fast way to increase your intake of fiber is to switch from white to whole-grain bread. One slice of the whole-grain variety contains 1.9 grams of fiber, as compared to one slice of white bread, which has only 0.6 grams.

Grab a V8 for C. When you're on the run, down a glass of vegetable juice for a quick daily dose of vitamin C. Six ounces

know what?

When it comes to fiber, not all beans are created equal. One-half cup canned vegetarian baked beans contains about 6 grams of fiber, while the same amount of canned black bean soup has more than 8 grams.

339

contain 50 milligrams, 84 percent of the Daily Value of 60 milligrams. Vegetable juice also contains less than half the calories than the same amount of orange juice, which makes it a good choice for weight-watchers.

Long-Term Tactics
To Tune Your Diet

In addition to the many day-to-day choices that can help ward off diabetes, you might want to consider some strategic changes in your eating patterns. For starters, follow the recommendations in Stop-Time Tactic No. 1 on page 3. In addition, here are some other nutritional strategies that can help.

Make for the Mediterranean Sea. Do you crave chicken cacciatore, a dish bursting with tomatoes, herbs, and sometimes wine? Do you love hearty bean salads? Then dig in. You are headed for a diabetes-beating future with a Mediterranean diet.

Based on the traditional cuisine of Mediterranean countries like Greece and Italy, the Mediterranean diet contains considerably less saturated fat than the traditional American diet and instead derives most of its fat from plant-based monounsaturated fats like olive oil. Besides being good for your heart, a Mediterranean-style diet may help regulate blood sugar, according to a study conducted at the General Clinical Research Center of the University of Texas Southwestern Medical Center. In the study, people with diabetes who consumed a high-monounsaturated-fat diet that contained 45 percent fat were better able to control their blood sugar than a group following a 30-percent-fat diet.

Get hooked on fish. Go ahead, order the catch of the day. Fatty fish like salmon and sardines may help prevent diabetes, according to a study conducted at Seattle Veterans Administration Hospital. Researchers analyzed the eating habits and blood sugar levels of 666 people over age 40 and found that those who ate salmon every day had a 50 percent lower risk of IGT than

340

Chromium or No?

For years, Richard A. Anderson, Ph.D., a researcher at the U.S. Department of Agriculture in Beltsville, Maryland, has insisted that the trace mineral chromium can control blood sugar levels in people with diabetes and can even prevent the onset of the disease. And for years, the American Diabetes Association has replied that taking chromium supplements to regulate blood sugar has "no known benefit."

Who's right? Fresh evidence shows that chromium, which helps the body break down fat and carbohydrates, may prevent diabetes by reversing impaired glucose tolerance (IGT), a precursor to diabetes. In a study conducted by Dr. Anderson, 180 Chinese people in the early stages of diabetes were given either 200 or 1,000 micrograms of supplemental chromium per day. After four months, both groups had near-normal glucose and insulin levels, with the most improvement seen in the 1,000-microgram group.

The Daily Value for chromium is 120 micrograms, yet most Americans get less than 50 micrograms a day. Part of the reason that we are chromium deficient, according to Dr. Anderson, is because we eat too many foods that leach chromium from our bodies, such as refined grains.

Good sources of chromium include broccoli, brewer's yeast, and black pepper. But because it's difficult to get enough chromium through food alone, Dr. Anderson advises taking a chromium supplement. "I recommend that people with diabetes or glucose intolerance take 400 micrograms of supplemental chromium per day," he says—adding that "blood sugar levels can drop within a month." But studies have shown that chromium can be toxic at doses above 200 micrograms, so you should talk to your doctor before you start taking larger doses.

people who ate it less often. Maybe the fatty acids in salmon help glucose penetrate the cells, researchers say.

Try a meatless menu. Eat more greens and grains and less meat, and you'll be planting the seeds for a longer life with less diabetes risk, according to a study conducted at Georgetown University in Washington, D.C. Researchers had one group consume a very low fat (10 percent fat) plant-based diet that provided 60 to 70 grams of fiber a day. They ate no meat, eggs, or dairy products. After three months, the fasting blood sugar lev-

341

els of these folks (that is, levels after fasting for 8 to 10 hours) had fallen 59 percent more than the levels of those in a group who followed a 30-percent-fat diet that contained less than half the fiber—about 30 grams. The vegetarian group also lost more weight—an average of 16 pounds, compared to an average of 8 pounds in the second group.

Give yourself an E. It's difficult to get enough vitamin E from food alone. So keep a bottle of vitamin E on the kitchen counter and pop a capsule every morning. Besides being good for the heart, vitamin E may also help insulin move sugar from the blood into the cells. Finnish researchers who studied 944 men found that those with the lowest levels of vitamin E in their blood were four times more likely to have diabetes than those with higher levels. Iswarlal Jialal, M.D., professor of internal medicine and clinical nutrition at the University of Texas Southwestern Medical Center at Dallas, suggests taking 400 international units of supplemental vitamin E a day. While that dose is more than 10 times the Daily Value of 30 international units, it's quite safe, says Dr. Jialal.

Walk Away from Diabetes

Whether it's old and beat-up or brand-spanking-new, that pair of walking shoes in your closet or under your bed is a powerful weapon against diabetes. "People who exercise appear less likely to develop diabetes than people who don't," says Susan Racette, Ph.D., a research instructor at Washington University School of Medicine in St. Louis.

Dr. Manson estimates that too little exercise accounts for 30 to 50 percent of all new cases of Type II diabetes. Studies support the idea that you will dramatically reduce your risk if you get moderate to vigorous exercise on a regular basis.

Researchers from the University of California, Berkeley, and Stanford University School of Medicine, who studied the exercise habits of 5,990 men found that for every 500 calories the men burned through exercise per week, their risk of diabetes dropped 6 percent. Men who had at least one risk factor for diabetes—such as a family history of the disease or being over-

342

weight—reaped the biggest benefits. High-risk men who burned 2,000 calories a week or more had 41 percent less risk than men who burned only 500 calories a week. In another study conducted in Sweden, researchers put 181 men with borderline diabetes on a weight-loss and exercise program. Five years later, 75 percent of them had improved glucose tolerance.

Exercise helps reduce the risk of diabetes by increasing your insulin sensitivity. It also helps lower blood pressure and low-density lipoprotein cholesterol levels and helps boost high-density lipoprotein cholesterol levels—and all of those benefits help improve your heart health. Working out can also help you lose weight and keep it off because it ratchets up your metabolism, so you burn calories more efficiently.

Since regular exercise makes your cells more sensitive to insulin, your pancreas doesn't have to churn out as much to move the sugar out of your blood. That is another strong vote for exercise since it is important to keep the pancreas from "burning out" if you're at high risk for diabetes. "Exercise helps lower blood sugar in people with IGT," says Dr. Racette. "Preserving the pancreas's ability to make insulin can help delay the onset of full-blown diabetes."

Makeover Minutes

To Mobilize You

When it comes to exercise, every little bit helps, from taking the stairs instead of the elevators to putting more muscle into household chores like vacuuming and mopping the kitchen floor. "Doing almost anything, as long as you're up on your feet and moving, is better than sitting around," says Dr. Racette.

See Stop-Time Tactic No. 4 on page 87 for starters. In addition, the following fast moves can help reduce your risk right away.

Park and walk. If you typically spend 20 minutes trolling the mall parking lot for a choice parking space, you are missing an opportunity to sneak a quick, convenient workout into a tight

343

Insulin Control—As Easy as Breathing

Striking down diabetes may be as simple as striking a pose.

"Yoga can help prevent and treat diabetes in a number of ways," says Robin Monro, Ph.D., a research biochemist and founder and director of the Yoga Biomedical Trust in Cambridge, England. "Stress elevates blood sugar levels, and yoga reduces stress. And like other forms of exercise, yoga may help the body use insulin more effectively." In addition, specific yoga poses and breathing exercises can help trim fat from around your belly. "This is important because people who carry extra weight around their middles rather than lower down are more likely to develop diabetes," says Dr. Monro.

A study in London showed that practicing yoga techniques, including breathing exercises, poses, and meditation, lowered blood sugar levels in people with diabetes. One-third of those who did yoga for 90 minutes a day (for two or more days a week) were able to reduce their medication.

The following breathing exercises are particularly helpful in the prevention or treatment of diabetes because they improve circulation to the abdominal area and help in the management of stress, says Dr. Monro. (The pancreas, which secretes

schedule. "If you want to shop at one end of the mall, park at the other end and walk the length of the parking lot and through the mall," suggests Dr. Racette. "Or when you go grocery shopping, park as far away from the entrance as you can and walk, especially if it's a nice day."

Make like Fred and Ginger. Too busy for an hour-long date with your treadmill? No problem. "Put on a CD and dance for 10 minutes," suggests Dr. Racette. Try dancing to three or four songs at a time, for a total of 30 minutes of energetic dancing a day.

Give yourself some rope. Ten minutes of jumping rope is equal to 10 minutes of jogging, says Dr. Racette. Jumping rope is an aerobic activity, meaning that it gets your heart pumping and your blood moving, so it strengthens your heart and lungs while it lowers your blood sugar.

Want some youthful lyrics to chant along while you jump? See "Hop To!" on page 256.

344

insulin, is located in the abdomen.) He suggests that these yoga exercises be performed once a day. Since these are advanced yoga exercises, he recommends consulting a yoga instructor to learn these practices and doing these exercises as part of an overall yoga program.

Udiyana (abdominal lock). Bend forward and put your hands on your knees. Exhale completely through your mouth. When your breath is gone, hold your breath so that no air can enter your lungs. Now expand your chest, as though inhaling, and suck in your abdomen tightly. At the same time, relax your abdominal muscles. Hold this position until you need to take a breath. Then release your abdominal muscles and inhale slowly. Repeat three times.

Abdominal pumping. Follow the first four steps of udiyana. But instead of sucking in your abdomen, pump it in and out until you need to take a breath. Repeat three times.

Because these breathing exercises affect the circulatory system, check with your doctor before you try them—and avoid them if you have high blood pressure or heart disease, warns Dr. Monro. He also advises special caution with these exercises if you have a hiatal hernia or other digestive problems.

To get the most from jumping rope, buy a proper rope, such as a segmented (beaded) or vinyl rope, at a sporting goods store. They are the most durable, and they are weighted for easy use. To protect your joints, wear aerobic or cross-training athletic shoes. And start off slowly. Jump rope for 1 minute, then march in place for 2 minutes, for a total of 12 minutes. You can do this routine three times a week.

Long-Term Tactics
To Stay in Action

To get a steady regimen of exercise in your schedule, be sure to follow the recommendations in Stop-Time Tactic No. 4 on page 87. You will also need to use some tactics that work over

345

Revamp Your Routine

While it has been shown that a low-fat diet, regular exercise, and weight loss can lower your risk of diabetes by as much as 75 percent, the question is how can you make it all happen? Well, if you follow a routine modeled on the one below, you increase your chances of staying diabetes-free, says David J. DeRose, M.D., a physician at the Lifestyle Center of America, a preventive health care center in Sulphur, Oklahoma. Here's a sample program for a brand-new day.

Breakfast: Make it your main meal of the day. Keep breakfast high in whole grains and complex carbohydrates but include some fat and protein to keep you satisfied until lunchtime. Example: one slice toast spread with 1½ tablespoons peanut butter, one ounce high-fiber cereal topped with one cup soy milk, and one piece of fresh fruit.

Mini-move: Take a brisk 15- to 20-minute walk.

Midmorning: Instead of grabbing a doughnut or even a bagel, sip a tall glass of water.

Lunch: Again, it's time for a good-size meal, with the emphasis on plant foods such as beans, whole grains, and fresh vegetables. Example: one cup brown rice or whole-wheat pasta topped with two-thirds cup vegetables with tofu stir-

---

the long haul. The following long-term strategies can help protect you from diabetes, say experts.

Garden with gusto. You can turn virtually any activity, even gardening, into a workout. To turn your garden into your own personal gym, plan at least three separate "exercises" for each gardening session—preparing flower beds, turning the compost pile, and raking the lawn, for example. Gardening should never turn into an endurance contest, however, especially in summer heat. Garden for 20 minutes to an hour, resting when you need to. To cool down, walk briskly around your garden or pick flowers or vegetables. Eventually, you might want to plant spring, summer, and fall gardens so that you can exercise nearly all year round.

Pump yourself up. Weight training may help control blood sugar levels because it diverts sugar from the blood to the muscles. It also burns fat as it builds muscle. You don't need to turn

346

fried in olive or canola oil, one-half cup cooked beans, one cup salad greens with two teaspoons fat-free salad dressing, one cup cooked vegetables, and one-half ounce nuts or seeds (any kind). Have a piece of fruit, too, if you like.

Mini-move: Reduce stress and improve circulation with 15 minutes of abdominal breathing exercises. (For more information, see "Insulin Control—As Easy as Breathing" on page 344.)

Midafternoon: Reach for the water bottle. A good-size lunch should eliminate the need for late-afternoon snacking.

Dinner: Keep it light; food eaten later in the day is more likely to be stored as fat. Aim for one serving of vegetable protein, one serving of whole grains, and one serving of fruit. Example: one-half cup cooked beans over one-half cup brown rice, with one piece of fresh fruit.

Maxi-move: Get in 30 to 45 minutes of moderate exercise as close to every day as possible. You can walk, jump rope, do yard work or garden (as long as it is moderately vigorous), or do circuit training—anything that gets you moving.

Note: Don't snack just before bed. Rising blood sugar at bedtime blunts production of important restorative hormones like growth hormone.

into a purple-veined hulk either. In fact, you don't need to lift any heavy weights. Muscle-builder-style training primarily builds muscles but doesn't do much for heart and lungs.

To get an aerobic workout—the kind that does benefit your hardworking heart and air-pumping lungs—choose circuit training with weights, recommends Dr. Racette. Use lighter weights, doing several repetitions per set. Move quickly from machine to machine, without long breaks in between, she advises.

Become a smoke-free zone. While the courts may be undecided, the health studies already agree: Smoking can lead to lung cancer, increased risk of heart disease, premature wrinkling of the skin, and other youth-sapping consequences. But here's something you may not know: Smokers may also be more likely to develop diabetes.

In one study, Japanese researchers studied 2,312 men for eight years and found that men who smoked 16 to 25 cigarettes

347

a day had more than triple the risk of developing diabetes as men who had never smoked. It may be that smoking leads to insulin resistance, researchers suggest. And there's some evidence that insulin-resistant smokers who quit may actually be able to reverse the condition. It may be hard to follow, but a smoking-cessation program is a must for diabetes protection.

Monitor your mood. If you have had a past episode of major depression, consider having your blood sugar checked. "There's evidence that depression increases the risk for Type II diabetes," says Patrick J. Lustman, Ph.D., associate professor of medical psychology in the department of psychiatry at Washington University School of Medicine. It's not known how depression might trigger diabetes, but biological processes may be at play. "For example, depression produces changes in the hormone cortisol, which in turn may affect glucose regulation," he says. "Or it may be that depressed people just don't take care of themselves. They may not eat right or exercise—and that increases their risk."

348

Protect Yourself from Digestion Problems

For tennis fans, one of the game's great thrills was watching Jimmy Connors, the winner of 109 career singles titles, take to the court against opponents less than half his age—and win. But even his most ardent fans would agree that Connors, at the age of forty-something, no longer had the same explosive speed and power that allowed him to dominate the game for so long.

Same goes for all of us. By the time we reach our forties, we are moving more slowly than we used to. But it's not only the legs and lungs that shift into lower gears. There are gut-level changes as well. The muscles of the intestines, like those in the arms and legs, gradually lose tone and get weaker.

That's not the only reason the digestive system gets crotchety as it ages. Prescription drugs can turn into a gut-wrenching experience. The average person between the ages of 55 and 64 spends about $500 per year on medicine—and that's almost twice as much as someone in his early forties. Follow that pattern, and your digestive lining could pay a price.

As we noted in Stop-Time Tactic No. 1, your digestive system may be headed for trouble if you eat too much fat and don't get enough dietary fiber. And if you are not getting enough exercise either, don't be surprised when your digestive system starts balking.

So it's really not surprising that as we get older we often experience a variety of digestive complaints. Older people, for ex-

349

Losing Acid

From what you read in magazines or see on TV, you might think that the biggest digestive problem facing Americans is too much stomach acid.

The solution? Well, if you believe the commercials, you might end up popping antacids as if they were some kind of after-dinner mints.

But if you're 60 years or older, chances are you have the opposite problem. Some older Americans actually have too little stomach acid, a condition called hypochlorhydria. While this usually isn't serious, it can cause you to feel full even when you haven't eaten much. It can also cause mild abdominal discomfort and, in some cases, interfere with your body's ability to absorb iron and calcium. And if all that's going on, the discomfort could easily make you feel older than your years.

Until recently, doctors assumed that acid levels declined as people aged. It was considered inevitable. But views on that subject are changing. A more recent theory suggests that bacteria called *Helicobacter pylori*, which is also associated with ulcers and stomach inflammation, may be to blame, says Susan Gordon, M.D., professor of medicine at Allegheny University Hospitals—Graduate in Philadelphia. "The bacteria cause you to lose the cells that produce acid in the stomach," she says.

To help reduce stomach discomfort, it's a good idea to eat less meat and less fat, which take longer to digest, Dr. Gordon says.

ample, are five times more likely to be constipated than their younger peers. Painful gallstones usually strike in the forties and fifties. And this is about the age when irritable bowel syndrome (IBS) is usually diagnosed. (Signs of IBS typically include cramping, diarrhea, and constipation.)

To top it all off, somewhere in your sixties there is a slowdown in the digestive system's efficiency. That's the decade when your stomach begins to secrete lower-than-normal amounts of stomach acid, which is likely to cause stomach pain. It can also inhibit the body's absorption of calcium and iron, causing osteoporosis and anemia.

But even as the years are beginning to add up, you can still improve your digestive health, says Samuel Meyers, M.D., clinical professor of medicine at Mount Sinai School of Medicine of the City University of New York in New York City. "More things tend to go wrong with your digestive system as you get older, but don't just accept it," he says. "For the most part, these problems are correctable. The main cause is usually a combination of poor diet, not taking in enough fluids, and inactivity." And the better you can maintain your digestion, the more you can turn back the clock on aging inward.

With some fast, effective strategies, you can prevent digestive problems from slowing you down. Here's how to halt digestive aging with some well-aimed tactics that are easy to swallow.

Countering Constipation

Regularity is one of those terms that is difficult to define since everyone's bowel habits are somewhat different. "There are some people for whom going once every three days is normal, and some for whom three times a day is normal," says Barry Jaffin, M.D., clinical instructor in the department of medicine and gastroenterology at Mount Sinai School of Medicine of the City University of New York. "So constipation is usually defined as what varies from the norm for you."

That said, if you're having fewer than one bowel movement every three days, or if you find yourself straining when you go, then you almost certainly have a problem.

Constipation isn't merely uncomfortable. Repeated straining can lead to hemorrhoids, a condition that sets in when veins around the rectum swell under pressure and turn painful and itchy. More serious is the risk of diverticulosis. This condition, which is especially common in people over 50, is a possible result of straining to have a bowel movement. Internal pressures in the colon sometimes cause the intestinal wall to bulge outward, according to Dr. Jaffin. Since the bulging occurs in little pouches called diverticula, the condition gets the name diverticulosis.

While diverticulosis is painless, it may lead to a painful condition called diverticulitis. If the intestinal bulges get infected, the inflammation can make your midsection feel miserable. Let this go on, and it might cause a perforation in the intestinal lin-

know what?

The small intestine is a mere 9 to 11 feet in length. But its interior surface is infinitely puckered and wrinkled. If the entire lining of the small intestine were opened up and spread flat, it would cover two tennis courts.

351

ing—what doctors call a blowout—which allows pus and bacteria to break through the colon wall and into the abdominal cavity.

While these and other problems caused by constipation can readily be treated, why not prevent them in the first place? You can do it just by making a few minor changes in your lifestyle and diet.

Makeover Minutes

For Easier Exiting

To reduce pain and get long-term gain, take a few minutes to reconsider your diet. Here's where to begin.

Feed on fiber. The number one cause of constipation is not getting enough fiber in the diet, says Dr. Meyers. Translated, that means "you need brussels sprouts and peas—all the things you hated as a kid," he says. "Fiber improves muscle function in the colon by making the stool bigger and stretching the intestinal muscles, which makes them contract better."

Dr. Meyers agrees with many experts who say that you should eat between 20 and 30 grams of fiber per day to maintain a healthy digestive tract and to stay regular. That's roughly the equivalent of three one-cup servings of raisin bran (each one-cup serving has about 9 grams). For other high-fiber food suggestions, be sure to check out the top 10 list for digestive health on page 13.

Take something extra. If you simply can't get enough fiber in your diet, Dr. Meyers recommends taking a fiber supplement. But don't start with a full dose the first time you take it, or your digestive system may rebel. "You can take wheat bran or oat bran tablets," he advises, "but start with one a meal, three times a day. Then increase to two a meal, and then to three a meal." That way, your bowels can start to adjust to the ever-increasing doses of fiber.

Drink plenty of water. Just a reminder: Drinking eight eight-ounce glasses of water a day makes the perfect complement to the fiber in your diet, says Dr. Jaffin. "You want a combination of water and fiber, which mix together to increase the bulk of the stool."

Shake a leg. Regular exercise stimulates your entire metabolism and helps stool move through your body more quickly, says Loren Cordain, Ph.D., director of the Human Performance Research Center at Colorado State University in Fort Collins. In a study of nine men ages 18 to 25 who were put on an exercise program, Dr. Cordain reported a dramatic reduction in the time it took for food to be passed. He found that exercise reduced the time from 35 hours to 24 hours. "The decreased time could have been the result of an improvement in nerve and muscle tone," he observes. "Or it could be that the jostling around of the bowel contents served as a stimulus."

But whatever the cause, people in the exercise group definitely benefited from speedier passage of food through their systems. And, Dr. Cordain adds, it doesn't take a lot of exercise to get the benefits. Among the exercises that improve digestion are walking, swimming, and riding a bike. If you do activities like those for about 30 minutes, three to five times a week, you'll get the benefit of speedier digestion.

If nothing's handy, try candy. In a pinch, eat a sugar-free candy sweetened with the artificial sweetener sorbitol, suggests Dr. Meyers. As bacteria in the colon feed on the sorbitol, they create acids that cause water to pour into the colon, helping the bowels move. "If you're constipated and going out for the evening and don't want to break out your Metamucil, you could just suck on a few sugar-free candies instead."

know what?

Just one slice of whole-wheat bread has almost 2 grams of fiber. And a cup of strawberries has nearly 3½ grams.

Long-Term Tactics

To Help You Move Along

In addition to the everyday things you can do to manage constipation, you might need to take a hard look at some of your lifestyle and health habits. Here are some other strategies to put into play.

353

How to Squelch a Belch

Kids think it's fun to belch—preferably as loud as possible. Adults, of course, don't have the same freedom of expression—which may be why Mother Nature, with her wicked sense of humor, makes adults much more prone to belching.

Respectfully called eructation by medical doctors, the belching that seems to assault us in middle age may be caused by ulcers, a hiatal hernia, or gallbladder disease. More commonly, it's simply caused by swallowing air, says Samuel Meyers, M.D., clinical professor of medicine at Mount Sinai School of Medicine of the City University of New York in New York City.

Every time you swallow, you take in about a third of an ounce of air, says Dr. Meyers. Most of the air passes into the stomach and out through the digestive tract. Some of it, however, simply hovers between the stomach and the esophagus—and periodically drifts upward as a burp.

While you can't stop belching entirely, you may be able to avoid it by steering clear of those things that make you swallow a lot of air. Eat more slowly and avoid carbonated drinks and chewing gum, and you have a better chance of keeping the eruptions under control, according to Dr. Meyers.

Go easy on the laxatives. There's nothing wrong with occasionally using laxatives for temporary constipation. But using laxatives once a week or more can make constipation worse, says Dr. Jaffin. "The gastrointestinal tract gets used to the laxative," he warns. "Your body's natural mechanism starts to rely on laxatives to prompt a bowel movement, and it can't work without them."

Question medications. Prescription medications such as the drugs for high blood pressure and anxiety are a common cause of constipation. If you're taking these or other medications, you may want to ask your doctor if there are substitutes that won't cause constipation, suggests James George, M.D., assistant professor of medicine in the department of gastroenterology at Mount Sinai School of Medicine of the City University of New York.

Check out other causes. You may need a checkup to see if certain physical problems are causing constipation. Sometimes diabetes or thyroid disease may be associated with intestinal problems. So be sure to talk to your doctor if you have tried a number of approaches but constipation problems still exist.

The Beastly Bellyache of IBS

When the tension is turned up too high, some folks get pounding headaches. Others can't sleep. But what if all that tension settles in your gut?

When people take stress deep down in the solar plexus, they're just asking for a condition called irritable bowel syndrome, or IBS.

Usually, IBS causes constipation, diarrhea, and cramping, according to Timothy Koch, M.D., chief of gastroenterology at West Virginia University Byrd Health Science Center in Morgantown.

Apart from this stress connection, the physical causes of IBS are still unclear. But people with this condition have intestines that either contract too vigorously, causing diarrhea, or not vigorously enough, causing constipation. Whichever the symptom, it's clear that stress plays a significant role, according to Dr. Koch. "For some of the people I see, all their good days are Saturdays and all their sick days are Mondays, so you know that work-related stress is involved," he observes.

Evidence shows that stress isn't the only thing that can set off IBS, however. Diet also plays a role. If someone is prone to IBS, too much greasy food or not enough fiber invariably sets off an attack.

Because the symptoms of IBS are similar to those caused by other digestive complaints, getting a diagnosis can be tricky, says Debra B. Jackson, Ph.D., acting dean of the graduate school for health education and human development and assistant vice-provost for research at Clemson University in Clemson, South Carolina. "Your doctor will rule out everything else that could also cause diarrhea and constipation," she says. In other words, you will get a very thorough examination for other kinds of gastrointestinal trouble. If no other problems turn up, there's a good chance you have IBS.

355

To Help Your IBS

Despite its mysterious origins and occurrences, IBS can be conquered even before an onset begins. Here are some quick tips to help stop the symptoms.

Beware of peppers. Both red and green peppers contain a chemical called capsaicin, which can aggravate IBS by making your colon go into spasms, says Dr. Koch. Drop them from your diet, he advises, then see if your bowel behavior improves.

Take advantage of fiber. The dietary fiber found in fruits, vegetables, legumes, and whole grains helps make digestion more comfortable, says Dr. Koch. "Fiber makes a larger stool in the colon. For many people—especially IBS sufferers—the large stool is easier to pass than a smaller, harder one."

Cut back on fried food. "Fatty foods send a message that tells the colon to contract," says Theodore Bayless, M.D., professor of medicine and clinical director of the Meyerhoff Digestive Disorders Center at the Johns Hopkins University School of Medicine in Baltimore. "The result could be abdominal pain and diarrhea," he observes.

Relax awhile. Because stress is a common trigger for IBS, teaching yourself to relax—even if just for short periods of time—is an important step in feeling better. "Meditation is a great way of clearing the mind, relaxing, and working on your stress," says Charles Lo, M.D., who practices traditional Chinese medicine in Chicago.

Meditation doesn't have to be complicated, Dr. Lo observes. All you have to do is find a quiet place, sit comfortably on the floor (using cushions if you want), and concentrate on your breathing rather than on your thoughts. Breathe slowly and deeply, keeping your mind focused on each breath. With practice, you'll soon find it's easy to create a little mental distance from the stressful events of the day. As stress levels subside, so should your IBS discomfort.

Look into lactose. Many American adults, not only those with IBS, have difficulty digesting lactose, which is the sugar found

356

in milk and other dairy products. If you have IBS, the lactose-intolerance symptoms can be particularly severe. Diarrhea and stomach cramps may occur frequently, says Dr. Koch.

Since the symptoms of IBS and lactose intolerance are very similar, you may want to ask your doctor to puzzle out the cause, suggests Dr. Koch. Your doctor can give you a test for lactose intolerance, and if you find that's not what's causing the symptoms, something else is to blame. IBS just might be the culprit.

Getting Out Gallstones

Some say the pangs that rack the upper abdomen during a gallstone attack can only be compared to childbirth. Judging from the agony expressed by gallstone sufferers, some doctors agree. Those stones burn like crazy. Nausea is common. And the pain is just—well—indescribable. But while the labor of childbirth results in a bundle of joy, all you get from gallstones is a war story to tell later.

The start of this rocky road to agony is a pear-shaped organ on the right side of the abdomen that collects bile from the liver. The gallbladder's job is to help digest fats by concentrating and storing bile. That bile is shipped to the small intestine when it's needed, according to Susan Gordon, M.D., professor of medicine at Allegheny University Hospitals—Graduate in Philadelphia.

For about one in five people over age 65, the gallbladder is also the repository for gallstones—hard, little deposits made from a mix of cholesterol, protein, and fat. While 80 percent of people with gallstones have no symptoms, others can suffer terrible discomfort, usually when a stone blocks one of the small ducts that are in the gallbladder or that lead into the small intestine, says Dr. George.

Most attacks occur soon after a fatty meal, when the gallbladder is pumping bile to the small intestine. And because the pain of gallstones is very similar to the discomfort caused by indigestion or ulcers, it's sometimes difficult to tell the difference. "Be aware of the patterns of the attacks," suggests Dr. Gordon. "If you always have them after a fatty meal, and the pain feels in-

what?

The largest gallstone ever removed weighed 13 pounds, 14 ounces. It was taken from the gallbladder of a woman in London in 1952.

357

tense—more like an attack than general discomfort—it's probably gallstones." To make sure, though, your doctor may recommend an ultrasound to verify the presence of stones.

In the past, removing stones from the gallbladder required major abdominal surgery. Today, the surgery is typically performed through tiny incisions in or near the navel, so the procedure goes faster, and the incisions heal more quickly.

Long-Term Tactics
To Hammer the Stones

Even if the procedure is less traumatic than it once was, your best policy is to make a few lifestyle changes that can help prevent the process from starting. Here are some ways to help stop the stones before they get rolling.

Reduce the fat in your diet. "Fat stimulates the gallbladder to release bile into the gastrointestinal tract for digestion," says Dr. Jackson. "So the more fat you eat, the more the gallbladder is stimulated to contract, and the more likely a stone will get stuck in the duct."

Some experts agree that you should get no more (and preferably less) than 25 percent of your total daily calories from fat. Of course, by eating less fat—particularly the saturated fat found in meat and most dairy products—you may also lower cholesterol and keep your weight in check. So what's good for your gallbladder could also be good for your waistline.

Put off the pounds. The heavier you are, the greater your chance of developing gallstones, says Dr. Gordon. Being overweight may cause bile in the gallbladder to become super-saturated with cholesterol. "That could affect the ability of the gallbladder to contract," she says. "If bile doesn't empty through the bile ducts, the chances of developing a stone increase."

But lose it slowly. While losing a few pounds is often good, losing too much too fast puts you in the gallstone danger zone, says Dr. Gordon. Rapid weight loss causes cholesterol levels in

358

the gallbladder to rise, making stones more likely to form. If you're trying to shed 10 percent of your body weight, for instance, try to lose 2 percent every month for five months—rather than 5 percent each month for two months, suggests Dr. Gordon.

Eat less rather than more. Eating several small meals throughout the day puts less stress on the gallbladder than having one (or two or three) big meals, says Dr. George. With more frequent and smaller meals, "the gallbladder doesn't have to process as much fat at one time, which makes it less likely to malfunction."

Figure on more fiber. Getting additional dietary fiber may go a long way toward keeping your digestion healthy. "Studies show animals with diets high in fiber have fewer gallstones," says Dr. Gordon.

Observe estrogen caution. Women who take estrogen are at higher risk for having high levels of cholesterol in the gallbladder, says Dr. George. If you're taking hormones, whether for birth control or as part of a hormone-replacement plan, ask your doctor if this may be a problem for you.

know what?

In 1987, doctors removed a record 23,530 gallstones from an 85-year-old woman.

Protect Yourself from Heart Disease

Roy Clarke is in his late fifties, but he has the heart of a much younger man. Not literally, mind you. He still has the heart he was born with. But he has taken such good care of it over the years that it shows few of the signs we associate with aging.

A dentist in Jacksonville, Florida, Dr. Clarke can swim a mile without being bludgeoned by the thump-thump of his heartbeat echoing in his ears. His blood pressure and cholesterol levels are enviably low. And his resting pulse is as calm and steady as a 25-year-old's.

"I feel great," says Dr. Clarke. "I'm more physically fit than I was in high school."

His secret for staying young at heart? He eats a low-fat diet, exercises five or six days a week, doesn't smoke, and makes sure he doesn't get stressed-out too often. In short, he does everything he should to keep heart disease at bay.

The formula used by Dr. Clarke is not unique. Follow suit, and you, too, can slow the clock on the body's most valuable pump. "I know a number of people like Dr. Clarke who do it right—eat the right diet, exercise, don't smoke, keep their blood pressure under control—who have hearts of much younger people," says Gerald F. Fletcher, M.D., a cardiologist, professor in medicine at the Mayo Medical School in Jacksonville, and a friend and sometime exercise partner of Dr. Clarke.

Attack the Attacker

Heart disease risk starts to zoom up in midlife and beyond. In fact, 95 percent of all heart attacks happen to people over 40.

And because of statistics like that, we tend to assume heart trouble is an unavoidable part of aging. We expect to get winded more easily, to develop high blood pressure, and to see our cholesterol readings get higher as we grow older.

But why be a slave to statistics? Your risk of heart disease does increase slightly as you grow older—but only slightly. If you eat well, exercise, and otherwise do right by your heart, you can more than compensate for the increase and steer clear of many problems, says Dr. Fletcher.

"A 75-year-old who has low cholesterol, is reasonably active, doesn't smoke or have high blood pressure or diabetes is still at higher risk than a 30-year-old, but still at a low risk overall," says Ira S. Ockene, M.D., professor of medicine at the University of Massachusetts Medical School in Worcester.

The truth is that heart disease is an entirely avoidable consequence of the way most of us live. The majority of us eat too much fatty food, get too little exercise, and suffer too much high anxiety. On top of that, too many of us smoke and are overweight. All these things increase your odds of developing heart disease.

Once the thumper starts balking, it brings up the curtain on a wide range of symptoms. Heart disease can truly make you feel older than your years. It can sap your stamina, leave you winded, and cause chest pain at the slightest exertion. Among both American men and women, heart disease is a leading cause of disability. Worse yet, it's the number one cause of death in the United States.

By the time we reach midlife, most of us are at a crossroads. And the traffic light at that crossroads is turning from green to yellow. Not enough exercise and too much fat in food will send us veering into the vigor-sapping, life-shortening lane toward heart disease. Fortunately, we can change direction, take a turn for healthier options, and protect or restore the former youthful power of those life-lending muscles. A number of Stop-Time Tactics will help you keep your heart in shape. So will the additional tips in this chapter. But in order for these tactics to work, you need to keep using them.

"I've seen people who have had heart attacks start doing things right and get very healthy and live long, satisfying lives," says Dr. Fletcher.

know what?

If all the blood vessels in your body were laid end to end, they would go around the Earth more than twice.

361

The Aging Effects of High Blood Pressure

To get your blood where it needs to go, your heart has to pump with considerable force. The fact is that by the time your blood has made the trip from your heart to the nether parts of your body and back again, it has traveled a distance that's the equivalent of two round-the-world trips.

Together, your heart's pumping force and the resistance force your blood vessels exert against the blood passing through them determine your blood pressure. If your heart pumps with too much force or if your arteries are too inelastic to give when your heart pumps a new batch of blood through, your blood pressure is sure to be too high.

As we age, we are at increased risk of developing high blood pressure, in part because our arteries stiffen and don't give as much as they used to. Research suggests that there may be a vicious-cycle effect: High blood pressure can actually worsen the problem by making arteries even stiffer.

Worse yet, high blood pressure can also damage the lining of the arteries leading to your heart, setting the scene for the accumulation of fatty plaque. If enough plaque accumulates, it can interfere with blood flow to your ticker. And if blood flow gets shut off completely, you move into heart attack territory.

High blood pressure can also contribute to something called hypertensive cardiovascular disease, which leaves your heart muscle thickened and weakened.

No one knows what causes most cases of high blood pressure. Though it's sometimes related to kidney or hormonal problems, "those cases are pretty rare," notes Eric Peterson, M.D., assistant professor of cardiology at Duke University in Durham, North Carolina. "Ninety percent of cases are what we call unexplained," he adds.

Researchers do know that certain factors—like age, heredity, race, sex, and weight—increase the odds that you'll develop high blood pressure.

Go with the Flow

Walk through the giant fiberglass heart at Philadelphia's famed science museum, the Franklin Institute, and you get a good idea of what your heart does all day. Arrows guide you through the two-story-high heart, as you follow the flow of blood that surges toward lungs and arteries with every beat.

Plus, you can actually inherit a tendency to have high blood pressure. If you are African-American or male, for instance, you run a higher risk than if you are white and a woman. (Though women, too, need to be very aware of heart disease risk since it's the number one killer of American women 65 and over.)

Other factors? Obesity certainly boosts your risk, as does inactivity. And heavy drinking also makes you a more likely candidate than someone who just drinks a glass or two of wine every day.

For reasons that aren't entirely clear, some people see their blood pressure rise significantly when they eat a lot of salt. In medical lingo, these people have "salt sensitivity."

Fortunately, many of the age-protecting tactics that will protect you from heart disease will also lower your odds of developing high blood pressure, and if you already have high blood pressure, these tactics will help bring it down a notch or two. The most important things that you can do are quit smoking, change your diet, lose excess weight, start exercising regularly, and manage your stress levels.

In addition, if you are salt-sensitive, cutting back on salt should help, suggests Fredric J. Pashkow, M.D., associate director of preventive cardiology and cardiac rehabilitation at the Cleveland Clinic Foundation in Cleveland and co-author of *50 Essential Things to Do When the Doctor Says It's Heart Disease.* For several weeks, stop adding salt to your food, he suggests. Also, buy only salt-free broth, bouillon, and soups and avoid any canned foods that have added salt. Choose low-sodium cheeses and ask that all your meals be prepared without salt. "If your systolic blood pressure (the top number of the reading) drops 15 to 20 millimeters when you do this, you are salt-sensitive," he says. That means that you should continue avoiding the stuff after the few weeks of testing are over.

The blood enters the right atrium that pumps it to the right ventricle, which squirts blood to the lungs where it picks up oxygen. The blood then enters the left atrium from which it flows into the left ventricle, the muscular pumphouse that sends newly oxygenated blood surging through blood vessels to the rest of the body.

363

Every part of you needs oxygen-rich blood to stay alive, and so does the heart itself. It comes equipped with three special blood vessels that keep it supplied. Shaped like the tubes on a coronet, they're known as coronary arteries.

Normally, the insides of your coronary arteries are slick and even, so blood flows smoothly to your heart. When you have heart disease, though, the inside of the arteries gets clogged with a waxy mixture of cholesterol and other substances, called plaque, that limits blood flow. Now the blood looks as if it's surging through rapids. If the flow gets dammed up altogether, the result is a heart attack.

Your heart isn't the only organ that can be affected by this pernicious clogging. The arteries to your brain and other key body parts, like your legs, can also get clogged with plaque. Cut off the blood flow to your brain, and the result is a stroke. Limit the flow to your legs, and you're almost guaranteed to have chronic cramps and leg pain. In men, too little blood flowing to the penis can cause another related problem—impotence.

Plaque gets a foothold when a certain type of cholesterol normally found in your blood—a type called low-density lipoprotein (LDL)—accumulates inside the arteries. Some research suggests that plaque is more likely to do this if the lining has been damaged. Once inside the artery wall, LDL can undergo a nefarious transformation called oxidation that makes it highly dangerous. Oxidized LDL causes inflammation and triggers a series of changes that usher immune cells and blood-clotting proteins into your arteries, where they turn into the sticky, messy play-school paste called plaque.

So anything that helps LDL to oxidize is the enemy. And among the enemy's forces are a breed of marauding opportunists called free radicals. Unstable molecules that are the unfortunate by-products of breathing and other essential metabolic processes, free radicals are what oxidize LDL.

Smoking, which unleashes extra free radicals in your body, seems to step up oxidation of LDL. So do elevated blood sugar levels associated with diabetes. It's obvious, then, that you should quit smoking if you smoke, and take care of your diabetes if you have diabetes, as your first measures to control heart disease.

What You Need to Know about Niacin

Inexpensive and readily available in health food stores, niacin in high doses can lower your "bad" low-density lipoprotein (LDL) cholesterol and triglyceride levels while giving your "good" high-density lipoprotein (HDL) cholesterol level a boost. Sounds ideal—but it can also be extremely dangerous.

To get the benefits of niacin therapy, you have to take amounts that may be hundreds of times higher than the Daily Value, says Ira S. Ockene, M.D., professor of medicine at the University of Massachusetts Medical School in Worcester. At these high levels, niacin may cause liver toxicity and other side effects. And a high dose of niacin can worsen diabetes.

"Niacin is a very good drug, but it's a real drug and at these dose levels can cause lots of side effects," he notes. "You shouldn't use it if you don't have a physician monitoring you."

It's also important to cut back on fat in your diet, particularly saturated fat, because that kind has a more marked effect on your LDL levels than anything else you eat. Saturated fat prompts your body to produce an excess of LDL, and the higher the level of LDL in your blood, the faster plaque builds up in your arteries, explains Eric Peterson, M.D., assistant professor of cardiology at Duke University in Durham, North Carolina.

Now, high LDLs are not entirely the result of high-fat diets. Some of us inherit a tendency to produce more LDL than we need, Dr. Peterson notes. But everyone can lower their LDL levels by eating less fat, particularly saturated fat.

Exercise is also a key part of disease- and age-proofing your heart because exercise prompts your body to produce a different kind of cholesterol, called high-density lipoprotein (HDL). The hero of our artery story, HDL actually cleans LDL from your artery walls, slowing and even reversing the buildup of plaque.

You're Never Too Old to Reverse

During the Korean Conflict in the 1950s, medical researchers performing autopsies on GIs found that roughly three-quarters of the men killed in the conflict had thick streaks

(continued on page 368)

365

Hazard Signs in Heart Attack Territory

The road to heart disease should be posted with dozens of warning signs—but it isn't. No bright, glaring posters to remind you—every mile—that you're closing in on your destination. In fact, most of the warning signs of heart disease are subtle, which means you have to be on the lookout for them. Here's what to look for.

High Blood Pressure

The American Heart Association suggests that you get your blood pressure checked at least once every two years. A test will give you two numbers, both expressed in terms of milligrams of mercury, or mm Hg. The first number, your systolic pressure, is the pressure in your arteries when your heart contracts to pump. The second is your diastolic pressure, the pressure in your arteries when your heart relaxes between contractions. If your doctor says your pressure is 120 over 85, for example, that means your systolic pressure is 120, and your diastolic is 80. Here's more on how to interpret your numbers, according to the American Heart Association.

Optimal: Less than 120 (systolic) over 80 (diastolic)

Normal: Less than 130 (systolic) over 85 (diastolic)

High: 140 (systolic) over 90 and higher (diastolic)

A single reading higher than 140 over 90 doesn't mean that you have high blood pressure—some people have temporarily higher blood pressure when they're nervous or upset. Doctors usually diagnose high blood pressure only after you have had two or more elevated readings in a row. If possible, those readings should be taken in a nonthreatening situation such as your home.

High Cholesterol

If you are overweight, smoke, have high blood pressure, diabetes, or a family history of heart disease, you should have your cholesterol levels tested yearly, says Fredric J. Pashkow, M.D., associate director of preventive cardiology and cardiac rehabilitation at the Cleveland Clinic Foundation in Cleveland and co-author of *50 Essential Things to Do When the Doctor Says It's Heart Disease*. If none of these risk factors apply, do it every two or three years, he suggests.

Make sure that the test you're getting will give you enough information. This means getting reports on two types of cholesterol. There's low-density lipoprotein (LDL), the "bad" stuff that can gunk up the arteries to your heart. And there's high-density lipoprotein (HDL), the "good" stuff that can clean your arteries.

Your results should tell you your LDL and HDL levels or your total cholesterol and HDL levels. Ask your doctor to tell you your LDL level if it isn't printed on the results. Here's how the numbers stack up, according to Dr. Pashkow.

Desirable total cholesterol: 200 milligrams per deciliter (mg/dl) of blood or lower

High total blood cholesterol: 240 mg/dl and higher

Desirable HDL cholesterol: 45 mg/dl and higher

If your total cholesterol level is higher than 200 mg/dl and your HDL is lower than 35 mg/dl, you should talk to your doctor about ways to lower your total cholesterol level while boosting your HDL level. Cutting back on the fat in your diet and exercising more often will help with both, says Dr. Pashkow.

If your total cholesterol level is not higher than 200 mg/dl but your HDL is less than 35 mg/dl, you should talk to your doctor about strategies for giving your HDL a lift. Regular exercise is the best approach, Dr. Pashkow says.

Some tests will report your ratio of total cholesterol to HDL. But if that's not in the report, you can figure it yourself. Divide HDL into total cholesterol. If you have total of 200 and HDL of 50, for instance, you have a ratio of 4 to 1. An optimum ratio is 3.5 to 1, and the goal is to keep your ratio below 5 to 1.

Angina

Angina—chest pain or discomfort—is one warning sign of heart disease that isn't subtle. Though angina usually doesn't last more than a few minutes, it can be extremely uncomfortable. It often feels like a heaviness or a squeezing pressure that starts behind the breastbone and sometimes spreads to your neck, jaw, and arms. But with some people the signals of angina include feeling breathless or having a temporarily erratic heartbeat, instead.

Both physical exertion and stress can bring on angina if you're a candidate for this problem. Advice: Heed the warning. It's a sign that your heart isn't getting the blood it needs, most likely because fatty plaque has built up in the arteries that feed your heart and has narrowed them to a threatening tightness. Not everyone with heart disease has angina, however. Some people don't have chest pain until they have a heart attack.

When angina persists, is extremely severe, or is accompanied by sweating, nausea, or weakness, you may be having something worse—an actual heart attack.

Even during a heart attack, however, not everyone has the same symptoms. Women, in particular, are likely to have atypical symptoms of heart attack—like stomach pain, heartburn, nausea, and shortness of breath. If you think you may be having a heart attack, call 911, says Dr. Pashkow. Heart attack requires immediate attention.

Itinerary for a Perfect Day in the Life of Your Heart

If you pampered your heart for a day—if you did everything you should to keep it youthful and protect it from heart disease—would you have to endure 24 hours of sweat and bran flakes? Never. As it turns out, the things you should do to be kind to your heart are probably the things you want to do anyway.

For the perfect day in the life of your heart, consider the following itinerary recommended by Fredric J. Pashkow, M.D., associate director of preventive cardiology and cardiac rehabilitation at the Cleveland Clinic Foundation in Cleveland and co-author of *50 Essential Things to Do When the Doctor Says It's Heart Disease*.

7:00 A.M.: Get up after a restful night's sleep and enjoy a breakfast of high-fiber cereal with fruit and skim milk.

7:30–8:15 A.M.: Go on a brisk walk through a park or scenic landscape.

9:00 A.M.–NOON: Work at a job you enjoy.

NOON–1:00 P.M.: For lunch, have a salad with lots of dark leafy greens, carrots, tomatoes, and broccoli florets, garnished with slivers of meat, a few olives, and a sprinkling of goat cheese. Grab a piece of fruit for dessert.

1:00–3:00 P.M.: Go back to your enjoyable job.

3:00–3:20 P.M.: Take a nap if your company allows this (it's probably one of the reasons you enjoy your job). If napping is frowned upon, just be ingenious and find a way to nod off somewhere. It takes no longer than a coffee break—and you owe yourself this stress relief.

3:20–4:05 P.M.: Spend another 45 minutes doing some aerobic activity you enjoy. A bike ride with your colleagues?

4:05–6:00 P.M.: Finish work feeling satisfied.

6:45–7:00 P.M.: Enjoy your dinner—pasta garnished with smoked salmon, lots of fresh vegetables, and a glass of your favorite wine.

7:15–8:00 P.M.: Enjoy intellectual discussion with guests or, if alone, meditate.

8:30–9:30 P.M.: Put on your favorite CD and listen to fine music.

10:00 P.M.: Go to bed—and doze off gradually into a sound, restful sleep.

of plaque in their coronary arteries. The soldiers' average age? A mere 22.

Though we rarely have symptoms before midlife, plaque starts building up in our arteries during youth. And it keeps ac-

Whole-Body Protection

cumulating, oh so quietly, over the course of many a fatty meal and many an indolent hour.

Angina, or chest pain, may be the first warning that plaque has built up to the point that it is shutting off blood flow to your heart. You may have this kind of chest pain only when you exert yourself—because exertion increases your heart's demand for oxygen—or when you are under stress. Or you might not experience angina at all. Some people have no symptoms of heart disease—don't even realize they have it—until they have a heart attack.

Researchers used to think that most heart attacks were the result of a gradual buildup of plaque that eventually sealed off blood flow to the heart. But more recent studies find the vast majority of heart attacks happen long before then, when plaque that only partially blocks an artery ruptures and triggers the formation of a blood clot that shuts off blood flow.

If you peered into a diseased blood vessel, you would notice that plaque isn't smooth and even. Unlike a healthy artery wall, a plaque-plagued artery is thicker in some places than others and tends to be knobby and uneven. "It looks disgusting, sort of like the surface of a cheese pizza," says Fredric J. Pashkow, M.D., associate director of preventive cardiology and cardiac rehabilitation at the Cleveland Clinic Foundation in Cleveland and co-author of *50 Essential Things to Do When the Doctor Says It's Heart Disease*. Any one of those thick spots might rupture.

As it turns out, plaque spots that block an artery by as little as 25 percent can rupture, says Dr. Peterson. Trouble is, most diagnostic tests can only detect blockages that fill 70 percent of an artery. "In part, this explains why a patient who has a test that shows nothing wrong on Monday can have a heart attack on Wednesday," explains Dr. Peterson.

But when you take care of your heart by changing your eating and exercise habits, you can actually shrink the plaque blisters in your arteries and make them less likely to rupture.

"It's like removing the fluid from a blister on your finger," Dr. Peterson says. "When that happens, the (plaque) is much less likely to burst open and cause a heart attack."

know what?

Most animals living in the wild don't live long enough to develop heart disease, and other animals, like dogs, have a genetic resistance to it. But pigs and monkeys that are kept in captivity and fed high-fat diets will get heart disease.

369

To Shelter Your Heart

The most important things that you can do to keep your heart healthy and youthful—quit smoking, change your diet, start exercising, lose excess weight—do take time. But there are a few things that you can do this very minute that will also lower your risk.

Ward off vampires. Garlic may or may not keep vampires at bay, but research suggests it can help stave off heart disease. "Garlic actually depresses the production of cholesterol in your body," says Yu-Yan Yeh, Ph.D., professor of nutritional science at Pennsylvania State University in University Park. To reap the benefits, Dr. Yeh says that you'll need to eat between three and five cloves a day.

Try adding garlic to soups, salad dressings, casseroles, stews, and sauces. If garlic is not your thing, consider garlic pills, also shown effective in studies. Take one to three pills daily, suggests Dr. Yeh.

Indulge in E. Some research suggests vitamin E supplements may also lower your risk of heart disease. (For more information, see "Superfoods to Guard Your Heart" on page 5.) Most studies indicate that you're better off getting antioxidants like vitamin E from foods since foods contain a variety of nutrients that seem to work together more effectively than any single magic bullet contained in a supplement. But even though researchers seem to agree about that, many people find that it's hard to get a lot of vitamin E in your diet without adding a lot of fat since oils are really the best food sources of vitamin E. And some research suggests that vitamin E supplements can be effective, says Dr. Peterson. "If you want to do everything you can to reduce your risk, taking vitamin E is probably reasonable," he says.

For foods that have vitamin E, be sure to look at the top 10 list on page 8. If you decide that you want supplements, check with your doctor since vitamin E can interact with some medications like the blood thinner Coumadin. But if your doctor

370

Sidestepping Side Effects

Drugs can help protect you from the vitality-stealing, life-threatening toll of heart disease, but they can also cause certain side effects that make you feel, well, old.

Most people have few side effects when they take commonly prescribed high blood pressure or cholesterol-lowering medications. But a number of high blood pressure drugs, beta blockers specifically, can cause weakness, dizziness, and even impotence, says Ira S. Ockene, M.D., professor of medicine at the University of Massachusetts Medical School in Worcester. Most people tolerate cholesterol-lowering medications well, he adds, but they can make some people feel weak or achy. And niacin can cause side effects like flushing, liver function abnormalities, and stomach upset, says Dr. Ockene, so don't take it without your doctor's supervision.

Unpleasant side effects may tempt you to stop taking your drugs or to cut back on your dose. But you shouldn't do either without also consulting your physician, advises Dr. Ockene.

If your doctor has prescribed a drug, assume it's because you need it. Most doctors will only prescribe cholesterol and high blood pressure drugs *after* you have tried lifestyle changes, Dr. Ockene says. If the changes don't bring your blood pressure or cholesterol levels down to the safe zone, you need medication.

If you're having trouble with side effects, talk to your doctor, says Dr. Ockene. The problem may be that you're taking too high or too low a dose. Your doctor can correct that or can prescribe a different drug that's a better match. There are a variety of different cholesterol and blood pressure drugs on the market. And different ones affect people differently, Dr. Ockene notes.

gives you the green light, you can shoot for 400 international units of vitamin E twice daily, according to Dr. Peterson.

Opt for an aspirin spritzer. Remember: Most heart attacks happen when plaque ruptures, triggering the formation of a blood clot that blocks blood flow. Aspirin, which inhibits clotting, can help keep that from happening.

If you have had a heart attack or stroke, or if you have chest pain (angina) or very high LDL levels, aspirin may be for you,

371

says Michael Criqui, M.D., professor of family and preventive medicine at the University of California, San Diego.

For anyone who weighs less than 130 pounds, a baby aspirin a day should do it. If you weigh in at 130 to 180, make it two baby aspirin. Heavier? Take one adult aspirin, says Dr. Pashkow.

Before you start taking aspirin regularly, though, be sure to check with your physician. A doctor is likely to advise you to steer clear of aspirin—at any dose—if you have a peptic ulcer, gastrointestinal bleeding, or any other bleeding disorder. People with liver or kidney disease are also advised to avoid aspirin. And, of course, if you have aspirin allergy, taking this blood-thinning agent is out of the question.

How to Pamper Your Pumper

In heart disease research, scientists are learning more every day about lifestyle changes and tactics that can keep your heart young. These strategies take more than a few minutes to make. In fact, lifestyle changes require long-term commitment. But you can begin right away to help lower your risk. Here's how.

Boycott tobacco. "Smoking is an incredibly potent accelerator of heart disease," says Dr. Ockene. The chemicals in cigarette smoke damage the lining of your arteries and contribute to high blood pressure, which does additional artery damage. Smoking can lower the level of "good" HDL cholesterol.

Adding injury to injury, smoking also promotes the formation of blood clots. All it takes is one clot to block the flow of blood through the arteries to your heart, triggering a heart attack. The risk associated with smoking may be further increased if you take birth control pills, since certain oral contraceptives also make your blood more likely to clot. If you take the Pill and smoke, you're issuing double invitations to trouble.

According to the American Heart Association (AHA), if you smoke, you can cut your risk of death from heart disease by a whopping 50 percent just by quitting. And you don't have to wait very long to see results. "Within three years of quitting, your risk of heart disease drops to that of a person who never smoked," says Dr. Ockene.

372

Not only that, your self-restraint can do a heap of good to the hearts of those closest to your heart. The effects of smoking impact those around you, too. Some evidence suggests that chronic exposure to secondhand smoke may increase risk of heart disease. (For specific tips on quitting, see "Toss Tobacco Out of Your Life" on page 301.)

Be a blood-sugar watcher. If you have diabetes, you know that you have to keep your blood sugar levels in line, but you may not realize just how much that monitoring helps your heart. High blood sugar levels can damage your artery linings and boost levels of harmful fats in your blood. (For more information on controlling your blood sugar, see Protect Yourself from Diabetes on page 333.)

Lose excess baggage. If you are overweight, you are more likely to have a bevy of problems associated with heart disease, including not only diabetes and high blood pressure but also a potentially disastrous combination of high LDL levels and low HDL levels. That's why it is important to lose the excess. (For some advice on doing just that, see Stop-Time Tactic No. 2 on page 36.)

Consider HRT. After menopause, a woman's risk of heart disease rises steeply. No one knows exactly why. But some evidence suggests the hormone estrogen is a key factor. Among other things, the hormone seems to help boost levels of "good" HDL cholesterol. After menopause, a woman's ovaries essentially stop making the female sex hormone.

Research shows that hormone-replacement therapy (HRT) can at least partly offset the increased risk of heart disease that kicks in with menopause. HRT helps build up levels of beneficial HDLs, and the therapy may also help prevent the formation of blood clots. "For most women past menopause, some type of HRT is important," says Dr. Fletcher.

Some women are concerned about the drawbacks of HRT, however. Hormone-replacement therapy can cause side effects such as weight gain, depression, or anxiety and may increase a woman's risk of developing breast cancer. If you're trying to decide whether to try HRT, you should discuss the pros and cons with your doctor.

know what?

An organ that's just a bit larger than your fist, your heart pumps 2,000 gallons of blood every day. That's enough to fill about 100 refrigerators with gallon jugs.

373

Discover the Lunch Counter of Youth

During World War II, heart disease rates took a nosedive throughout Europe. Researchers were puzzled—until they analyzed what Europeans were eating during wartime. Or, rather, what they *weren't* eating.

"People were deprived of butter and fat," says Dr. Ockene. "While things like stress, smoking, and high blood pressure may make it more likely that you get heart disease, too much fat is the real problem. What you *must* have to get coronary disease is too much fat, especially saturated fat."

Unfortunately, most of us in postwar America eat too much meat, which is regrettably high in fat, and we also eat too much fat from other sources—including dairy, baked goods, and processed foods.

Adding to the problem, we eat too few whole grains, vegetables, and fruits. Since people who eat lots of fruits and vegetables are less likely to have heart disease, we are giving up an ounce of prevention every time that we munch on potato chips instead of apples or chomp on cheeseburgers instead of broccoli.

Based on heart studies of the last few decades, the AHA has come up with these guidelines: Eat five or more servings of fruits and vegetables every day, and be sure you have at least six servings of whole grains, breads, pasta, and starchy vegetables. In order to limit your intake of fat, the guidelines suggest that you have only two to four servings of low-fat or nonfat dairy products and no more than six ounces of lean meat, chicken, or fish daily.

Long-Term Tactics
To Bless Your Heart

Although we are likely to respect the advice of the American Heart Association, the question is—how can we make practical use of their guidelines? Here are some ways that you can go about it.

374

Fat versus Fiction in Fast-Food Land

When investigators with the Center for Science in the Public Interest (CSPI) analyzed the nutritional content of meals served at Big Boy, Chi-Chi's, and half a dozen other big chain restaurants, they found a lot more fat than the chains were claiming.

Take the Big Boy's stir-fry, for instance. According to the menu, the stir-fry should have included no more than 16 grams of fat. The total was almost twice as much—27 grams—in the stir-fry that CSPI analyzed. Tests at other restaurant chains turned up similar results.

Now, this doesn't mean every Big Boy stir-fry has 27 grams of fat, says CSPI senior staff attorney Leila Farzan. But you can't be sure what you will get—there's a good chance that the chef cooking your meal might not follow the recipe to the letter and could add more fat than the recipe calls for.

"A restaurant may have good intentions when it devises its recipes, but when you have 1,000 different chefs preparing those recipes, a chef with a heavy hand can change the numbers," says Farzan.

Since May 1997, restaurants have had to meet certain guidelines when using a heart symbol or words like "heart smart" to describe items on their menus. To qualify for this labeling, a main dish is supposed to include no more than 19.5 grams of fat, 6 grams of saturated fat, 90 milligrams of cholesterol, and 720 milligrams of sodium. Since the actual content is bound to vary from chef to chef, though, you should always specify that you want a light hand with the oil.

"You can't rely blindly on the symbol," says Farzan.

Keep a bead on calories. Excess calories add up to excess weight, which can raise your risk of heart disease. When you are carrying around excess weight, your heart has to work harder, your HDL levels are depressed, and your blood pressure rises. To lose weight and keep it off, keep tabs on your calories, says Dr. Fletcher.

It's easy to calculate the number of calories you need daily. Just follow the guidelines in "Some Shape-Up Math" on page 44. In general, you won't need as many calories—that is, you don't need to eat as much—as you get older. But you'll still need those calories if you keep active, says Penny Kris-Etherton, R.D., Ph.D.,

The American
Heart Associ-
ation sug-
gests that you
get no more
than 10 per-
cent of your
daily calories
from satu-
rated fat. If
you already
have heart
disease,
make that
7 percent
or less.

professor of nutrition at Pennsylvania State University in University Park. The main reason we tend to need fewer calories as we get older is that we get sedentary and lose muscle mass, she observes. And since muscles are big-time calorie burners, you should cultivate big ones by working out regularly. (For more information on exercising, see "Moving toward a Vigorous Heart" on page 387.)

Eating a diet that's low in fat and high in complex carbohydrates—such as whole grains, fruits, and vegetables—will help keep your calorie count within reasonable range, says Dr. Kris-Etherton. That's because a small quantity of fat packs a lot of calories, while complex carbohydrates fill you up without filling you out.

Say, "30 or bust." The American Heart Association suggests that you get no more than 30 percent of your day's calories from fat. If you have been diagnosed with heart disease, Dr. Fletcher suggests that you limit yourself to a leaner 15 percent.

Know your fats. While a low-fat diet is generally advisable for heart health, it helps to know that there are three kinds of fats that affect your heart in different ways. Most foods with fat in them contain saturated, polyunsaturated, and monounsaturated fats, but in varying amounts. Animal fat; dairy fat; coconut, palm, and palm kernel oils; and cocoa butter are mostly saturated. Safflower and corn oils are primarily polyunsaturated, while peanut, canola, and olive oils are mostly monounsaturated.

Saturated fat has the worst effect on your cholesterol profile, insidiously boosting your LDL with every drop you eat. By substituting fats that are mostly polyunsaturated and monounsaturated for mostly saturated ones, you can lower your LDL levels. But you still need to watch your total fat intake since all fats have a high calorie concentration, which means that you will be plumping up your fat cells even if you aren't necessarily raising LDL levels.

Do some trans spotting. Most vegetable oils are monounsaturated and polyunsaturated, but the vegetable fats that turn solid at room temperature fall into another category—a bad one. The manufacturing process that turns vegetable oil into margarine

376

and vegetable shortening creates compounds called trans fatty acids. These can also boost your LDL levels. Though they are not as damaging as saturated fats, trans fatty acids can do considerable harm, which is why you should use oils instead of solid fats whenever possible. If you have to use solid margarine or vegetable shortening, choose the brands that are softest at room temperature since these contain fewer trans fatty acids than the firmer kinds.

Limit your brains... And your kidneys, livers, egg yolks, and whole-fat dairy products. All these foods are high in dietary cholesterol, which can also boost your LDL levels (though not as much as saturated fat does). The American Heart Association suggests that you limit yourself to 300 milligrams of cholesterol daily. If you have heart disease, make it 200 milligrams a day or less. You will stay within that range if you eat no more than six ounces of lean meat, fish, or poultry a day. As a matter of cholesterol-dodging policy, also follow the AHA guidelines and forgo all full-fat dairy products.

Eggs are among the worst offenders since a single egg yolk provides a staggering 213 to 220 milligrams of cholesterol. If you follow the AHA's recommendations, you will limit yourself to three to four egg yolks a week—no more. Opt for omelets made with egg whites only or an egg substitute whenever you can.

Fish in cold water. If you're going to eat meat, the American Heart Association recommends eating fish. In general, fish is lower in fat than chicken and red meat. So follow the advice in Stop-Time Tactic No. 1: Eat the cold-water fish like mackerel, tuna, and salmon containing special kinds of polyunsaturated fat acids called omega-3 fatty acids. (For more information, see "Superfoods to Guard Your Heart" on page 5.)

Research suggests that omega-3s protect you from heart disease, in part because they inhibit the formation of nasty blood clots. The American Heart Association suggests that you eat cold-water fish several times a week. Supplements might help, but it's not clear that fish oil supplements work as well as the real thing. And some experts worry that taking the high doses of omega-3s found in supplements could disrupt the balance of fatty acids in your body and cause some side effects such as pro-

377

know
what?

Ocean fish
are higher
in omega-3s
than farm-
raised fish.
That's
because
ocean fish
eat plankton
while farm-
raised fish
are often fed
fish chow
made of soy-
beans and
corn.

longed bleeding or upset stomach. So, until omega-3 supplements are proven safe and effective, researchers suggest that you skip the supplements and eat the fish.

Dine on broccoli-spinach lasagna. Or whole-wheat vegetarian pizza with low-fat cheese. Or any other dish combining low-fat dairy and vegetables.

If you follow the recommendations under Stop-Time Tactic No. 1 on page 3, you will be getting the nutrients you need to help ensure a healthy heart. Here is a reminder about what these heart-smart foods provide: Low-fat dairy products give you lots of calcium. Broccoli and most other vegetables and fruits are good sources of potassium. And dark green leafy vegetables like spinach pack a lot of magnesium. All three of these nutrients are good to your heart.

In a study sponsored by the National Heart, Lung, and Blood Institute of the National Institutes of Health, researchers switched volunteers with high blood pressure to diets with a lot of magnesium-, potassium-, and calcium-rich foods—and saw the volunteers' blood pressures drop significantly.

But apparently, you need the whole food to get the full benefits. In other studies, scientists gave supplements containing magnesium, potassium, or calcium to people with high blood pressure and found little or no change. "So we think it may not be these three minerals specifically, but a combination of all sorts of things in these foods that does it," says Marlene Windhauser, R.D., Ph.D., a research dietitian at Pennington Biomedical Research Center in Baton Rouge, Louisiana.

Like some other doctors who have observed the impact of nutrition on heart health, Dr. Windhauser suggests that you aim for four to five servings of vegetables, four to five servings of fruit, and two to three servings of low-fat or nonfat dairy daily—recommendations that surpass even the AHA suggestions. Need to ease into this routine? First, include one serving of fruit or vegetable at each meal, says Dr. Windhauser. After a few days, make sure you get two servings at each meal. And, finally, make it three.

"You can have juice and cereal with fruit for breakfast," Dr. Windhauser suggests. "At lunch, have a salad, some vegetable

Whole-Body Protection

juice, and a piece of fruit. And at dinner, have a couple of servings of vegetables with fruit as dessert or a snack."

Brighten your diet with color. Citrus fruits and dark green leafy vegetables are good sources of folate (the natural form of the supplement folic acid), Dr. Kris-Etherton says. This is yet another good reason to eat them every day. Make at least one of your fruits or vegetables a bright orange, yellow, or red one, she suggests. Not only do those fruits and vegetables provide folate, they are also good sources of beta-carotene and vitamin C, two important antioxidants. And make sure that at least one vegetable is dark green and leafy to provide you with folate, vitamin E, potassium, and magnesium. (For a top 10 list of foods that are high in folate and other important nutrients, see page 8.)

Ingrain a grain habit. Like fruits and vegetables, whole grains provide fiber. Fiber is the part of an edible plant that you can't digest—but far from being useless, it's a star player in the match against LDL. Plant foods, as we have mentioned, provide two types of fiber—soluble and insoluble. Sources of soluble fiber include peas, citrus fruits, barley, beans, oatmeal, strawberries, and apples. You can get insoluble fiber from whole-grain breads and cereals, bran, cabbage, beets, carrots, cauliflower, and similar sources.

For years, researchers have been trying to determine which kind of fiber needs greater attention in heart disease prevention. "But new studies show fiber in general is beneficial," says Dr. Kris-Etherton.

Ideally, you should get 25 grams a day, according to Dr. Kris-Etherton. Eat six servings of whole grains and five or six servings of fruits and vegetables, and you'll do that easily. To make it even easier, have some high-fiber cereal for breakfast. You will get 10 grams or more in a one-cup serving.

Go Meatless

Take 500 high-fat food eaters, put them on a strict vegetarian diet for 12 days, and what do you get? Significant drops in their total cholesterol levels and blood pressures. That's what researchers in California found when they switched 500 people who ate a typical American diet (high in fat and low in fresh fruits, vegetables, and whole grains) to a low-fat, meatless diet combined with stress management and moderate exercise.

Though noteworthy, those results didn't surprise many heart specialists.

Numerous studies have found that vegetarians run a lower risk of heart disease than meat-eaters do. Because a vegetarian diet tends to be lower in total fat, saturated fat, and dietary cholesterol, the vegetarian set tends to have lower LDL levels than the average omnivore. Also, since vegetarian diets are usually lower in calories and higher in fiber than meat-eaters' diets, vegetarians are less likely to be overweight. Their svelte profile could help explain why vegetarians have lower blood pressures than meat-eaters. Plus there are nutrient factors. Because vegetarians tend to eat more fruits and vegetables and grains than carnivores, they also tend to get more folate and antioxidants in their diets.

Of course, there is more than one kind of vegetarian. Ovolactovegetarians are the type who eat dairy products and eggs but no other animal foods. Vegans are strict vegetarians who eat no animal foods whatsoever. The interesting thing is that people in both groups do better in heart disease ratings than meat-eaters.

Long-Term Tactics

Cultivate Your Garden Tastes

Since meatless eating is a good way to protect your heart, why not try out some vegetarian routes? Here are some ways to get started.

Switch and bite. Serve vegetarian versions of old favorites, suggests Reed Mangels, R.D., Ph.D., nutrition advisor for the Vegetarian Resource Group in Baltimore. Try veggie burgers instead of hamburgers, bean burritos in place of the carnivorous variety, vegetarian lasagna instead of lasagna bolognese.

Don't panic over protein. Among other things, protein supplies us with amino acids, substances our bodies need to make hormones, enzymes, and muscle. If you don't eat meat, dairy, or eggs, you can get your protein from grains, beans, peas, nuts, and seeds. As long as you meet your calorie needs and consistently eat a variety of these foods, you can easily meet your protein requirement, says Dr. Mangels.

Over the course of a day, two slices of whole-wheat toast, one tablespoon peanut butter, one cup soy yogurt, two tablespoons almonds, one baked potato, one cup each of lentils and bulgur should give vegans their full complement of protein, says Dr. Mangels. But remember to vary your choices each day, she adds.

If you are going ovo-lacto, you can easily meet your daily protein needs by substituting a couple of servings of low or nonfat yogurt for the soy variety and try an omelet made with a couple of egg whites instead of eating peanut butter, says Dr. Mangels.

Say, "low-fat cheese." Vegetarian fare isn't automatically low in fat, especially if you're eating dairy foods. If there's Brie, ice cream, and quiche in your diet, you'll be eating a lot of fat, including saturated fat and cholesterol.

Instead, look for low-fat and nonfat dairy products and have some low-fat tofu, which you'll find next to the full-fat variety in most supermarket produce sections. Choose fat-free mayonnaise and other spreads. Bake, broil, and steam your food—but don't fry it, says Dr. Mangels.

Fortify your heart's health. Low and nonfat dairy products are good sources of calcium, which helps keep your blood pressure in reasonable range in addition to promoting bone health. If you go the ovo-lacto route, shoot for three servings of low-fat or nonfat dairy every day to get the calcium you need, says Dr. Mangels.

If you're eating vegan, you can get calcium from plant foods, but it's a bit harder. Broccoli, kale, collards, and mustard greens contain calcium. But for some people, says Dr. Mangels, fortified foods may be a more realistic way to meet calcium needs. She suggests that you aim for at least three servings of calcium-rich nondairy foods like calcium-fortified tofu, fortified orange juice, and fortified soy milk. Otherwise, she adds, try a calcium supplement.

381

Read the label to make sure that you're getting the calcium you need. The optimal calcium requirements recommended by the National Institutes of Health Consensus Panel are 1,000 milligrams for men 65 and under, women under 50, and women older than 50 who receive hormone-replacement therapy. Women over 50 and men over 65 should aim for 1,500 milligrams a day. Women who are pregnant or nursing should get between 1,200 and 1,500 milligrams a day.

Iron out nutritional wrinkles. A key ingredient in red blood cells, iron is a mineral we can't live without. Red meat is a particularly good source of heme iron, the most easily absorbed form. Cooked dried beans and other plant foods provide smaller amounts in what's called the nonheme form, a kind of dietary iron that isn't as easily absorbed, Dr. Mangels says.

You can boost your absorption of nonheme iron if you eat nonheme-iron foods along with foods that are high in vitamin C—a nutrient that helps your body absorb iron. Accompany iron-rich plant foods like soybeans, other dried beans, and dark leafy vegetables with foods high in vitamin C like peppers, tomatoes, and citrus fruits, Dr. Mangels advises. To make sure that you are getting the Daily Value of iron, ask your doctor whether you should be taking a daily multivitamin/mineral supplement that includes this mineral.

But don't go overboard on iron. Some research suggests that too much iron can contribute to heart disease by stepping up the oxidation of LDL.

Turn to the yeast. Vitamin B_{12}, which is found naturally in foods of animal origin, plays a key role in the production of blood and DNA, your body's built-in instruction manual. Plus, when combined with vitamin B_6 and folic acid, B_{12} can help lower homocysteine levels in the blood and reduce your risk for heart disease, says Killian Robinson, M.D., a staff cardiologist at the Cleveland Clinic Foundation in Cleveland. You can also find vitamin B_{12} added as an extra ingredient in fortified soy milk, in certain cereals, and in some nutritional yeast. Read labels to make sure the brand you are buying has vitamin B_{12}. (If you use the yeast, sprinkle about one heaping tablespoon a day on pasta, sauces, or salads. It adds a cheesy taste.)

Long-Term Tactics
For World-Class Dining

Culinary adventure can keep you young at heart—particularly if you seek it among the traditional cuisines of Latin America, Asia, and the Mediterranean.

People who regularly eat these cuisines have famously low rates of heart disease. All three cuisines use an abundance of vegetables, fruits, and grains. Latin and Asian fare are low in fat and very low in saturated fat. While Mediterranean cuisine is higher in total fat, most of the extra fat comes from monounsaturated olive oil.

It's not hard to eat the Latin, Asian, and Mediterranean way. All the food supplies you need are tucked away on the shelves of your supermarket, but you need to know what you're looking for. Here are some tips.

Say "¡Viva America Central!" As you may have guessed, the Latin food we're talking about isn't the stuff that you'll find at the local burrito joint. Too heavy on the fat and meat and too stingy with the vegetables and grains, burrito-shop fare is American-style Latin food.

But you can eat heart-smart cuisine if you skip the meat and stir in the vegetables, fruits, and grains that are often used in Central and South America.

Among the complex carbohydrates making up heart-smart Latin cuisine are tomatoes, eggplants, squash, pumpkins, plantains, cooked dried beans, papayas, citrus fruits, grapes, potatoes, corn tortillas, and other corn dishes. As we've mentioned, it's okay to accompany this repast with a moderate amount of alcohol—a glass or two for men, a glass for women.

Eat Eastern. While Oriental fare is basically low-fat, too, be aware of the differences between American-style Asian food and traditional Asian cuisine. Traditional Asian meals include very small quantities of vegetable and nut oils. Fish and dairy products get on the menu once a day, at most. Eggs and poultry might appear weekly, while meat is eaten once a month or so.

383

In a hearty
Greek meal
including
whole-wheat
bread, salad,
grilled fish,
zucchini
stew, fresh
figs, and red
wine, you get
a hefty 28
grams of
monounsatu-
rated fat—the
healthful kind
of fat that's
found in
olive oil.

Featured roles go to noodles, rice, and other grains. The Oriental menu includes a lot of vegetables—as well as sea vegetables like nori, the dark green, dried seaweed often used in sushi. Some fruits and many bean products like tofu are also on the menu.

Since calcium-rich foods like dairy don't make regular appearances in traditional Asian meals, include calcium-rich foods in your meal or take a daily calcium supplement for insurance when you eat Asian, suggests Doris Derelian, R.D., Ph.D., former president of the American Dietetic Association.

Feast as the Romans did. Goodbye, extra-cheese pizza with pepperoni. Hello, ratatouille with risotto. Traditional Mediterranean fare is altogether different from what you'll find at the local pizzeria. It's lower in fat, but not quite as low as you might expect, given the low incidence of heart disease among Mediterraneans who eat the traditional way.

A traditional Mediterranean diet gets between 25 and 40 percent of calories from fat, roughly the same proportion of calories that the standard American diet gets from fat. But the difference, which has been mentioned before, that is most of the fat in traditional Mediterranean cuisine is monounsaturated fat from olive oil.

When researchers compared the effects of a diet that followed the American Heart Association guidelines with a traditional Mediterranean diet, they found that both led to reductions in LDL cholesterol. Everything wasn't equal, however. The AHA-based diet led to a drop in "good" HDL cholesterol and a slight increase in triglyceride levels. But the Mediterranean diet led to a much smaller drop in HDL and had no effect on triglycerides.

So the Mediterranean way may be the better way if you have high triglyceride levels and low HDL levels, Dr. Kris-Etherton says. It's also a good option for many people with diabetes, who have a higher risk for developing heart disease, she adds.

Most Mediterranean cuisines include red meat only once or twice a month. If meat appears more often, it's in very small portions that add flavor but not much saturated fat (think of pasta with marinara sauce).

384

In Mediterranean-style cooking, there's not much dairy either. The emphasis is on vegetables, fruits, grains, and cooked dried beans and peas.

Shift from Low to Very Low

By the summer of 1985, John Cardozo had already had one heart attack. So when he started having chest pains again, he decided to make some big changes. A retiree who lives in San Francisco, Cardozo enrolled in a study headed by Dean Ornish, M.D., assistant clinical professor of medicine at the University of California, San Francisco, and president and director of the Preventive Medicine Research Institute in Sausalito.

Cardozo and others who enrolled in Dr. Ornish's program ate a very, very low fat vegetarian diet, exercised regularly, stopped smoking, and learned techniques to control their stress levels. As part of the program, they attended regular support group meetings.

Cardozo—and others in the study—reaped true rewards from the Ornish experience. A year later, more than 80 percent of those enrolled in the study had cleaner arteries than when they started. Their blood pressure and LDL levels had dropped. Nearly all said their chest pain had almost completely disappeared. The study, in fact, was the first to provide hard evidence that following a very low fat diet and making other lifestyle changes could reverse heart disease. Follow-up studies have confirmed the results.

More than a decade after he started, Cardozo still follows the program religiously. It's given him a new lease on youthfulness. "I'm able to do more, I'm in much better shape than I was before I started," says Cardozo. "It really works."

A similar low-fat diet is at the heart of the Pritikin program, another successful regimen that combines dietary reform with exercise and stress management. In studies, people who have followed the Pritikin plan have seen their cholesterol levels and blood pressures drop significantly. One study even showed that blood flow improved significantly enough to be measured.

With all these benefits, you might wonder why more people

know
what?
Blood shoots out of the heart into the aorta at a speed of 1.5 feet per second. If the Mississippi River moved at this speed, it would have taken Huckleberry Finn (traveling by raft) just 42 days to get from Hannibal, Missouri, to Baton Rouge, Louisiana.

385

don't adhere to the Ornish or Pritikin programs. The toughest trick with these plans is to make them part of your lifestyle so that you don't go back to old habits.

"If a patient with heart disease adopted the Ornish diet, I'd think that's great," says Dr. Peterson. "My worry is that people will adopt these types of diets for a very short period of time. But heart disease is a lifetime disease. If you stick with the diet for a year, then go back to high-fat eating habits, that's not positive behavior."

Long-Term Tactics

To Get with a Program

Many people with heart disease have attended Ornish or Pritikin programs, but you don't have to travel. You can get many of the benefits by adhering to the basic game plan. Here's how.

Eat like John Cardozo. The Ornish diet gets a skinny 10 percent of calories from fat. That means no butter, margarine, or added oil allowed. No meat, poultry, fish, or egg yolks either. You are, however, allowed one to two servings of skim milk, nonfat cheese, or other nonfat dairy foods daily.

While the Ornish diet limits fats and high-protein foods, it's liberal with vegetables, grains, fruits, beans, and peas. You are encouraged to eat three or more servings of dark green, leafy, dark yellow, and cruciferous vegetables daily. (The cruciferous group includes broccoli, cabbage, and cauliflower.) To that, add two to four servings of dark yellow and citrus fruits and six or more servings of whole-grain bread, cereal, potatoes, rice, and pasta.

On the Ornish program, you can also include two to four servings of beans and peas—or have some dish made with egg whites, which give you similar nutrients in fat-free form. If you have a sweet tooth or enjoy a glass of wine with dinner, you're in luck. The diet also permits one drink and a small fat-free dessert daily.

Pick some Pritikin tips. Similar to the Ornish plan in most respects, the Pritikin diet nixes any butter, margarine, or added oil. But it does allow you to eat some meat, as long as it's lean and as long as you eat no more than 3½ ounces daily. That's a portion of meat about as big as a billfold. If you already have high cholesterol, the Pritikin diet steers you away from meat and suggests 3½ to 7 ounces a day of fish, like salmon or mackerel, instead.

If you are a vegetarian, you can substitute ⅔ cup beans, four to six ounces of tofu, or one ounce of nuts or seeds for the meat portion in your meals.

On the Pritikin plan, you can include two servings of nonfat dairy in your diet, but you will probably need to rein in salt. The plan limits you to 1,600 milligrams of sodium daily. Sodium is not just in table salt—it's also in most canned and packaged foods.

The Pritikin plan limits salt because excessive salt intake is a major factor in raising blood pressure and prompts your body to excrete more calcium, increasing your risk of osteoporosis, says James J. Kenney, R.D., Ph.D., a nutrition research specialist for the Pritikin Longevity Center in Santa Monica, California.

Moving toward a Vigorous Heart

Not more than a couple of generations ago, doctors advised people with heart disease to go home, put their feet up, and rest—more or less permanently.

Of course, that kind of advice was just the thing to make you feel old before your time. And not only that, we now realize that putting your feet up can easily make the problem worse. "Even if you're not overweight, inactivity is still a risk factor for heart disease," says Dr. Fletcher.

Getting active can lower your risk for a number of reasons. Exercise has been shown to boost HDL levels and to lower blood pressure and triglyceride levels, Dr. Fletcher notes. And studies find that people who exercise regularly have lower levels of blood-borne fibrinogen, which is a major player in blood-clot formation.

Exercise can also help you lose excess weight and manage stress. And it can help strengthen your heart. With training,

know what?

On the Pritikin plan—one of the optimal programs for heart protection—people eat five or more servings of whole-grain cereals, breads, pastas, lentils, and brown rice; four servings of vegetables; and three servings of fruit every day.

387

your heart will pump more blood per beat and will beat more slowly. A slower beat is a sign of a younger heart.

And if you already have heart disease, exercise can lower your risk of having a heart attack, research shows. Studies find that people who exercise regularly following heart attacks have better survival rates than those who head straight for the lounge chair afterward.

Long-Term Tactics

For Heart-Smart Flexing

You should never start an exercise program without checking with your doctor first. But once the checkup is out of the way, you have a wide range of exercise choices. For general advice on starting an exercise program, see Stop-Time Tactic No. 4 on page 87. In addition, here's some advice that can help you customize your routine for heart-targeted workouts.

Go for brisk. You'll need some aerobic exercise like walking, jogging, cycling, or dancing to help strengthen your heart, says Dr. Fletcher. Such activities really benefit you twice: They help control your weight, and they help your heart. Aim for 30 to 45 minutes of aerobic exercise five to six times a week, he says.

Weight up. Include moderate weight-training sessions two or three times weekly, advises Dr. Fletcher. Doctors used to think that resistance training was out of bounds if you had high blood pressure because they thought lifting weight could trigger a heart attack. But several studies show that blood pressure rises only slightly during weight training. Moreover, research suggests that in people over age 60 with mild hypertension, resistance training can ultimately lower blood pressure.

Know when to quit—and call. Exercise should leave you feeling moderately fatigued, says Dr. Fletcher. It shouldn't cause chest pain, fainting or near fainting, dizziness, or severe shortness of breath—which might actually be signs of a heart attack. If you begin to experience any of those warning signals,

388

Just Scent Flowers

Visit the cardiac care unit in a British hospital, and odds are, you'll smell alpine lavender or rose or sweet marjoram. It's all part of the treatment.

"The British have used aroma-therapy in heart treatment for years," says Jane Buckle, R.N., a certified aromatherapist and aromatherapy teacher in England and author of *Clinical Aromatherapy in Nursing.*

Aromatherapy is based on the premise that fragrant essential oils can have therapeutic effects. Studies, in fact, have shown that the essential oils extracted from various plants do have distinct physiological and psychological effects. Oils from euca-lyptus, spike lavender, and rosemary, for instance, act as stimulants. Those from alpine lavender, sandalwood, and rose have been found to have sedative effects.

Most British cardiac intensive care units offer patients a choice of different soothing essential oils, like alpine lavender and sweet marjoram, says Buckle. The staffers routinely rub small amounts of the essential oils on patients' hands and feet. Not only do the oils soothe the patients, she adds, the fragrance also lowers the stress levels among the staff.

"To lower your risk of heart disease, it's very important to work on some stress management," Buckle says. "And aromatherapy can be very useful for highly stressed people."

Most people find the scents of alpine lavender, sweet marjoram, and frankincense very soothing. But you should sniff before you buy any of them, Buckle says. Odors have different effects on different people, and often our responses are influenced by past experience. If, for example, you associate the scent of lavender with the teacher who terrified you all the way through third grade, you won't find the scent very relaxing.

Once you find the oils you like, use them in any number of ways, says Buckle. Add a drop or two to a table-spoon of grapeseed or almond oil and ask a friend to gently massage the oil into your hands or feet, she says. Add a few drops of the essential oil to a va-porizer. Or mix a couple of drops with a tablespoon of milk, then add the mixture to your bathwater, Buckle suggests. (Since oil won't dissolve in water, you need to emulsify it in milk first.)

389

stop what you are doing and call your doctor or the emergency room immediately, he says.

Unfurrow Your Brow, Lighten Your Heart

When Dr. Clarke starts getting stressed-out, he goes for a run or a bike ride or, if the weather is nice, a swim in the ocean near his oceanside home. He also asks himself whether he can influence the thing that has him uptight. If the answer is no, then he tries to shift focus and stop worrying about it.

That's good age-protection-thinking because research has shown that stress can take a toll on your heart.

"Emotional stress is not a major risk factor, but several studies show that it does aggravate heart disease risk," says Dr. Fletcher.

Stress seems to boost levels of fibrinogen, the blood-clotting factor, in your arteries, Dr. Pashkow says. And it appears to affect blood pressure. In an Iowa study, African-American men and women with high blood pressure saw their pressure drop when they practiced meditation.

Doctors used to think that so-called type A people—who tend to be stressed-out, competitive, and often mistrustful—were at greater risk of heart disease than people with more mellow temperaments. But other research has pointed the finger at one particular element of type A behavior—specifically, hostility. According to one study, people who score high on tests of hostility are more likely to need repeat surgery for heart disease than those who score low.

Long-Term Tactics
For Taming a Temper

For general advice on managing stress, see Stop-Time Tactic No. 7 on page 168. If you're inclined to get hot under the collar, you might want to consider some other strategies as well. Here are some approaches to mellowing out.

Grill yourself. When you're getting hot, ask yourself a few questions, suggests Redford Williams, M.D., professor of psychiatry and director of the Behavioral Medicine Research Center at Duke University Medical Center in Durham, North Carolina, and author of *Anger Kills*. Start with "Is this important?" If the answer is yes, ask yourself a second question, "Is my anger justified?" If the answer is again yes, ask yourself a final question, "Do I have an effective response?"

If you do have an effective response, of course, the next goal is to act on it, says Dr. Williams. If you're angry because you just heard that the local school district plans to do away with art classes, for instance, you can write a letter to the school board, show up at the board's next meeting, start a petition drive. Go ahead and list those things—then act on them in sequence.

Do take no for an answer. If you conclude that your anger is neither important nor justified, the next step is to talk yourself out of being upset, Dr. Williams explains. Remind yourself that roiling in fury, when there's nothing to be done, hurts only you. Tell yourself that your anger won't change the situation. By reasoning with yourself this way, you can often manage your anger.

Protect Yourself from Hormonal Changes

In 1889, the eminent French physician Charles-Edouard Brown-Sequard stunned the world with a bold pronouncement. He had revitalized himself. He had managed this feat, the 72-year-old Brown-Sequard explained, by injecting himself with extracts from dog and guinea pig testicles. Not only did this treatment reinvigorate him, he noted, it also improved his bladder and bowel control.

As you might or might not expect, the news set off an animal-testicle injection craze. Without waiting for confirmation of Brown-Sequard's results, physicians began using the therapy—to treat everything from tuberculosis to senility.

Though studies eventually proved his animal testicle treatment wholly ineffective, Brown-Sequard's life's work ultimately laid the foundation for what became endocrinology, the study of hormones. As scientists looked more closely at these chemical messengers secreted by the testes and other glands, they discovered that hormones influence a whole range of key processes involved in reproduction and development.

In an ironic twist of fate, it is present-day research in endocrinology that promises to shed new light on the aging process and raises the possibly that we might one day reverse at least some signs of aging. What started with Brown-Sequard's animal testicle research may ultimately help revitalize us after all.

"This is a very exciting time for researchers in this field," says Stanley Slater, M.D., deputy associate director for geriatrics

392

at the National Institute on Aging in Bethesda, Maryland, where a number of studies examining the hormone/aging connection are underway.

Our Hothouse of Hormones

No doubt about it, hormones are potent stuff. We all produce an assortment: dehydroepiandrosterone (DHEA), growth hormone, melatonin, testosterone, to name just a few. (Although we think of testosterone as a quintessentially male substance, women also manufacture it.) Secreted by various glands, hormones travel the bloodstream, influencing virtually every cell in your body.

Researchers like Dr. Slater are excited about the hormone/aging connection for a couple of reasons. For starters, studies show that many of us produce smaller quantities of certain hormones as we age. After menopause, women's ovaries essentially stop producing the sex hormone estrogen. Many men produce a bit less testosterone, manufactured in the testes, at 75 than they did at 25.

Other hormonal changes come along as we age. We all churn out less human growth hormone, which is a product of the pituitary gland, a marble-size organ in our heads. Many of us produce somewhat smaller quantities of the hormone melatonin, a sleep-pattern regulator, manufactured by the pineal gland. As the years pass, we also have less DHEA, an adrenal gland hormone.

These downturns in hormone production coincide with the changes that we associate with aging—like loss of muscle and bone density, lowered immunity, and increased risk of heart disease, diabetes, and cancer. But that doesn't mean hormone shortages cause aging. We can't automatically assume that giving older folks replacement doses of these hormones will reverse aging.

But research suggests that there might be a connection between hormonal changes and aging, and that hormone supplements could help combat some age-related changes.

Over the years, studies have shown that giving post-menopausal women supplemental doses of estrogen can not

393

what?

In the
United States,
doctors
usually
prescribe
growth
hormone
solely for
children with
human growth
hormone
deficiency
or for people
who have lost
their pituitary
glands.

only alleviate menopausal symptoms but also help ward off heart disease, osteoporosis, even Alzheimer's disease. There are on-going studies to explore whether hormones—like human growth hormone and testosterone—can afford similar clock-beating benefits.

Does this news warrant a trip to your local health food store, where bottles of DHEA and melatonin supplements glisten on the shelves, alongside best-sellers hyping their anti-aging powers? "We advise people not to take these products until we know more about them," says Dr. Slater.

There appear to be considerable benefits for post-menopausal women in taking hormone-replacement therapy (HRT), he explains. And that has turned out to offer a trade-off of benefits and risks.

By contrast, we know very little about the consequences of popping supplemental doses of DHEA, melatonin, human growth hormone, and the like. The data we have is preliminary and comes from short-term studies.

Since some of the studies have already found unpleasant side effects associated with the supplements, there's obviously more work to be done. What we really need, he says, are long-term studies. "This is a wonderful field of research for the future, but the future is not now," says Dr. Slater. Here are some things that research has already uncovered.

Getting the Measure of Melatonin

Despite the media hype that accompanied melatonin's arrival on the scene a few years back, research has yet to prove that melatonin supplements will keep us forever young.

One well-publicized study found that mice given water spiked with the hormone lived 40 percent longer than those who got plain water. But there was a problem with the research. "The study used mice that don't normally produce melatonin," says Andrew Monjan, Ph.D., chief of neurobiology of the Aging Branch of the National Institute on Aging.

So why did the rodents live longer? A possible explanation is that melatonin spoiled the animals' appetites, he says. The

394

mice given the melatonin-spiked water ate less than usual during the study.

And previous studies have found that rodents on calorie-restricted diets live longer than those that eat heartily. Claims that melatonin supplements can enhance immune function haven't panned out either, Dr. Monjan says.

Some studies have found that, at high doses, melatonin does have an antioxidant effect. The hormone appears to have a talent for disarming free radicals, highly destructive molecules that can damage cells and set the stage for diseases such as cancer. But these studies have looked at the effects of extremely high doses of melatonin, "higher than those found in healthy young people," he says.

On an encouraging note, research suggests that melatonin can help you get to sleep and recover from jet lag. (For more information, see "The Hormone Shortcut to Dreamland" on page 396.) Whether you can use it indefinitely is another matter, however. We have no long-term data on efficacy or safety, says Frank Bellino, Ph.D., endocrinology program administrator at the National Institute on Aging.

Growth Hormone: Good for Grown-Ups?

By comparison, studies examining the effects of human growth hormone supplementation have turned up more promising results.

Human growth hormone helps regulate blood sugar levels and stimulate bone, cartilage, and muscle growth. In preliminary studies, older adults given growth hormone supplements have lost fat and added muscle, says Martin I. Surks, M.D., head of the division of endocrinology at Montefiore Medical Center in Bronx, New York.

In a study at the University of California, San Francisco, men in their seventies and eighties added significant muscle and lost fat after six months of treatment. These findings are particularly encouraging because even a modest gain in muscle strength can reduce the rate of falls and fractures among older people, he says. Among older folks, fractures can lead to deadly complications.

The Hormone Shortcut to Dreamland

The ancient Greeks believed that sleep was ruled by a god who dwelled deep down in the underworld. Surprisingly, they were wrong on this point.

Sleep, it seems, is at least partly under the influence of melatonin, the hormone produced by your pineal gland, located way up in your head.

Melatonin seems to work by influencing your circadian clock, or body clock, the internal timepiece that tells your body when it's day and when it's night. High levels of melatonin in your blood tell you it's sleep time. Low levels tell you it's wake time.

When everything's working as it should, your pineal gland produces melatonin when the light dims in the evening. And it stops production when daylight resumes, so melatonin levels nose-dive at dawn.

Of course, everything doesn't always work as it should. If you stay up late with the lights on several nights in a row or fly through several time zones in the course of an evening, you can throw your circadian clock way out of sync. You may find that your melatonin levels rise and fall out of synchrony with your body clock's sleep/wake timing and that you are wide-awake in the dead-quiet dark of night.

This is where melatonin supplements can come in handy. In a number of studies, melatonin has been shown to help reset people's circadian clocks, says Andrew Monjan, Ph.D., chief of neurobiology of the Aging Branch of the National Institute on Aging in Bethesda, Maryland. It's helped insomniacs doze off and jet-setters avoid the sleeplessness and fatigue of jet lag.

If you're having trouble sleeping, though, better talk to your doctor before popping some melatonin. Insomnia may be a symptom that's caused by something specific—such as a side effect of medication, notes Quentin Regestein, M.D., a sleep disorders physician at Brigham and Women's Hospital in Boston. And

Unfortunately, preliminary studies have also turned up some undesirable side effects. In one study, a third of those who were given growth hormone supplements developed carpal tunnel syndrome, which is a painful or tingling feeling in the hands or fingers, usually caused by excessive wrist movement. Growth hormone supplementation can also cause fluid retention, which can lead to high blood pressure and heart failure and can worsen diabetes in those people who already have it, research finds.

melatonin supplements may not mix with other medications that you're taking. If these factors are taken into account, however, and your doctor recommends melatonin, you might give it a try, he says.

There's one caveat. The Food and Drug Administration doesn't regulate the manufacture of melatonin supplements. So it's hard to know what's in the stuff on the shelves. In one study, researchers examined the contents of various supplements and found "evidence of all sorts of substances that weren't accounted for" on the label, says Dr. Regestein.

If you decide to take melatonin, nonetheless, have it at bedtime if insomnia is the problem. Try a dose of a milligram or less, every night, at the very same clock time. Then be patient. It may take a week or two to get results, especially if your circadian clock is way out of sync, notes Dr. Regestein.

If you're trying to prevent jet lag, you have to consider the direction in which you'll be traveling in order to determine when to take your pill, he says. Let's say you're flying west toward Hong Kong. A few weeks before your trip, you should start moving your bedtime so that it's closer to what it will be when your reach Hong Kong. Then, when you're in flight, you should take your melatonin halfway between your usual bedtime and your bedtime in Hong Kong.

If you're traveling east—say, to Rome—take your melatonin as soon as the flight attendant clears away your dinner tray. "Then skip the movie and see if you can get to sleep," advises Dr. Regestein.

One more caveat: Melatonin isn't for chronic insomnia. Because we don't know the long-term effects of taking melatonin supplements, anything more than occasional use is too risky, says Dr. Monjan. If you haven't been able to get regular sleep for weeks or months, be sure to talk to your doctor.

"Most of these side effects can be managed by lowering the dose," says Dr. Surks.

Because the side effects are so serious, you shouldn't take growth hormone unless you're participating in a supervised study, Dr. Slater says. And in the United States, it's available only by prescription. But despite official restrictions, there have been reports of people sneaking in the hormone from foreign clinics and through the mail. "And this concerns us," he says.

397

Is DHEA Really Okay?

In aging mice, dehydroepiandrosterone (DHEA) supplements appear to boost immunity. In rats, doses of the hormone seem to reduce the incidence of obesity. Other animal studies suggest that DHEA may also help protect against diabetes, heart disease, even cancer, Dr. Bellino says.

But there's no guarantee that DHEA supplements will have the same effect in people. In fact, results from trials with people have been inconsistent. In some studies, people have reported feeling better while taking DHEA. In other studies, they haven't. And a few studies suggest that the hormone may help folks beef up and build muscle, but still other ones suggest that it won't.

"Some research has found DHEA affects the immune system, but the magnitude of the effect has been small, and the meaning hasn't been obvious," Dr. Bellino says. "All told, we haven't seen the results we would need to see in order to start recommending this."

At this point, no one has any idea why DHEA might have any beneficial effect either. "We don't know the mechanism," Dr. Bellino says. Since your body converts DHEA into estrogen and testosterone, it's quite possible that estrogen and testosterone supplements might yield the same results.

And because your body converts DHEA into estrogen and testosterone, it's possible that DHEA supplements could also cause serious side effects. Elevated testosterone levels in men can speed the growth of cells in the prostate gland, thereby boosting risks of both prostate cancer and benign prostatic hyperplasia (BPH), a noncancerous but extremely uncomfortable swelling of the prostate. Because high testosterone levels also speed production of red blood cells, they can thicken the blood and raise the risk of stroke, says Dr. Slater.

For women, a DHEA-assisted boost in estrogen could pose other problems. More estrogen might mean a higher risk of breast and uterine cancers, notes Leon Speroff, M.D., professor of obstetrics and gynecology at Oregon Health Sciences University in Portland.

People who volunteer for clinical trials with any hormone are carefully monitored for harmful changes in their health status, Dr. Slater points out.

Although some medical doctors are recommending DHEA to their patients, Dr. Bellino advises against it because the potential risks are too high.

Testing Testosterone

Most of us have a fairly Freudian response to testosterone: We hear the word, and all we think of is sex. But testosterone plays a number of key roles in the male body. It fuels development of male sex characteristics, and it adds fuel to the fire of a man's sex drive. But it also helps build and maintain muscle and bone, perhaps even mood and mental agility.

Doctors have long prescribed supplemental testosterone for men with a severe testosterone deficiency condition called hypogonadism. Men with the condition tend to have small muscles, fragile bones, and lagging libido, and testosterone supplements help build all three. Studies suggest that the supplements may also help older men with testosterone levels at the low end of normal. In a study at the University of Washington in Seattle, men in the low-normal range gained muscle and bone density and said they felt friskier after three months of treatment. (For more information, see "A Woman's Guide to Testosterone" on page 400.)

Researchers at both Emory University in Atlanta and the University of Pennsylvania in Philadelphia are conducting longer-term studies of older men with low-normal testosterone levels. They are tracking changes in the men's body composition, bone density, strength, and mental ability. And they are watching for side effects in these men, especially changes in cholesterol levels. They are also monitoring levels of prostate-specific antigen, a chemical substance that warns of changes that may be indicative of developing BPH and prostate cancer.

At this point, testosterone replacement is strictly experimental. Because elevated testosterone levels pose risks, it's not

399

A Woman's Guide to Testosterone

Your biology teacher may have called testosterone the male sex hormone, but women produce this substance, too.

Testosterone, manufactured by the ovaries and adrenal glands, fuels a woman's sex drive. That's why doctors often prescribe testosterone supplements—along with hormone-replacement therapy (HRT)—for post-menopausal women who complain of flagging libidos.

But it isn't clear whether most postmenopausal women need testosterone supplementation or can benefit from it. "I think it's a myth that testosterone declines with age in all menopausal women," says Peter R. Casson, M.D., assistant professor in the department of obstetrics and gynecology in the division of reproductive endocrinology and infertility at Baylor College of Medicine in Houston, who is studying testosterone-replacement therapy for women. He

has found little evidence that a woman produces significantly less testosterone after natural menopause. And there's little evidence that testosterone supplements will enhance her sex drive or offer other benefits, he says. If a woman's sex drive is waning after menopause, it could be for any number of reasons, including assorted psychological ones, he notes.

On the other hand, there is plenty of evidence that a woman who has had her uterus and her ovaries removed—and gone through the surgical meno-pause that follows—will see a steep decline in testosterone production. Since the ovaries produce testos-terone, levels plummet after the surgery. Some studies do show that, in these circumstances, testosterone supplements help improve sex drive and may alleviate some menopausal symptoms.

But there's still a problem. These

for men with normal hormone profiles—or for men with prostate abnormalities or heart disease either.

In the Emory study, doctors are screening out men with prostate cancer, BPH, and high risk of heart disease, according to Joyce Tenover, M.D., head of the study and associate professor of medicine in the university's geriatrics division. During the study, she and her colleagues regularly tested volunteers' prostate-specific antigen and cholesterol levels.

Testosterone replacement will probably never be as wide-

Whole-Body Protection

studies have looked at the effects of very high doses of testosterone, far higher than a woman would naturally produce, says Dr. Casson. At these levels, testosterone supplements may wreak havoc with a woman's cholesterol levels, causing growth of facial hair, acne, and other unhappy side effects. The testosterone pills usually prescribed for women may also have the potential to cause liver dysfunction, he says.

A number of research centers, including Dr. Casson's, are now studying the risks and benefits of a low-dose testosterone patch for women who have had their uteruses and ovaries removed. One of the benefits of the patch is that it delivers testosterone in a fashion that doesn't affect the liver.

What to do until the results are in? If you have had both your uterus and ovaries removed and can trace a dip in libido to surgery, Dr. Casson suggests that you wait before you even consider trying testosterone.

And he has another suggestion. The drop in estrogen production following surgical menopause can cause vaginal dryness, which can also interfere with sex drive. Since hormone-replacement therapy can alleviate the dryness and may help boost libido, consider HRT before you consider testosterone, Dr. Casson says.

If you try HRT, still have a problem, and want to give testosterone a shot, make sure that your doctor prescribes the lowest dose. And ask your doctor to check your cholesterol every six months and your liver function every year, Dr. Casson recommends.

"Testosterone replacement should be limited to women who have had their ovaries and uteruses removed, who are on good hormone-replacement regimens, and who are still having problems," he says. "Even then, they should get a low dose of testosterone."

spread among men as hormone-replacement therapy is among women because many men see no noticeable change in testosterone production until they are well into their seventies, says Dr. Slater.

"For most men, it's never a problem," agrees Dr. Tenover.

Whether testosterone deficiency is a problem for many women isn't yet clear. Since testosterone also drives the female libido, doctors often prescribe testosterone supplements, along with hormone-replacement therapy, for postmenopausal women

401

Adjusting to Hormone-Replacement Therapy

Karen Giblin was in her early forties when she checked into the hospital for a hysterectomy and an ovariectomy. She was prepared for the surgery, but not for what followed.

"A few days after the surgery, I was having hot flashes, night sweats, chills, and heart palpitations," recalls Giblin, who lives in Ridgefield, Connecticut.

Giblin's surgery, which involved removing both her uterus and her ovaries, had triggered what's called surgical, or immediate, menopause. Women who go through natural menopause often have hot flashes and night sweats, too, caused by the drop in estrogen production, but they usually don't have the extreme symptoms that come with the abrupt surgical menopause. When it's happening naturally, women see a more gradual decline in estrogen production than those who go through the immediate version. A woman's ovaries produce the lion's share of estrogen, so estrogen levels crash after the kind of surgery that Giblin had.

To alleviate Giblin's symptoms, her doctor prescribed estrogen-replacement therapy (ERT) just before she left the hospital. When she got home, though, Giblin realized that the dose wasn't right. She was still experiencing chills, memory loss, hot flashes—

who complain of flagging sex drive. But the evidence that women produce less testosterone after menopause is shaky, says Peter R. Casson, M.D., assistant professor in the department of obstetrics and gynecology in the division of reproductive endocrinology and infertility at Baylor College of Medicine in Houston, who is studying testosterone supplementation among women. And the long-term benefits of doling out the supplements remain to be seen, he says.

What Women Should Know about Estrogen

If the history of hormone-replacement therapy is any indicator, it may take researchers years to answer the big questions

402

and her heart was racing. She called her doctor, who adjusted the dose.

"It took me about a year to get the proper dose," says Giblin, whose experience led her to start an educational and support program for menopausal women called PRIME PLUS/Red Hot Mamas Menopause Management Education program. It's now offered in more than 35 hospitals and in various HMOs and medical practices nationwide.

More than five years after her surgery, Giblin still takes ERT—for the heart and bone protection it affords and to improve her quality of life. Now that the dose is right, she says, she no longer has any noticeable side effects.

Hormone-replacement therapy (HRT) is similar to ERT, but instead of using just estrogen, the formulation includes a synthetic version of the female sex hormone progesterone. But HRT may also require some adjustment, Giblin says. The synthetic progesterone leaves some women feeling queasy and bloated and can trigger monthly vaginal bleeding. But changes in dosage and formulation can ease and even eliminate these side effects, she says.

"Your physician should be able to tailor the ERT or HRT to your needs and how you're feeling," she says. "You should definitely talk to your doctor if you're having side effects."

about other hormone-replacement regimens. Though researchers have done considerable tinkering with doses and formulations of HRT over the years, the current formulation still offers a mixed bag of benefits and risks.

Doctors started giving menopausal women estrogen supplements back in the 1960s. The idea was that estrogen-replacement therapy (ERT), as it came to be known, would ease the hot flashes and night sweats so often associated with menopause. It made sense. Levels of estrogen and other sex hormones start fluctuating a year or so before a woman has her last menstrual period. As her ovaries produce less estrogen, the drop in production can trigger some nasty symptoms. Restoring estrogen can ease these symptoms.

403

But years of research have also shown that long-term estrogen replacement poses risks. Initially, physicians gave all women estrogen only, and in relatively high doses. As it turned out, this raised their chances of endometrial cancer, or cancer of the uterine lining. So researchers cut back on the estrogen content and reformulated the mix.

Doctors now give women with uteruses a combination of estrogen and progestin—a synthetic version of the sex hormone progesterone. When a woman has a hysterectomy, her uterus is surgically removed, so she usually doesn't need the progestin. Estrogen and progestin make up the formula known as hormone-replacement therapy, or HRT. Subsequent research has shown that the added progestin offsets estrogen's negative effect on endometrial cancer risk.

Studies have found that long-term HRT offers a wide range of benefits. The best documented long-term benefit is the protection HRT offers against osteoporosis, a thinning of the bones that can lead to serious fractures. HRT appears to slow the rate at which calcium leaches from bones, a process that usually speeds up after menopause. Studies have also found that hormone-replacement therapy not only prevents bone loss, but can actually reverse it.

Years of study suggest that hormone-replacement therapy can lower a woman's risk of heart disease and stroke. It seems to help in a number of different ways—by lowering levels of low-density lipoprotein cholesterol (the "bad" stuff) and boosting levels of high-density lipoprotein cholesterol (the "good" stuff), by keeping arteries supple, and by elevating levels of substances that prevent blood clots from forming inside arteries.

HRT may also possibly lower a woman's risk of colon cancer and prevent the thinning of vaginal and urinary tract tissues, halting changes that can take the joy out of sex and can contribute to incontinence. There's evidence that estrogen might help prevent wrinkles as well by keeping skin plumper and more elastic.

Some research suggests that estrogen may even improve

404

memory and lower a woman's risk of Alzheimer's disease. Researchers at Columbia University in New York City have found that women who take estrogen have a lower rate of Alzheimer's. Among women who do develop the disease, those on HRT get Alzheimer's significantly later in life than those who have never taken the hormone.

"Estrogen appears to alter the relationships between neurons," says Robert Barbieri, M.D., chairman of obstetrics and gynecology at Brigham and Women's Hospital in Boston. "In some studies, the connections among neurons appear to become more complex when estrogen is present."

For a long time, researchers worried that the added progestin might also offset estrogen's beneficial effect on heart disease risk. But a number of large-scale, long-term studies suggest that it doesn't, says Trudy Bush, Ph.D., adjunct professor of epidemiology at Johns Hopkins University School of Medicine in Baltimore and an internationally known expert on HRT and ERT.

Even in its new, improved incarnation, hormone-replacement therapy has its downside since it can put a woman at increased risk of developing gallstones in her gallbladder and blood clots in her veins. What most worries women, though, is the effect that long-term hormone therapy may have on breast cancer risk. Here, the clinical studies are maddeningly contradictory.

Reviewing five years' worth of studies conducted between 1992 and 1997, Dr. Bush found six that she considered large and well-conducted enough to be worth serious evaluation. "One found significant decrease in breast cancer risk (with hormone replacement), one found a significant increase in breast cancer occurrence, and four found no effect whatsoever on breast cancer," she says.

The contradictory findings have divided researchers. Some argue that there is a link between hormone replacement and breast cancer, but it's a weak link that will be hard to detect in all but the largest studies. Others argue that if there were a link, research findings wouldn't be so inconsistent.

Finding New Options

At menopause, many women feel torn between two polar options, getting hormone-replacement therapy (HRT) or getting nothing at all.

But there are all sorts of other possibilities in between, says Tori Hudson, doctor of naturopathy, a naturopathic physician and professor of women's health at the National College of Naturopathic Medicine in Portland, Oregon. You might, for instance, opt for herbal remedies instead of HRT. Or choose vitamin therapy. Or ultimately decide to combine all three. "Different approaches work for different women, so every woman needs to be evaluated individually," says Dr. Hudson.

Dr. Hudson suggests the following six-step regimen to her patients. Every woman starts with step 1. Whether she goes on to the next and subsequent steps will depend on whether she is getting the results she wants given the steps she has already taken. Of course, you should check with your doctor first before beginning this or any type of new treatment.

Step 1: Diet, Exercise, and Stress Reduction

Diet: Eat a low-fat, low-cholesterol diet, with plenty of complex carbohydrates and soy foods, like tofu, soy milk, and roasted soy beans. Shoot for one or more soy servings daily. The serving size depends upon the form of soy you are eating or drinking. One cup soy milk, a half-cup tofu, or a quarter-cup roasted soy nuts are all eligible to meet your daily serving. Soy foods are good sources of phytoestrogens, plant compounds that act like weak estrogens and protect against various health problems. Studies show that soy can alleviate hot flashes, lower "bad" cholesterol levels, prevent osteoporosis, and lower risks of breast cancer.

Exercise: Work your way up to 30 minutes of exercise daily. In an Australian study, women who exercised regularly reported fewer menopausal symptoms—fewer night sweats, hot flashes, sleep problems, and mood swings—than sedentary types. Exercise can also lower risks of heart disease, osteoporosis, and breast cancer, Dr. Hudson says.

Stress reduction: Since stress can make menopausal symptoms worse and raise blood pressure, Dr. Hudson recommends stress-management techniques. (For more information, see Stop-Time Tactic No. 7 on page 168.)

Step 2: Nutritional Supplements

Various vitamin and mineral supplements can ease menopausal symptoms and can help alleviate hot flashes, Dr. Hudson says. "Everyone has different needs, so recommendations are on a case-by-case basis," she says. Check with your doctor.

Step 3: Herbs

Various botanical remedies can also help relieve menopausal symptoms and lower risk of heart disease, says Dr. Hudson. Black cohosh, for instance, can reduce hot flashes. And herbs like garlic can lower cholesterol and blood pressure levels. Again, what works for one woman may not be right for another, so recommendations are case-by-case.

Step 4: Natural Hormones

If you are at medium or high risk for heart disease or osteoporosis, you may want to add hormone-replacement therapy to your regimen, Dr. Hudson says.

There are different types of estrogen and progesterone therapies out there, she points out, and there are some considerable differences between them. Natural hormones, which are manufactured from ingredients found in plants and biochemically identical to the hormones produced by the ovaries and adrenal glands, tend to cause fewer side effects, like nausea, than conventional hormones.

Step 5: Natural and Commercial Hormones

Natural hormones are less researched than conventional HRT however, so they may not do the trick if you're at very high risk of osteoporosis or heart disease. You may need a combination of natural progesterone and a more well-studied commercial form of estrogen, Dr. Hudson says. These friendlier estrogen drugs are also manufactured from plant extractions, but they are not biochemically identical, as are the natural hormones.

Step 6: Commercial Hormone Preparations

If you don't get results with the previous five steps, your best bet may be to try typical, long-studied commercial preparations of estrogen, but then combine these preparations with oral natural progesterone, Dr. Hudson says.

This six-step approach is fairly complex, she notes. So you'll need professional help if you want to give it a try. To find a practitioner well-versed in these options, she suggests that you contact the American Association of Naturopathic Physicians at 601 Valley Street, Suite 105, Seattle, WA 98109. Ask for the name of a naturopathic physician near you.

Since all naturopathic doctors don't have the same areas of expertise, interview prospective doctors before making an appointment. Look for a naturopathic doctor who is familiar with herbs, natural hormones, and menopause issues, she recommends.

Measure the Pros and Cons

Even with years of research data to go on, it's clear that doctors still don't have all the answers about hormone-replacement therapy. So what should you do if you are trying to decide whether long-term hormone replacement is for you? The experts recommend the following:

Study yourself. Each woman needs to weigh her concerns and risk of breast cancer against her risks of heart disease and osteoporosis, says Sherry Sherman, Ph.D., chief of the geriatrics program at the National Institute on Aging. In addition, there is the additional burden of monthly bleeding to be considered if a woman has not had her uterus removed. Do some research, she advises. Find out whether osteoporosis, heart disease, or breast cancer run in your family and have your risk factors for these diseases evaluated. Discuss the pros and cons with your doctor, says Dr. Barbieri.

Match form to function. Hormone-replacement treatments come in a variety of forms—pills, patches that deliver the hormones through your skin, and vaginal creams. Depending upon the dosages, skin patches and pills may have roughly equivalent effects, says Dr. Sherman. Since only small quantities of the hormones in the vaginal creams are absorbed into your blood and make their way throughout your body, these forms of hormone treatment can ameliorate problems such as vaginal dryness without significantly affecting other tissues. Again, discuss your options with your physician, says Dr. Barbieri.

Never say never. Even if it has been years since you went through menopause, you can still give hormone replacement a try. "It's a misconception that you have to start at menopause; you can start years later," says Dr. Barbieri.

Unfortunately, women tend to have a harder time getting used to hormone replacement when they start at an older age, says Dr. Bush. And older women miss out on years of heart disease and osteoporosis prevention. If you are at high risk of either heart disease or osteoporosis, the sooner you get HRT, the better.

Whole-Body Protection

Tuning In to HRT

No matter when you start taking hormone-replacement therapy, it can take some getting used to. Though the treatment can cause a number of unpleasant side effects, you can take steps to alleviate those effects. Here are some guidelines.

Some women feel queasy and headachy when they start taking estrogen. If you do, tell your doctor. Lowering the dose can help, says Dr. Barbieri.

If you're taking estrogen and progestin, the progestin in the mix can make you feel bloated and uncomfortable, and some women dislike HRT for that reason. Others object because it can trigger monthly vaginal bleeding. (It's like getting your period all over again.) A lower dose of progestin may help with the bloating. And changing your HRT regimen may eliminate the bleeding, Dr. Barbieri says.

There are various ways to time the doses of HRT. On one regimen, you take estrogen every day of the month and progestin just 12 days a month. On another, you take both estrogen and progesterone every day. This "combined-continuous" regimen is much less likely to cause vaginal bleeding after it is used for six months to a year, says Dr. Sherman.

Holding Out for More Info

Studies examining the risks and benefits of various hormone-replacement regimens are in the works, so you can count on more information in the future. Researchers expect to have considerably more answers after 1999 when the National Institute on Aging starts wrapping up ambitious five-year studies of hormone supplementation and aging.

In the meantime, the expert advice is to discuss the pros and cons of HRT with your doctor before deciding whether that's for you. And don't make a habit of taking any of the other hormones—even if they are touted as miraculous—unless you are participating in a scientific study.

Since no one knows the long-term consequences of gulping down hormones like melatonin and DHEA, you may well wonder what these supplements are doing on the shelves of health food stores. If you are familiar with the term *dietary supplements*, you have your answer. Federal legislation lets merchants sell any manner of dietary supplement, as long as they make no specific health claims for the product, says Dr. Monjan.

When hormones are labeled "dietary supplement," it's a misnomer, however. "These hormones are produced by our bodies," Dr. Monjan points out. "Since we don't depend on the food supply to get them, you shouldn't be getting them from a bottle either," he says.

Protect Yourself
from Loneliness

In the 1984 comedy *The Lonely Guy*, Steve Martin plays a nice, ordinary guy who gets dumped by his girlfriend. He goes into a crash-and-burn, flat-out, down-in-the-dumps, ain't-worth-nuthin-to-no-one slump.

It's not long before Martin's similarly afflicted buddy introduces his lovelorn friend to a flourishing underground club—the Lonely Guy Society of New York. Turns out, the membership roll is extensive. Our hero discovers that, far from being alone in his misery, he has plenty of company.

Point well taken, says Judith Beck, Ph.D., director of the Beck Institute for Cognitive Therapy and Research in suburban Philadelphia. "Everyone feels lonely now and then. It's a basic human experience."

When Loneliness Is Old Hat

Firsthand experience with loneliness begins pretty early, studies show. In fact, it's the teenage years—a no-person's-land where we don't know who we are or who we want to be with—when many of us have been loneliest of all.

But adulthood can be plenty lonely, too—and when it sneaks up later in life, loneliness exacts a health toll that can make you feel a lot older than you would care to.

Loneliness, studies show, is stressful. It contributes to mental health problems like depression and addiction, and it figures in a variety of stress-related physical ills. Like other types of emotional stress, the stress of loneliness prompts your body to re-

411

lease a surge of hormones that can elevate your heart rate and suppress your immune system. Several studies have found that people who feel socially isolated are considerably more likely to die of heart disease—the number one cause of death in the United States—and other potentially fatal illnesses.

"Loneliness may be a leading cause of premature death in America," says James J. Lynch, Ph.D., a psychologist and author of *The Broken Heart* and *The Language of the Heart*, two books about loneliness and health.

How the Hurt Hits You

Any number of life events can lead to loneliness. We are likely to feel lonely when relationships fail, when career changes force us to pull up stakes, when a marriage ends, when children fly the coop, and when parents die. An opportunist, loneliness also seizes on less-dramatic life events: Loneliness can sneak in when friends grow distant, when a partner leaves for a weekend convention, or when we are left off the guest list of a good friend's party.

But whatever initiates it, loneliness can be a painful experience—varying parts fear, sorrow, hopelessness, emptiness, isolation, boredom, and self-doubt.

Hanging out with other people might not be the ticket to an instant cure. In fact, feeling lonely doesn't seem to have a whole lot to do with the number of people who surround you. When you're left alone after a busy day or after an exhausting party, for instance, the peace and silence of that time by yourself can feel downright delightful. At the other extreme, if you find yourself in a hubbub where you don't know anyone—a room full of strangers, a street crowd, a noisy restaurant—you can end up feeling as lonely as a wayfarer. So...why is it you can sometimes be *alone* without feeling lonely?

"Loneliness is essentially a state in which you feel that you don't have enough close interpersonal contact," says Craig Anderson, Ph.D., a loneliness researcher and professor of psychology at the University of Missouri at Columbia.

But the feeling of loneliness may be increased by the stigma

412

Pet Therapy

They never call at the last minute to cancel dates, they don't criticize your taste in shoes (though they may, occasionally, taste your shoes), and they never hold grudges.

All things considered, pets make good company. In fact, research has shown that dogs, cats, and other household pets are actually pretty good at chasing away loneliness and keeping it at bay.

In a study at the University of California, Davis, women with pets reported feeling significantly less lonely than women living alone. Pet ownership is inversely related to depression, scientists have concluded—meaning that you're a lot less likely to become depressed if you have Fido to feed and Kitty to cut capers with. According to researchers, pets can fill a combination of emotional needs, sometimes substituting for human attachments.

Pets can also extend the range of your relationships. If you have ever walked a curious, friendly dog down a crowded street, you know from experience how easy it is to strike up a conversation with passersby. "Other pet owners can relate to you; they ask you questions about your pet," explains Judith Beck, Ph.D., director of the Beck Institute for Cognitive Therapy and Research in suburban Philadelphia.

that's attached to *being* alone. "In our culture, a relationship is viewed as an achievement," observes Cecilia Solano, Ph.D., professor of psychology at Wake Forest University in Winston-Salem, North Carolina. Since "achieving" a relationship is a sign of winning in our society, some people feel as though they're losing out if they don't have friends or a partner. "It's different in more communal cultures where you have lots of relationships 'given' to you—for instance, in cultures where you have arranged marriages," she observes.

Unfortunately, many of us are reluctant to acknowledge loneliness—and this reluctance can prolong it, notes Daniel Perlman, Ph.D., professor of family science at the University of British Columbia in Vancouver and co-editor of *Loneliness: A Sourcebook of Current Theory, Research, and Therapy.*

"If you hide your loneliness, other people don't know to reach out," Dr. Perlman says.

413

Sizing Up Your Situation

For most of us, loneliness is a sometime thing. It is likely to be a very fleeting feeling if you are momentarily lonely because a friend cancels a lunch date at the last minute or someone doesn't return a call. After a divorce or a death, though, most people feel a more prolonged loneliness that lasts for months, even years.

Whatever its cause, researchers label loneliness "situational" if there's clearly an initiating event that prompts it. As the name suggests, situational loneliness is the type that's brought on by a particular situation like a broken date or a broken relationship or a death. But if the loneliness doesn't fade, you're probably experiencing something the experts call chronic loneliness.

"Chronically lonely people are lonely regardless of the situation," explains Dr. Solano.

Some of us, research shows, are more susceptible to chronic loneliness than others. People who have low self-esteem, are shy, introverted, or afraid to take social risks are more likely to be chronically lonely. So are people who lack social skills—or believe that they do.

Dealing with chronic loneliness is usually more difficult than coping with situational loneliness, Dr. Perlman says. If you identify with the description of chronic loneliness, you may need the help of a psychiatrist or counselor. Therapists have a good track record in treating loneliness, he says.

But if you think your loneliness is situational, it's likely that you can deal with it yourself. For that, Dr. Perlman recommends two important strategies. One way to give loneliness the slip is to spend your time alone doing things that are engrossing and rewarding, he says. The other way is to go out and meet people and get to know them. Both methods seem to work.

Making Space for Your Own Thing

Free-floating astronauts caught up in their work can shrug off the loneliness of the void.

Al Worden, for example. The command module pilot in the

414

Apollo 15 mission, Worden spent three days orbiting the moon alone. That remote accomplishment earned him a spot in the *Guinness Book of World Records* as the most isolated human being in the known universe. While Worden was in orbit, his crewmates—his nearest neighbors—were exploring the moon's surface more than 2,000 miles away.

But Worden's feelings on that occasion defied expectations. "I enjoyed that time alone," he says. "It helped me concentrate on what I had to do."

Doing something engaging on your own helps ease loneliness because it occupies and satisfies you, says Dr. Perlman.

And there's a side benefit, as Worden discovered when he got back to Earth. If you spend time alone pursuing your interests, you are likely to become more interesting to other people—and to yourself.

The more interests you have, the more you have to share with other people, and the more easily you can relate to them, notes David Broder, Ph.D., a clinical psychologist and co-author of *The Art of Living Single.*

Of course, many of us wonder what interests can be compelling enough to pull us out of loneliness. If you want to get more in touch with things you enjoy doing—and can do alone—make a list of those things you'd like to remember to do during those spells of loneliness, Dr. Broder suggests. The list might read: "Rent *The African Queen* and pop popcorn" or "Go to gym and have a swim and sauna" or "Find good book on Druids." Next time you're going solo, refer to the list. When you have a checklist of recommended activities at hand, you're less likely to sit at home feeling lonely, Dr. Broder says.

Meeting People

If you find that activities aren't enough to banish that lonely feeling, maybe you should try another, equally important option—trying to meet people you might like and who might also like you.

If you're saying to yourself "easier said than done," you're not alone. Meeting people takes effort and more than a tad of

415

Solace in Soulful Company

Think you're alone with the so-alone blues? As long as people have been writing songs, they have been writing songs about loneliness.

And it doesn't take much guessing to understand why so many I'm-so-lonely songs have headed up the Top 10 lists of the past few decades—loneliness loves company. These are the tunes that millions of listeners have related to.

- Crazy (Patsy Cline)
- Eleanor Rigby (Beatles)
- Heartbreak Hotel (Elvis Presley)
- I'm So Lonesome I Could Cry (Hank Williams)
- Lonely Days (The Bee Gees)
- Lonely Night (The Captain and Tennille)
- Lonely People (America)
- Lonely Street (Andy Williams)
- Lonely Teardrops (Jackie Wilson)
- Lonely Teenager (Dion)
- Lonesome Loser (Little River Band)
- Lonesome Nights (Benny Carter and His Orchestra)
- The Lonesome Road (from *Show Boat*)
- Three Days (k.d. lang)

persistence. Just don't throw in the towel, experts advise. By starting with the right attitude, looking in the right places, asking the right questions, and cutting yourself some slack, you'll increase your odds of success.

Makeover Minutes

To Break the Ice

Meeting people isn't something that you can leave to chance. Sure, once in a while you might have a fortunate encounter with someone who instantly triggers in you feelings of ease—and you hit it off right away. But the fact is, your chances improve if you make a consistent, concerted effort to meet more people as often as you can. Here's what experts advise to get you started.

Chat yourself up. Attitude counts. If you want to meet people who might become friends, you have to convince yourself it's going to happen, says Dr. Anderson. "People who feel lonely tend to tell themselves, 'It's my fault I'm lonely. I just can't get along with people,' They're telling themselves, 'I'm going to fail.'"

Prophecies like this tend to undercut your self-esteem, Dr. Anderson observes. So instead of blaming yourself and predicting failure, give yourself a pep talk. "Tell yourself, 'I'm feeling lonely, but there are things I can do to improve the situation.'"

Research shows it works. A study of lonely college students found that those who went on to establish satisfying relationships had a higher self-esteem and were less likely to assume that their loneliness was the result of some irreparable personal flaw.

Do what you like. Yes, it might be helpful to join a group like Parents without Partners or go to a meeting place like the Nice 2 Meet U Bar N Grill—but there's a drawback to places that are intended to introduce people to one another. Since everyone knows the sole purpose is to meet people, that can make a lot of us very self-conscious, says Dr. Perlman.

A less stressful, more natural way to meet people is to join a group that's involved with something that interests you. "If you join a bridge group or an investment group, you have something to do. The emphasis is on the task at hand, and there's less of a self-conscious quality to the get-together," Dr. Perlman says. "That can be quite freeing. Sometimes you click into relationships incidentally. The focus on the activity makes the formation of the relationship a bit easier."

Even if you don't become best buddies with anyone in the group, Dr. Solano points out, you still have a good time.

Raise your hand—and volunteer. When you volunteer your services, expertise, and talent for a cause or for other people, you'll build your self-confidence. In addition, any kind of volunteer work makes you feel good and gives you opportunities to meet people, Dr. Anderson says.

Wondering where to volunteer? Call city hall and tell whoever answers the phone that you want to help, suggests Dr. An-

know what?

Studies show that shy and anxious people give themselves lower grades for social skills than objective observers give them. The message: Give yourself a break—you may look more skilled than you feel.

417

The Writing Cure

If you think journal writing is best left to retired royalty and lame-duck presidents, maybe you should open the book and consider again.

Studies find that journal writing can help many of us deal with difficult situations. Some effortless stream-of-conscious scribbling may help you deal with loneliness, too, says James Pennebaker, Ph.D., professor of psychology at University of Texas at Austin and author of *Opening Up: The Healing Power of Expressing Emotion*.

Keeping a journal helps you make sense of your experiences, see them more clearly, and put them in perspective, explains Dr. Pennebaker. When you write about a problem, it isn't the same as simply thinking about it. Writing forces you to slow down, and when you do that, you work things out in a more deliberate fashion.

"If a person felt lonely, I'd probably tell them that they should explore, in writing, their deepest thoughts and feelings about loneliness," says Dr. Pennebaker.

Just turn to a blank page—and consider these key questions.

▌When did I start feeling lonely?
▌What may have brought it on?
▌What's happening in my relationships with friends and family?
▌How do I feel about myself—am I comfortable with the kind of person I am?

derson. "Usually, they have a list of volunteer opportunities." Or, if you have some teaching skills, call the Board of Education and ask whether they are looking for volunteers. The answer will usually be yes.

Use a question or two. Once you're where the people are, you have to make your presence known. If you have trouble getting conversations going, Dr. Beck suggests that you rely on a number of stock ice-breaker questions. One easy question focuses on the group or the meeting itself: "Have you ever been to this lecture series before?" Or you can break the ice with a question about vacation: "Will you be going away for Labor Day weekend?"

That second one is particularly effective as an ice-breaker. "People always like talking about their vacations," Dr. Beck observes.

Whole-Body Protection

- What circumstances have made me feel lonely before? What's helped in the past?
- What would make me feel less lonely now?

"After doing this sort of exercise, most people say, 'I understand myself and my emotions better,'" observes Dr. Pennebaker.

To get the most out of journal writing, set aside 20 minutes a day for at least three or four days, he advises. Go somewhere quiet, where you won't be interrupted, then write continuously, without stopping to correct grammar, sentence structure, or spelling. No need to worry if you don't have a thesis statement or don't follow outline form.

"I tell people to write with the expectation that they'll throw away what they have written when they finish," says Dr. Pennebaker.

Of course, you don't have to throw it away—you can save it and read it a day or a month or a year later, if you like. The point is, don't write for an imaginary audience of literary critics or for posterity.

While your journal can be an important helpmate in times of loneliness, Dr. Pennebaker cautions against using your journal as a substitute for action. You still need to do things you enjoy on your own and get out and meet people, he says. But he has observed that journal writing can help you do both.

Listen some, gab some. A conversation should allow for give and take—which means listening and talking. The idea is to get to know the other person and let him get to know you. So, ask questions, but don't forget to talk about yourself, Dr. Beck says.

If the other person neglects to ask you about yourself, go ahead and volunteer information anyway, Dr. Beck suggests. "Don't let the other person's lack of social skills inhibit you."

Note the weather. Conversing gets easier the more you do it. Practice starting conversations with people in the elevator, in line at the bank, on the commuter train. These won't be long conversations, of course, but they're still good practice.

Want a topic? Well, there's a reason that talking about the weather is such a standard opening for conversation: It's something you have in common with everyone. "You'll be surprised

419

by the high percentage of people who are glad to talk if you ask about the weather," Dr. Beck says.

Jot down your jerky behavior. If you're shy, maybe you're talking yourself out of social opportunities with self-defeating predictions like "I'll look like a jerk if I start to dance" or "I'll say something stupid if I get up and talk at the meeting." Sound like familiar voices?

Next time you catch yourself making predictions like that, test your hypotheses, Dr. Beck recommends. "Ask yourself, 'How often have I acted like a jerk in the past?'" If you think it has been fairly often, try keeping an actual record of your "jerky behavior" for a week. Odds are, the record will have zero entries, Dr. Beck predicts.

Expect some hits—not home runs. Even an all-star hitter doesn't expect to slam every pitch out of the ballpark. "If you're at a gathering and approach 10 people and get enthusiastic responses out of two of them, you're doing wonderfully," Dr. Beck says.

In other words, you can't expect overwhelmingly positive responses from everyone. If you've had a couple of good conversations, that's as much as you can hope for. And if it so happens that you don't meet anyone you liked, well, there's always the next gathering.

Getting, and Staying, Close

Meeting people is only half the story, of course. What you really want when you feel lonely is to be close to someone. And to get close to someone, you have to let your hair down, share some cherished beliefs, and—what's hardest for many of us—reveal some deeper feelings.

"Intimacy is about being able to share things that are usually difficult to share with others, unless you feel close to them," Dr. Broder says. Sure, it's fine to talk about celebrities or to admit your preference for hamburgers over hot dogs. But if you want to get closer to someone, you have to talk about a lot more.

Of course, there's always a chance that the other person won't listen or won't share anything in return. But just suppose you try? What if you tell the other person that a piece of music

420

really means a lot to you because of the memories it evokes? Or what if you tell that person what you want out of life? Chances are, the other person will respond sympathetically, and you're on your way to greater closeness.

Once you have established a close relationship, though, the work is far from over. You have to keep listening, talking, sharing, and doing things together—as long as you want the closeness to last.

Long-Term Tactics
To Keep the Doors Open

Since the things that keep you close to another person don't happen automatically, researchers have looked at some of the factors that keep people close. Although we would all like to trust our instincts, the fact is we can use some reminders from time to time. Here's what experts recommend.

Open up—but don't overflow. When you're getting to know someone, share some of your beliefs and feelings, but not all of them at once. If you start by revealing your most painful feelings or unnerving thoughts, for instance, you might overwhelm the other person.

"If you're lonely after a divorce, it's better to talk about a particular problem related to it," notes Dr. Beck. For instance, you might say, "I really have trouble planning meals for myself." "That's a lot less overwhelming than to say, 'I'm extremely lonely from six to midnight every night, and I'm thinking of killing myself,'" he says.

Ask for what you need. It would be convenient if we all had partners and friends with superpowers of perception, who could understand intuitively how we feel and what we want. Unfortunately, it's hard for most of us to know our own minds, let alone someone else's. To avoid misunderstandings when you're in a close relationship, you have to ask for what you want and need, says Dr. Beck.

421

For example, if you like to garden and your spouse doesn't, you can't expect your partner to be a mind reader and realize that you need help with weeding. Ask for what you need: "I'd really like it if you could help pull weeds for an hour next Saturday." This approach is a lot more effective than stomping around the house in your gardening boots trying to get the attention of a spouse who's perfectly content in the lap of a lounge chair.

But asking isn't a one-way street. "Be mindful that you have to offer something in return," Dr. Beck says. So if you get the cooperation you requested, you should also say, "I'm really glad you're going to help me out, and I'd like you to tell me what I can do that would be of interest to you." Compromise may be the key.

Be really specific. When you make a request, the more specific you are, the better, Dr. Beck says. If you feel neglected, you might not get the attention you want if you just say, "I want some attention." Dr. Beck recommends that you try this instead: "I'd love it if every night we could sit for five minutes and talk about what happened to each of us during the day."

Do things together. "If you're not spending time together, eventually you drift apart," says Dr. Broder. To avoid letting that happen, reserve time for friends and for your partner, he advises.

Plan your dates. If you and your partner are busy people, set aside at least one date night every week or two, Dr. Anderson suggests. "It's understood that nothing takes precedence over the date," he says.

When you're planning your date, make a list of things you enjoy doing together. "One couple I know disappears for a weekend at a local bed-and-breakfast every two months," Dr. Anderson says. "They leave all work behind; they talk to each other, take hikes."

It's sometimes hard to make time that way, Dr. Anderson acknowledges. "But it's essential."

Reveal the hidden "I." While conflicts are inevitable in any relationship, it's how you resolve those conflicts that helps determine whether the relationship stays good or heads south.

Next time a conflict raises its snarly head, Dr. Beck suggests the following approach.

- Avoid accusations that will make the other person defensive. Examples are "You always put me down!" or "All you do is sit and watch TV."
- Instead, talk about how the other person's behavior makes you feel. Examples are "I feel rotten when you criticize my taste in clothing" or "I really like to spend some time with you, and when you watch TV, I feel left out."
- Don't criticize. "If you criticize, the other person will feel defensive," Dr. Beck says.

Protect Yourself from Memory Loss

Years ago at a dinner party, Congresswoman Clare Boothe Luce of Connecticut was seated next to David Burpee, chairman of the famous seed company that bears his name. Midway through the evening, Burpee realized that even though he had been introduced to Luce earlier, she had already forgotten his name. To help his dining companion avoid an awkward moment, Burpee leaned toward Luce and whispered, "I'm Burpee."

Unfortunately, even that blatant reminder didn't jog the memory of the glamorous, urbane, and socially adept congresswoman. Luce looked at her dinner companion, gently patted his hand, and said, "That's all right. I get that way sometimes myself."

Everyone forgets—often with humorous or embarrassing consequences. It's just part of being human. Whether you are 6 or 86, you can lose a book, forget the key to your house, or have trouble remembering someone's name.

Yet memory does seem to worsen with age. According to a 1995 survey, 80 percent of people age 35 and older reported having at least some difficulty with memory or concentration. By age 45, 56 percent of American adults say they habitually lose things and 45 percent say they have trouble remembering familiar names, according to a survey commissioned by the Charles A. Dana Foundation.

But even though most of us can count on memory declining with age, that doesn't mean we are on a fast track for senility. Far from it, says Barry Gordon, M.D., Ph.D., a behavioral neurologist at the Johns Hopkins University School of Medicine in Bal-

424

Is There Brain Drain?

Even though senility isn't in most people's future, the brain is affected by aging in less dramatic ways, say Barry Gordon, M.D., Ph.D., a behavioral neurologist at the Johns Hopkins University School of Medicine in Baltimore and author of *Memory: Remembering and Forgetting in Everyday Life*. After about age 45, it does take longer to recall things. It also takes the brain longer to digest new information.

Older people can still learn, but they need more time than younger people, notes Richard Mohs, Ph.D., a memory researcher and professor of psychology at Mount Sinai School of Medicine of the City University of New York in New York City.

Neurologists have observed that, as people age, some alterations in the brain make it more difficult to concentrate and retain recent memories, such as what was for lunch yesterday. But long-term memories are relatively unaffected, says Daniel Alkon, M.D., a neurologist and chief of the Laboratory of Adaptive Systems at the National Institute of Stroke and Neurological Disorders in Bethesda, Maryland, and author of *Memory's Voice*.

One part of the brain in particular—the hippocampus—has been closely studied for its role in memory. "The hippocampus is one of the structures in the brain that gets hit hard by aging," Dr. Alkon says. "That may be because it's very sensitive to a lack of oxygen. So it could be as people grow older and the heart doesn't pump blood to the brain as efficiently as it once did, the hippocampus sustains damage."

But even though changes in the brain may be responsible for some memory loss, the physical changes that occur in normal aging are generally slight, says Tora Brawley, Ph.D., a neuropsychologist at Duke University Medical Center in Durham, North Carolina. "The brain shrinks as we get older, just as the spine shrinks," she says. "But these changes should be easy to deal with as long as people understand that they are a part of the normal aging process."

timore and author of *Memory: Remembering and Forgetting in Everyday Life*.

With the exception of serious neurological problems like Alzheimer's disease, most memory loss is not severe, Dr. Gordon says. A person in his twenties, for instance, might be able to recall seven digits of a phone number that he just looked up. That

425

same person at age 60 may be able to recall six. Hardly an earth-shaking change.

"Memory isn't perfect at any age," says Donald Kausler, Ph.D., professor emeritus of psychology at the University of Missouri at Columbia. "But the losses of memory as you age are small. In fact, some types of memory like vocabulary and general knowledge can actually increase throughout the life span. It's not as if old age means you drift off into a mental void. It may take more effort to learn and remember things, but you can reach the same level as any younger person."

Where Memories Begin

Used to be, everyone believed that old people turned senile. It's not true, Dr. Gordon says. Although some brain cells, called neurons, do die off with age, scientists are pretty sure that the multitude of remaining neurons become adventurous networkers, branching out to form new connections in the brain. With these new connections clicking along, memories stay intact.

When you remember something, it's like switching on a tape recording. The neurons are the tape that memory is recorded on, and a region of the brain called the hippocampus is the "Record" button. Most of the time, your hippocampus is turned off—so information that is only momentarily important, like the name "Burpee," flies quickly out of your mind. But when your brain wants to remember, the hippocampus starts the recording process, and neurons begin "taping" the information.

So if you want to remember, right now, the name of the woman sitting next to Burpee, your hippocampus is switched on to that "recording" mode.

But many of us simply can't remember who was sitting next to whom at the last dinner party. And, usually, that's nothing to worry about. In fact, few people really worry if they lose their car keys or forget names from time to time. But some kinds of memory loss can be disturbing, at best, and sometimes terrifying. For example:

426

An Herb to Remember

Ginkgo has been used in Asia for thousands of years—for treating asthma and improving circulation.

Research now suggests that this herb, which is extracted from the leaves of the ginkgo tree, also may help strengthen memory and improve concentration, says David Edelberg, M.D., the Chicago-based founder of American Whole Health, a national network of integrated medical centers.

By enhancing blood circulation, ginkgo helps additional oxygen and vital nutrients to reach brain cells, enabling them to work more efficiently. In European studies, the active ingredient in the herb was found to enhance mental performance and short-term memory. In fact, German doctors commonly use the herb for treating a number of problems associated with poor circulation—not just memory loss but also headaches and dizziness. It is unlikely, however, to relieve memory trouble caused by alcohol or drugs like antihistamines or blood pressure medications, says Dr. Edelberg.

If you've been having memory problems, Dr. Edelberg suggests taking 40 milligrams of the concentrated extract three times daily (look for a content of 20 to 24 percent ginkgo heterocide on the label). Ginkgo is available in most health food stores and is nontoxic.

▮ Getting lost while driving a familiar route

▮ Forgetting important appointments

▮ Telling the same stories repeatedly during a single conversation

▮ Being unable to manage simple finances—like balancing the checkbook—when you didn't have problems before

▮ A sudden change in artistic or musical abilities

If you have experienced any of these problems, or if you're losing memory to such a degree that it's getting difficult to function, then you need to check with your doctor, says Vernon Mark, M.D., a neurosurgeon in Newport, Rhode Island, and co-author of *Reversing Memory Loss.*

A physical problem—as well as age—can contribute to memory loss, and sometimes that problem is treatable or reversible,

427

says Dr. Gordon. There are more than 70 conditions that can trigger or worsen memory loss, he adds. The conditions include some that you might expect and many that you wouldn't—from hearing loss, vision problems, thyroid conditions, and stress to high blood pressure and depression. If you have been more distracted than usual, ask your doctor for a complete physical examination before you jump to the conclusion that your mind is failing you.

Check out your medications, too, suggests Dr. Gordon. Distractibility, poor attention span, and memory problems can be side effects of drugs like tranquilizers and antidepressants, he says. Ask your doctor if your prescription or over-the-counter medications may be hampering your memory.

Apart from finding a medical cause, there's a whole laundry list of things that we can do every day to help avoid memory loss. Here are some things to remember.

Doing Away with Distractions

Distraction is one of memory's greatest foes. For example, take a moment to read the following paragraph in a quiet room.

John Adelbert Kelley rose at 6:00 on the morning of April 19, 1935. Not yet married, he was living at home with his parents in the town of Arlington, Massachusetts, a northwestern suburb of Boston. His mother prepared him a breakfast that morning that included steak.

All done? Close your eyes and try to recall as many details as you can about the story. No peeking allowed.

Now turn on the television or radio while you read the following paragraph—then try to recollect the details with the same degree of accuracy.

On Pioneer Drive, Pat Davis, mother of three children, was busy in her kitchen preparing the spice cake she had promised to take to a guild meeting at St. Joseph's Church that evening. By 2:30 P.M., when she put the spice cake in the oven and set the timer, it was raining heavily.

428

Chances are, you remembered more details from the first story than the second one, says Janet Fogler, a clinical social worker at Turner Geriatric Clinic at the University of Michigan Geriatrics Center in Ann Arbor and co-author of *Improving Your Memory*. Why?

Short-term memory is fragile. It often lasts no more than 30 seconds. Unless the hippocampus in the brain has time to switch on the recording mechanisms, the memory won't be stored. When you're distracted by another thought, sound, or sight, your most recent short-term memories—like the details of what you just read—will be wiped out like chalk erased from a blackboard, Dr. Gordon says.

Distractions can invade your thinking at any moment, and even though you may believe you can erase them, don't be too sure. If you have ever hurried away from the cash register without counting your change, it's probably because you were concerned about the next errand you had to run. If you have absentmindedly left a bag of groceries at the checkout counter, maybe it was because you were thinking about getting to the post office before it closed—or you were in a hurry to make an urgent phone call.

The tendency to be distracted gets more pronounced with age because our ability to concentrate on a single task begins to slip, says Dr. Gordon, possibly because we lose much of our ability to filter out stray thoughts. As a result, memory lapses may occur more frequently.

But maybe those lapses don't have to happen. "If you are motivated and your brain is working well, you can remember almost anything you want at age 20, 40, 60, or even 80. It's really just a matter of focusing your attention," Dr. Mark says.

know what?

According to a University of Texas survey, people remember only 20 percent of what they hear, but 70 percent of what they say.

Makeover Minutes

For Clearer Focus

Want to leap the distraction barrier? You can do it by using some learnable techniques to focus your concentration. Here are some ways to make that happen.

429

Catch up on sleep. Getting a good night's sleep—at least six to eight hours a day—will make your brain more efficient at processing and storing information, according to Dr. Gordon.

When you're tired, you have more trouble focusing your attention, and your memory is sure to suffer, says Fogler.

Keep using your head. Try memorizing lists, names, and other important information. That can help keep your memory sharp and fend off distractibility as you get older, says Alan S. Brown, Ph.D., professor of psychology at Southern Methodist University in Dallas and author of *How to Increase Your Memory Power*. Written lists can be helpful, but they also can be a crutch that can actually diminish your ability to concentrate and recall, he says. So if you use a grocery list, for example, leave at least three or four items off the list—and try to keep track of those items in your head.

Get organized. Chaos is a memory buster—and clutter is a distraction that can leave you more confused than you need to be. If you just tuck the mail somewhere, toss the car keys on the counter, and leave newspapers wherever you happen to drop them, you may be forced to hunt for items or clean up the chaos later on—and that's certainly going to be distracting. Instead of just setting things aside, Fogler recommends that you choose some designated spots for these everyday items. A bowl on the table, for example, might be the one place you always put your keys—never anywhere else.

As for old magazines and newspapers, toss them once a week, Fogler suggests. And when you sort through your mail, keep a wastebasket handy. If you have a designated spot for all the usual items that come in the door—and you don't hesitate to toss the things you don't need—you'll keep distractions to a minimum, she says.

Build up your tolerance. Unless you live alone on a remote island, there's no easy way to eliminate distractions from your life. But you can teach yourself to concentrate more effectively despite the distractions, says Fran Pirozzolo, Ph.D., a neuropsychologist and sports psychology consultant to the New York Yankees.

Two or three times a week, put your concentration to the test, Dr. Pirozzolo suggests. Try reading a book, but do it with

430

Lest We Forget

The most-feared kind of memory loss—Alzheimer's—affects an estimated four million Americans. Nearly 1 out of every 10 people will have it past the age of 65, and 1 out of 2 over the age of 85. So far, no one has discovered how to reverse the progress of the disease, but researchers are beginning to find clues to the discovery of effective therapy.

For unexplained reasons, the disease causes certain proteins in the brain to twist together and form fibrous tangles. These tangles may clog the normal signaling pathways of brain cells. As a result, people who have the disorder progressively lose memory and their ability to think rationally.

Although the evidence is slim, keeping people with Alzheimer's mentally active seems to slow the progression of this disease, says Leonard Berg, M.D., professor of neurology and founding director of the Alzheimer's Disease Research Center at Washington University School of Medicine in St. Louis. "There's plenty of reason for optimism," he says. "The research about the causes and mechanisms of Alzheimer's disease has been so productive in the past few years that early in the twenty-first century we might have a new generation of drugs that could slow its progression substantially."

Research also suggests that hormone-replacement therapy may help prevent or delay the onset of the disease. In a 14-year study of 8,877 women, researchers found that those taking estrogen were 35 percent less likely to develop Alzheimer's disease, says Annlia Paganini-Hill, Ph.D., co-author of the study and professor of preventive medicine at the University of Southern California School of Medicine in Los Angeles. Preliminary studies have also shown that estrogen might slow the onset of symptoms in women who already have the disease, she adds.

"A five-year delay in onset would reduce the prevalence of Alzheimer's disease by at least one-third," according to Dr. Paganini-Hill. "For many individuals, such a delay would mean they would escape Alzheimer's disease altogether. Others might still develop the disease, but they would have additional symptom-free years."

the television turned to high volume. After reading for a couple of minutes, put down the book, watch television for a couple of minutes, then pick up the book again. After 10 minutes, turn off the television, put down the book, and see how much you can remember from each source. Do this two or three times a week, and gradually your ability to block out distractions should improve.

Speak out. Talking to yourself as you do something can help focus your attention and make things easier to remember, Fogler says. If you talk your way through a problem, you'll reinforce the memory because you're using your senses as well as your mind. When you say something aloud, you're using your voice and hearing as well as your memory. Next time you park your car at a shopping mall, try saying the location aloud, for instance, "The car is parked in section 3C, space 22." When you return—even if you're still dazed from shopping—you're more likely to remember "section 3C, space 22" because it's more strongly imprinted on your memory.

Make the most of sounds and smells. Memory depends on all of the senses. So use them, says Danielle Lapp, a memory training specialist at Stanford University and author of *Don't Forget*. When you take a walk in an unfamiliar neighborhood, don't stop with noting the street names. Look around and note: Are there are any flowers nearby? What are their colors and scents? Listen for sounds of the neighborhood—kids laughing, radios playing. Touch the fire hydrant at the corner. With your eyes, ears, and fingers at work, you'll absorb the neighborhood more vividly with all your senses—and quickly recognize the landmarks when you pass that way again.

Write a short story. One way to remember a short list of items is to transform it into a story, Fogler says. The story becomes a focusing technique: It links some unrelated items, and as long as you're telling yourself the story, you'll concentrate on moving from item to item. "It's one of my favorite memory techniques," she says.

The story doesn't need to be elaborate, Fogler notes. "Suppose I need to call my sister about my niece's birthday, and I need to call a mechanic about repairing my car. I would make up a one-sentence story like, 'My sister is going to buy my niece a new car for her birthday.' The two phone calls I need to make are in that one story."

Slow down. We have all experienced anxious instants when

432

A Mental Metal?

When news leaked out that aluminum cans might contribute to Alzheimer's, some Americans swore never again to sip from a suspect can. Others have gone to even greater lengths—avoiding aluminum cookware and aluminum-containing products like antiperspirants and antacids, says Barry Gordon, M.D., Ph.D., a behavioral neurologist at the Johns Hopkins University School of Medicine in Baltimore and author of *Memory: Remembering and Forgetting in Everyday Life.*

This pattern of avoidance began when some researchers discovered that people with Alzheimer's disease have elevated levels of aluminum in their brains. Some scientists speculated that aluminum in food-storage containers might be contributing to the condition.

Subsequent research, however, suggests that the disease causes the metal to accumulate rather than the other way around, Dr. Gordon says. In people with Alzheimer's, abnormal protein buildups called plaques form in the brain. "We think that the protein in the plaques does soak up the aluminum, but the aluminum itself is not damaging," he says. "My best advice at this point is, don't worry about aluminum."

we couldn't remember something important—like whether we locked the door or turned off the coffeemaker. Usually, that's a sign you were distracted when leaving your home. So before dashing out the door, Lapp suggests, take a moment to concentrate. Pause for a moment, take a deep breath, close your eyes, and relax. Ask yourself, "Where am I going? What am I doing? What do I need? Have I forgotten anything?"

Zero in on the eyes. It happens all the time at weddings, high school reunions, and other social occasions. You're talking with someone when all of a sudden you spot a longtime friend on the far side of the room. Odds are, you don't remember half of what follows in the conversation you're having.

When your gaze wanders, so does your attention. "You're more apt to recall what people say if you maintain eye contact with them," says Tora Brawley, Ph.D., a neuropsychologist at Duke University Medical Center in Durham, North Carolina. To avoid being distracted—and to better remember what

433

someone's saying—be sure to keep looking at the person you're talking to.

Take advantage of props. Every day is so full of things to remember, it's hardly surprising that a few details fall by the wayside. To keep things more keenly focused in your mind, place some attention-getters in your path, Fogler says.

For example, she once woke up in the middle of the night and realized that she needed to mail a package the next day. "I didn't want to get out of bed and write myself a note, so I took a slipper that was on the floor and put it on top of my lamp," Fogler says. "The next morning, there was the slipper on top of the lamp. I thought, 'Oh yeah, I need to get that mailing out.'"

A good reminder, Fogler notes, can be unconventional or even weird. It should be so out of the ordinary that it will grab your attention—and trigger some association in your mind.

Avoiding Information Overload

In the Stone Age, the stones actually had a chance to gather some moss. Now, they're more likely to be rolling—24 hours a day. With mobile telephones, computers, televisions, radios, and a bevy of digital devices bombarding our senses, we can find out everything from the weather in Katmandu to the politics in Panama in minutes or less.

As the information supply reaches staggering proportions, it's no wonder our minds start to stagger under the overload. A weekday edition of the *New York Times* contains more information than an average person in seventeenth-century England learned in a lifetime. The number of books in the nation's best libraries doubles every 14 years. Even the English language is exploding with variations: A dictionary now has more than 500,000 words, five times more than when Shakespeare's Hamlet struggled to express himself.

"There is so much information available through television, newspapers, magazines, books, mail, and the Internet these days," says Richard Mohs, Ph.D., a memory researcher and professor of psychology at Mount Sinai School of Medicine of the City University of New York in New York City. "That

know what?

Memories of adolescence and old age are more vivid than memories of the middle years— presumably because middle age is a more routine time of life.

434

Tales from the Champ

For most of his life, Dominic O'Brien had a memory like Teflon—nothing stuck.

"I had lots of trouble remembering names and faces, I was always losing my car keys, and I rarely showed up for appointments on time because I couldn't remember when they were. It was quite embarrassing," says O'Brien, a former x-ray film recycler who lives near London.

Today, O'Brien is a four-time world memory champion who can memorize a 500-word poem in 30 minutes and recall 1,392 random numbers an hour after seeing them for the first time. He also can memorize 100 names and faces in 20 minutes, recite 200 random words in sequence, and recall the precise order of 40 decks of shuffled playing cards.

His quest for perfect memory began in 1988 after he saw a man on television memorize a pack of shuffled cards in three minutes. "I was fascinated by that, so I began investigating my own memory. Within three months, I found I could do it, too," O'Brien says. And in 1996, he set a world record by memorizing the order of a deck of cards in 38.29 seconds, according to the *Guinness Book of Records*.

To achieve these kinds of feats, O'Brien mastered a slew of powerful memory techniques.

To remember numbers, for instance, O'Brien imagines shapes. A two looks like a swan, a four like a sailboat. So to remember a simple number like 2,248, he pictures two swans getting into a boat moored next to an hourglass.

To memorize the faces of cards, he associates each card with relatives, friends, or celebrities. Then he imagines taking a walk through his village, meeting each person (card) along the way.

"Anyone can learn to do this," says memory master O'Brien. "You just need to learn a few basic techniques and then practice a bit."

places heavy demands on the memory that just weren't there in the past."

Handling this new tidal wave of information is truly a challenge. To filter out the unnecessary and flee from what experts

435

are calling information anxiety, you need to figure out what's too trivial to keep in mind. "If you want to tame information anxiety, you first need to realize that you can't remember everything and that no one expects you to," says Dennis Gersten, M.D., a psychiatrist in San Diego and author of *Are You Getting Enlightened or Losing Your Mind?* "The best thing you can do in this age of information overload is decide what is personally relevant to you and discard the rest. More than likely, you can find that forgotten information later in an almanac, book, or other source."

Makeover Minutes

To Glean Clear Info

As you pick and choose the information you want to keep—and discard—you can follow some general guidelines to help decide what matters to you. Here are some strategies to reflect on while you collect your thoughts.

Make it meaningful. To siphon off the details that you want to keep clearly in mind, connect the information to something that's significant to you. Imagine, for example, that a friend tells you that she just bought a 15-acre farm. Is that big or small? Unless you can visualize exactly an acre, then multiply it (mentally) by 15, you probably can't guess. And without some image as a reference, that information is likely to get jumbled up with other numbers that are equally difficult to recall, Dr. Gersten says.

To help yourself remember, ask questions that clarify the information, he advises. For instance, you might ask, "How big is an acre compared to a football field?" When you learn that an acre is about the size of a football field without the end zones, your mind can start to play with images of 15 football fields jammed together to make a farm. At that point, the information becomes easier to remember, Dr. Gersten says.

"If information isn't understandable or personally meaningful, and you can't use it, that's when you can feel overwhelmed," Dr. Gersten says.

Think in question marks. Which are you more likely to remember: 1 picture that you studied for 10 seconds, or 10 pictures that you only got to see for 1 second?

One way to avoid information overload is to make the speaker slow down—and to hear more about one particular topic. Don't be afraid to let your ignorance show, Dr. Gersten suggests. The next time someone mentions a book, author, politician, or event that you are unfamiliar with, stop the conversation and start asking questions. Otherwise, the other person is likely to skip on to topic number two before you have really heard enough about topic number one.

"Too many people measure their knowledge against others," Dr. Gersten observes. "They think other people know so much more than they do, and they end up feeling anxious and overwhelmed." If you're not afraid to ask questions, people will probably respect you for being courageous and curious, he says. And, ultimately, you'll understand and remember better because you get a longer look at the whole picture.

Lessening Stress

If you can vividly remember what you were doing when you heard John F. Kennedy was dead or when Ronald Reagan was shot, it's largely due to stress. In traumatic situations, you get a stress reaction that triggers a rush of adrenaline and other hormones. Sometimes, the active hormones can help etch memories forever in your mind.

But when stress fills everyday life, it isn't so helpful as a memory preserver. In fact, when you have too much steady stress every day, your powers of memory can take a beating, according to Paul Rosch, M.D., clinical professor of medicine and psychiatry at New York Medical College in Valhalla and president of the American Institute of Stress in Yonkers, New York.

Unrelenting stress causes the hippocampus to shrink, making it harder to hold on to recent memories, Dr. Rosch says. Much of this damage is probably caused by cortisol, a hormone secreted when you are under emotional strain. In one study, older men and women were asked to make speeches that—

know what?

Nearly 62 percent of Americans say that they have had the experience of going into a room to get something only to forget what they were looking for.

each was told—would be shown to a large audience. While they spoke, researchers measured their cortisol levels. The study showed that those with the highest rise in cortisol levels also had the most difficulty recalling what they had said.

Makeover Minutes

To Stamp Out Tension

When you take steps to tame stress, you're likely to help your powers of recollection, according to Dr. Rosch. The only hitch is finding a stress-taming technique that's right for you. "There is no single stress-reduction strategy that will work for everyone," he says. "Anything that helps you feel more in control of your life will reduce stress and quite likely help to improve your memory." Here are some approaches that Dr. Rosch and other experts recommend.

Go for baroque. Listening to slow baroque music can help soothe stress and enhance the recording portion of your memory, Lapp says. And she means *really* slow—music that has about 60 beats per minute. If you want to memorize a proverb, for instance, try playing the slow portion—the largo movement—of a piece written by Handel, Bach, Vivaldi, or one of the other baroque composers. As the music plays, Lapp says, try to feel relaxed, in control, and in harmony with the music. Then read the phrase aloud in rhythm to the music. Stop and just listen to the music for a moment. Then repeat the process until the information is locked into your brain.

Plan ahead. Before going to a gathering, take a few moments to think about who's going to be there and to review their names and faces in your mind, Dr. Brown says. Visualize where you first met each person. Doing this in advance will help you be more relaxed and more apt to remember important details.

Don't worry if you can't remember *all* the names the first time that you try this technique. By priming your mental pump ahead of time, your mind will continue searching for informa-

438

Let the Band Play Long

Researchers are discovering that music can help people with brain damage recover speech, memories, and other intellectual skills, according to Connie Tomaino, certified music therapist and director of music therapy at Beth Abraham Health Services in New York City.

While the recovery may be temporary, the effects can be dramatic. Tomaino recalls one stroke victim who started responding to a song "Tumbalalaika." At first, the patient just hummed along, but as his recovery continued, he finally burst into song.

"Within a month, the patient was singing the full lyrics spontaneously," Tomaino recalls. Apparently the music evoked memories that, in turn, prompted a whole chain of responses. "I found out from his wife this was a song that he used to sing to his kids at bedtime," she says. "Once he got the words to the song back, he began recovering other language skills."

In a study where Tomaino worked with Oliver Sacks, M.D., a neurologist in New York City and author of *The Man Who Mistook His Wife for a Hat*, the researchers played familiar music to 30 people with severe memory problems. Afterward, more than half were better able to remember names, dates, and recent events, Tomaino says.

Those results suggest that music may have power that we can realize when we're trying to jog our memory. After all, music automatically triggers recollections. Listen to "I've Been Workin' on the Railroad," and you can probably remember scenes from your childhood. Sing "Plop, plop, fizz, fizz, oh, what a relief it is," and you're sure to visualize a bottle of Alka-Seltzer.

While researchers aren't sure how music triggers memories, some suspect that sounds, emotions, and memory are processed in the same areas of the brain, Tomaino says. And this can be helpful if a loved one has a memory problem. She recommends that caregivers try playing a familiar tune four to six times a day.

"It's not uncommon for a man with severe memory impairment not to recognize his wife," Tomaino says. "But if they sing a song together, he might say at the end of it, 'Mary, that was really great. Thank you.'"

tion even without conscious effort. So when you see that person at the party, her name will probably come to you.

Reduce the tension. Relaxation techniques like deep breathing can reduce stress and boost your ability to remember things,

It takes about
eight seconds
of uninter-
rupted atten-
tion for your
mind to form
a long-term
memory.

Lapp says. If you find that important matters have been slipping your mind, you may want to take a few minutes to de-stress. According to Lapp, here's one way.

▌ Sit comfortably, letting your arms and legs go limp.
▌ Keeping your mouth closed, inhale deeply and gradually through your nose until your lungs are full.
▌ Exhale slowly, again through your nose, until all of the air is out.
▌ Continue breathing deeply, listening to the rhythm of your breathing.

As air rushes in and then slowly oozes out, notice how your breathing sounds like waves crashing gently against the shore. Visualize the motion of the waves, their sound, and the smell of the sea breeze. Enjoy the sensations.

Feel better? If you practice this technique often, particularly when you're tense or angry, you'll dispel some of the tension that may be interfering with your powers of concentration and memory, says Lapp.

Lend your worries to a friend. If you're worried about an upcoming event or you're stressed-out by pressure, try handing off some of that worry to a friend. Sound difficult? Well, think in terms of setting aside your worries so that you can concentrate on what's important to you. "I do that with some of the professional athletes I work with," Dr. Pirozzolo says. "I'll tell them, 'Don't worry about next year's contract today. I'll do all the worrying for you.' It sounds silly, but it works. It relieves stress, helps you focus on other things, and eliminates a barrier that blocks memory."

Of course, you can't literally pass off your worries. If you have a friend who will listen to what's worrying you, that's a good way to help put your worries in perspective so that you can concentrate on what you have to do. And by concentrating, you help improve your memory, notes Dr. Pirozzolo.

Beating Blues to Bolster Brainpower

Stress and depression often are silent partners. If you feel one, the other is probably stalking you, too. In fact, the same hormone that appears to dampen memory during stress also floods the brain when you feel depressed, Dr. Rosch says. And the feelings that go along with depression can severely plug up memory.

"Depression almost always makes everything in the brain work much more slowly," says Harry Prosen, M.D., chairman of the department of psychiatry and mental health services at the Medical College of Wisconsin in Milwaukee. "It takes more time to recall memories, and it becomes much harder to retain new information. A person who is depressed may only remember something for a minute or two—then, poof, it's gone."

Serious depression may require counseling and medications. If you're just feeling low, on the other hand, you may find that the blue mood will pass—and when it does, it will be easier for you to concentrate and remember things, says Dr. Prosen. (For a list of the symptoms that often accompany serious depression, see "When to Get Help" on page 322.)

Makeover Minutes

To Knock Out the Negatives

Sometimes all you need is a shift of focus to lift your spirits and reinvigorate your memory, Dr. Prosen says. Certainly, a good experience can help erase the lingering effects of negative feelings—and there are quick ways to lift your mood with minimal effort. Here are some tricks of the feel-better trade.

Give your mind a break. When we are blue, we tend to brood—and that's no time to put your memory to the test. In fact, if you forget something like making a phone call or buying a loaf of bread, you might take it too seriously and plunge into a deeper funk. So even if you normally have a good memory, rely more on lists and written reminders until you feel better, Dr. Prosen suggests. At least you'll get through the day-to-day things you have to do while you're feeling low.

Match pluses with minuses. Whenever you catch yourself saying something negative, write it down, suggests Fogler. Then jot

441

a more positive thought to replace it such as "I may be having trouble remembering some things right now, but it's only a temporary problem. I still have a good memory for faces and dates." Doing that helps to stop the cycle of negative thoughts ("Oh, I can't remember anything!") and reminds you that there is an upside.

Sweat it out. Walking, running, swimming, and other forms of aerobic exercise will help improve memory, Dr. Gordon says. Doing any aerobic activity for at least 20 minutes, three times a week, can improve memory 20 to 30 percent, he says.

Put humor to work. Laughter is one of the best antidotes for depression and memory problems, says William F. Fry, M.D., a psychiatrist and clinical professor emeritus at Stanford University School of Medicine. Clip cartoons, stockpile funny newspaper and magazine articles, and watch humorous videos. When you're feeling low, these weapons can do wonders for your mood. And as your mood improves, so will your powers of recall, he notes.

Protect Yourself from
Osteoporosis

You don't have to be a little old lady to get osteoporosis. Ask Judy Simon.

Simon, a computer programmer in the Baltimore area, was 45 when she discovered that she had osteoporosis, a disease that makes bones fragile and likely to break. The bone-density scan that she had requested revealed that the bone in her lumbar spine—the small of the back—was 25 to 30 percent below normal for the young adult population. "While my osteoporosis was not advanced, it was pretty bad for someone who was only 45 and had not yet entered menopause," says Simon.

She knew that if she didn't do something, her bones would continue to deteriorate, increasing her risk of a spine or hip fracture later on. The thought scared her. "My husband and I are avid golfers, and we had always envisioned our retirement years as playing a lot of golf and being active," she says. "All of a sudden, I saw myself not being able to do that—my husband having to take care of me, our not being able to do things together. That was disturbing."

Simon got busy; she wasn't going to be a pain-ridden husk confined to a bed or an armchair. She consulted a nutritionist, who recommended that she begin consuming 1,500 milligrams of calcium a day. She joined a health club and started hitting the weight machines because strength training protects bone. She also began taking alendronate sodium (Fosamax), a drug approved in 1995 for the prevention and treatment of osteoporosis. "I was extremely aggressive in treating my osteoporosis; I did everything I could," says Simon.

443

Supplement Your Knowledge

You thought choosing a cold remedy was tough? Try standing in any drugstore's vitamin aisle and picking a calcium supplement. Should you opt for calcium carbonate, calcium citrate, or calcium citrate malate? Tablets, chewables, or liquids? With or without vitamin D or added minerals?

While it might seem like you need a degree in nutrition to choose a calcium supplement, all you really need are a few facts. First of all, look for the amount of elemental calcium on the label. The most common type of calcium used in supplements, calcium carbonate, contains the most elemental calcium. And calcium carbonate is also the least expensive, says Mark B. Andon, Ph.D., chief of the Mineral Nutrition Laboratory at Proctor and Gamble in Cincinnati.

Calcium carbonate supplements, however, do have some drawbacks. Researchers say that these supplements can cause gas, constipation, or bloating; that the calcium they contain can be hard to absorb; and that they must be taken with meals.

By contrast, supplements that contain calcium citrate or calcium citrate malate contain less calcium but may be better absorbed than calcium carbonate. These supplements have another advantage as well: You can take them whenever you want or whenever you remember to.

Those are the basics. Beyond that, you can personalize your selection based on your age, personal habits, and other special circumstances. Here's the selection recommended by Robert Mascitelli, M.D., a member of the National Osteoporosis Foundation in Bethesda, Maryland, and director of

Two years later, she had increased her bone density by 7½ percent. For every 1 percent increase in bone mass, the risk of a fracture from osteoporosis decreases by 6 percent. That means Simon had slashed her risk of an osteoporosis-related fracture by 45 percent. "My bone density no longer meets the definition of osteoporosis," she says. "I'm one of the first who can say, 'I used to have osteoporosis.' And there will be many more to follow."

It's Never Too Late

Unlike Simon, who understood the potential seriousness of her slowly weakening bones, few of us think of the aging that oc-

the Osteoporosis Prevention and Treatment program at East 72nd Street Health Management Specialists in New York City.

If you don't already take a multivitamin: Consider a calcium supplement that contains 400 international units of vitamin D (100 percent of the Daily Value, or DV), 100 milligrams of magnesium (25 percent of the DV), and 15 milligrams of zinc (100 percent of the DV). Many of us are deficient in these bone-sparing nutrients.

If you're over 60: Consider calcium citrate or calcium citrate malate, which do not require stomach hydrochloric acid to be absorbed. This makes them a good choice for people over 60, whose stomachs tend to make less of this acid.

If you can't swallow pills: Try chewable calcium carbonate supplements like Tums or Rolaids or calcium citrate chewables. You might also opt for a liquid supplement like Liqui-Cal or a fizzy tablet that you plop into a glass of water such as Citrical Liquitab.

If you like to take supplements with meals: Opt for a calcium carbonate supplement. Its calcium is best absorbed if you take it with food.

If you often forget to take supplements: Consider calcium citrate or calcium citrate malate supplements; their calcium can be absorbed on an empty stomach.

If you take prescription drugs: Talk to your doctor or pharmacist before taking any supplement. Calcium supplements can impair the absorption of certain drugs, such as the antibiotic tetracycline.

curs in our skeleton—or the importance of strong bones and a straight spine in keeping our youth.

Maybe it's because we can't see our bones in the way we can a new wrinkle or a fresh gray hair: Out of sight is out of mind. Or maybe we tend to think of bone as more dead than alive—a calcified structure that supports the malleable, less reliable parts of our body. Whatever the reason, the condition of our bones just doesn't register on our "age-o-meters."

But it should. In the decades to come, your youthful appearance, vigor, and independence will ride on the health of your bones. A fracture in later years takes much longer to heal and costs much more in terms of mobility than a broken bone

445

in your twenties or thirties. It's essential to guard against that—by taking steps now to help prevent bone loss.

Despite what you may think, osteoporosis is not an inevitable consequence of aging. "If that were true, every older person around the world would have osteoporosis. And that simply doesn't happen," says Susan E. Brown, Ph.D., director of the Osteoporosis Education Project in Syracuse, New York, and author of *Better Bones, Better Body.* "For example, the Japanese live longer than any people in the world, but the rate of hip fractures in elderly Japanese is less than half that of Western countries. And the Chinese, who have thinner bones than we do, suffer fewer fractures even into old age."

That's not to say that osteoporosis itself is completely preventable. Some factors beyond our control are known to increase risk—such as being a woman and having a family history of the disease. You are also at greater risk than others if you are small-boned, underweight, or light-complected. And poor nutrition is a significant risk factor.

But even if you are among the high-risk group, you can take significant steps to avoid the consequences of osteoporosis. And there is a big difference between developing osteoporosis and sustaining an osteoporosis-related fracture. "Unfortunately, in the majority of cases, a person discovers that he has osteoporosis only after suffering a fracture," says Robert J. Mascitelli, M.D., a member of the National Osteoporosis Foundation in Bethesda, Maryland, and director of the Osteoporosis Prevention and Treatment program at East 72nd Street Health Management Specialists in New York City. So early detection is key, he says.

Like many doctors, Dr. Mascitelli recommends that women request a bone-density test at the start of menopause so that if bone loss is detected, it can be treated before it leads to a fracture.

Plus, you can take many steps to prevent the bone loss that leads to fractures. It's estimated that once we attain our peak bone mass, fully half of all bone loss is caused by unhealthy lifestyle habits. So eating a healthy diet, using nutritional supplements as necessary, getting regular exercise, and avoiding

446

health-damaging behavior like smoking and ingesting excessive protein, sugar, and alcohol can significantly reduce our risk, says Dr. Brown.

It's never too late to hang on to the bone you already have. "Even if you already have thinning bones, there's a lot you can do to halt further bone loss," says Dr. Brown. "You need never suffer a fracture."

The Life and Death of Bone

Though the old Grim Reaper is usually portrayed as a skeleton, that image is an insult to every bone in our bodies. A hard, durable shell wrapped around spongy inner layers teeming with blood vessels and nerves, every bone we have is very much alive. Every week, we recycle from 5 to 7 percent of our bone mass. In effect, we are replacing our entire skeleton every three months or so.

From the day we are born until the day we die, our bones undergo a constant cycle of breakdown and regeneration, a process called remodeling. Until we reach the age of about 30, we make more bone than we lose. At that age, we reach what researchers call peak bone mass, the point at which our bones arc as dense and strong as they will ever be.

In our late thirties, however, we start losing more bone than we make. At first, we lose a portion of bone slowly, perhaps 1 percent a year. But the older we get, the more we lose.

For women, the greatest bone loss occurs in the years after menopause, when their stores of bone-protecting estrogen begin to wane. This erosion of bone can be drastic: Women can lose up to 20 percent of their bone density in the five to seven years following menopause. It's for this reason that some postmenopausal women, particularly those with a family history of osteoporosis, opt for hormone-replacement therapy (HRT), which has been shown to reduce the expected risk of fractures by 50 to 60 percent. (For more information on HRT, see Protect Yourself from Hormonal Changes on page 392.)

"The advent of menopause is the critical moment when significant bone loss begins," says Ethel Siris, M.D., director of the

know what?

At its peak, human bone possesses nearly half the strength of steel when it's resisting compression —and bone is equal to steel in resisting tension.

447

Toni Stabile Center for the Prevention and Treatment of Osteoporosis at Columbia-Presbyterian Medical Center in New York City. "The bone you bring to menopause, and how rapidly you lose bone during menopause, are very important factors in determining what's going to happen to you later."

But for all men as well as pre- and postmenopausal women, you can follow the lead of Judy Simon to protect your bones now. Here's how to begin.

Grow a Milk Mustache

For decades, parents have admonished their kids to drink their milk to build strong bones. But we grown-ups have come to realize that our middle-aged bones also need milk's bone-building calcium.

Calcium helps you build bone when you're young and hang on to it as you grow older. Yet surveys show that many Americans don't meet recommended guidelines for optimal calcium intake. The optimal calcium requirements recommended by the National Institutes of Health Consensus Panel are 1,000 milligrams for men age 65 and under, women under age 50, and women older than 50 who receive hormone-replacement therapy. Women over age 50 and men over age 65 should aim for 1,500 milligrams a day. Women who are pregnant or nursing should get between 1,200 and 1,500 milligrams a day.

Women, who don't drink as much milk as men and who consume fewer calories, are especially likely to fall short on calcium. That's bad news for bones, which serve as a storehouse for 99 percent of the body's calcium. The skeleton's supply of calcium is much like money in a bank account; it's continually "deposited" and "withdrawn" from the bones as the body needs it. If you don't get enough calcium from your diet, your body will pull it right out of your bones, setting the stage for a thin, frail skeleton. So consuming enough calcium is a kind of overdraft protection for your bones; it can help prevent further bone loss.

You don't have to chug glass after glass of milk to protect your bones, however. Yogurt, beans, broccoli, calcium-fortified orange juice, turnip greens, Chinese cabbage, seeds, and nuts are all sources of calcium. (So is cheese, though you will need to pick out the low-fat kinds to avoid getting too much fat while you're trying to get calcium.)

Calcium from food is the preferred choice, so be sure to check the top 10 list for bone protection on page 24 in Stop-Time Tactic No. 1. But if you don't get enough calcium from your diet, you can make up the difference with a daily calcium supplement, says Patty Packard, R.D., a nutritionist at the Center for Osteoporosis Research at Creighton University in Omaha, Nebraska.

A reminder: Your bones require other vitamins and minerals besides calcium. Dr. Brown names vitamins D, C, and K, and a number of minerals as essential to bone health.

As we have noted, the most essential is vitamin D, found in vitamin D–fortified milk and in fatty fish like salmon. Vitamin D increases absorption of calcium in the intestine. "Without adequate vitamin D, you can take in all the calcium in the world, and it won't be absorbed," says Packard.

Vitamin C, abundant in fruits and vegetables, helps form collagen, a tough, stringy tissue into which minerals are packed—and these are the minerals that get turned into bone. Vitamin K, found primarily in green leafy vegetables, helps make osteocalcin, a bone protein that is thought to assist in the bone-building process.

When you are mining minerals for bone strength, take a good look at magnesium, zinc, manganese, copper, and boron, advises Dr. Brown. Magnesium, found in whole grains, wheat germ, and dark green leafy vegetables, stimulates the production of calcitonin, a bone-preserving hormone. Zinc, found in whole grains, milk, lean beef, and shellfish, may affect the bones' ability to make new bone. Manganese, abundant in whole-grain cereals, nuts, fruits, and green leafy vegetables, appears to help develop strong, healthy cartilage and bone. "Copper and boron have only recently been found essential for bone health," says Dr. Brown. Excellent sources of copper include oysters, shiitake mushrooms, sesame seeds, and cashews. As for boron, you can get this valuable mineral from all fruits and vegetables.

449

The Bad News on Bone Loss

The most poignant symbol of age is the dowager's hump, the curving of the spine that develops after multiple spinal fractures. And that's a direct result of osteoporosis, notes Ethel Siris, M.D., director of the Toni Stabile Center for the Prevention and Treatment of Osteoporosis at Columbia-Presbyterian Medical Center in New York City. "You wind up with your head tilted down, so you can't look at the world the way you used to," she says. "You get shorter. Your clothes don't fit. Your rib cage moves very close to your pelvis. That means there's less room in your abdomen for your abdominal contents, so you get a belly."

When an older person does get a bone fracture, there's often a cost in terms of morale as well as a physical cost. People who have suffered a spinal fracture are often so terrified of having another that they are afraid to do anything or go anywhere, says Dr. Siris. You're more likely to stoop to hug your grandchildren, engage in a spontaneous session of lovemaking with your spouse, or go country line-dancing if you're not afraid that you'll crush a vertebra in your spine.

The other "hidden punishment" of osteoporosis is the potential loss of independence for older people. Sustaining a hip fracture, for example, almost always requires hospitalization and major surgery. While some people recover well enough to be independent again, 15 to 20 percent are still in a nursing home a year after their fractures.

Beware the Bone Robbers

Oddly enough, some nutrients that help build and maintain a strong skeleton seem to harm bone indirectly if you eat too much of them.

Protein, particularly the animal protein abundant in meat and eggs, is one such nutrient, says Dr. Brown. Unfortunately for advocates of milk, animal protein is abundantly present there, too. When the body breaks down protein, it produces sulfuric acid, which must be mixed with calcium before it can be passed in the urine. Consuming too much protein and too little calcium requires bones to release calcium to transport this acid out of the body. The result is calcium-poor bones.

How much protein is too much? The Daily Value for protein

450

is 50 grams for women and men who eat 2,000 calories per day, but the average American consumes nearly double that amount.

Consuming too much phosphorus may also contribute to bone loss by affecting the body's ratio of phosphorus to calcium. When you take in excess amounts of this mineral, calcium is pulled from the bones to balance the blood's elevated phosphorus levels, according to Dr. Brown. Excess phosphorus also binds with magnesium and prevents it from being fully absorbed. The government recommends that we consume equal amounts of calcium and phosphorus. But the average American, who consumes large amounts of phosphorus-laden soft drinks and processed foods, may take in up to 4,000 milligrams of phosphorus a day, about four times the recommended amount.

And then there's salt. Mounting evidence indicates that a high-salt diet causes large amounts of calcium to be excreted in the urine, effectively stealing calcium from the bones. Researchers at the University of Western Australia in Nedlands followed 124 postmenopausal women for two years and found that those who consumed the most sodium lost the most bone in their hips and ankles.

**know
what?**
The average American woman currently consumes 3,200 milligrams of sodium a day, 800 milligrams over the Daily Value.

Makeover Minutes

To Boost Your Calcium

To start beating osteoporosis right now, take some nutritional action based on the advice of experts. Here's what they say you can do.

Mix up some mega-milk. When it comes to calcium, milk really is the perfect food as long as you try to drink low-fat or skim milk—high in calcium, low in fat. One cup of skim milk contains 316 milligrams of calcium, and low-fat milk has 300 milligrams, which is even more than whole milk's 291 milligrams. Depending on your calcium needs, you would have to drink three to five glasses a day to get your Daily Value of calcium.

But there's a sneaky way to boost the calcium content of the

451

Drink Up—In Measured Amounts

Too much caffeine can contribute to bone loss, which is a strike against coffee and colas. And soft drinks contain phosphorus, another calcium-depleting substance. All in all, it might seem as though you should swear off those beverages.

But maybe you don't have to go cold turkey just yet. The idea that coffee and carbonated soft drinks deplete bone of calcium "is a myth that just doesn't die," says Patti Packard, R.D., a nutritionist at the Center for Osteoporosis Research at Creighton University in Omaha, Nebraska. In a study that appears to let coffee off the hook, researchers at the University of California, San Diego, studied the association between coffee drinking and bone density in 980 postmenopausal women. While women who drank two or more cups of coffee a day had significantly thinner bones, those who drank at least one glass of milk a day (along with the same amount of coffee) for most of their adult lives did not.

What about soft drinks? When researchers at the University of California, San Diego, examined the association between past and current consumption of carbonated beverages and bone loss in 1,000 postmenopausal women, they found that drinking a moderate amount of soda did not appear to adversely affect bone.

But moderation is necessary. The more coffee and soda you drink, the less room you have for healthier beverages like skim milk, says Packard. So drink no more than two cups of coffee or two servings of soda a day, she advises—and don't forget to get your calcium. If you drink coffee, you're better off with a latte than an espresso. One tablespoon of milk will offset the amount of calcium lost after drinking one cup of coffee, says Packard.

milk you drink: Stir one-quarter cup nonfat dry milk into one cup of your milk, mashed potatoes, soups, muffin mixes, or meat loaf. That adds 220 milligrams of calcium, says Packard.

Scream for extra calcium. Frozen yogurt was never a good source of calcium—until now. Dreyer's and Edy's Grand Ice Cream have reformulated their frozen yogurt to include more calcium. A four-ounce serving contains 450 milligrams of calcium—more than what's in an eight-ounce glass of skim milk. (Look for Edy's brand name if you live east of Colorado and

452

Dreyer's if you live in or west of Colorado, including Alaska, Hawaii, and Texas.)

Get juiced. If you just plain hate milk, say a prayer of gratitude for calcium-fortified orange juice. An eight-ounce glass of Tropicana Pure Premium with calcium contains 350 milligrams of calcium, 35 percent of the Daily Value. Tropicana Pure Premium with calcium is the only orange juice fortified with calcium citrate malate, which may be particularly beneficial.

Researchers at Miami Valley Laboratories in Cincinnati found that women who drank about nine ounces of orange juice fortified with calcium citrate malate absorbed 36 percent of its calcium. By contrast, from 25 to 30 percent of the calcium in milk is absorbed.

Open, sesame seeds. To turn a green salad into a bone builder, stud it with sesame seeds, which are a good source of calcium. One-half ounce contains 140.4 milligrams of calcium, 14 percent of the Daily Value.

Pucker up every morning. To help offset the bone-depleting effects of the typical American diet, drink the juice of one lime or lemon in a cup of hot water every day and consume two cups of vegetables with both lunch and dinner, recommends Dr. Brown. A diet heavy on meat, caffeine, sugar, and processed foods is highly acidic, and a high-acid diet can leach calcium from your bones, according to Dr. Brown.

Limes and lemons leave alkaline residues in the body. In fact, many fruits and vegetables have an acid/alkaline balance that is closer to the body's normal internal environment, says Dr. Brown. She also recommends regular consumption of alkaline foods, such as yams, sweet potatoes, lentils, kale, squash, sea vegetables, ginger, and most spices.

Forgo that extra cola. The next time you find yourself reaching for a diet soda, opt for a cup of herbal tea or a glass of skim milk instead. Most sodas contain both caffeine and phosphorus, and neither of these benefit your bones. Sodas are okay as long as they don't keep you from quenching your thirst with drinks like milk or calcium-fortified orange juice—as well as other calcium-fortified drinks, says Packard.

Lick your salt habit. In a country where the landscape is dot-

453

**know
what?**

Some re-
searchers
believe that
we need
significantly
more vitamin
D than the
Daily Value
of 400
international
units to
protect our
bones.

ted with burger huts and whole supermarket aisles are devoted
to salty snack foods, it can be difficult to avoid salt overload.
But many people aren't aware that high-salt foods include fast-
food burgers, canned soup, and many other prepared foods.
So read labels and try to eat fresh foods because they are naturally lower in salt than prepared and packaged foods, says
Packard.

Down some D, too. As we mentioned, we can't absorb calcium
without adequate vitamin D. And people who live in northern
states, where the sun's rays are weak for a large part of the year,
may need the most D of all. Researchers at the Jean Mayer U.S.
Department of Agriculture (USDA) Human Nutrition Research
Center on Aging at Tufts University in Boston conducted a study
to see whether consuming extra vitamin D would stave off bone
loss in postmenopausal women. The 247 women, who were already getting an average of 100 international units (IU) of vitamin D from their daily diets, received an additional 100 IU or
700 IU of vitamin D daily, along with 500 milligrams of calcium.
After two years, women who consumed the most vitamin D had
lost 1½ percent less bone in their hips than the women who had
consumed the least. This finding led the researchers to recommend consuming up to 800 IU a day.

To get this much vitamin D, you'll need to take supplements. But since high doses of vitamin D may have some side effects that cause health problems, you should consult your doctor before consuming more than 600 IU of vitamin D a day.
Consider taking a calcium supplement or multivitamin/mineral
supplement that contains 400 IU of vitamin D, then take another 400 IU of vitamin D later in the day, suggests Dr.
Mascitelli. But don't go much higher than that without your
doctor's recommendation.

Make like a snake. Since our bodies manufacture 80 to 90
percent of their vitamin D upon exposure to sunlight, what
more pleasant way to get your D than to bask in the sun? Sit in
the sun (without sunscreen) for 15 minutes, and you'll get your
Daily Value of vitamin D, says Packard. But be sure to apply sunscreen immediately after your 15 minutes of rays in order to
avoid skin damage.

For a Stronger Structure

In addition to the Makeover Minutes that put you on the road to stronger bones, you will do even better if you make more-lasting changes in your eating patterns. The first step is to follow the recommendations in Stop-Time Tactic No. 1 on page 3. In addition, here are some other nutritional strategies that can help.

Consume "whole" foods. Consuming whole grains, such as brown rice, barley, and whole-grain bread and pasta, can help you meet the Daily Value for such minerals as calcium, zinc, and magnesium. Bread, pasta, and low-fat baked goods made with white flour, for instance, contain virtually none of these nutrients, notes Dr. Brown. In the process of refining whole-wheat flour to make enriched white flour, the grain loses more than 80 percent of its vitamin B_6; more than 70 percent of its fiber, zinc, and potassium; and more than 60 percent of its calcium. So eat your sandwiches on whole-grain bread and opt for fiber-rich breakfast cereals. Though brown rice takes longer to cook than white, the extra wait is worth it. Or look for quick-cooking brown rice that is easy to prepare, she says.

Trade beef for beans. Research shows that people who consume plant-based diets have lower rates of cancer and heart disease than meat-eaters. All those grains and greens may benefit their bones as well. There is evidence that people who consume plant-based diets, including eggs and dairy products, have stronger, denser bones than their carnivorous counterparts.

In one nutrition study, researchers at Andrews University in Berrien Springs, Michigan, compared the bone density of 1,600 ovo-lactovegetarian women between the ages of 50 and 87 with that of their meat-eating sisters. They found that over a period of 40 years the meat-eating women had lost 35 percent of their bone mass, while the vegetarian women had lost only 18 percent.

Discover the joy of soy. Just a reminder: Soy is not only a supportive bone builder but also one of the top 20 foods for overall good health. (For more information, see the list of foods on

455

page 32.) If you have been reluctant to try soy foods like tofu and soy milk, do it for your skeleton's sake. Isoflavones—substances in soy that have estrogen-like effects in the body—may help protect your bones in a similar way as estrogen-replacement therapy.

As studies have shown, eating soy protein containing 140 milligrams of isoflavones resulted in a 2 percent increase in the bone mass of women's lumbar spines—effectively reducing their risk of spine fracture by as much as 50 percent. (For more information, see "Superfoods to Save Your Bones" on page 22.)

It's not hard to get the equivalent amount of isoflavones as the women who were included in the studies. One cup of tofu contains 70 milligrams of isoflavones, and one cup of soy milk has 30 milligrams. You can also buy isolated soy protein in powdered form in health food stores.

Take out calcium insurance. Virtually everyone can benefit from taking a daily calcium supplement, says Dr. Mascitelli. He recommends taking from 1,000 to 1,500 milligrams a day in supplement form. "Then, any calcium you're getting from your diet is icing on the cake," he says. (For tips on choosing a calcium supplement, see "Supplement Your Knowledge" on page 444.)

Revving Up for Bone Care

In 1980, Flora Lovely's bone-density test revealed bad news: The 49-year-old was losing bone. "They said that I was the perfect candidate for osteoporosis because I'm a small-boned, light-complected woman," says the Chelsea, Massachusetts, resident, now in her sixties. In the decade-plus following the discovery that she had osteoporosis, Lovely never suffered a fracture. And she wanted to keep it that way. So in 1991, she enrolled in a Tufts University study to find out whether a twice-a-week regimen of strength training would help protect her bones.

It did. After a year in the gym, Lovely—along with a group consisting of 19 other women—found that the bones in her hips and spine had actually become denser. Another group of women, a control group that did not exercise, lost bone during that time.

456

The Tufts study ended in 1993, but Lovely's strength-training program didn't. She still buckles weights around her wrists and ankles twice a week for 45 minutes of weight-bearing exercise. "It's something I'll do for the rest of my life," she says.

Bone adapts to physical stress by becoming denser and stronger, explains Miriam Nelson, Ph.D., associate chief of the Human Physiology Laboratory at the Jean Mayer USDA Human Nutrition Research Center on Aging at Tufts University and author of *Strong Women Stay Young*. Exercise also builds muscle, which cushions bone, and also improves balance, which reduces the risk of falls. "If you have a lot of muscle and good balance, you're at a much decreased risk for falling and breaking a hip," she says.

The best bone-strengthening workouts involve strength training along with weight-bearing, impact-loading exercises. Weight bearing means that you're on your feet, letting your skeleton support the weight of your body, and impact loading means that impact, or force, passes through your bones as you exercise. Walking, for instance, is a weight-bearing, impact-loading exercise.

Dr. Nelson stresses resistance training as the most effective component to preventing bone loss. In one of her studies (the same one in which Lovely was enrolled), a group of postmenopausal women from 50 to 70 years old lifted weights twice a week for 45 minutes. After a year, the density of the bones in their hips and spines had increased an average of 1 percent. In effect, they had the bones of women five years younger, says Dr. Nelson. By contrast, a second group of women told not to exercise lost from 2 to 2½ percent of their bone mass after a year.

Resistance training didn't just improve the condition of the women's bodies and bones. It transformed their spirits as well. While the nonexercising women had become 25 percent less active after a year, the activity level of the women who pumped iron increased by 27 percent.

Dr. Nelson was not surprised. "Once older people get stronger and improve balance, they naturally take up a more physically active lifestyle," she says. "Imagine being 65 and all of a sudden getting stronger, feeling great, sleeping better, feeling less depressed. It's a pretty amazing transformation."

Basketball Bones

Paul Saltman, Ph.D., professor of biology at the University of San Diego, has former NBA great Bill Walton—actually, Walton's left foot and ankle—to thank for helping him study the role of trace elements in healthy bone.

It was 1979. "I was at a sports medicine conference, and Bill Walton's physician was showing x-rays of Walton's foot and ankle," recalls Dr. Saltman. "The bone looked like Swiss cheese. I said to his physician afterward, quietly, 'Pardon me, it looks like your boy has osteoporosis.' He said, 'Men don't get osteoporosis.' I said, 'You can call it whatever you want—osteopenia, fragile bones—your boy's got fragile bones.' He said, 'Oh, yes, that's true.'"

Dr. Saltman asked if Walton, then playing for the San Diego Clippers, would allow him to test his blood level of trace elements. Manganese, copper,

and zinc are necessary to synthesize the reinforcing material in bones, including collagen and elastin to give structural strength, explains Dr. Saltman, and he suspected that Walton was deficient in these trace elements. "So Walton came in, and it turned out that his blood contained zero manganese, half the normal amount of zinc, and half the normal amount of copper," he recalls.

Walton's blood also contained an abnormally high amount of calcium, which meant that it was being pulled out of his bones. There were several possible explanations for Walton's deficiency, including his stringent diet and his active life as an athlete—since profuse sweating may deplete the body of trace elements.

Intrigued, Dr. Saltman and a colleague hypothesized that giving Walton extra amounts of trace

---

If you want to start a strength-training regimen, first check with your doctor before you begin. As for getting started, there are several ways to go. You can work out at home, using hand-held dumbbells and ankle weights, or you can join a health club or gym, says Dr. Nelson. If you choose to join a fitness center, Dr. Nelson recommends looking for Keiser, Nautilus, or Cybex strength-training machines. Other good equipment is made by Universal and Life Fitness. You should also make sure that the equipment is in good repair and that there are attentive instructors to help you.

elements might help heal his foot and ankle. So they concocted two beverages fortified with calcium, manganese, copper, and zinc and gave them to Walton to drink every day.

Two weeks after Walton began drinking these mineral "cocktails," his left foot began to heal. In another two months, he was playing for the Clippers regularly for the first time in two seasons.

By 1987, Dr. Saltman and his colleagues had tested their hypothesis in rats. They first deprived the animals of copper and manganese to give them osteoporosis, then halted the disease by dosing the rats with trace elements.

They also tested people. In one of their studies, they had two groups of postmenopausal women consume 1,000 milligrams of supplemental calcium. One group took calcium alone, while the second group consumed calcium along with trace minerals.

After two years, the spines of the women taking calcium alone had lost bone more slowly than they would have otherwise. But the group who consumed supplemental manganese, copper, and zinc along with the calcium showed no bone loss at all.

While most of us will never have as severe a deficiency in trace elements as Walton did, chances are that you're not getting the recommended amounts of these bone-healthy nutrients. To ensure that you get enough, take a multivitamin/mineral supplement that contains the Daily Value for these trace minerals: 2 milligrams each of manganese and copper and 15 milligrams of zinc, advises Dr. Saltman. "Think of a supplement as a nutritional insurance policy," he says.

Long-Term Tactics

To Keep You in Good Standing

If strength training isn't your thing, you can still protect your bones with other types of physical activity. Consider these other bone-preserving workouts.

Tai one on. The better your balance, the better your odds of avoiding a bone-shattering fall. And that's one good reason to learn tai chi. Research has shown that this graceful Chinese discipline, often called moving meditation, significantly reduces the risk of falling.

459

Are Steroids Depleting Your Bones?

If you take corticosteroids for a chronic condition, but your doctor hasn't recommended a bone-density test, ask for one. Pronto.

"Without question, anyone taking oral corticosteroids for more than 90 days should have a baseline bone-density study," says Robert Mascitelli, M.D., a member of the National Osteoporosis Foundation in Bethesda, Maryland, and director of the Osteoporosis Prevention and Treatment program at East 72nd Street Health Management Specialists in New York City. If you haven't yet started on the drug, but it's likely that treatment will extend beyond 90 days, "I would not wait; get the bone-density study before you start treatment," he says.

Corticosteroids, used to treat a variety of chronic diseases including asthma, inflammatory bowel disease, multiple sclerosis, and rheumatoid arthritis, can cause bone loss—as much as 10 to 20 percent in the first six months of use. More than 30 million Americans are estimated to have a condition commonly treated with long-term corticosteroids, which increase bone loss, reduce the formation of new bone, and lower levels of bone-protecting estrogen and testosterone. As many as 25 percent eventually suffer a fracture from thinning bones.

Besides undergoing a bone-density test, there's even more that you can do to protect your bones from the effects of corticosteroids. If you are a postmenopausal woman, for example, you may want to consider either estrogen-replacement therapy or, if you're uncomfortable with the idea of taking hormones, a nonhormonal osteoporosis-preventing drug such as alendronate sodium (Fosamax), says Dr. Mascitelli. The American College of Rheumatology also recommends that people on long-term corticosteroid treatment consume 1,500 milligrams of calcium and 800 international units (IU) of vitamin D a day.

But since high doses of vitamin D may have some side effects that cause health problems, you should consult your doctor before consuming more than 600 IU of vitamin D per day.

To find out whether tai chi is really effective, researchers at Emory University in Atlanta had one group of people age 70 and older take a 15-week course in tai chi to improve their balance, while a second group used computerized balance training. When the study was over, the tai chi group was

47½ percent less likely than the other group to suffer multiple falls.

As a first step in getting familiar with tai chi, have a look at books such as *Step-by-Step Tai Chi* by Master Lam Kam Chuen. To find a tai chi class, look under "karate and other martial arts instruction" in your local yellow pages.

Swim bones strong. If you would rather work out in water than on land, here's some good news: Water exercise, which is neither weight bearing nor impact loading, may still help preserve bone. Researchers in Japan had 35 women take one 45-minute water-workout class, once a week, in which they performed simple arm and leg movements, using the water as resistance. A year later, all of the women had gained bone density in their spines.

Women who had just begun the workout showed the most gains; their bone mass increased about ¾ of 1 percent. (Women who had been doing the program an average of three years had higher bone mass from the beginning, which explained the different rate of change.)

Like the women in Dr. Nelson's study, Japanese women reported that they felt more upbeat and had become more physically active as a result of activity in the study.

Take your bones for a stroll. When you walk, the heel of your foot hits the ground with a force equivalent to 1.3 times your body weight. All that pounding is good for bones. Researchers at the Jean Mayer USDA Human Nutrition Research Center on Aging at Tufts University polled a group of 239 postmenopausal women between the ages of 43 and 72 on their exercise habits. They also measured the women's bone mass twice over the course of a year. The researchers found that women who walked about a mile a day (7.5 miles a week) had denser bones than women who walked less than a mile a week.

Butts, Booze, and Bones

If you smoke or drink a lot, you have probably heard your fill of warnings against these health-damaging habits. So maybe bone loss just seems like an additional cost.

461

Even so, the cost of these indulgences in terms of bone loss is very high.

With every puff of a cigarette, a bit more bone goes up in smoke. "There's no question that smoking is a risk factor for osteoporosis," says Dr. Mascitelli. Smoking appears to lower levels of bone-protecting testosterone in men and estrogen in women, which accelerates bone loss. In one study, researchers in Australia studied the bone mass of 41 pairs of female twins. They found that the bone mass of the twin who smoked more heavily was 2 percent lower at the lumbar spine and 1 percent lower at the hip for every 10 "pack-years" of smoking. (To get pack-years, the researchers multiplied the number of years of smoking by the average number of cigarettes smoked per day and divided by 20.)

Even more striking was the study's conclusion: Women who smoke a pack of cigarettes a day throughout adulthood will enter menopause with an average of 5 to 10 percent less bone mass than women who don't smoke. Dr. Mascitelli's advice: "Obviously, throw out the cigarettes."

Excessive alcohol consumption is another potential bone robber. Alcoholism, for instance, clearly takes its bone toll: Researchers have long known that alcoholics are more likely to develop osteoporosis than the general population. And since people who drink to excess are often malnourished, they don't consume enough bone-building nutrients. Excessive drinking may also "poison" osteoblasts, the cells responsible for making new bone.

Moderate drinking poses no threat to bone, however, and it may even help. "There are a few very nice studies that show that two to three ounces of alcohol per day is actually beneficial," says Dr. Mascitelli. "Many of our patients are delighted to know that a glass or two of wine in the evening is perfectly safe."

Whole-Body Protection

Protect Yourself
from Pain

Before you could walk or talk—even before you knew you felt hungry or needed a diaper change—you could tell something was wrong.

Perhaps you rolled over on a toy, touched something hot, or felt a bit of indigestion. Without knowing the actual word for what you experienced, you knew darn well when something hurt. Then with an earth-shattering scream, you probably let somebody else know about it, too.

You may not think so when you feel it, but pain is a good thing—your body's natural alarm system. You're born with this system to protect you from danger. Your body catapults a message through the twists and turns of your nervous system to the brain, which then sends you a quick reply that grabs your attention. "It gets you to stop what you are doing and makes you deal with the problem. It's a survival mechanism," says Robert J. Gatchel, Ph.D., professor of psychiatry and rehabilitation science at the University of Texas Southwestern Medical Center at Dallas.

Despite pain's wonderful contribution to the survival of humankind, however, none of us goes out of our way to find it. And as you get older, your body starts to wear down, says Dr. Gatchel, leaving you susceptible to more jolting reminders that your sensitive alarm system is still in top working order.

Much of the pain that accompanies aging seems to emanate from bones and muscles that just do not work as well as they used to. "We see more cumulative effects from the strain of doing the same kind of work over and over again as we reach

463

our forties," says Fred N. Davis, M.D., vice president of Michigan Pain Consultants in Grand Rapids.

Preventing the Wearing and Tearing

Just like any alarm system, pain can go a bit haywire. Sometimes pain sensations overload your nervous system. Your body responds by sending out more pain signals—even if there isn't a real reason. "Pains that go on for long, long periods of time are bodily defenses that have gone out of control and start having negative effects on the person. Just as taking too much of anything can be harmful—the same thing holds true for chronic pain," observes Jayson A. Hymes, M.D., medical director of Conservative Care Specialists Medical Group in Beverly Hills, California.

But getting older doesn't mean you have to suffer more pain—it just means you have to work a little harder to prevent it. "It's a misconception that aging is inevitably associated with pain," says Margaret Caudill, M.D., Ph.D., co-director of the Arnold Pain Center at the Beth Israel Deaconess Medical Center West in Boston and author of *Managing Pain Before It Manages You.*

Being pain-free will also keep your lifestyle freed up for all the things you want to enjoy in your golden years. Chronic pain can wear down your zest for life and can even age you prematurely, Dr. Hymes says. "People who have a pain-related lifestyle may come to obsess on their pain. They clearly tend to age faster from both the psychological and physical standpoints. Physically, they can become invalids, disconnected from life. And they will not be getting the exercise they need to stand the rigors of aging. Mentally, they can become more withdrawn and angry."

Exercise, stretching, and relaxation methods tend to minimize many stress-related symptoms including pain. But specific pain problems require specific treatment plans. You can prevent many of the most common pain problems—headaches, neck pain, and back pain—by taking a few extra steps in your pain-prevention program, says Dr. Caudill.

know what?

A study by McNeil Pharmaceuticals found that more than 17 percent of Americans—34 million—suffer from mild to moderate chronic pain. Of those who suffer pain, 56 percent have lower back pain, 46 percent have arthritic pain, and 27 percent suffer from mild to moderate chronic migraine headaches.

464

Showing Some Flexibility

You have heard the saying "No pain, no gain," when it comes to exercise. Well, when it comes to pain, this saying should be turned around. If you are out of shape, you are more likely to be in a lot more chronic pain than you ever would be during an aerobics class or a long-distance run.

With regular exercise you can build up muscle tone and increase your flexibility. A fit body can better sustain the wear and tear of daily living and make you less likely to get hurt playing sports, lifting heavy objects, or digging in the garden, says Dr. Hymes.

Also, a well-conditioned muscle bounces back from an injury much faster than an out-of-shape one. "If you are fit, your injuries will tend to be less severe, and you will most likely recover much faster," adds Dan M. Mankoff, M.D., a partner with Michigan Pain Consultants.

In addition to building strength, exercise starts your brain's production of natural painkilling chemicals called endorphins, the body's own version of over-the-counter pain medicine. "I know a colleague who had bad facial pain. She found that running was the only way to relieve her headaches. So she ran all the time and became an accomplished marathon runner," says Mark L. Gostine, M.D., president of Michigan Pain Consultants.

Makeover Minutes

To Start the Ball Rolling

You have to get away from believing that exercise means going into a gym every day, says Shane P. Watson, a former clinical physical therapist and educator with Michigan Pain Consultants and current president of RE-PT Physical Therapy Consultancy Service in New South Wales, Australia. Sprinkle your day with one- and two-minute exercises by making a few small changes to your routine.

Take a walk. Simply putting one foot in front of the other de-

465

creases your chances of pain and suffering. "Even just walking regularly has been found to improve health," Dr. Caudill says. Walk 15 minutes in the morning, 10 minutes after lunch, and another 10 minutes before dinner. Take a nightcap walk a few hours after dinner if time is a problem. Get some friends involved and make it a group exercise.

Do the small things. Park farther away from the office or the supermarket so that you have a longer walk. Take the stairs at work instead of the elevator. Challenge yourself on the stairs by taking two steps at a time. Take a break and walk some laps around the office. "Something is better than nothing," Dr. Caudill says.

Try a beginner program. Start small and work your way up. Do something you enjoy for 10 to 15 minutes a few times a week, suggests Dr. Caudill. As you feel more fit, increase your time and distance.

Long-Term Tactics
To Stay on Course

When you get into longer workouts, they should be fun and enjoyable so that you stick with them in the long term. You're trying to prevent pain—not create more suffering by pushing yourself too hard. "Staying in shape and moderation go hand in hand. A lot of people think staying in shape means excessively exercising. It doesn't—especially when we get older," Dr. Gatchel says.

Here are some things that you can do regularly for fun as well as relief.

Do the bike stuff. Start by doing 1 to 2 miles, three times a week. Work your way to 3 to 5 miles, and then 6 to 8, suggests Dr. Gostine. Once you feel as though you can tackle that easily, increase your miles from 6 to 9 miles, riding at least four times a week. When you reach your peak, move it up to 10 to 15 miles, four times a week.

466

Be like Fred or Ginger. Dancing the night away is just as good a workout as a step-aerobic class. Sign up for dance classes, Dr. Caudill suggests. You can have fun and improve your chances against pain at the same time. Look into all kinds of dance forms—ballroom, line dancing, international.

Enroll in a yoga class. Yoga combines exercise with stretching, another activity that protects you from pain. These age-old techniques reduce stress as well, Dr. Caudill says. Sign up for a class at a local community center or gym. Study other ancient exercises such as tai chi, a Chinese system of physical exercises especially designed for meditation.

Get wet. Want the workout without the sweat? Dive in—the water's fine. Working out in water spares your joints from the constant pounding of aerobics, Dr. Caudill says, and the extra buoyancy allows you a wider range of motion. If you already feel pain because of an injury, water aerobics enables you to work out without aggravating the injury.

Keep moving. If you are recovering from some injury, get moving again as soon as you can. The longer you stay sedentary, the more your muscles will grow weak, leaving you even more prone to pain, says Dr. Gatchel. "If we don't use muscles, they go away. If you have an injured knee, for instance, and you don't move around for weeks, all of the supportive muscles—the thighs and calves, for example—are no longer there. When we go to use the knee, we don't have that support structure to protect it, and we are more prone to reinjure it. It develops into a vicious cycle."

Under the supervision of your doctor or physical therapist, rest for only a minimum amount of time (usually 48 hours) after an injury, Dr. Gatchel advises. After that, move around carefully and keep active without overdoing it.

Stretch to Ward Off Pain

As a species, humans were created to roam free in the wild, hunting and gathering food. Nature didn't foresee that we would plunk our bodies in desk chairs for hours on end. "We are not designed to be sedentary individuals," Watson says.

know what?

Do your joints dread the drizzle? People who have chronic joint pain are likely to feel worse when the weather turns cooler and damper, according to a study that included more than 500 people from San Diego, Nashville, Boston, and Worcester, Massachusetts.

467

Your muscles don't react very well when the most lively part of your day is a walk to the coffeemaker. If you already have some stress and pain and you are seated upright and immobile every day, your muscles recoil instinctively. After years of tensing up, those muscles become chronically over-tense, and they may even get shorter.

Stretching exercises may make your muscles less prone to spasm and better able to respond to normal daily usage. "Instead of taking pills, people can take a short break and stretch their muscles," Dr. Hymes says. And he has found that the stretching exercises can be as effective as pills in counteracting certain types of pain.

Daily stretching doesn't require a major time commitment. If you just grab the opportunities whenever you can, you'll discover how a few minutes of stretching can really make a difference. But remember, consistency is the key to a successful stretching regimen. A regular schedule of short stretch and exercise breaks is more beneficial than longer sessions performed infrequently. To get the most out of loosening up, see Stop-Time Tactic No. 4 on page 87.

Makeover Minutes

For Better Stretches

Whether you do small, quick stretches throughout the day or more-extensive stretching routines, you'll want to make sure that you do enough to stay limber. Here are some ideas to get you started.

Take breaks. Buy a timer and put it on your desk, in your workspace, or wherever you do anything that places stress on the muscles. Set the timer to go off every hour for your stretch breaks. "Just get up for three to five minutes and stretch your arms and legs," Dr. Hymes says. "The few minutes you spend doing that can make a big difference in your overall pain outlook."

The Medium Is the Massage

Refuge from muscle pain could lie in the palm of your hand—or someone else's. The gentle, yet deep rubbing, kneading, and pushing of massaging fingers can set you free from a good deal of discomfort.

"It's really pretty elementary. Muscle pain is caused by a lack of oxygen to the tissue—a lack of circulation. The rubbing and the kneading get the oxygen flowing and restart the circulation to the muscles," says Will Green, president of the International Massage Association and owner of Georgetown Bodyworks in Washington, D.C.

A good massage can loosen those muscles right up, says Robert J. Gatchel, Ph.D., professor of psychiatry and rehabilitation science at the University of Texas Southwestern Medical Center at Dallas. "A tense muscle is sort of like tying a knot and pulling it really, really tight. When you go to untie it, you have to work at it. If you keep working at it, the muscle will rebound into a relaxation mode."

Those magical fingers can also rub out some of the stress that you store in your muscles. Stress tenses up the muscles, leaving open a pathway for pain and soreness. But a massage can calm you down and work out some of life's daily strains. "Tension is a major killer when it comes to pain," Green says, adding that some of his clients are the most stressed-out people in the country—politicians and a litany of big-time Washington lawyers.

What's the best way to find a quality massage therapist? Ask your friends. "Word of mouth is the best source of a massage professional," Green says. And the therapist should be accredited with a professional organization—the International Massage Association, the American Massage Therapy Association, or the Associated Bodywork and Massage Professionals Association.

But you don't need to call up a professional every time you feel some pain. Your very own fingers can do the trick. "Any time you rub and knead your muscles, you'll help alleviate pain," Green says.

For example, Green recommends the following self-massage relief after a day of strenuous typing.

- Lay your hand flat on the desk, palm down.
- Using the fingers on your other hand, rub the area that hurts.

And there you go—you've just given yourself a pain-relief massage.

Extend your body. Do a full-body stretch at least once a week to find out which muscles are tight, then stretch those muscles once a day, says Barry Carlin, a chiropractor and injury-prevention consultant from Future Industrial Technologies in Santa Barbara, California. When planning your stretches, start with your head and work down, says Carlin. Make a list of your daily 'custom' stretches for that week. Hold each stretch for five relaxing breaths. "By finding your tight muscles, then relaxing them, you will reduce stress and fatigue, prevent injury, and enhance your future health," says Carlin.

Do some preemptive stretching. Don't delay stretching until the moment when you begin to feel pain. Instead, get a jump on pain by stretching a bit each morning when you get up and again before you log on to your computer at work, suggests Watson. Whenever you feel muscle tension, it's a signal telling you that pain may develop—so take that as a warning to stop and stretch. Also, make sure to limber up with stretches before you do any heavy lifting and before you exercise.

Sit Back and Relax

Stress and pain both play their parts in a vicious cycle. The more anxious you get, the lower your pain threshold becomes. Then you feel more pain, and that's likely to make you even more anxious. If this cycle goes unchecked, it can wear you down both physically and mentally.

Stress lowers your natural defenses. When your muscles tense up, you are more prone to injury than someone who is completely relaxed. Your immune system is affected, too: When stressed-out, you become susceptible to disease. Also, when you are battling anxiety, you're less likely to live a healthy lifestyle, eating right and exercising regularly—the habits that normally help keep you pain-free.

"I've heard this so many times," Dr. Caudill says. "People say to me, 'I was just leaning over to brush my teeth, and my back went out.' Invariably, you find out they were under increased stress at this time in their lives. They have had marital problems or problems with their children. They have been at a level of in-

470

creased tension, and then—whammo!—something simple is the straw that breaks the camel's back."

Besides the physical hurt you are facing, your mind is likely to be flooded with thoughts of "Why am I in pain? Will it ever go away? What am I going to do?" These reflections snowball, raising your agony level. "Pain is a stress that wears at the body, mind, and spirit without people knowing it," Dr. Caudill observes.

Relaxation techniques protect you from pain in two ways: First, they keep your stress level down, guarding you from increased tension. Second, when you are in the throes of pain, these exercises help reduce its intensity, thus reducing your stress. When you can calm yourself down, you begin to break the vicious cycle.

The simplest relaxation technique is deep breathing. Just take a few very deep breaths every few hours or so—and as you do so, relax your shoulders, your arms and stretch. You will find that you can't remain tense and breathe deeply at the same time. "Check in with yourself on a regular basis so that you can let the tension go, which you can do by taking a deep breath," advises Dr. Caudill. "Do these mini-relaxations throughout the day so that you don't have a whole 12-hour-day stress level in your body before you attempt to unwind."

Long-Term Tactics

To Melt the Discomfort

With a little attention, relaxation exercises can become a habit, says Dr. Caudill. Like brushing your teeth and taking vitamins, maybe stress relief needs to become part of your everyday lifestyle to help protect you from aches and pains. If you think so, here are some techniques that can work wonders.

Go somewhere great. Picture yourself in the cool, breezy mountains, sitting by a babbling stream. Or imagine yourself walking along a sunny beach, the sand sifting through your toes.

471

Who's Complaining?

Some time ago, President Clinton proudly proclaimed to the American people, "I feel your pain." That might be an agonizing proposition for the commander in chief. According to a study at Stanford University, Americans feel—or at least complain about—a lot more pain than other cultures do.

While working for the United Nations in Vietnam years ago, Eugene Carragee, M.D., associate professor of orthopedic surgery at Stanford University, noticed that Vietnamese patients had a high threshold for pain. "These people received very little narcotics after surgery, and they didn't seem to mind," he says.

So he decided to compare the pain reactions of 25 patients in the United States to another 25 in Vietnam. Dr. Carragee chose to compare people from the two cultures who had one par-ticular type of injury—a broken femur bone in the leg. No matter what culture you live in, he figured, breaking your leg really hurts. But despite the "equivalent" pain, he found some startling differences in the way people in the two cultures deal with that pain.

Though the Americans patients received pain medication dosages about 30 times higher than the Vietnamese, 80 percent of the Americans still weren't happy with the level of drugs. Only 8 percent of the Vietnamese patients felt the same way. "Most of the Americans thought they had received too little medication, despite the fact that compared with the Vietnamese they had received a huge amount," Dr. Carragee says. Several Vietnamese, he adds, actually believed they had received too much medication.

Though you can't physically transport yourself to these places on the strength of wishing, you *can* get to the destinations in your own mind, says Dr. Caudill.

Imagery calms you down, relaxes your muscles, and even increases your blood flow, says Dr. Caudill. Just create a peaceful image in your mind and place yourself in the picture. Don't just think of what it looks like—imagine the smells and the sounds as well as the sights.

Tackle your pain with imagery. Sometimes, imagery can help you "capture" pain and conquer it as well. Dr. Caudill has a patient who pictures her migraine headaches as a big red ball.

472

Then he asked the subjects, "Did this hurt about what you figured it would if you broke your leg?" A whopping 85 percent of Americans responded that it hurt much more than they thought it would. Fewer than 4 percent of the Vietnamese people considered the pain that severe. Also, unlike the Vietnamese, the Americans had definite ideas about why they felt so much more pain than they thought they should: they blamed their medical care.

The difference between the two cultures was not how much pain they felt, Dr. Carragee says, but how much pain they think they should have felt. "Since both groups of patients had the same type of fracture, the stimulation that prompted the pain was the same for the Americans as it was for the Vietnamese. But what they thought about the pain was very different," says Dr. Carragee. The Vietnamese patients understood that having a broken leg was no walk in the park, while the Americans held strongly to their belief that medication and medical care could control almost any pain.

How can Dr. Carragee's study help you the next time you have some kind of injury—a broken toe, a sprained ankle, or even something that requires surgery? Set realistic pain expectations for yourself, he suggests. "A lot of the discontentment with the American medical system is based on inappropriate expectations, such as 'I'm going to have this thing done, and everything is going to be fine.' Whereas the doctor or surgeon is thinking, 'I'm going to do this thing, and it's going to make them 25 percent better,'" Dr. Carragee says.

Whenever she feels a migraine coming on, she imagines the red ball behind a glass wall. Then, in her own mind, she builds an igloo around the ball. "Many times she is able to abort the headache this way," she says.

Repeat after yourself. Practice an exercise that can elicit the relaxation response, to teach yourself how to calm down when you feel stress and anger coming on, Dr. Caudill suggests. "We all have this innate ability to counteract stress," she says.

First, pick a quiet place where you won't be bothered. Make yourself comfortable, lying down with a pillow under your head. Breathe deeply, and with each exhalation, silently repeat a word

473

The Sakhalin
Ainu people
of Japan give
different an-
imal names to
headaches
depending on
how they feel.
"Bear"
headaches
feel like the
heavy
sounding
steps of a
bear; the
"deer"
headaches
feel like the
much lighter
sounds of a
running deer;
and
"woodpecker"
headaches
feel like a
woodpecker's
constant
pounding into
a tree trunk.

or phrase. It can be something with no meaning, or it can be a word or a phrase that has significance. Continue to repeat the phrase for 10 to 20 minutes. If you repeatedly practice, you'll learn how to start the day relaxed and how to stay relaxed just by repeating the words that bring about this response.

Distract yourself. Pain by its nature grabs your attention and forces you to focus on your problem. But all that attention can actually make the pain worse. "If we start focusing on it, we become more aware of it," Dr. Gatchel says. Count the ceiling tiles on the wall, focus on your inhalations and exhalations, or look at a pretty picture to get your mind far off your discomfort. Even watching television or taking a walk can get your mind off your pain.

Relax one muscle at a time. Allow some quiet time for yourself once or twice a day to loosen up your muscles and calm your mind. The following relaxation procedure is suggested by Dr. Gostine.

- Sit with your feet elevated. Clench each group of muscles in your feet and lower legs. When you clench, hold until the count of 10, then relax.
- Move on up your body, from your calf muscles to your front and back thighs, then your hands, forearms, chest, shoulders, and neck.

"It's a very good way of getting in a meditative mood. After you tense all of the muscle groups, then you just let it all out. You just relax," Dr. Gostine says.

De-stress before you hit the pillow. To protect yourself from pain, you consistently need a good night's sleep. But worries, fears, and stress can keep you tossing and turning all night. Get them out of your mind before you hit the sack. "Using relaxation techniques before bedtime will help people get into a more deep and peaceful sleep," Dr. Caudill says. If relaxation techniques don't work for you, write down your thoughts on paper. "Getting all those stresses out on paper can do amazing things for eliminating the unresolved issues that spin around our brains before we go to sleep," she says.

Whole-Body Protection

Heal Your Head

It may feel as if your brain is about to explode with the force of Mount St. Helens, but your pounding headache has nothing to do with gray matter. When the blood vessels and the muscles surrounding your brain get irritated, they fight back by making your head feel like a bongo drum.

Everyone gets hit with a splitting headache from time to time. In fact, more than 40 million people in the United States have experienced a severe headache at least once, and about 16 million of us suffer from headaches frequently. But whether you get a headache once a year or once a day, you can take some preventive measures to help keep them away or stop them in their tracks.

Makeover Minutes

To Pamper the Noggin

Take the first steps to eliminating your next headache while sitting at your desk, watching TV, or going to the grocery store. Here are the quick tactics.

Train your teeth to stay apart. Are you grinding your teeth as you read this? Some of us do it instinctively. But whenever your teeth clench, you create tension that builds right into a headache. "Once I tell people that their teeth are not supposed to be together, they ask me, 'What are you talking about? I thought you were supposed to have your teeth together,'" says Michael L. Gelb, D.D.S., director of the TMD (temporomandibular disorder) and orofacial pain program at the New York University College of Dentistry in New York City.

Dr. Gelb suggests keeping your lips together, but your teeth apart to prevent headaches. "If your teeth are not clenched together, you're basically relaxing your muscles," he says.

Send your tongue to the roof. Believe it or not, you can use your tongue to keep your head relaxed. Place the tip of your

475

know what?

Nigerians use phrases like "it seems as if pepper were put into my head" or "things like ants keep on creeping in various parts of my brain" to describe different kinds of headaches.

tongue to the roof of your mouth, right behind your upper row of front teeth. (This place is called the rugae.) The reason? "If your tongue is there on the roof of your mouth, you won't clench," Dr. Gelb says.

Quit the nail-biters' club. You might as well be grinding your teeth together with all your might if you're among the nail-biters of the world, Dr. Gelb says. Any oral fixation facilitates a headache by creating tension in the jaw. "Chewing gum, sucking on pens, and licking your lips will all contribute to the perpetuation of headaches and sometimes even daily headaches," he says. "A lot of people are like this—they need something in their mouths. They have to be clenching, and they are not even aware of it."

Ice your head. When you have a headache, it sometimes helps to apply ice. Ice treatment is especially beneficial for headaches caused by muscle, nerve, and joint irritation, says Dr. Gostine, because the cold anesthetizes the nerves causing pain and tension in the muscles.

But if the thought of using ice cubes makes your blood run cold, you might be more comfortable with a bag of frozen peas.

"Take the peas out of the freezer, bang the bag a few times with your fists, and then you can mold it into the back and side of your head," Dr. Gostine says.

Long-Term Tactics
To Track Down the Ache

Along with the quick-and-easy variety of tactics, you can also try out a long-term approach to help relieve your headache pain, says Dr. Gostine. Changing your diet and sleeping habits can make a big difference—and so can some other lifestyle changes. Here's how to get on track for more permanent headache relief.

Keep a headache diary. Each time you feel a headache coming on, reach for a pen and paper. Record all the details about

476

your headache, Dr. Gostine suggests. The diary will help you identify—and then avoid—headache triggers. "Maybe every time you watch *Gilligan's Island* or have to deal with a neighbor, you get a headache," he says. "Or maybe every time you eat fish, you get a headache. A diary will help you find those triggers."

Stay away from the food triggers. Avoid the classic headache triggers. Alcohol, caffeine, chocolate, and highly fermented foods such as blue cheese can start a drumbeat pounding inside your head. Women should be especially wary of these foods around their menstrual periods, Dr. Gostine cautions, because that's when many women are more prone to headaches.

Don't light up. Reaching for a cigarette to stave off a headache will only bring you more misery, Dr. Gostine says. To prevent headaches, you want to keep the blood vessels from getting tight by avoiding smoking. Try a relaxation technique or walk around the block instead of taking a puff.

Be prepared for menstrual changes. Women who suffer from the monthly agony of menstrual headaches can seek solace in magnesium and calcium. Your menstrual changes deplete the body of these two minerals, which help act as muscle relaxants and prevent the tightening of your blood vessels.

Take 400 milligrams of magnesium and 1,500 milligrams of calcium a day beginning three days before your period, Dr. Gostine advises. And he recommends that women continue taking their supplements throughout their periods. Be aware, however, that doctors advise against taking supplemental magnesium if you have heart or kidney problems.

Go prone. If you feel a big migraine come on, why not go to bed? "Sleep is a time-honored treatment for migraine headaches," Dr. Gostine says. But you need more than a catnap. "We're talking about three to four hours. So go to bed early and sleep it off," he says.

Watch where you're headed. When you snooze face down, your head is at a 90-degree angle all night long. "That is just a horrible way to sleep at night," Dr. Gostine says. When you place a lot of strain on your neck that way, it builds up pressure on the muscles leading to your head.

477

If you're waking up with a headache, this could be the prime reason. Make a conscious effort to sleep on your back or side.

Change your pillow. Throw out Grandma's old feather pillow. When your head sinks into the feathers, or you turn and lie on your side, your neck ends up in a stressful position that can cause a headache in the morning. A good pillow should fill the hollow between the tip of your shoulder and the bottom of your head, Dr. Gostine says. Next time you're in the bedding department, check out some foam pillows of various sizes until you find one that suits you.

Makeover Minutes

Stave Off Stiffness

If you have stared at a computer screen for long hours or watched an epic saga from the front row of your local cinema, you're probably familiar with the stiff, painful feeling you get afterward when you try to turn your head. That's all the more unsettling when you consider that your neck has a very important job to perform—namely, keeping your head on straight. After a while, the neck muscles get tired of all this head-holding activity and start to tense up, Dr. Gelb observes. That's when you put your hand at the back of your neck to try and coax it to loosen up.

But you don't have to wait until you have a stiff neck to begin battling neck pain. The key to preventing it is to keep the neck muscles from getting tense in the first place. Try these simple stretches designed specifically for the neck muscles. If you just remember to stretch your neck a few minutes a day, you'll save yourself hours of pain in the long run.

Smell your armpit. Gently tuck your left arm behind your back. Then move your nose toward your right armpit, as if you were trying to smell it. Meanwhile, reach down and behind with your left hand—as though you were reaching for the floor. "You'll feel a nice pull on the left side and the back of the neck,"

478

Watson says. Sustain the stretch for 10 seconds. Repeat about four times, then switch sides.

Listen to your shoulder. Tilt your head to the right side, as if you were trying to place your ear on your shoulder. With your right hand, gently pull down your head toward the shoulder. At the same time, keep the left shoulder lowered. Hold for about 10 seconds. Repeat about four times, then stretch the other side the same way, suggests Watson.

Tuck in your chin. Find an object that's at eye level and stare at it while you tuck in your chin by pulling your head back to create a double chin. (When you do the chin tuck, don't lower your head.) Without straining, hold this position for about 10 seconds. Repeat four to six times. Sure, you'll look something like a pigeon when you do the stretch correctly, but the indignity of the posture is worth the payoff. "It gets to the muscles under the back of the skull," Watson says.

Long-Term Tactics
For Neck Correction

Sometimes self-awareness is your ace in the hole. Some of your normal daily habits may be leading to neck ache—but if you institute some consistent changes, your neck will feel better in no time. Here are long-term approaches to help make life easier on your neck.

Keep your head up. Your neck strains really hard to make sure that your head doesn't fall right down to the ground. And that means some major weight lifting since a 10- to 15-pound head weighs about as much as a bowling ball.

To save your neck from agony, keep your head straight up as much as possible. "If the head is in front of the body, it feels like it even weighs more. Your ears should be over your shoulders. Most of us have our ears way in front of the shoulders," Dr. Gelb says.

Learn how to breathe. Breathe in. Breathe out. Seems simple

479

(continued on page 482)

"Ouch" Is Not Enough

"It hurts." Two words that send millions of people a year to their doctors looking for answers. But you have to say a lot more than that if you want your doctor to help. You need to get down to the cause of your agony. "You have to be a little bit of a detective about yourself with pain," says Fred N. Davis, M.D., vice president of Michigan Pain Consultants in Grand Rapids.

First, Dr. Davis suggests, be thorough. Think about the when, where, and why of your pain. When does the pain start, and when does it end? What did you do right before it struck you?

To help the doctor help you, expand your vocabulary, Dr. Davis advises. "It hurts here" isn't as enlightening as "The pain covers my legs like a stocking" or "It's a sharp, sudden feeling." Without a detailed and accurate description of your ailments, doctors can't really get a feel for what's going on inside your body.

To help get it all in order, write out the details of your pain before you ever set foot in the doctor's office. "Sometimes it is easy to jumble up your symptoms with how it all started, and you never really get to a good descrip-tion of what you are feeling. So before you go to the doctor, write this down. It helps if you have things listed," Dr. Davis says.

Here's a 16-point list of information that a doctor needs to diagnose your pain, suggested by Dr. Davis.

1. Location: Where is the pain in the body? Pinpoint the area. "If it is in the leg, which part of the leg—the front, the thigh, the buttock?" Dr. Davis asks.
2. Coverage: Does it cover like a stocking or is it a narrow stripe?
3. Radiating quality: Tell your doctor where pain travels. "Does it start some place and then go anywhere? That's really important," says Dr. Davis.
4. Consistency: Does the pain come and go, or is it always present?
5. Influencing factors: "What activities make it worse? Bending, twisting, lifting, stair climbing, walking, lying down, or doing key job tasks? Do certain foods increase pain? Does sexual intercourse?"
6. What helps the pain: Tell your doctor what you do that lessens

Whole-Body Protection

the pain, such as lying down or changing positions.

7. **Time of day:** When does the pain hit? Is there a pattern?

8. **Weather:** Are you more likely to get the pain on a cloudy or rainy day? When the temperature shoots up? When the barometer plummets? Try to keep track.

9. **Where it happens:** Dr. Davis says that doctors need to know this, in case there's something in your home or work environment that might be related to painful episodes.

10. **Other bodily functions:** Does the pain prevent you from doing things such as going to the bathroom or having sex?

11. **Effect on sleep:** Dr. Davis notes that with some kinds of pain, you might have a problem getting to sleep, but once you are asleep, the pain doesn't bother you. If that's how it is for you, make a note.

12. **History of the pain:** Tell your doctor when the pain started and what triggered the pain. "Can you recall a specific incident that started it?" Also,

note if the pain has changed since it began. For example, if it used to be in your calf but now is in your thigh, make a note of that.

13. **Treatment:** Has the pain been treated before, and how? Tell your doctor as much as you can and bring along any records and test results. "The more information people can bring with them, the better we can treat them," Dr. Davis says.

14. **Medication:** Bring a list of all the pain medication you have taken along with a list of all the medication you currently take for *any* condition. "We don't want to use a medication that's been used unsuccessfully before," Dr. Davis says.

15. **History of surgeries and other medical problems:** In addition to listing surgeries, tell the doctor about any other illness, even if it doesn't seem related to your current pain.

16. **Family history:** Find out if anyone else in your family has had problems with pain or with certain pain-related conditions such as back injuries.

enough. But even though your everyday breathing keeps you alive, it may not be helping you relieve your neck pain. When you breathe more with your upper chest rather than your diaphragm, you force your neck muscles to work harder than they should. Over time, the increased strain causes chronic neck pain and can even induce headaches, according to the interactive CD-ROM *The Headache Clinic,* designed by Dr. Gostine and Dr. Davis.

How do you know if you're giving your neck the best deal by breathing correctly? Lie down on your back and place your right hand on your upper chest, with your left hand just below the ribs, says Dr. Gostine. Take a few deep breaths. If your left hand rises up, then you are breathing correctly using your diaphragm. But if your right hand rises more, then you are breathing with your upper chest, which places additional strain on your neck. To fix this, focus on reducing the movement in your upper chest while increasing the action in your diaphragm. After practicing this lying down, work on it while sitting, then, finally, while standing up.

Baby Your Back

If you don't already suffer from a bad back, it's very likely that you know someone who does. About 70 percent of women and 80 percent of men will experience back pain at some time in their lives. Back pain is the most frequent cause of restricted activity among people under 45. As a reason to see the doctor, back pain is right behind colds and flu.

Your back suffers more than most other body parts because it supports your entire body, says Watson. It gets stressed to the max when you lift heavy boxes; it bends and twists when you lean way over to look under the bed; and it's the structural support that keeps you erect rather than slumped when you are sitting down.

With long work hours and few vacations, no wonder your back gets stressed. Before you know it, the littlest bend or pull can send your back muscles into a spasm. "These things don't spontaneously explode on us. They take the wear and tear of daily living," Watson says.

But even though back pain is a modern-day epidemic, your number doesn't have to come up. By taking care of your back and relieving some burdens on your spine, you can enormously improve your chances of avoiding back pain.

Makeover Minutes

Along the Spine Line

Though it takes just a second to hurt your back, you can keep that from happening if you just take some customary precautions. Here are some quick measures to stop a lot of back trouble before it starts.

Give yourself a back roll. You don't have to purchase an expensive special seat or pillow to give your lower back the proper support it needs. Roll up an old towel and bind it with masking tape. Put it in the small of your back when you are sitting in a car or desk chair for hours on end, says Carlin. The towel will support your lower back, making it less susceptible to an attack of pain.

Keep legs on the go. "I spend a lot of my time training my patients to use their legs again," Watson says. To help your back, you need to find ways to use your legs more effectively in many everyday activities, Watson says. For example:

- Don't grab the armrests when you try to get out of a chair. To make your legs do more of the work, "get your balance and drive your feet into the floor," Watson says.
- Avoid using railings when climbing the stairs. "As long as you don't feel dizzy or off-balance, you can climb the stairs without lifting a hand. Use your legs," says Watson.
- If you have to look down into a cabinet or underneath a desk, don't stand there with stiff knees and bend from the waist. "Get down into a squat position and get back up using leg power," Watson says.

483

To Get Back on Track

Fight the long-term abuse your back takes day after day by lightening its load. Here are some lifestyle tips from doctors that will give your back a holiday and help keep it healthy.

Get rid of the extra baggage. Take off the extra pounds in your belly, and you will take a mound of pressure off your back. "One of the heaviest loads that your spine has to routinely deal with is the weight of your stomach. If you are overweight, you are putting a lot of strain on your back and fatiguing your muscles. If the muscles are already fatigued, and you go to lift something, then the muscles are going to give," Dr. Gatchel says. See Stop Time Tactic No. 2 on page 36 to help you along.

Strengthen your gut. A strong abdomen can lighten your spine's load, and we automatically think of situps as tummy tighteners. But normal situps miss a group of abdominal muscles that can carry a lot of the back's workload, Watson says. To get the most out of your situp, lie on a padded surface with your knees bent and your feet planted on the floor—but not pinned down. Then follow these steps.

1. Slowly curl up, raising your head and shoulders off the floor about six inches or so. You don't need to curl up into a sitting position—just curl as far as you can.
2. Once you are up, slowly rotate your trunk toward your left. To make sure you exercise the correct muscle group, try to keep your belly as flat as possible rather than letting it bulge out as you rotate. Hold this for a few seconds, then rotate back to the middle and return to the starting position.
3. Repeat the situp, but this time turn to the right.

Each situp should be done at a measured pace, Watson advises. "Do it slowly without throwing yourself up using your body weight. It's not a race. You're going to be doing yourself a favor if you go for quality over quantity," he says. As with any exercise, if the situps cause you pain, you should stop doing them immediately.

Don't overdo it. Unless you are competing for the strongest-person-in-the-world championship, you should not lift more than your body can handle. Lift what you can, then ask for help or just get someone else to do it, Dr. Gatchel says. Overdoing it could strain your back and renew old pain or prompt a new one.

One thing at a time. "A lot of people try to lift something from the ground and then place it on a surface off to the side. When you do that, you are straining your back two ways," Dr. Gatchel says. With your first action, lift the load using your legs and knees. Then use your legs, not your back, to turn toward where you want to place the object.

Consider a career change. If you work with your back, you may need to consider a new career. "You may find that you have entered a career that is good for someone in their twenties or thirties, but once you start hitting your forties and fifties, it's not a sustainable career anymore," Dr. Davis says. This isn't an option for everyone, of course—but if you have been considering a career change without making a move, your back may be telling you that it's time to take action.

485

Protect Yourself from Sexual Problems

Imagine having unlimited zest for sex.

Now imagine having unlimited *time* for sex.

Chances are, the older you get, the harder it is to imagine having either of those things—much less both.

That's too bad. A good sex life is right up there with sleeping, eating, and breathing on the happiness scale. Furthermore, if retirement is off in the future, the best may be yet to come.

Many people don't fully appreciate that sex as you get older can be better than it ever was before. While your zest may not be quite as rampant, the time factor does improve. Kids move out. Things quiet down a bit. And eventually, along comes retirement. So—what could be a better way to enjoy all that free time?

"For the majority of people, sex gets better—not worse—with age," says Barry McCarthy, Ph.D., a clinical psychologist and sex therapist at the Washington Psychological Center in Washington, D.C., and co-author of *Sexual Awareness*.

That's not to say that people aren't faced with some sexual difficulties as the years pass by. Both men and women experience physical changes that come with aging. An exhausting job and a less-than-sexy self-image can also take a toll on one's sex life.

But sex counselors and other experts have some strategies that can help you thwart the physical conditions of aging that may put a damper on your sex life. By following a few simple steps, you can maintain your sexual spirit with all the sprightliness of youth as the years roll by. "When it comes to sex, you can conquer time. It's something that you can continually improve on during the years. And you should value sex as an energizing

486

force that can help you keep young," says Martin Goldberg, M.D., a psychiatrist and director emeritus of the Marriage Council of Philadelphia at the University of Pennsylvania School of Medicine.

Of course, if there's one thing we know for sure about sex, it's that men and women have different points of view on the subject. Here's some expert advice for couples—plus exclusive advise for women and for men.

For Couples:
Finding the Time for Making Love

In the world of today's family, time is as valuable as money. In the crunch to get everything done in a 24-hour day, sex gets pushed to the back burner while we try to fit other things in.

When you finally get a break, however, you might find that bringing sex to the forefront won't be as easy as imagined. "Frequently, sexuality has suffered during the child-rearing years. Couples give sex a low priority and keep putting it off until tomorrow," says Dr. Goldberg. When we get to our forties and fifties and try to rekindle the flames, we might find it harder than expected.

That's why you have to make sex a priority just like work, children's activities, and household chores. "If we don't see to it that we give sex enough time, we do ourselves a great disservice," Dr. Goldberg says.

Makeover Minutes

For Couples on the Go

Making time for your love life might be easier than you think. Here is what the experts recommend for you and your partner.

Call the babysitter. If you have kids at home, put the babysitter on speed dial and press that button when you feel that you need to be alone with the one you love. Even if the sitter only watches the kids for an hour or two, that's found time for you

continued on page 490

487

Get Away to Romance

A young couple walks hand in hand on a beach as a blazing red sun sinks into the blue waters behind them.

For many people, this image immediately conjures the word *honeymoon*. But strolls on the beach needn't be reserved exclusively for those who just walked down the aisle.

"You should get away as often as you can as a couple—and not just because you are on your honeymoon. You need to think of yourself again. Do what you want," says Sherryl Robinson, owner of Robinson Travel Services in Manhattan Beach, California. "A perfect way to do that is to take a romantic trip."

It's not just travel agents who espouse the need to take a vacation—even sex therapists encourage romantic interludes. Couples need to get away from life and experience each other in a romantic setting to keep their relationship—and their sex life—healthy, says Al Cooper, Ph.D., an expert in sexuality who is a psychologist and clinical director of the San Jose Marital and Sexuality Centre in Santa Clara, California.

Resorts all around the world, especially in the Caribbean, cater to these couples who want to temporarily get away from their children and their jobs in order to find each other again, says Sally McCorrison, a certified travel consultant and director of AAA Travel Services in Allentown, Pennsylvania. In fact, many resorts are marketing these vacations to the 40-to-60 crowd, a group that is more likely to go for hassle-free travel arrangements and first-class accommodations.

The list of possible getaways is endless, and your choice depends on what you and your partner consider romantic. But here are a few ideas that got top billing from travel agents who recommend these settings for romance, intimacy, and a lot of fun.

▌ Want to be treated like the royalty you really are but no one will acknowledge? A vacation to all-inclusive resorts such as a Sandals or a Superclubs resort in the Caribbean should do the trick.

"All-inclusives are my idea of really getting away," says McCorrison. "They have everything you need, and you don't even have to leave the premises." At these beautiful oceanfront resorts, you pay one price up front. After that, everything is covered—meals, drinks, and activities. The resorts make sure that your every desire is met, whether you yearn for a day of snorkeling or want a perfect setting for a dinner for two, McCorrison says.

■ Maybe you really want to get away—no water sports, no talking with other happy couples—no anything. Then Little Dix Bay on Virgin Gorda in the British Virgin Islands or the Sonesta Resort on Anguilla are for you. "These resorts are perfect for romantic interludes. The islands are quiet. They are upscale but very secluded, and there's not much to do but be together," McCorrison says.

■ Perhaps your idea of a romantic evening is a formal dinner by the beach every night. Then the island of pink beaches may be calling. "Bermuda has a lot more of a conservative atmosphere, but it's a wonderful getaway," according to McCorrison. "The guest houses in Bermuda are upscale cottages on the beach—very romantic."

Bermuda gets formal at night, so bring your classy dinner clothes. One resort, The Reefs, sits atop a cliff overlooking the ocean, giving couples a view so awesomely romantic that it's almost guaranteed to revive the most passionate strains of love.

■ If you can't, or don't want to, leave the kids with relatives as you and your spouse cavort around the globe, some resorts have family places where you can enjoy romance and bring the kids. Most cruise lines and resorts now offer family packages where the younger ones are kept busy with camp activities such as arts and crafts, nature and field trips, and swimming and snorkeling classes. This allows the two of you to have time alone, McCorrison says, while the children have a ball learning new things and making friends.

■ Unlike Caribbean counterparts that may be seen as only honeymooners' paradises, the cruise industry has been typecast as the vacation for the older folks. Well, watch out for typecasting, warns Robinson. These floating palaces offer a lot to rekindle your love.

"We find couples going on cruises because it is the ultimate pampering getaway," says Robinson. "You have a lot of choices on a big cruise—card playing, golf, Hollywood shows, a piano bar. But you can also spend time alone and have a dinner for two." Smaller cruises can dock into beautiful, romantic ports in the Mediterranean that the bigger boats can't get into.

and your partner, notes Al Cooper, Ph.D., psychologist and clinical director of the San Jose Marital and Sexuality Centre in Santa Clara, California. You can go out, have dinner, or just lounge around in bed.

Close your door. What some people see as a lack of time for sex is actually a lack of privacy. "I've worked with couples afraid to close the door on their children. They think it's wrong for them to do that. And this really impairs their time for sexuality," says Dr. Goldberg. Make it clear to your children that when your door is closed, that's "mom-and-dad time" unless a real emergency happens. "Kids have to get used to the fact that you need privacy. It's a part of life," he says.

Make dinner together. Ask your spouse to help you make a meal. This chore can become a time of togetherness. "People can get in touch with each other by cooking and eating meals together. A lot of couples don't do this anymore," says Shirley Zussman, Ed.D., sex and marital therapist in New York City and editor of the newsletter, *Sex Over 40*.

Mark your calendar. Most couples hate this idea, but it works, says Dr. Cooper. Schedule sex or a date time with your partner every week. "People don't do things anymore if the event isn't scheduled in the date book," he says. To keep it spontaneous, make rules that each night has to be different from the last. Each week, trade off the responsibility of making plans for your night out. You might go to a symphony one week, have dinner in bed the next, or spend part of an evening reading a favorite book aloud.

Make love in the morning. Set the alarm clock for a half-hour earlier than usual and open up that time for sex. In the morning, you will be well-rested and more eager to pursue pleasure than you're likely to be after a 10-hour workday. "Make sexual dates early in the morning when you are awake and you have more energy rather than when you are tired and you've just turned off Jay Leno," says Dr. McCarthy.

Forget the laundry. "I'm always amazed to hear what people do with their Saturdays," says Dr. Zussman. "It's a precious day—and they do nothing but errands." Saturdays should be time for the two of you to hang out and talk, share a common interest, or take a class together.

Whole-Body Protection

Accept those wedding invites. Something about watching a bride and groom start their lives together gets people in the mood for love. "I have many clients who tell me that they always have sex after they have gone to a wedding," Dr. McCarthy says.

The trigger isn't just the wedding, but the memories and feelings that the ceremony revives in a couple. Bring out the wedding album, go to places where you had your first date or where you first spoke of marriage. You can also just talk about special times the two of you had and what you were feeling—and how you want to feel that way again. "Old memories and special feelings that you have had during your relationship can be used as sexual turn-ons. Be aware of what those things are," says Dr. McCarthy.

Do everything but. For some, sex becomes routine when they follow the same pattern—kissing, touching, and intercourse. But this same old thing can lead to boredom. "What kills sexuality is that it becomes very routine and predictable," says Dr. McCarthy.

In fact, studies have shown that when people are exposed to the same sexual stimulation over and over again, they become almost immune to it. Researchers found that when men in one study were shown the same erotic film more than 18 times, they were less aroused with each showing. Another study found that women who engaged repeatedly in the same sexual fantasy had a decrease in arousal.

To fight the boredom problem, sex therapists recommend nonsex sex nights for new clients. This takes the pressure off the performance and puts the focus on finding new ways to pleasure your partner. "Once a month, a couple should get together to talk and play sexually. But the play doesn't lead to intercourse. If you take intercourse away, it forces them to do something other than the routine. It asks them to be playful and creative," Dr. McCarthy says.

Read erotica to each other. Not only is this a way to get in the mood, it can also give you some great ideas. In addition to the multitude of modern erotica in bookstores, you can also check out historical erotica such as *The Perfumed Garden* by Sheikh Omar al-Nafzawi and *The Devil in the Flesh* by Andrea de Nerciat. Both were chosen by editors of the *Book of Lists* as two of the most erotic books in history.

(continued on page 494)

know what?
According to a survey in 1995, 40 percent of people age 65 and older are sexually active. They have sex on average 2½ times a month, compared with 7 times a month for those under 65.

491

Bound Together in the Snow

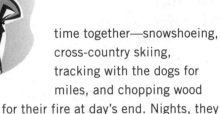

After five years of marriage, Tammy and Don Downs hardly saw each other anymore. Most of the time, Don stuck to his job in the payroll department while Tammy divided her time between work and classes at Western Connecticut State University, where she was working toward a degree in counseling. Then there were household chores, errands, and the other things that slowly erode away a couple's time. "It was actually rare that we saw each other," Tammy says.

Enough was enough, the couple finally decided. They determined to slow down their lives and spend some quality time together. A sex counselor might have encouraged Tammy and Don to develop intimacy by getting away from it all. When the Downs contemplated "getaway," however, they weren't thinking ocean cruises.

Instead, they gathered every piece of winter clothing they had and trekked to the snowy woods of Minnesota, where they braved −22°F temperatures to go dogsledding with two other couples. Over the course of a week, Tammy and Don spent a lot of time together—snowshoeing, cross-country skiing, tracking with the dogs for miles, and chopping wood for their fire at day's end. Nights, they slept on a bed of snow to the accompaniment of howling wolves.

It was all planned that way. Tammy and Don took a couples course through Outward Bound, an international nonprofit education organization that runs adventure programs to inspire self-esteem, self-reliance, concern for others, and care for the environment. The course encourages couples to handle the challenges of nature together, and in so doing, gives them a chance to examine and strengthen their relationships, says Steven McGaughey, admission coordinator for the Voyageur Outward Bound School in Minneapolis.

In most cases, the Outward Bound instructors leading the troop are a couple, McGaughey says. "Our focus on the couples course is building self-esteem and self-confidence in a couple. A lot of them have never been through something like this together. Couples get challenged, and then they

492

examine how they worked together through the challenge—and they grow from that," he says.

There's nothing like trudging through snow behind a pack of dogs to teach a couple how much they depend on each other. "If you go off one of the tracks or trails through the woods and you fall, you are falling into many feet of snow. And you can't get back up when you have a backpack on your back. You need someone there to lend a hand," Tammy says.

At the end of the course, the couple wrote down what they learned about themselves and each other. Tammy's and Don's answers surprised each other. "We both learned the same thing without knowing it," Tammy observed. "I found that I get a lot more support from Don than I thought. Then he showed me what he wrote—that he learned he gets so much support from me, that he didn't know if he could do without it. We both thought we were so independent, yet we both depended a lot on each other during the course."

Now that they are home from the snowdrifts, and wolves no longer sing their lullabies, that sense of appreciation carries over to their everyday lives. "It brought out a lot of things that we were not aware of. We realized we do an even split when it comes to housework and chores. And I get a ton of moral support from him with school. One of the things we realized when we were out there is that we take each other for granted," Tammy says.

At home, Tammy and Don incorporate one of the nightly rituals of the Outward Bound course in their lives. On the trail, every night the couples had to choose some passage to read to each other. "It's just one of those simple things that doesn't take a lot of energy but means a lot to the relationship," Tammy says.

Many couples, ranging in age from 20 to midfifties, have come back rejuvenated from their wilderness travels, McGaughey says. Interested couples can also take expeditions in whitewater canoeing, canoe expeditions, desert backpacking, and canyon exploration in addition to the dogsledding. To contact Outward Bound, write to R.D. 2, Box 280, Garrison, NY 10524.

493

For Couples:
Bringing Up a Touchy Subject

Deciding to improve your love life isn't always an easy task. It's one thing to suggest setting time each week for sex. It's another thing to ask for a romantic weekend away without the kids. It's yet another to come home with a black lace negligee from Victoria's Secret or suggest watching an erotic movie together.

If you think those things may be difficult to bring up with your partner, imagine suggesting, "Honey, I think we need to see a sex therapist." More often than not, it's the female half of the couple that has to ask this question—if she can get up the gumption to do so.

"I have couples who should have been here 20 years ago, but it took 19 years for the women to get up the courage to ask their partners to come," says Theresa Crenshaw, M.D., a sex therapist in San Diego and author of *The Alchemy of Love and Lust*.

Many men balk at the idea of going to a sex therapist, Dr. Crenshaw says, because they tend to want a quick medical fix. "They don't want anyone messing with their heads," she says. Women are typically more open to the idea of therapy.

So when do you decide that something more interesting than underwear is needed to spark your libido? A couple may want to seek sex therapy if a problem persists for more than six months and they have tried all possible solutions without success, says Dr. Goldberg.

But the big sign that you need help is when bedroom problems spill out into the living room, dining room, the kitchen, and everywhere else. "If you feel the frustration spinning off into your relationship and beginning to cause hostility elsewhere in your marriage, then it's a good time to go for help," Dr. Goldberg says.

Many partners won't even hear of it. In fact, one of Dr. Crenshaw's clients only got her husband to go to sex therapy after she rowed the two of them out to the middle of a lake and threatened to throw the oars overboard if he didn't go. He went.

To explore somewhat more practical ways of convincing your partner, try the prevention approach, Dr. Crenshaw sug-

494

gests. "Tell him, 'I've seen so many marriages that have gone bad. Why don't we become the exception and get some help so that we don't develop any problems?'"

Or if problems have already developed, ask him to help you with *your* therapy. Dr. Crenshaw says that many men will attend sessions if they believe they are going to help their partners, and not themselves. "Even if there isn't a problem in your eyes, I am concerned and I want you to humor me," she suggests telling your significant other. Once a partner comes in and participates, he usually keeps coming, she says.

Once your partner is thinking about sex therapy, he may start to ask what it is—and it helps to have an answer.

In sex therapy, instant groping is not the way. Sex therapists do assign "homework" in the form of touching exercises, but talking is bigger than touching—at least at first. A lot of sex therapy is helping the couple communicate their problems with each other, Dr. Crenshaw says.

At no time—be assured—will you be asked to have sex with each other in front of or with the therapist. "Couples do sexual exercises, but they're done in the privacy of their own home," says Dr. McCarthy.

There's no reason for any touching at all during a therapy session. "If a therapist attempts to touch you, leave as fast as you can," adds Dr. Zussman.

For Couples: Getting Good Guidance

Finding a good sex therapist isn't as easy as opening the phone book. It takes a little guidance and the ability to ask the right questions to find quality professional help, so here are some suggestions.

The therapist should be a licensed professional, such as a social worker, psychologist, or marriage psychiatrist, Dr. McCarthy says. These professionals have the standard background, but when they decide to specialize in sex therapy, they get advanced training and study. There's no such thing as a licensed sex therapist. So if a sex therapist claims to be licensed, you might want to find someone else.

Word of mouth is the best way to find mechanics, babysitters, and doctors—and the same goes for finding a sex therapist. Get a recommendation from a family doctor, a minister, or other patients, if possible. Couples looking for help often first go to their family doctor or minister, so they may already know of a good therapist, Dr. McCarthy says.

If you can't get a lead from these sources, call area hospitals or universities and ask if they have specialists in sex therapy, Dr. McCarthy suggests. Many institutions have started sex therapy programs, or they can direct you to a well-regarded therapist. You can also get a list of certified counselors in your area by sending a self-addressed, stamped envelope to the American Association of Sex Educators, Counselors, and Therapists at P.O. Box 238, Mount Vernon, IA 52314.

Ask the therapists you interview how much training they have had and where they studied sex therapy. Also, find out if sex therapy is their primary area or if they only dabble in it. Any therapist can treat sexual problems, but it doesn't mean she specializes in it. "You need to know if they have had strong training and a lot of experience. Don't just go to any therapist who may have dealt with some sexual problems," says Dr. Cooper.

Be very cautious or suspicious if a sex therapist guarantees that a service or product will work. Many not-so-good therapists will be quick to offer a guaranteed miracle cure, Dr. Goldberg says.

A good therapist, on the other hand, will need to spend time with you and your partner to understand your unique situation. "If they say, 'I'd be happy working with you to try and help your problem,' that's fine. But if they claim, 'I know exactly what your problem is, and your troubles are over,' then that's a clear warning that you are going to be wasting your money," Dr. Goldberg says.

For Women: Setting the Stage

Maybe there is a reason that two separate groups have had a hit with the song, "You've Lost That Lovin' Feelin'." As the years roll by, the spark that used to be there every night can fizzle out,

496

and sex can turn into a chore. "What happens more than anything else is that the couple takes sex for granted and get into boring, dull routines," Dr. McCarthy says.

But sex doesn't have to turn into something like feeding the cat and taking the kids to school. Just do a few things for each other during the week, and you can easily get romance, intimacy, and adventure back into a relationship.

Makeover Minutes

What Women Can Do

Of course, "setting the stage" is a man's responsibility as well as a woman's, but here are some things that a woman can do to encourage that "lovin' feelin'."

A fast stop at the florist and a pack of matches are all you need to get the fires burning. Here's how.

Buy him a rose. One of the biggest problems women have with romance is that they keep waiting for it to happen to them—not by them. If more romance is what you want, you can get things rolling by buying him a rose, surprising him with silk boxers, or taking him out to a candlelit dinner. "Each person must take responsibility for his or her sexuality and can't depend on their spouse to cure the problem," Dr. McCarthy says.

Get what you want. You can take the first steps when it comes to sex, too. Culture has taught women that, like romance, men initiate sex while women just accept. But these roles confine a couple's sexual pleasure. "When both people are comfortable initiating sex, their sex life is likely to be much better," says Dr. McCarthy.

Light a candle. Let him walk into a darkened room with just the candlelight illuminating your face, and your favorite music playing in the background. It's the little things that can spark a love-filled night.

497

For Women: Image Enhancement

Open any fashion magazine, and you'll see the popular definition of sexy: tall, skinny, glamorous, and most of all, *young*. When you constantly compare yourself to an 18-year-old runway model, you are probably not going to feel that attractive. And if you don't feel attractive, chances are that you won't be in the mood for sex.

Don't be fooled by all these false images of sexiness, Dr. McCarthy says. Your sexual attractiveness depends more on how you feel about yourself than on how you look. The definition of sexiness varies from person to person and encompasses not just looks but also intelligence and personality, he adds.

Whatever the current level of your sexual interest, here are some tips to help make sure that your self-image is as flattering as it can be.

Double up for workouts. To make exercise a sexy event, work out with your partner. That way, the two of you are improving your bodies, while you are spending time together, says Beverly Whipple, R.N., Ph.D., associate professor of nursing at Rutgers, the State University of New Jersey, in Newark and president of the American Association of Sex Educators, Counselors, and Therapists. The combination of togetherness and warm afterglow is sure to increase your sex drive.

Wear what you want. For some women, the lacy teddy— or flannel nightgown—is the sexiest garment around. For others, it's a business suit. Whatever the selection, you're the one who decides what makes you feel sexy, Dr. McCarthy says. For many women, there is no bigger turnoff than trying to squirm into a skimpy piece of fabric that seems to highlight their imperfections. Being sexy is a state of mind, and if an old torn-up smock is what you feel sexy in, then it will probably turn him on, too.

Rent a movie. Find a movie that portrays older adults as sexual beings, such as the Clint Eastwood/Meryl Streep movie, *The*

Bridges of Madison County, says Dr. Cooper. "You really need to be looking for older role models who are sexy and passionate," he says. You can even buy instructional sex videos featuring people over 40. So what if the models are overweight or the men are balding? "These videos show people who are really enjoying themselves sexually," he says.

Long-Term Tactics

For Women in Menopause

With menopause come physical changes that directly affect a woman's sex life. Many are related to lack of estrogen. Sexual intercourse might become painful because of vaginal dryness. Or the vagina might not be as flexible as it used to be. A woman might even experience a loss in the desire to have sex.

But that doesn't mean your sex life is over. A trip to the drugstore or a trip to the doctor can get your love life back in shape. "Menopause doesn't mark the end of sexuality. If you were interested in sex when you were young, you'll be interested in sex way after menopause," Dr. Whipple says.

Experts say that there are things you can both do before and after menopause to help make sure your sex life stays alive. Here are their suggestions.

Keep lubricants beside your bed. Use lubricants as part of your everyday sexual life—not just at times when you anticipate vaginal dryness. If the lubricants are always near at hand, you won't have any interruptions. "When the lubricant is always there, it's part of the sexual scenario," says Dr. McCarthy. "It doesn't mean, 'Oh my God, it's not working now, and a lubricant is what I use when it doesn't work.'"

Get a whiff of anticipation. The old standby K-Y jelly does work, Dr. McCarthy says. But why not turn picking a lubricant into something that's fun for you and your partner to do? Dr. McCarthy tells his clients to go to the store together to pick out

499

sweet-smelling lubricants. "The trick is to find a lubricant that smells good, feels good, and is hypoallergenic," he says.

Don't stop now. One way to prevent painful intercourse after menopause is to keep having sex. Doctors aren't sure why, but the more you have sex, the less you will experience physical problems such as vaginal dryness. "Women who are sexually active before and after menopause have better vaginal lubrication and elasticity than those who aren't," Dr. Whipple says.

Ask about hormone-replacement therapy. Estrogen treatments such as hormone-replacement therapy or estrogen creams can help restore vaginal lubrication and elasticity, Dr. Whipple says. Treatment may also help keep sexual desire up as well, she adds. Talk to your doctor about whether or not these treatments are right for you.

What Men Need to Know

One of the most common reasons that a couple comes to sex therapy is that the woman suffers from "inhibited sexual desire," says Dr. McCarthy. In other words, she just doesn't feel like it all that much.

People used to call this frigidity and blamed it all on the woman. But now people realize that it's a problem that the couple has to face together. Some of the time, it's because a woman is tired or doesn't feel desired by her mate anymore. So don't give up on her and your sex life, experts warn. Just make a few changes to get you both back in sync.

Long-Term Tactics

For Men: Getting Intimate

Some steps toward sweet love may take a bit more than a few minutes. But it will be worth it in the long run if you go the distance.

Tell her she's beautiful. You may think these words every day, but do you tell her?

"Don't say, 'I love you.' Tell your partner what you love about her," Dr. Whipple says. If she's not in the mood, it's possible that it has nothing to do with you but with how she feels about herself. A quick reminder from you about why you love her will make her feel better.

Dr. McCarthy suggests that a husband tell his wife five things that he loves and admires about her before he asks for sex. That way, couples think about why they love each other, and they also learn to express their love.

Give her a hug, just because. A hug here and there, a small smooch, or even a kiss on the cheek can show your partner that you care about her and that you love her. "It doesn't have to lead to sex. If the woman is getting a lot more physical affection, she'll feel sexier. And physical contact is needed to live and thrive; you need it just like you need air and water," says Dr. Cooper.

Keep her guessing. Just by doing little things every once in a while, you can keep the love alive between the two of you. Here are some suggestions from sex therapist Ellen Kreidman, author of *Light Her Fire*.

- Put notes saying "I love you" everywhere.
- Hold hands in public.
- Send a gift for no reason.
- Read poetry to her.
- Take her to a drive-in movie.
- Make a cassette of love songs for her.

Let her buy the lingerie. It spoke to you from the window of Victoria's Secret—that black lace teddy with matching thong underwear. You say to yourself, "She'll love it," as the salesgirl wraps it up.

But what you really mean is "*I* love it!" And with that imprinted on your brain, maybe you can't understand why she has a look of fear and disgust as she holds the teddy up against her body.

For some, lingerie is a sexy turn-on. But for other women, lingerie is a constant reminder of their not-so-perfect bodies. It makes some women feel less sexy, if not downright ugly, which

501

can dampen the mood very quickly. "Anything that is going to intimidate her or makes her feel self-conscious will be a big turnoff," Dr. McCarthy says.

So if you want to buy her something sexy, take her with you. Go on a shopping spree and let her pick out what makes her feel desirable, Dr. McCarthy advises.

Do the dishes. A man may complain that his wife doesn't want to anymore, that she's too tired. Well, maybe that's because she's gone to work, cleaned the house, taken the kids to school, cooked dinner, and put the children to bed.

So, maybe the best aphrodisiac is for a man to pick up the slack. "Let her know you care, that you see her stress and frustration. Then do something practical about it," Dr. Cooper says. Do the housework, freeing her of some time. Or draw her a bath after dinner and say that you'll clean up. "Don't just complain; be part of the solution," he says.

Learn some massaging techniques. Take the opportunity to sign the two of you up for a couples massage course at a community college. You will show her that you care enough to want to learn, and as a bonus, you will learn how to use touch to please each other.

Have a pillow fight. Many women complain to sex therapists that there is no afterplay, Dr. McCarthy says. They want the intimacy to carry on after sex as well. Keep the romance going after sex by having a playful pillow fight, for example, or by making her a cup of tea.

Long-Term Tactics
For Erection Problems

It may be a man's worst fear, even worse than losing his hair. The word has taken on such a meaning that sex therapists now ask that you say "erection problems" instead of the dreaded "impotence."

Whole-Body Protection

Sampling Some Sultry Sutra

"Seizing her head with his hands, he applies his mouth forcefully on hers, without violence...holding him loosely, she closes her eyes and covers his eyes with her hands. She then rubs her lover's lips with her tongue."

Although this passage might have come straight from of the pages of a popular pulp romance novel, this particular steamy scene is actually more than 2,000 years old. Try some more where that came from, and you might introduce ginger as well as sugar to the spice in your sex life.

The *Kāmā Sūtra* is an ancient sex manual compiled in fourth century A.D. by a delightfully open-minded religious scholar named Vātsyāyana. In his text, the scholar covers a multitude of sexual issues—from marriage to sexual positions. Open this book up, and you'll find age-old advice on everything from how to embrace your love to the preludes and conclusions to the game of love. He even wrote about how to make love in water.

"For those who want to give it a try, the *Kāmā Sūtra* can help a couple and give them some ideas," says Martin Goldberg, M.D, a psychiatrist and di-rector emeritus of the Marriage Council of Philadelphia at the University of Pennsylvania School of Medicine.

For instance, in the section called "Amorous Advances," the author gives some tips on how to get your partner in the mood. "In order to arouse his desire, she embraces him and wakes him with a kiss, so that he immediately understands her intentions. This kind of kiss is called the inflamer." Following the basic inflaming instruction comes information on the art of biting and scratching to induce pleasure.

In the "Acquiring a Wife" chapter, the author lets us know that even two millennia ago, a wife who didn't get signs of affection wasn't too happy. "A woman who has not received any signs of love is wounded and becomes hostile, an enemy of men."

But to take on the *Kāmā Sūtra* may take a lot of time and patience. In some versions, the text runs as long as 550 pages. Of course, depending on why you are reading it, you can skip over the sections on how to sexually conquer other men's wives or the section about how to obtain the right courtesans.

Although most men think that it's in their heads, many erection difficulties stem from physical problems such as diseases and medications—problems that can be almost completely avoided. In fact, the very things that rob you of your health and youth—drugs, alcohol, bad diet—can rob you of an erection.

Erection problems can develop over time or occur suddenly. But by following a few simple pointers, you can prevent many of these problems.

Lay off the alcohol. It may increase the desire, but it decreases the performance, and especially so over time, says Robert N. Butler, M.D., professor of geriatrics at the Mount Sinai School of Medicine of the City University of New York in New York City and author of *Love and Sex after 60*. A few drinks before sex can make an erection less firm and more difficult to achieve, Dr. Butler says. Up to 80 percent of men who drink heavily suffer sexual side effects including erection problems, sterility, and loss of desire. Even heavier drinking over time destroys testicular cells, leaving men with shrunken testicles and a reduced sex drive.

Start working out. Regular exercise will do the obvious by improving your body and, therefore, improving your self-image. But researchers have found that exercise may be an aphrodisiac in itself. A study conducted at the University of California, San Diego, found that men who exercised 60 minutes a day for about three days per week improved their sex lives. The men reported having more sex and even more-satisfying orgasms. As the men improved their fitness levels, they said the sex kept getting better. But don't overdo it, warns Dr. Crenshaw, because exercising to the extreme can be detrimental to sex.

Also, you should start from a modest pace and build up, says Dr. Butler. If you're not already in good physical condition, you might do more harm than good if you start with an exercise plan that's too rigorous.

Throw out the smokes. If cancer doesn't scare you, how about smoking's effects on sex? Nicotine constricts blood vessels, making it hard for blood to flow to the penis. Long-term smoking can severely hamper erections, says Dr. Cooper, "When smokers stop smoking, many of the erection problems disappear."

504

Check out your medicine cabinet. Your medication could be robbing you of that erection. "Many prescription medications eliminate sex drive and erections," says Dr. Crenshaw, who is also the author of *Sexual Pharmacology.* The most common perpetrators include antidepressants (Prozac and Elavil), blood pressure medications (Atenolol, Besimil, and Diupres), and anti-ulcer drugs (Tagamet and Pepcid AC). Even over-the-counter drugs such as antihistamines and Dramamine can cause erection problems or can reduce sexual desire. If you suspect your medication is hurting your love life, ask your doctor to switch to another type of medication or to lower your dosage, she says.

Keep healthy. Heart disease, cancer, high blood pressure, obesity, and diabetes can all make men impotent. To help prevent these diseases, use the strategies in Stop-Time Tactics No. 1, 2, 7, and 11 on pages 3, 36, 168, and 242.

Remember your member. It's a cycle, says Dr. Cooper. In order to have healthy erections, men have to keep having erections. "Young men have five to six erections every night because it gets needed oxygen to the penis through the blood. As a man gets older, he gets less and less of these nocturnal erections, and it really affects the health of the penis," Dr. Cooper says. So to make up for the erections that you're not having during the night, it's good to have more during your waking hours to keep the penis healthy. "It's not just for fun, it's for health," he says.

Think of it as longer, better sex. Even if you are the picture of perfect health, it's going to take you longer to get an erection as you get older. So work with it, Dr. McCarthy says. It means that you and your partner will have to spend more time fooling around before intercourse, and of course, that's far from bad. "You have to get used to a different rhythm. Become more sensuous instead of overreacting to it," he says.

If you don't adjust to this change, then you could be in for real problems. Many men who don't accept this fact of life end up panicking with every sexual experience. Some men can't get an erection because they get so nervous about not being able to get an erection.

know what?

At the age of 70, novelist Victor Hugo carried on an affair with a 27-year-old laundress, seduced the young daughter of a famous novelist, allegedly dallied with actress Sarah Bernhardt, and maintained his 50-year relationship with actress Juliette Drouet.

505

Don't rush into implants. Although still a viable option for those who need penile implants, men with erection problems should not rush into surgery before exploring other options, says Dr. McCarthy. Many times, there might not be a major problem at all. "In their teens, twenties, and early thirties, men get easy, automatic erections. Basically, they don't need anything from their partners to get erect. But with aging, that changes—and a fair number of people get distracted by that," he says.

In the rush to quickly save their sex lives, men may take actions that actually harm them in the end, Dr. McCarthy warns. The penile implant treatments "are not really user-friendly," he says. "It is so artificial. And the woman often resents it more than the man because she feels left out of the process," he says. Make sure that you and your partner get all the facts and make the decision together.

Protect Yourself from
Vision Problems

Want to take a good look at your eyes? Easy—gaze in the mirror. Without even intending to, you'll make immediate eye contact.

The eyes—whether our own or other people's—are magnets for attention. Not only that, they're the only part of your body that can actually look at itself. It's like having a built-in self-examining device.

What you actually see, however, is only about one-sixth of a very complex organ. The white background, called the sclera, covers the largest part of the eyeball. The blue, green, hazel, or brown doughnut surrounding the midnight-black center is the iris. The pupil, that black circular doorway, leads to the all-important lens. And the clear, shiny dome forming the eye's glistening outer bulge is the cornea.

While the eyes may be amazing to look at, what they actually do is more incredible still. The beautifully colored iris is made up of muscle tissue that contracts and expands to change the size of the pupil. In turn, the deep pool of the pupil permits just the right amount of light to enter the eye. And the crystal-clear cornea and lens bring the world into focus by concentrating that light on its journey into the spherical interior.

The miracle of our vision is something we tend to take for granted. But with age comes a set of eye concerns that you may never have encountered before. If you are lucky, an extra pair of glasses will be the worst inconvenience. If you are not so fortunate, more serious vision problems may crop up.

Good eye care is an important part of aging well. And while it

507

Know Your O's

Even if you've never had a reason to visit an eye doctor before, you should start getting annual eye exams beginning at age 40, says Gerald Fishman, M.D., professor of ophthalmology at the University of Illinois Eye and Ear Infirmary in Chicago. Around that time, age-related vision problems often begin to show up. "This is a good time to get what's called a baseline checkup," he says.

For the most thorough examination, and for management of any serious eye disease, Dr. Fishman recommends that you choose an ophthalmologist. This is a medical doctor who has also done a residency in ophthalmology. Ophthalmologists are licensed to give exams during which they routinely check for signs of eye disease by using dilating drops to carefully inspect the inside of the eye. And some specialize in specific eye conditions such as glaucoma or cataracts, performing surgery when needed.

If you have your eyes checked at a walk-in vision center, you're more likely to be in the hands of an optometrist. Having attended four years of optometry school, an optometrist is licensed to perform eye exams or to screen for certain eye disorders such as lazy eye or glaucoma. They are just fine if you're only looking for a prescription for glasses or contact lens; however, the treatment of eye disease requires the attention of an ophthalmologist, says Dr. Fishman.

Opticians are the ones who actually make corrective lenses and fit them into glasses frames. An optician can help you select the best frame and can give you information on bifocals. They repair eyeglasses, and many opticians can fill prescriptions for contact lenses. They're not trained to diagnose eye problems or prescribe medication, however. Some opticians work side by side with optometrists in storefront-type eyeglasses shops, so you can get your eyes examined and get glasses at the same place.

doesn't take a crystal ball to see into the future, when it comes to your eyes, it's wise to arm yourself with a little special knowledge.

Embracing the Inevitable

Remember when you were a kid and you could focus on the tip of your nose? (Remember when you even wanted to?) Compare that early feat of vision to the short-arms syndrome of our

508

adult years—when diners start asking waiters to recommend a dish, not because they really want their opinion but because they can't see the menu.

This extremely common condition is known as presbyopia, or loss of visual range. An age-related variation of farsightedness, presbyopia usually sets in around the age of 40. It's an unavoidable sign of aging, according to Jane F. Koretz, Ph.D., professor of biophysics at Rensselaer Polytechnic Institute in Troy, New York.

The classic symptoms come slowly. Type on a page starts looking a little fuzzy—in the phone book, on a recipe card. Precision chores like threading a needle become next to impossible. You'll notice (with some relief, most likely) that the horizon is still nice and sharp. But look down to check your watch and, well, you get the idea.

These changes in focusing ability are directly related to changes in the lens, the normally clear, usually flexible, little lentil-shaped flying saucer located just behind your iris. The muscles surrounding the lens are like the fine-tuning knob on a microscope. When these muscles contract, your lens gets thicker and close objects are brought into focus. As the muscles relax, your lens is pulled taut and made thinner, and you can see into the distance.

As we and our lenses age, this neat arrangement changes. That's because the lens continually grows new layers as we get older, says Dr. Koretz. Like an M&M candy being dipped into color over and over again, the new layers pile on top of the originally squishy core. This eventually causes the lens to lose much of its youthful flexibility, limiting its ability to contract when you need it to. At age 40 or 50, your lenses can't dance like they did at 20.

Makeover Minutes

See What You Can Do

While you can't stop the clock on aging, you can do some things to help your eyes grow old gracefully, and in the meantime, keep your vision as sharp as possible. Here's what experts suggest.

509

A Workout Like No Other

Vision therapy, eye exercises, the Bates method—if none of these terms sound familiar to you, you are not alone. The practice of therapeutic eye exercises is an uncommon, even controversial, approach to optical health.

Although vision therapy is hardly accepted as scientific fact today, in ancient times it was a staple of good eye care, according to Robert Abel Jr., M.D., professor of ophthalmology at Thomas Jefferson University in Philadelphia. "In Japan, Tibet, and India, there are written records of eye exercises from thousands of years ago," he says.

Eye exercises have been associated primarily with helping to correct refractive error—that is, near- or far-sightedness. The reasoning is that certain eye muscles need to "unlearn" bad focusing habits. Vision exercises have no proven effect on eye disease.

A typical vision exercise is called tromboning, or pencil pushups. To try it, hold a pencil at arm's length and focus your vision on it. Slowly bring the pencil toward your nose while maintaining your focus. Then, just as slowly, extend your arm again. Maneuvers like this one are thought to develop focusing ability to the point where corrective lenses may no longer be necessary.

While many experts feel that eye exercises offer little more than distraction, others believe that the evidence is in the effects. "There may be no hard scientific proof that this stuff works," says Dr. Abel, "but the value is obvious in people who have been helped by vision therapy."

Join the reading-glasses club. The ideal answer to age-related loss of visual range is—you guessed it—longer arms. But most people turn to reading glasses. It's fine to start off with the dime-store variety of reading glasses, says Dr. Koretz. Check the racks at drugstores or grocery stores for a low-price introduction to a wide selection of low-powered lenses. But don't be surprised if you find yourself eventually needing a stronger prescription.

Brave the world in bifocals. If you already wear glasses, you may want to consider bifocals to combine your near and distance prescriptions. There are even "invisible" bifocals available

510

now, blending different strengths without telltale lines where the lens thicknesses meet.

At the next level of high-tech optics, trifocals are yet another option for those who need prescriptions to cover three distances—for things like reading, cooking, and driving. For any of these prescription lenses, you'll first need an exam and a written prescription from an optometrist or ophthalmologist. Then an optician can help you choose styles.

Prevent the worst. Your eyes are at risk from age, disease—and baseballs and soapsuds, too. Nearly 2.5 million preventable eye injuries occur each year. That's about three-fourths as many injuries as occur in traffic accidents. So wearing eye protection should be as automatic as stopping at a stop sign.

Experts advise that you wear eye protection whenever there is any chance of injuring your eyes. Weed whacking, nail pounding, and even scrubbing the kitchen floor with household cleaners are everyday endeavors that call for eye protection. If you don't have safety goggles handy, a pair of sunglasses will do, says Norman A. Saffra, M.D., director of the Retina Center at Maimonides Medical Center in Brooklyn, New York. The idea is to keep dust, sharp objects, and dangerous chemicals out of the eyes. All it takes is one flying speck to do serious damage.

Post a number. Look up the phone number of your local poison control center (check the blue pages of your phone book) and keep it handy for emergencies. Call the center immediately for more information and a referral in an eye emergency. Or get someone to call for you, if necessary.

Act carefully in an eye emergency. If you get something in your eye, resist the impulse to rub it. Instead, gently pull the upper lid over the lower one and try blinking a few times, says Dr. Saffra. If you rub your eye, you might damage it, he warns. If the speck is still there, keep the eye closed and get help.

If you have splashed a dangerous liquid into your eyes—like chlorine bleach, ammonia, paint thinner, or even vinegar—immediately rinse the eyes with cool running water for at least 15 minutes, says Dr. Saffra.

Get regular eye exams. Give your eyes a gift—thorough

know what?
The largest eye of any animal belongs to the Atlantic giant squid—and it's bigger than a basketball. An ostrich eye is roughly the size of a tennis ball. The human eye, puny by comparison, is not even as big as a golf ball.

511

Modernize Your Eyes

There's nothing like a pair of glasses with "Coke bottle" lenses to make you feel old — even if you're still in your thirties. Mike Byrne, a production control planner from Long Island, New York, was extremely nearsighted and had been wearing glasses since about the fifth grade. "I literally couldn't see across the room without my glasses or contacts."

He had always been curious to know what it would be like to live with perfect vision. And he was concerned about an upcoming police force exam because the police department required applicants to have good eyesight. Deciding that the newest eye surgery technique was worth the risk, Byrne, who is in his thirties, opted for a procedure called photorefractive keratectomy (PRK), also known as excimer laser surgery.

The term *laser surgery* is actually only half correct since there's no surgery involved. PRK brings vision into focus without a single incision. A laser is used to vaporize a very small amount of corneal tissue from the surface of the eye, reducing the curve of the cornea by just the right amount.

The procedure was mostly painless, according to Byrne, but far from fun. "It was like a scene from the movie, *A Clockwork Orange*," says Byrne about the device used to hold the eyelids open. The eye is numbed with anesthetic eyedrops so that you can't feel the laser. And although the treatment itself only takes about a minute per eye, the discomfort lasts for about three days after the initial numbness wears off.

To prevent infection and help the cornea heal properly, anyone who has

checkups every other year. "For those without evidence of glaucoma or other ocular disease, an eye exam every two years is sufficient unless new eye symptoms develop," says Gerald Fishman, M.D., professor of ophthalmology at the University of Illinois Eye and Ear Infirmary in Chicago. During an exam, an optometrist or ophthalmologist can detect early eye problems like glaucoma before symptoms can appear—and when detected in the early stages, such eye problems are most treatable. Even if

Whole-Body Protection

PRK has to use eyedrops religiously for several months. And since the eye becomes more light sensitive, dark glasses are a must. "They offered me those wraparound glasses made for people who have had cataract surgery," says Byrne, "but I chose to wear my Ray-Bans."

The success rate for PRK is very good, says Eric Donnenfeld, M.D., Byrne's surgeon and medical advisory board member of 20/20 Laser Centers in Rockville Centre, New York. Most people wind up with 20/40 vision or better—good enough to drive a car without needing corrective lenses, according to Dr. Donnenfeld. Results are even more impressive for people with relatively mild nearsightedness.

After complete recovery, Byrne had 20/20 vision in one eye and 20/25 in the other—pretty close to perfect. But complications remain a possibility, his doctor notes. The main reasons that some people will not end up with ideal vision are over- or under-correction. Over-correction causes farsightedness, which means the person might still need glasses. Under-correction, however, can sometimes be fixed with a "touch-up" laser treatment.

Other problems can occur, but luckily, most complications are rare, says Dr. Donnenfeld. Some people will experience glare or halos surrounding concentrated sources of light, especially at night. This condition usually lessens over time. And infection or clouding of the cornea can occur if it doesn't heal properly.

For Byrne, who was aware of the risks, the procedure was worthwhile. "This definitely changed my life. In fact," he adds, "there are days I don't even think about my eyesight—and I used to think about it all the time."

your eyes get a clean bill of health, that regular checkup will ensure that your prescription is always up-to-date.

Clear Away the Clouds

The key word for dealing with eye disease is prevention—and, as with many other health conditions, good prevention begins with good nutrition. Once problems start, however, early

513

Don't Ever Forget Your Sunglasses

Experts agree that wearing sunglasses is more than just a way to look sharp—it's also one of the best steps that you can take to protect your eyesight. Over a lifetime, the sun's ultraviolet radiation causes cumulative damage to the eye lens, which can ultimately lead to cataracts and macular degeneration.

Ultraviolet light is divided into two major types. UVA is the type of radiation that causes the skin to tan and age more rapidly. UVB rays are responsible for causing sunburns, and they contribute to skin cancer. Both types are bad for the eyes.

Although no federal regulations apply to sunglasses, most carry some sort of label indicating their protective ability. For the best protection, the American Academy of Ophthalmology recommends choosing sunglasses that block between 99 to 100 percent of ultraviolet light—including both UVA and UVB.

As for price, it's a myth that expensive shades offer better protection than cheaper ones, according to Jeffrey Spitzer, M.D., associate clinical director of the New York Eye and Ear Infirmary in Manhattan. While it's true that designer glasses may offer a flashier fashion statement, your eyes won't know the difference. In the long run, it's better to select affordable, flattering sunglasses, he says. That way, you'll be more likely to wear them regularly—rather than leave them home for fear of losing your investment.

detection can make all the difference. So you are helping to protect your vision—possibly in a major way—if you get an appointment for an eye exam on this year's calendar right now.

Although cataracts are one of the most common causes of vision loss affecting older adults, they can often be counteracted with modern techniques of surgery or with medications. Prompt treatment can slow the progress of cataracts, allowing people to maintain their vision.

Cataracts develop in the lens. This normally clear disk behind the cornea is the part that focuses light rays on the interior of the eye, the retina. Under certain circumstances, proteins in the lens clump together, clouding the disk and scattering incoming light.

The majority of cataracts occur as a result of aging. In fact, statistics show that over half of men and women over age 65 will

514

have cataracts at some point. "Everybody would eventually develop cataracts if they lived long enough," says Dr. Saffra. People using steroids for long periods of time and those with diabetes are at risk for developing cataracts even earlier.

Looking at the world through a cataract is like trying to see through a sheet of waxed paper—things look milky or hazy. There may be also a pronounced glare, especially at night.

An interesting early symptom is something known as second sight. This is the strange experience of suddenly being able to read without your reading glasses, after years of relying on them. Second sight seems at first, a change for the better, but the improvement is temporary, lasting only a few months. And as the cataract worsens, sight gradually goes downhill.

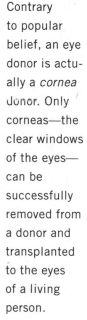

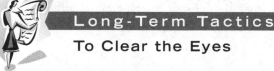

Long-Term Tactics

To Clear the Eyes

Since aging is the strongest risk factor for cataracts, the most reliable prevention tactic would be to turn back the calendar. Barring that, you'll have to resort to other, more practical ways of clearing the clouds from your sight.

Consider a replacement. When a cataract begins to hinder your vision, the afflicted lens can be replaced by a synthetic lens known as an intraocular lens (IOL). This surgery is considered one of the most effective medical procedures done today. But as with all surgical procedures, discussing the alternatives with your doctor first is key.

Through a technique known as extracapsular surgery, a small incision is made in the eye. The cloudy lens is removed through the front of the membrane that encases it, leaving the rear wall in place. The clear plastic IOL, which is smaller than a dime, is carefully inserted and comes to rest firmly against the back of the membrane. Two loops attached to the new lens help to keep it securely in place.

The IOL implant is permanent. If you get one, you won't

515

Vision Quest

How far would you go to heal your sight? Well, fifty-something performance artist Spalding Gray traveled the world in search of a healing miracle rather than submit to eye surgery. He tells the bizarre story of his quest for clear sight in his monologue, *Gray's Anatomy*.

Like many people his age, Gray was less than eager to see a doctor. "I hadn't had my eyes examined in a long time, and I was fantasizing about all sorts of things," Gray recounts in his monologue. After reluctantly being examined by an ophthalmologist on the Upper West Side of Manhattan, Gray was diagnosed with a "macula pucker"—a rare and strange-sounding age-related problem—in his left eye.

Before finally submitting to surgery, he spent a harrowing night in a smoky, smelly Native American sweat lodge and witnessed a gory session with a psychic surgeon in the Philippines. And it should be mentioned here that none of his exotic experiences had any beneficial effect on his eyesight.

Ultimately, reason won over and Gray scheduled the surgery—and got his sight back. "Suddenly, I realized that my eyesight is really important," he writes. "I'm very protective of it. I'm very cautious."

have to worry about cleaning your new lens, and you may not even be aware of it. But since the new lens can't stretch and contract to help you focus on different distances, you'll still need reading glasses.

Have it made in the shade. Research shows that too much sun does damage not only to your skin but also to your eyes. A study in Rome, Italy, compared 1,008 people with cataracts to 469 people without them. Participants answered questions to determine their lifetime sun exposure. Those whose eyes had racked up the most unprotected time in the sun were more than twice as likely to develop cataracts, the study showed.

Keep your eyes safely in the shade by making it a habit to wear UV-protective sunglasses and a brimmed hat whenever you find yourself outdoors for any length of time. UV-protective sunglasses can help reduce your risk of cataracts, says Marco Zarbin, M.D., Ph.D., professor and chairman of ophthalmology at the University of Medicine and Dentistry of New Jersey in Newark.

516

Eat for eyesight. If you need yet another good reason to stock up on broccoli, consider this news. Certain nutrients found in vegetables may help prevent cataract progression. In one eye study, researchers at the University of Wisconsin Medical School in Madison analyzed the diets of nearly 2,000 older men and women living in Beaver Dam, Wisconsin. Researchers found that people who had the lowest incidence of cataracts were the ones who got the most antioxidants, powerful nutritional substances like beta-carotene and vitamin C. These antioxidants, as we've noted, come from many food sources—especially green vegetables—and you can also reinforce your intake with vitamin supplements to help protect the body from damage associated with aging.

Looking at Risks of Macular Degeneration

Age-related macular degeneration (AMD) may sound more like an automotive problem than an eye disease. But, unfortunately, the name of this vision-threatening disease is very familiar to the one-quarter of people over 65 who show signs of developing it.

AMD affects the macula—the bull's-eye in the center of the retina, the light-sensitive lining of the eye. Located on the back wall of the eye's interior, the macula contains the densest concentration of nerve cells, called cones, that are sensitive to light and color.

To get an idea of the macula's importance, think of what you are doing at this very moment. The word you are reading right now—the one that is in clearest focus—is the only one hitting your macula's bull's-eye. All other words—the ones in your peripheral, or side, vision—are slightly blurred. That's because the light coming from them is not aimed directly at the center of your macula. Clear, detailed, central vision relies on a properly functioning macula.

Ninety percent of people with AMD have a form of the disease known as the dry, or non-neovascular, type. In this form, as the macula ages it gradually gets thinner and begins to break down. As cells in the macula stop working, a blurred or blind spot will develop in the center of vision, making it hard for you

517

to read or to recognize faces. Most people with dry AMD will not lose their sight completely, although there is presently no way to restore lost vision or stop this disease from progressing once it starts.

The other 10 percent of people with age-related macular degeneration have a form called wet, or neovascular, AMD. This more serious form of the disease can develop at any time in someone who already has dry AMD. The term *wet* is used because new blood vessels grow within the eye and leak blood and other fluids under the retina. As more and more blood and fluid leak under the retina, the delicate macula gets damaged, eventually causing loss of vision.

When someone has wet AMD, straight lines may start to appear wavy, and central vision deteriorates rapidly. Sight fades much more quickly than with dry AMD. This type of the disease can lead to severe vision loss within two to three years.

Like cataracts, risk for age-related macular degeneration increases with age. About 2 percent of people in their fifties get some form of macular degeneration, and about 30 percent of those over 75 have the condition. You are probably at greater risk if you have a family history of the problem, says Dr. Zarbin.

Unlike treatments for cataracts, there's no reliably effective treatment for the majority of people with either type of AMD. "I don't have any doubt that we will have better treatments in the near future," says Dr. Zarbin. "But for now, it's smart to take whatever steps you can toward prevention."

Long-Term Tactics
To Lessen Degeneration

Taking on some of the habits of a typically healthy lifestyle can do a lot to minimize your risk for macular degeneration, says Dr. Zarbin. Here are a few of the best ways to start.

Don't smoke. This is one you have heard before. But it may surprise you to learn that cigarette smoke is a definite offender when it comes to eye health. "You're at greater risk of both cataracts and AMD if you smoke," says Dr. Zarbin. "Don't start—and if you already have, it's a really good idea to quit right away."

Go the healthy-heart route. "When patients ask me what they should do for AMD, I recommend they make dietary changes similar to the changes they would make to treat heart disease," says Frederik Van Kuijk, M.D., Ph.D., associate professor of ophthalmology at the University of Texas Medical Branch at Galveston. That includes eating more leafy greens, whole grains, and more fruits and vegetables in general, he says. The nutrients found in such foods may help avoid or reverse early damage to the eye that can lead to macular degeneration, he says.

See about laser surgery. For a small number of people with wet AMD, doctors may be able to do laser surgery that stops the leakage of fluid under the retina, slowing vision loss. The treatment does have side effects and may not be appropriate for everyone with this condition. Ophthalmologists who are experienced in laser surgery should help you weigh the risks if you ever have wet AMD.

Get a Grip on Glaucoma

At least two million Americans have glaucoma—and half of them don't even know it. That's because in glaucoma's early stages there are no symptoms to tell you that your sight is in danger.

Glaucoma refers to a condition in which the pressure normally found within the eyeball is high. This increased intraocular pressure, or IOP, comes from a built-up excess of the fluid called the aqueous humor. (Though it's a fluid in the eye, aqueous humor isn't the same as tears, which are produced by ducts outside of the eye and don't enter the eyeball itself.) To better understand glaucoma, you need to know what the aqueous humor is and how it works.

The lens and the cornea are the only parts of the body that don't receive blood flow. Instead, the eye produces clear aqueous humor—about a teaspoonful every 24 hours—that flows out of the iris and over the cornea and lens. This fluid delivers nu-

519

Make the Most of Low Vision

You may know someone who has been cut off from the world because of low vision—sight so poor that it can't be corrected with ordinary eyeglasses. Such faltering eyesight is most common in people over 60, although children can also suffer from it.

Low vision is usually the result of progressive eye diseases like macular degeneration. Many of those with low vision are considered legally blind—and can see only the big E on the eye chart while wearing their glasses.

For people with low vision, day-to-day pastimes such as watching TV or reading a novel become frustrating, if not impossible. Many give up leaving their homes because they are afraid of falling down or getting lost.

But it doesn't have to be quite this bad. There are aids available to help people with low vision make the most of what sight they do have—and by doing so, regain some of their independence, says Marco Zarbin, M.D., Ph.D., professor and chairman of ophthalmology at the University of Medicine and Dentistry of New Jersey in Newark. For instance:

▐ Handheld magnifiers are helpful for identifying money or reading menus. They are inexpensive and portable. Look for models with lighted handles.

▐ Ring telescopes are handheld mini telescopes. Slipped over a finger, the telescope is hidden, but when you need it, you just open your hand and lift the telescope to your eye. They're best for magnifying distant objects. Your eye doctor can help you find one that's right for you.

▐ High-powered reading glasses are convenient because they leave the hands free. One drawback, however, is that they are heavier than normal eyeglasses.

In addition to finding the right device for you, there are other ways to make low-vision living less limiting. High-wattage lightbulbs can make your home safer and easier to navigate. Large-print books and magazines are available at many libraries and bookstores. There are even oversize games and playing cards for a vision-friendly game of bingo or pinochle.

trients and removes waste products, serving the same role played by blood circulation in the rest of the body.

Normally, the aqueous humor drains out of the eye through a meshwork of tiny channels called the trabecular network, and after exiting, it's carried away by the bloodstream. But when someone has glaucoma, the trabecular network gets blocked. Like a tiny water balloon being filled by a steady trickle, the aqueous humor soon has nowhere to go. So it builds up and pushes outward on the eye.

If the situation isn't corrected, increased pressure will eventually damage the sensitive optic nerve—the cablelike bundle of nerves leading from the back of the eye to the brain. With the death of fibers in the optic nerve, vision gradually gets stolen away. At first a person loses sight at the outer edges of the visual field. During the following two years, or so, the damage becomes more noticeable. But by then, it's often too late to prevent the condition from getting worse.

Glaucoma appears mostly in people over 50, although if you are African-American, your age of peak risk occurs nearly a decade earlier than if you are Caucasian. Still, you might be able to prevent vision loss if you catch it early.

Long-Term Tactics

Against Glaucoma

If your eye doctor detects significant signs of glaucoma, chances are that you are having even more vision problems. Glaucoma is also known as the quiet thief because many people do not even notice they have it until some sight is already lost. To help treat it, you need to do all you can to help lower eye pressure, which will increase the chances of saving your sight. Here's how.

Find out about family. If you know that glaucoma runs in your family, give it the slip by getting annual exams with an ophthalmologist. Be sure the doctor gives you a tonometry (eye pressure) test at each exam as well as a comprehensive eye exam of the optic nerve and a visual function test, says Alon Harris, Ph.D., director of the Glaucoma Research and Diagnostic Center at Indiana University School of Medicine in Indianapolis.

Work off the pressure. Exercise seems to help lower intraocular pressure, says Dr. Harris. A study performed by Dr. Harris

521

showed that pressure in the eye was significantly reduced after only 10 minutes of moderate exercise. "Pressure was lower after both aerobic and isometric exercise," he says. "Regular physical activity may have real, long-term benefits for eye health."

Do the drops. Older people may be less likely to stick to their treatment regimen. In the case of glaucoma, however, the medications need to be used on schedule to have the best effect on eye pressure. Medication for glaucoma usually comes in the form of eyedrops. And while the drops may be uncomfortable to use, they tend to cause fewer side effects than pills.

Be sure to ask your ophthalmologist for clear instructions on how to use your medicines. Also ask what side effects you should expect. And never stop using these eyedrops without asking your doctor first.

Dealing with Diabetic Retinopathy

Diabetes causes high levels of blood sugar—glucose—to build up in the bloodstream. Over time, these unusual amounts of glucose can cause changes to the delicate blood vessels in the retina. The result may be a vision-threatening condition known as diabetic retinopathy. So common is this disease among people with diabetes that anyone with diabetes has a three out of four chance of also developing the eye disease.

At first, retinopathy causes weak spots in the retina's blood vessels that bulge out and tend to sprout leaks. But some people may develop an even more serious condition called proliferative retinopathy, when new blood vessels begin to grow out of control, invading the fluid-filled back portion of the eyeball called the vitreous.

Even in its advanced stages, retinopathy often occurs without the visible evidence of symptoms. That's why anyone with diabetes needs to see an ophthalmologist at least once a year, says Dr. Saffra. And if the eye doctor observes changes associated with retinopathy, treatment should be started as soon as possible. Prompt treatment could mean the difference between losing your sight and saving it.

522

Most people with diabetes don't realize the seriousness of their risk for retinopathy, says Dr. Saffra. Because it is such a threat, anyone who has diabetes should stick closely to their treatment—both diet and medication, he cautions. "If someone was diagnosed with cancer, you wouldn't let them cheat on their chemotherapy, right? But some people with diabetes cheat, losing control of their blood sugars at times. All those little snacks can add up in the form of permanently lost vision."

Research clearly shows that sticking to your treatment can drastically lower your risk for developing retinopathy. In one study, the Diabetes Control and Complications Trial, researchers followed 1,441 people with diabetes in the United States and Canada for 10 years. The study showed that intense therapy reduced the risk of *any* retinopathy by more than 25 percent. And those who followed the regimen were only one-quarter as likely to see the disease progress as those who did nothing for their retinopathy.

If you already have some symptoms of retinopathy, prompt treatment is crucial. A procedure known as laser photocoagulation can stop or reverse sight loss for most people if it's done early enough, says Dr. Saffra.

During this office procedure, a laser is used to close off the new blood vessels as well as leaky blood vessels that tend to grow into the back portion of the eye. The laser treatment can help reduce the risk of further vision loss.

For those who already have some leakage from these blood vessels in the eye, laser treatment improves vision about 10 percent of the time, and even if it doesn't lead to sight improvement, photocoagulation cuts the odds of further vision loss in half.

Index

Underscored page references indicate boxed text. **Boldface** references indicate illustrations. *Italicized* references indicate tables. Prescription drug names are denoted with the symbol Rx.

American Association of Sex Educators, Counselors, and Therapists, 496
Angels, belief in, <u>261</u>, <u>267</u>
Anger, stress from, 391
Angina, as sign of heart disease, <u>367</u>, 369
Animals. *See also* Pets
  diabetes in, <u>337</u>
  heart disease in, <u>369</u>
  for stress reduction, <u>185</u>
Ankles, range-of-motion exercises for, 287, **287**
Antidepressants, <u>325</u>
  erection problems from, 505
  side effects from, <u>325</u>
Antihistamines, erection problems from, 505
Anti-inflammatory drugs, for arthritis pain, 277, 289
Antioxidant(s)
  benefits of
    arthritis relief, 279–80
    cancer prevention, <u>299</u>
    cataract prevention, 517
    diabetes control, 338
    mental acuity, 35
  sources of, 15
  vitamin E as, 10
Apnea, sleep. *See* Sleep apnea
Aquacise. *See* Water, exercising in
Arm/shoulder stretch, 105, **105**
Arnaz, Desi, smoking-related cancer and, <u>304</u>
Aromatherapy, for cardiac patients, <u>389</u>
Arterial plaque
  formation of, 364
  heart disease from, 368–69
Arteries, causes of damage to, <u>364</u>
Arthritis. *See also* Osteoarthritis; Rheumatoid arthritis
  in ancient Greece, <u>274</u>
  cause of, 274
  devices for reducing pain of, <u>278</u>
  overweight and, 39
Arts, challenge from, 207–11
Asbestos removal, for cancer prevention, 316

Asian diet, for preventing heart disease, 383–84
Asparagus, heart protection from, <u>9</u>
Aspirin
  for heart disease prevention, 371–72
  for osteoarthritis, 277
  for rheumatoid arthritis, 289
Atenolol (Rx), erection problems from, 505
Atherosclerosis
  diabetes and, 336
  strokes from, 27
Athletics. *See* Sports
Attitude, youthful appearance and, 59–60

B

Back
  lower, stretch for, 104, **104**
  pain, 482–85
  range-of-motion exercises for, 287, **287**
Bagels, toppings for, <u>48</u>
Baldness
  ancient cures for, <u>73</u>
  causes of, 69–70
  grooming for, 72
  treatment for, 73–76
Bananas, for protecting brainpower, <u>31</u>
Batt, Bertram Clifford, challenge and, <u>201</u>
Beans
  for boosting immunity, <u>20</u>
  for diabetes prevention, 339
  fiber in, <u>339</u>
  for protecting
    bones, <u>25</u>, 26
    brainpower, <u>30</u>
    heart, <u>9</u>
    intestines, <u>13</u>
  suggestions for eating, <u>32</u>
Beef, lean, 49
Belching, <u>354</u>
Benign prostatic hyperplasia (BPH), testosterone and, 398, 399, 400
Bent-knee pushups, 116, **116**
Benzene, as carcinogen, 316

525

Breathing

diaphragmatic, for
preventing neck pain, 479, 482
stress reduction, 169, 180–81,
288
for improving posture, 86
in relaxation techniques, 178,
179–81, 471
during weight training, 120

**Bright light therapy, for sleep disor-
ders**, 146–47

Broccoli

for boosting immunity, 21
health benefits of, 15–16
in meals, 16–18
for protecting
bones, 25
brainpower, 31
heart, 8
intestines, 13
suggestions for eating, 33

Broiling, for low-fat cooking, 52

**Brynner, Yul, smoking-related
cancer and**, 304

Bulgur wheat

intestinal protection from, 13
suggestions for eating, 33

Burnout, job, signs of, 219

Butter, alternative to, 52

Buttocks stretch, 102, **102**

B vitamins

for boosting immunity, 19, 20
food sources of, 7, 10
heart protection from, 7
for mental functioning, 136

C

Caffeine

effects of
bone loss, 452
depression, 332
insomnia, 163, 164
stress and, 183–84

Calcium

for blood pressure control, 34,
378
consumption of, 448
food sources of, 448–49, 451–454,
455–56
for headache prevention, 477

heart protection from, 7
recommended intake of, 25–26,
448
sources of, in vegetarian diet,
381–82
supplements
choosing, 444–45
recommendations for taking,
456
vitamin D for absorption of, 24, 26

Calcium carbonate, 444, 445

Calcium citrate, 444, 445

Calcium citrate malate, 444, 445

in orange juice, 453

Calf stretch, 103, **103**

Calisthenics, 114–17, **115–17**

Calories

burning, 40–41
calculating daily requirement for,
44–46, 375–76
counting, 43
in fat, 46

Cancer

alternative treatments for, 312,
313
breakthroughs in prevention,
detection, and treatment of,
293–95, 293
breast
estrogen and, 398
exercise for preventing, 89, 311
fiber for preventing, 299
hormone-replacement therapy
and, 405, 408
mammography for detecting,
296
overweight and, 305–6, 307
survival rate with, 295
celebrity deaths from, 304
cervical, survival rate with, 295
from cigar smoking, 302
colon
death rate from, 12
exercise for preventing, 89,
310–11
hormone-replacement therapy
for preventing, 404
inactivity and, 310
insoluble fiber for preventing,
14–15

527

Underscored page references indicate boxed text. **Boldface**
references indicate illustrations. *Italicized* references indicate
tables. Prescription drug names are denoted with the symbol Rx.

529

<u>Underscored</u> page references indicate boxed text. **Boldface** references indicate illustrations. *Italicized* references indicate tables. Prescription drug names are denoted with the symbol Rx.

Index

Underscored page references indicate boxed text. **Boldface**
references indicate illustrations. *Italicized* references indicate
tables. Prescription drug names are denoted with the symbol Rx.

531

Underscored page references indicate boxed text. **Boldface** references indicate illustrations. *Italicized* references indicate tables. Prescription drug names are denoted with the symbol Rx.

Index

constipation, 352
diabetes, 337–38
gallstones, 359
heart disease, 379
irritable bowel syndrome, 356
soluble, 12
supplements, for constipation, 352
water drinking and, 15
Fingers, range-of-motion exercises for, 286, **286**
Fish
for boosting immunity, 19, 22
for preventing
diabetes, 340–41
heart disease, 5–6, 377–78
rheumatoid arthritis, 290–91
Five a Day for Better Health program, 28–29
Flavonoids, in tea, 23
Flexibility
emotional, 250
exercises, 99, 102–5, **102–5**
guidelines for, 100–101
Flonase (Rx), for nasal problems, 158
Fluoride
bone strength from, 26
in water, 76
Fluticasone propionate (Rx), for nasal problems, 158
Folate
heart protection from, 7, 379
for mental functioning, 35
Folic acid, for boosting immunity, 19
Food. *See also specific types*
allergies, rheumatoid arthritis and, 289–90
shopping, for low-calorie foods, 47–49
Foot massage, for stress reduction, 177
Forgetfulness, 437. *See also* Memory, loss
Forgiveness, emotional benefits of, 256–57
Fosamax (Rx)
with corticosteroid use, 460
for osteoporosis, 443
Foundation, for concealing wrinkles, 65

Fractures
from bone loss, 445–46, 447, 462
effects of, 450
Fragrances, for stress reduction, 190
Free radicals, 15–16
arthritis and, 279
cancer and, 299
skin damage from, 61, 62
Free weights, machines vs., 120
Friendships
emotional benefits of, 253
starting, 255
Fruit preserves, fat in, 48
Fruits
for brainpower, 135–36
dried, 29
increasing consumption of, 28–29
for preventing
cancer, 299
diabetes, 338, 339
heart disease, 378–79
removing pesticides from, 315
serving size of, 29

G

Gallstones
with aging, 350
from hormone-replacement therapy, 405
preventing, 358–59
record-setting, 357, 359
symptoms of, 357–58
Gardening, as exercise, 346
Garlic, health benefits of, 23, 370
Gasoline, carcinogen in, 316
Gatewood, Emma, exercise and, 95
Genetics, weight and, 42
Ginkgo, for memory improvement, 427
Glasses, for vision correction, 510–11
Glaucoma, 519–22
Glucosamine supplements, for osteoarthritis, 290
Grable, Betty, smoking-related cancer and, 304
Grains, whole, minerals in, 455
Grief, vs. depression, 329
Grilling, for low-fat cooking, 52
Guilt, depression from, 331

533

Underscored page references indicate boxed text. **Boldface** references indicate illustrations. *Italicized* references indicate tables. Prescription drug names are denoted with the symbol Rx.

Index

Hip(s)
fractures, from bone loss, <u>462</u>
range-of-motion exercises for, 284, **284**, 285, **285**
replacement surgery, 282
Hobbies, emotional benefits of, 330
Homocysteine
B vitamins and, 7
heart disease and, 7
Hormone-replacement therapy (HRT). *See also* Estrogen-replacement therapy (ERT)
adjusting to, <u>403</u>
alternatives to, <u>406</u>
analyzing pros and cons of, 408
benefits of, 393–94, 394, 404–5
for bone loss prevention, 25, 447
gallbladder and, 359
for heart disease prevention, 373
for improving sex drive, <u>401</u>
risks from, 405
side effects from, 409
skin and, 66–67
vaginal lubrication from, <u>401</u>, 500
Hormones. *See also specific types*
aging and, 393–94
anti-aging
DHEA, 398–99
future of, 409–10
hormone-replacement therapy (*see* Hormone-replacement therapy)
human growth hormone, 395–98
melatonin, 394–95, <u>395–97</u>
testosterone, 399–402, <u>400–401</u>
commercial, for menopausal symptoms, <u>407</u>
elevated, by rushing, 236
natural, for menopausal symptoms, <u>407</u>
Hosiery, support, for varicose veins, 81
Housecleaning, time spent on, 232–33
HRT. *See* Hormone-replacement therapy
Hugo, Victor, sex and, <u>505</u>
Human growth hormone
anti-aging effects of, 395–98
conditions requiring, <u>394</u>
side effects from, 396–97

Humor
emotional benefits of, 244–45
longevity from, 173–74
methods of stimulating, 245–46
for stress reduction, 173–76
therapeutic effects of, <u>248–49</u>
Humor Project, <u>249</u>
Hydroquinone, for age spots, 64
Hypertension. *See* High blood pressure
Hypertensive cardiovascular disease, <u>362</u>
Hypochlorhydria, <u>350</u>

I

IBS. *See* Irritable bowel syndrome
Ibuprofen
for osteoarthritis, 277
for rheumatoid arthritis, 289
Ice cream
fat in, <u>47</u>
weight gain from, <u>17</u>
Ice pack, for
arthritis pain, 276–77
headache pain, 476
IGT. *See* Impaired glucose tolerance
Imagery
for pain relief, 472–73
as relaxation technique, 471–72
Immune system
cancer and, <u>294</u>
effect of rushing on, 236
laughter for strengthening, <u>248</u>
sleep loss and, 142
stress and, 171
superfoods for protecting, 18–22
Impaired glucose tolerance (IGT), 335, 340, <u>341</u>
Implants, penile, for erection problems, 506
Impotence, 502, 504–6
from diabetes, 336, <u>336</u>
Infections, yeast, from diabetes, 336
Information overload, avoiding, 434–37
Inhibited sexual desire
overcoming, 500–502
reasons for, 500
Injuries
exercise after, 467
preventing eye, 511

535

Insomnia, 153, 161–64
  melatonin for, 396–97
Insulin, diabetes and, 335
Intercourse, sexual. *See* Sex
Internet, prayer service on, 264
Intestines, superfoods for
      protecting, 12–18
Intimacy, for overcoming loneliness,
      420–23
Intraocular lens (IOL), in cataract
      surgery, 515–16
Iron
  for boosting immunity, 19
  sources of, in vegetarian diet, 382
Irritable bowel syndrome (IBS), 355–57
  with aging, 350
Isoflavones
  bone protection from, 26
  bone strength from, 456
Izumi, Shigechiyo, working and, 225

J

Japan, stress reduction in, 195
Jelly, as butter substitute, 52
Jet lag, 148–49
  melatonin for preventing, 395,
      396–97
Job(s). *See* Careers; Work
  burnout, 219
Joint(s)
  pain, from damp weather, 467
  replacement
      alternatives to, for knees, 275
      for osteoarthritis, 282–83
  synovial fluid in, 279
  weeping lubrication in, 283
Journal writing, for analyzing
  depression, 331
  loneliness, 418–19
Jumping
  pressure on thighbone from, 112
  rope
      chants for, 256
      as exercise, 344–45
      for stress reduction, 186

K

Kama Sutra, sexual advice in, 503
Kekulé, Fredrich August, dreaming
      and, 164

Kickboxing, for stress reduction, 187
Kidney beans
  for boosting immunity, 20
  for protecting
      bones, 25, 26
      brainpower, 30
      heart, 9
      intestines, 13
  suggestions for eating, 32
Kneeling, osteoarthritis from, 277
Knee(s)
  range-of-motion exercises for, 284,
      284, 285, **285**
  replacement, 282
      alternatives to, 275

L

Labels, nutrition
  calorie counts on, 43
  reading, 48
Lactose intolerance, irritable bowel
      syndrome from, 356–57
Lacy, Will, challenge and, 198
Lamb, lean, 49
Laminates, porcelain, for teeth, 79
Landon, Michael, smoking-related
      cancer and, 304
Laser surgery, for
  age-related macular degeneration,
      519
  diabetic retinopathy, 523
  skin improvement, 67–68
Latin diet, for preventing heart dis-
      ease, 383
Laughter
  benefits of, 172, 244–45, 248–49
      memory improvement, 442
      stress reduction, 173–76
  methods of stimulating, 245–46
Laxatives, for constipation, 354
LDL cholesterol
  arterial plaque from, 364, 364
  reducing, with
      hormone-replacement therapy,
          404
      monounsaturated fat, 22
      niacin, 365
      soy protein, 7
      tea, 23
  from saturated fat, 365

Underscored page references indicate boxed text. **Boldface**
references indicate illustrations. *Italicized* references indicate
tables. Prescription drug names are denoted with the symbol Rx.

537

Muscle(s)
contraction, energy expenditure and, <u>100</u>
expansion, <u>99</u>
loss
metabolism slowed by, 41–42
with weight loss, 43–44
stretching neck, 186
shrinking, <u>99</u>
tension, effect of rushing on, 236, 237
Music
for memory recovery, <u>439</u>
for overcoming depression, 332
stress from rock, <u>178</u>
Mustard greens
for boosting immunity, <u>21</u>
heart protection from, <u>9</u>

N
Naps, 166–67
Edison, Thomas Alva, and, <u>138</u>
insomnia and, 164, 166
refreshment from, 250–51
Narcolepsy, <u>154–55</u>
Nasal problems, snoring from, 157–58
National Zoo, time spent at, <u>236</u>
Nature, praying in, 266
Neck
muscles, stretching, 186
range-of-motion exercises for, 286, **286**
pain, 478–79, 482
Negative thinking, depression from, 331
Niacin, side effects from, <u>365</u>, <u>371</u>
Nicotine
gum, for smoking cessation, 305
patch, for smoking cessation, 304–5
tooth damage from, 79
Noise, stress from, 191
Nutrition
anti-aging effects of, 3–4
labels (*see* Nutrition labels)
from superfoods (*see* Superfoods)
Nutritional supplements, for menopausal symptoms, <u>406–7</u>

Nutrition labels
calorie counts on, <u>43</u>
reading, 48
Nuts, cooking with, 50

O
Obesity. *See also* Overweight
as diabetes risk factor, 334
high blood pressure from, <u>363</u>
Oils
best choices of, <u>50</u>
cutting back on, <u>51</u>
olive, health benefits of, <u>22</u>
Olive oil, health benefits of, <u>22</u>
Omega-3 fatty acids
heart protection from, 5–6, 377–78
in ocean vs. farm-raised fish, <u>378</u>
for rheumatoid arthritis, 290–91
in water-packed seafood, 19, 22
Ophthalmologists, <u>508</u>
Opticians, <u>508</u>
Optimism
emotional benefits of, 251, 255
mental functioning and, 139–40
in stressful situations, <u>251</u>
Optometrists, <u>508</u>
Orange juice, calcium-fortified, 453
for protecting
bones, <u>25</u>
brainpower, <u>31</u>
Organization, for improving memory, 430
Ornish program, for heart disease prevention, 385, 386
Osteoarthritis, 274–76
age at occurrence of, 273
chondroitin sulfate for, <u>290</u>
devices for reducing pain of, <u>278</u>
diet for, 279
glucosamine for, <u>290</u>
in knees, <u>275</u>
pain relief from, 276–80
with social support, <u>122</u>
preventing, 280–83
Osteoporosis
alcohol and, 462
from corticosteroids, <u>460</u>
depression and, 319
hip fractures from, <u>462</u>
incidence of, 23

539

Osteoporosis *(continued)*
prevention, 443–62
diet and, 448–56
exercise and, 89–92, 459–61
hormone-replacement therapy
and, 404
resistance training and, 113
strength training and, 456–58
trace minerals and, 458–59
smoking and, 461–62
Outer thigh and torso stretch, 102,
102
Outward Bound adventures
challenge of, 196–98, 197
intimacy from, 492–93
Overeating, avoiding, 54–55
Overhead shoulder stretch, 105, **105**
Overweight. *See also* Obesity
arthritis and, 39
cancer risk from, 305–7
effects of
back pain, 484
heart disease, 373, 375
varicose veins, 81–82
gallstones and, 358
health risks from, 37–38
Oysters, for boosting immunity, 20

P

Pain, 470
aging and, 463–64
back, 482–85
chest, from angina, 367, 369
chronic
effects of, 464
statistics on, 464
cultural expectations of, 472–73
describing, 480–81
function of, 463
headache, 475–78
joint, from damp weather, 467
neck, 478–79, 482
preventing, with
exercise, 465–67
massage, 469
stretching, 467–68, 470
relieving arthritis, 276–80
stress and, 470–71
Papaya
for boosting immunity, 21

for protecting
brainpower, 31
heart, 9
suggestions for eating, 32
Paralysis, sleep, with narcolepsy,
155
Parkinson's disease, depression
with, 320
Paxil (Rx), side effects from, 325
PEA, love and, 502
Peas, black-eyed
for boosting immunity, 21
for protecting
bones, 25, 26
brainpower, 30
heart, 8
intestines, 13
suggestions for eating, 32
Penile implants, for erection prob-
lems, 506
Pepcid AC (Rx), erection problems
from, 505
Peppers, irritable bowel syndrome
from, 356
Periodic limb movement disorder
(PLMD), 153, 160–61
Pessimism
mental functioning and, 138–39
in stressful situations, 251
Pesticides
alternatives to, 316
cancer risk and, 314
removing, from fruits and vegetables, 315
Pets. *See also* Animals
emotional benefits from, 329
for overcoming loneliness, 413
Phenylethylamine (PEA), love and,
502
Phosphorus
bone loss from excess, 451, 452
bone strength from, 24, 26
Photorefractive keratectomy (PRK),
512–13
Phytochemicals, 16
Phytoestrogens, in soy protein, 7, 11
Pitt-Turner, Thelma, exercise and, 96
Plants, for stress reduction, 190–91
Plastic surgery, for improving skin,
67–68

540

Play
    finding opportunities for, 246–47
    at work, <u>244</u>
        for stress reduction, <u>192</u>
PLMD. *See* Periodic limb movement
        disorder
Poetry writing, as creative challenge,
        210
Points of Light Foundation, 328
Poison, in eyes, 511
Polyps, intestinal, preventing, 15
Pork, lean, 49
Posture
    arthritis pain and, 277–79
    effects of, 82–83
    improving, 84–86
        with Alexander Technique, <u>83</u>
Potassium
    for controlling blood pressure, 34,
        378
    heart protection from, 7
Potato chips, fat in, <u>46</u>
Potatoes, for protecting brainpower,
    <u>31</u>
Pott, Percival, cancer and, <u>297</u>
Poultry, lean, 49
Prayer, 265–66
    belief in healing from, <u>262</u>
    centering, 266–67
    health benefits of, 260, 261, 262
    online, <u>264</u>
    physical effects of, 263–64
    requests for, <u>263</u>
Presbyopia, vision loss and, 509
Preserves, fruit, fat in, <u>48</u>
**Pritikin program, for heart disease
        prevention**, 385, 386, 387,
        <u>387</u>
Privacy, preserving, 492
PRK, <u>512–13</u>
**Progesterone, in hormone-replace-
        ment therapy**, <u>403</u>
Progressive relaxation, 288–89
Prostate cancer
    fiber for preventing, <u>299</u>
Protein
    bone loss from, 450–51
    for boosting immunity, 19, <u>20</u>
    for brainpower, 135
    sources of, in vegetarian diet, 381

Prozac (Rx)
    for depression, <u>325</u>
    erection problems from, 505
    side effects from, <u>325</u>

R

Race car driving, age advantage in, <u>205</u>
**Rapid eye movements (REM),
        during dreaming**, <u>145</u>, 165
Reflexology, for stress reduction, <u>177</u>
Relationships
    developing closeness in, 420–29
    emotional benefits of, 253
Relaxation
    emotional benefits of, 247–49
    for irritable bowel syndrome, 356
    from prayer, 261
    techniques for
        improving memory, 439–40
        massage, 249
        pain relief, 471–74
        progressive relaxation, 288–89
        stress reduction, 176, 178–82,
            439–40
        yoga stretching, 249–50
Religion
    beliefs about, <u>267</u>
    choosing congregations and, 268–70
    emotional benefits of, 330
    health benefits of, 260–62
    importance of, to Americans, <u>262</u>
REM, during dreaming, <u>145</u>, 165
**Remick, Lee, smoking-related
        cancer and**, <u>304</u>
Renova (Rx), for skin care, 64
Repetitive motion disorders, from
    rushing, 236–37
    smoking, 241
Resistance training
    benefits of, 112–13
        for women, 113
    for depression, 322–23
    exercises
        with weights, 117–19, **118–19**
        without weights, 114–17, **115–17**
    for preventing
        diabetes, 346–47
        heart disease, 388
        osteoporosis, 456–58
    in weight-loss program, 43

541

<u>Underscored</u> page references indicate boxed text. **Boldface**
references indicate illustrations. *Italicized* references indicate
tables. Prescription drug names are denoted with the symbol Rx.

Index

Resorts, all-inclusive, for romantic getaways, <u>488–89</u>
Restless legs syndrome, 161
Retin-A (Rx), for skin care, 63–64
Retinopathy, diabetic, 522–23
Retirement
    depression during, 318, 323–24
    planning for, 326–30
Revelations, religious, <u>261</u>
Rheumatoid arthritis, 283
    age at occurrence of, 273
    controlling, 288–91
    range-of-motion exercises for, 284–87, **284–87**
Riboflavin, for mental functioning, <u>136</u>
Risk taking, willingness for, 204–6
Rivers, Joan, depression and, <u>318</u>
Rock music, stress from, <u>178</u>
Rogaine, for baldness, 73
Romance
    gestures of
        by men, 500–502
        by women, 497
    getaways for, <u>488–89</u>
Rope jumping
    chants for, <u>256</u>
    as exercise, 344–45
    for stress reduction, 186
Ruts, breaking out of, 200–201

S

Salad dressing, calories in, <u>44</u>
Salmon
    for boosting immunity, 19, <u>20</u>, 22
    for protecting
        bones, <u>24</u>
        brainpower, <u>30</u>
        heart, <u>8</u>
        suggestions for eating, <u>32</u>
Salt. *See also* Sodium
    sensitivity, high blood pressure from, <u>363</u>
Sclerotherapy, for varicose veins, 82
Selenium, for
    boosting immunity, 19, <u>20</u>
    cancer prevention, <u>300</u>
Self-confidence, building, <u>247</u>
Serotonin
    antidepressants for increasing, <u>325</u>
    relaxation from, 183

Serving size
    of fruits and vegetables, <u>29</u>
    on nutrition labels, 48
Serzone (Rx), side effects from, <u>325</u>
Sesame seeds, calcium in, 453
Sex
    after age 65, <u>493</u>
    diabetes affecting, 336
    drive
        aging and, 486–87
        exercise for improving, <u>88</u>, 498, 504
        testosterone and, <u>400–401</u>, 401
    erection problems and, 502, 504–6
    finding time for, 487, 490–91
    frequency of, <u>492</u>
    in *Kama Sutra*, <u>503</u>
    during menopause, 499–500
    overcoming inhibited desire for, 500–502
    romance and, 497, 500–502
    therapists, finding, 495–96
    therapy, 494–95
Sexual attractiveness, in women, 498–99
Sexual desire, overcoming inhibited, 500–502
Sherbet, fat in, <u>47</u>
Shopping, for low-calorie foods, 47–49
Shoulders
    overhead stretch for, 105, **105**
    range-of-motion exercises for, 285, **285**
Shyness, social skills and, <u>417</u>
Singing, worship with, <u>269</u>
Situps, for preventing back pain, 484
Skin
    aging of, 57–59
    cancer (*see* Skin cancer)
    care
        in ancient Rome, <u>64</u>
        in foreign countries, <u>62</u>
        guidelines for, <u>58</u>, 59–65
        long-term tactics for, 65–68
    composition of, 57–58
    protecting, from sun damage, 60–62
    statistics about, <u>61</u>
Skin cancer
    development of, 307–10
    melanoma, 295, <u>308</u>

<u>Underscored</u> page references indicate boxed text. **Boldface** references indicate illustrations. *Italicized* references indicate tables. Prescription drug names are denoted with the symbol Rx.

preventing, with
low-fat diet, 298
sun-protective clothing, <u>309</u>
smoking and, 66
Sleep
accidents related to changes in,
<u>148</u>
aging and, 165
apnea (*see* Sleep apnea)
average amount of, <u>161</u>
biological clock and, 148–50
deprivation, signs of, 145
disorders (*see* Sleep disorders)
dreaming during, <u>145</u>
in earlier times, 144–45, <u>144</u>
headaches and, 477–78
immune system and, 142
importance of, 141–42
longevity and, 143
for memory improvement, 430
mental functioning and, 138
metabolism during, <u>165</u>
napping (*see* Naps)
obstacles to, 143–44
onset of, 152–53
position for, for arthritis sufferers,
280
paralysis, with narcolepsy, <u>155</u>
problems (*see* Sleep problems)
relaxation before, 474
requirement for, <u>143</u>
stages of, 164–66
waking up naturally from, 145–48
Sleep apnea, <u>156–57</u>, 158–60
deaths from, <u>158</u>
Sleep disorders, 153–64
advanced-phase syndromes,
<u>146–47</u>
bright light therapy for, <u>146–47</u>
delayed-phase syndromes, <u>146–47</u>,
162
insomnia, 153, 161–64
narcolepsy, <u>154–55</u>
periodic limb movement disorder,
153, 160–61
sleep apnea, <u>156–57</u>, 158–60
Sleeping pills, <u>162</u>
Sleep problems
effects of, 141–42
melatonin for, <u>396–97</u>

in shift workers, 150
solutions for, 151
from snoring, 154–58
Sleepwalking, <u>153</u>
Small intestine, size of, <u>351</u>
Smoking
effects of
diabetes, 347–48
erection problems, 504
eye disease, 518–19
heart disease, 364, 372–73
lung cancer, 301–2
osteoporosis, 461–62
skin damage, 66
time urgency, 241
tooth discoloration, 77, 78, 79
headaches and, 477
quitting, <u>301</u>, 303–5
secondhand smoke and, 315–16,
373
sleep apnea and, 159, 160
Smoking-cessation products, <u>301</u>
Snoring, 154–58
nasal problems and, 157–58
sleep apnea and, 159, 160
Socializing, for overcoming depres-
sion, 323–24, 326
Soda, bone loss from, 451, <u>452</u>, 453
Sodium
average consumption of, <u>451</u>
bone loss from, 451, 453–54
high blood pressure from, <u>363</u>
Soft drinks, bone loss from, 451,
<u>452</u>, 453
Sorbitol, for constipation, 353
Soups
broccoli in, 17
skimming fat from, 54
Soy protein
bone strength from, 26, 455–56
cholesterol reduction from, 7
heart protection from, 6–7
sources of
tempeh, 11–12
tofu, 11, 12
Spareribs, avoiding, <u>17</u>
SPF, in sunscreen, 60
Spider veins, 79–82
Spinach
for boosting immunity, <u>20</u>

543

<u>Underscored</u> page references indicate boxed text. **Boldface**
references indicate illustrations. *Italicized* references indicate
tables. Prescription drug names are denoted with the symbol Rx.

Index

Spinach (*continued*)
  for protecting
    bones, 24
    brainpower, 30
    heart, 8
    intestines, 13
  suggestions for eating, 32
Spirituality
  in children, 259
  emotional benefits of, 330
  health benefits of, 261
Spontaneity, emotional benefits of,
    257
Sports
  adventure, 202, 204
  challenge from, 202
  for overcoming depression, 324
  starting, 203–4
Squash, acorn
  for boosting immunity, 21
  for protecting
    bones, 25
    brainpower, 30
    heart, 9
  suggestions for eating, 33
Squats, 116, **116**
Standard time, traffic accidents and,
    148
Steaming, for low-fat cooking, 52
Steroids, osteoporosis from, 460
Stews, skimming fat from, 54
Stomach acid, lack of, 350
Storytelling, creativity of, 258
Strawberries, fiber in, 353
Strength training. *See* Resistance
    training
Stress
  in caregivers, 180–81
  heart disease and, 390
  of loneliness, 411–12
  mental effects of, 171–72
    memory loss, 437–38
  from movies, 191
  pain and, 470–71
  physical effects of, 168–71
    irritable bowel syndrome, 355,
      356
    weakened resistance, 171
  sleep prevented by, 474
  techniques for reducing, 438–40

  animal companionship, 185
  aromatherapy, 389
  breathing, 169, 180–81, 288
  challenge seeking, 199–200
  diet, 182–84
  exercise, 184–88
  faith, 261–62
  guidelines for, 172–73, 390–91
  home environment, 188–91
  in Japan, 195
  laughter, 173–76
  long-term tactics, 179–82
  in menopause, 406
  organization, 187
  reflexology, 177
  relaxation, 176, 178–79
  at work, 191–95
  from work, 219–20
Stretching, 106–7
  bar, for improving posture, 85–86
  for flexibility, 99–101
  of neck muscles, 478–79
  for pain prevention, 467–68, 470
  routine, 101–5, **102–5**
  for stress reduction, 186
  yoga, as relaxation technique,
    249–50
**Stretching bar, for improving
    posture**, 85–86
Stroke
  from arterial plaque, 364
  diabetes and, 336
  preventing, 27
    diet and, 34, 34
    hormone-replacement therapy
      and, 404
Styron, William, depression and, 319
Sun damage, to
  eyes, 514, 516
  skin, 60–62
Sunflower seeds
  for boosting immunity, 20
  intestinal protection from, 13
  suggestions for eating, 33
Sunglasses, for protecting
  eyesight, 514, 516
  skin, 61
Sunlight
  biological clock and, 149
  for stress reduction, 188–89

544

545

Tomatoes, suggestions for eating, <u>33</u>
Tooth grinding, headaches from, 475
Torso stretch, 102, **102**
Trace minerals, osteoporosis from deficiency of, <u>458–59</u>
Transcutaneous electrical nerve stimulation (TENS), for arthritis pain, 280
Trans fatty acids, damage from, 376–77
Transplants
  cornea, <u>515</u>
  hair, 74–76
Travel
  as challenge, 211–14
  romantic destinations for, <u>488–89</u>
Trifocals, 510–11
Triglycerides, lowering, with niacin, <u>365</u>
Trips. *See* Travel
Trust, regaining, 254
Tuna
  for boosting immunity, 19, <u>21</u>, 22
  canned
    bone protection from, <u>25</u>
    suggestions for eating, <u>32–33</u>
  fat content of, <u>5</u>
  heart protection from, <u>8</u>
TV watching. *See* Television watching
Type A personality, heart attacks and, 236

U

Ulcer medications, erection problems from, 505
Ultraviolet rays
  eye damage from, <u>514</u>
  skin damage from, 60–61
Upright rows, 118, **118**
U.S.A. Masters Track and Field Committee, 203
U.S. National Senior Sports Organization, 203
Uterine cancer
  estrogen and, 398
  fiber for preventing, <u>299</u>
UVA rays
  eye damage from, <u>514</u>
  skin damage from, 60

UVB rays
  eye damage from, <u>514</u>
  skin damage from, 60

V

Vacations. *See* Travel
Vaginal dryness, in menopause, 499, 500
Varicose veins, 79–82
Vaughn, Sarah, smoking-related cancer and, <u>304</u>
Vegan diet, health benefits of, <u>6</u>
Vegetable(s)
  four most popular, <u>35</u>
  increasing consumption of, <u>28–29</u>
  juice, for
    brainpower protection, <u>31</u>
    diabetes prevention, 339–40
  for preventing
    cancer, <u>299</u>
    diabetes, 338
    heart disease, 378–79
  protein, heart protection from, 6–7
  removing pesticides from, 315
  serving size of, <u>29</u>
  sizzling, in own juices, 53
  steaming, 52
Vegetarian diet
  bone strength from, 455
  for preventing
    diabetes, 341–42
    heart disease, 379–80
  switching to, 380–82
  vegan diet as, <u>6</u>
Vegetarians, famous, <u>10</u>
Veins
  spider, 79–82
  varicose, 79–82
Vision
  aging and, 508–9
  low, <u>520</u>
  protecting, 509–13
  therapy, <u>510</u>
Vision problems
  causes of
    age-related macular degeneration, 517–19
    cataracts, 514–17
    diabetes, 336–37

glaucoma, 519–22
low vision, <u>520</u>
correcting, with
glasses, 510–11
photorefractive keratectomy,
<u>512–13</u>
presbyopia, 509
preventing, 513–17
with eye exercises, <u>510</u>
screening for, <u>508</u>
search for miracle cures for, <u>516</u>
Visualization
as relaxation technique, 178
for releasing bad work memories,
<u>222</u>
Vitamin A, for boosting immunity,
19, <u>20</u>
Vitamin B$_6$
food sources of, 10
heart protection from, 7
for mental functioning, 35
Vitamin B$_{12}$
food sources of, 10
in vegetarian diet, 382
heart protection from, 7
for mental functioning, 35, <u>136</u>
Vitamin C
benefits of
arthritis relief, 279, 280
bone strength, 449
boosting immunity, 19, <u>20</u>
improving memory, 35
mental functioning, 35
cream, for treating wrinkles,
61–62
Vitamin D
calcium absorption and, <u>24</u>, 26,
449, 454
with corticosteroid use, <u>460</u>
daily requirement for, 454, <u>454</u>
Vitamin E
for arthritis relief, 279–80
for boosting immunity, 19, <u>20</u>
for diabetes prevention, 342
food sources of, 10
heart protection from, 10
for mental functioning, 35
supplements, for heart disease
prevention, 370–71
Vitamin K, for bone strength, 449

Vitamins. *See also specific types*
for mental functioning, <u>137</u>, *137*
side effects from, 18–19
Volksmarching, for stress reduction,
188
Volunteering
emotional benefits of, 327–28
meeting people through, 417–18
statistics on, <u>328</u>
**Vumsa, Bhandanta Vicittabi,
memory and**, <u>130</u>

W

Walking
as exercise, 111
for beginners, 98–99
meditation, for stress reduction,
186
for preventing
depression, 321
diabetes, 343–44
osteoporosis, 461
pain, 465–66
Wallace, Mike, depression and, <u>318</u>
Water
for brainpower, 137–38
for constipation prevention,
352–53
exercising in, 111–12
for osteoporosis prevention,
461
for pain prevention, 467
fiber and, 15
fluoridated, <u>76</u>
importance of drinking, <u>14</u>,
137–38
for stress reduction, 183
**Wayne, John, smoking-related
cancer and**, <u>304</u>
Weight
control
exercise for, 43–44
health benefits of, 37, 38, 39
principles of, 36
determining ideal, 46
gain
with age, reasons for, 40–41
average, in men and women, <u>37</u>
cancer risk from, 305–7
from ice cream, <u>17</u>

547

Underscored page references indicate boxed text. **Boldface**
references indicate illustrations. *Italicized* references indicate
tables. Prescription drug names are denoted with the symbol Rx.

Index